WELSH NOT

WELSH NOT

ELEMENTARY EDUCATION AND THE ANGLICISATION OF WALES

Martin Johnes

UNIVERSITY OF WALES PRESS
2024

© Martin Johnes, 2024

All rights reserved. No part of this book may be reproduced in any material form (including photocopying or storing it in any medium by electronic means and whether or not transiently or incidentally to some other use of this publication) without the written permission of the copyright owner except in accordance with the provisions of the Copyright, Designs and Patents Act 1988. Applications for the copyright owner's written permission to reproduce any part of this publication should be addressed to The University of Wales Press, University Registry, King Edward VII Avenue, Cardiff CF10 3NS

www.uwp.co.uk
British Library Cataloguing-in-Publication Data

A catalogue record for this book is available from the British Library.

ISBN   978-1-83772-180-1
e-ISBN   978-1-83772-181-8

The rights of authorship of this work have been asserted in accordance with sections 77 and 79 of the Copyright, Designs and Patents Act 1988.

Typeset by Richard Huw Pritchard
Printed by CPI Antony Rowe, Melksham, UK.

CONTENTS

Preface	ix
Abbreviations	xi
List of Illustrations	xiii
List of tables	xiv

1 The Welsh Not in History and Memory — 1
- Remembering the Welsh Not — 3
- The Welsh Not beyond living memory — 10
- Historians and the Welsh Not — 22
- This book — 27

2 The Age of the Welsh Not: Language and Punishment before 1862 — 37
- The first schools and teachers — 39
- The Welsh Not, Note, Lump and Stick — 45
- A culture of punishment — 52
- The Welsh Not's origins — 58
- The influence of training schools — 62
- Conclusion — 67

3 Learning without Understanding: The Problems of Education before 1862 — 77
- Learning without understanding — 79
- The practical challenges of teaching — 83
- Welsh in the classroom — 90
- Sunday schools and popular literacy — 98
- Conclusion — 99

4	**The Welsh Not's Afterlife: Punishing Welsh-Speaking after the 1862 Revised Code**	**109**
	The professionalisation of teaching	114
	The Welsh Not after 1862	117
	Punishments for speaking Welsh	130
	Teaching: 'a very hard occupation'	137
	Caring power and Welshness	141
	Conclusion	146
5	**The Employment of Welsh in Schools after the 1862 Revised Code**	**157**
	Using Welsh in the classroom	159
	Ongoing challenges and the evolution of the curriculum	168
	The formal recognition of Welsh	179
	Conclusion	186
6	**Enemies of the Welsh Language? Her Majesty's Inspectors and the British State**	**197**
	Promoting the use of Welsh: Longueville Jones and the Welsh paper	199
	Other voices and the Reverend Shadrach Pryce	205
	The inspectors at work	212
	The influence of inspectors	222
	Conclusion	226
7	**Victims and Rebels: Children and the Welsh Not**	**239**
	Remembering school and the Welsh Not	240
	Fighting back: children's agency	252
	The failures and indignities of education	261
	The power of education	267
	Conclusion	270
8	**Parental and Community Attitudes towards Education and the Welsh Language**	**279**
	Parental attitudes to education	280
	Parental agency and attitudes to punishment	288
	Parents and the Welsh Not	293
	School boards and managers	300
	Conclusion	308

9	**Education and the Anglicisation of Wales**	**317**
	Language and communities	320
	The decline of Welsh	325
	The resilience of Welsh	335
	The influence of education on language choices	339
	Britishness beyond English	352
	Conclusion: the Welsh Not, the state, colonialism and language shifts	355

Bibliography		373
Index		419

PREFACE

This is a book about language in elementary (i.e. primary) schools in nineteenth-century Wales. It looks at how use of the Welsh language was restricted and sometimes forbidden in those schools using a variety of methods and punishments, the most infamous of which was known as the Welsh Not. The book also examines how the complete exclusion of the language was not possible and gradually Welsh found a limited place in elementary classrooms. It goes on to consider the role education did, and did not, play in the spread of the English language and the retreat of Welsh. Very few children went on to intermediate (i.e. secondary) school and language policies and practices in those institutions are not examined.

The research for this book has been enabled by archivists, librarians and museum professionals across Wales and the UK. They are the preservers of knowledge, and all historical research depends on their expertise and on governments to fund them properly.

I have also been much helped and supported by colleagues at Swansea University. In a world where higher education is much under pressure, I am particularly fortunate to work in such a supportive and genial environment. I am particularly grateful to Kirsti Bohata, Tomás Irish, Leighton James, Simon John, Alex Langlands, Gethin Matthews, Louise Miskell, Vivienne Rogers, Matthew Stevens and Daniel Williams, who all offered specific advice and feedback on aspects of the project. The book could not have been completed without being given a semester away from teaching and I am grateful that Swansea University understands how essential sabbaticals are for research in the arts and humanities.

Beyond Swansea, Simon Brooks, Darren Chetty, Neil Fleming, Lucie Matthews-Jones, Chris Millington, Lynda Mugglestone, Paul O'Leary and Robert Smith all provided specific advice. The University of Wales Press's anonymous reviewer offered invaluable and constructive feedback and I am especially grateful for their thoroughness and diligence. The AHRC-funded Victorian Literary Languages network ran two of the most stimulating conferences I have ever attended and helped me think through and reconsider many of my ideas. The network was an important example of why the funding of research collaborations and exchanges matters. I am also grateful to delegates at the History of Education Society conference for their discussion of a paper I presented on part of this book.

Outside academia, the community of dogwalkers on the parks of Penylan and Roath helped keep me sane during the isolation of my sabbatical. Andrew, Jenny, Giulia, Julie, Margaret, Pete and Ryan now all know more about Victorian education than they wanted to, but I am very grateful to them for their listening and friendship every morning. My daughters, Bethan and Anwen, helped in their own ways, which did once include coming to an archive with me. Finally, my thanks and love go to Heather, who did, and does, far more for me than she knows.

Martin Johnes
Cardiff and Swansea

ABBREVIATIONS AND NOTES ON REFERENCING, AND THE ORGANISATION OF SCHOOLS

AA	Anglesey Archives
CA	Ceredigion Archives
CwyA	Conwy Archives
CCE	Committee of Council on Education
CmA	Carmarthenshire Archives
CRO	Caernarfon Record Office (Gwynedd Archives)
GA	Glamorgan Archives
MRO	Meirionnydd Record Office (Gwynedd Archives)
NEWAR	North-East Wales Archives (Ruthin)
NEWAH	North-East Wales Archives (Hawarden)
NLW	National Library of Wales
PA	Powys Archives
PbA	Pembrokeshire Archives
RBA	Richard Burton Archives, Swansea University
WGA	West Glamorgan Archives

All archival references in endnotes refer to school logbooks unless otherwise stated.

Modern spellings of Welsh place-names have been used.

Standards refer to the how schools were divided after 1862. These were based on merit rather than age groups but Standard I often began at around age seven. Standard VI was the highest group, until 1882 when Standard VII was introduced, although not all schools used this. Children below Standard I were referred to as infants. Some schools also grouped standards into classes, with Class 1 consisting of the higher standards.

LIST OF ILLUSTRATIONS

1. 'Y *Welsh Note*'.
2. Welsh Not found at Capel Pen-rhiw, Drefach Felindre, Carmarthenshire (Courtesy of Amgueddfa Cymru).
3. Welsh Not found at Garth school, Bangor (Courtesy of Storiel).
4. A depiction of a school in the 1820s from Charles Dickens, *The Old Curiosity Shop* (1840–1). Note the Dunce's Cap on the shelf.
5. British Infants School, Newport, built 1856 (Courtesy of Amgueddfa Cymru).
6. A rural post-1870 school in New Radnor (Courtesy of National Library of Wales).
7. Regulations of the Abergwili National school. Probably from the first half of the century (Courtesy of Carmarthenshire Archives).
8. Pupils of Y Wern school, Llanbryn-mair, Montgomeryshire, 1890s (Courtesy of National Library of Wales).
9. Extract from the 1875 logbook of Aberffraw Board school noting the introduction of a form of Welsh Not (Courtesy of Anglesey Archives).
10. Extract from the 1877 logbook of Llanddoged school. Note how children were being subject to a Welsh Not and taught a song in Welsh (Courtesy of Conwy Archives).

LIST OF TABLES

4.1. Tywyn school logbook entries detailing attempts to stop children speaking Welsh (MRO).

5.1. Percentage of school masters, mistresses and teachers born in Wales, 1891 and 1901 censuses.

7.1. Language ability by age, 1901 census.

7.2. Percentage of children in Meirionnydd recorded as monolingual Welsh by age, 1901 census.

9.1. Number and proportion of Welsh and English speakers, 1891 and 1901 censuses.

9.2. Home language of secondary schoolchildren, 1927.

1

THE WELSH NOT IN HISTORY AND MEMORY

In 1906, Owen M. Edwards, a writer, historian and, briefly, a Liberal MP, published an autobiographical book in Welsh in which he recalled his first day at school. Although he knew no English, the teacher told him he was not to speak his mother tongue. The other boys set out to provoke him and he lost his temper, shouting at them in Welsh. The children then laughed at him and he was 'given a string about my neck, with a heavy wooden token on it'. He did not know what it was. At lunchtime, the children pointed him out to the schoolmistress, who smiled and said something he did not understand. She did not hit him and instead took the token away. Edwards recalled he then understood he had been given it for speaking Welsh.

After that day, the token was, he stated, put around his neck hundreds of times. He was supposed to tell the teacher if he heard anyone else speaking Welsh so it could be transferred to them. But he was proud to recall that he never passed it on and was instead caned at the end of every day. Such things were done, he said, because teachers believed that their main duty was to teach English to the children and that the best way to do this was to force children to only speak the little of the language they had learned from books or picked up from others. But the result of his treatment, and not being able to understand his teachers, was that he hated school and was unable to sleep. He argued that such experiences made children look upon everyone who spoke English as a natural enemy.[1]

Edwards was not the first to complain about what others called the Welsh Not, but his is the only first-hand memory of the practice that is widely known. Yet his account is problematic. Plaid Cymru-founder Saunders Lewis thought Edwards's account of his early life was journalism, romanticised and coloured by his readings of poets.[2] Hazel Davies, a biographer of Edwards, said the 'memories' were highly coloured and that the account was 'a deliberate and clever piece of publicity designed to right a wrong'. Edwards was exaggerating the deficiency of his schooling, it was suggested, in order to highlight the need for change in Welsh education.[3]

Edwards was certainly a man deeply committed to promoting and protecting Welsh culture. He was the author and editor of books, magazines and periodicals intended to promote a love of Wales amongst children and the wider population. In 1907, a year after the story's publication, Edwards became chief inspector of schools in Wales. In that job, he set about trying to ensure the new Welsh department of the Board of Education promoted the Welsh language and identity in schools. Edwards's story of the Welsh Not had helped establish both the need for change and was a statement of his own commitment to making that happen.

Whatever the problems of Edwards's account, one of his biographers argued that it became part of Welsh folklore.[4] In 2003, it was given a stamp of authority, when it became the basis of a bilingual textbook for primary schools.[5] By then, accounts of the Welsh Not were common in schools and popular culture. They were also passed down within families and invoked during controversies around the Welsh language and the status of Wales. People in Wales may have been hazy on the details, but the vast majority seemed to know what the Welsh Not was. In the telling and retelling of its story, the nature and effects of the Welsh Not grew. It started to be assumed that it was some kind of official policy. As fewer and fewer people spoke Welsh, the Welsh Not became a widely accepted explanation for this linguistic change. The language was beaten out of our ancestors, the saying went.

The idea that the blame lay at the feet of the British state owed much to how people think about history backwards, seeing the past through the prism of present-day conditions. The fact that the state runs education today has led to assumptions that has always been the case. Present-day understandings of the relationship between Wales and England have also shaped popular views of the Welsh Not. Those who feel Wales has been mistreated or oppressed by rule from London are likely to see the Welsh Not as another example of that relationship. One historian summed up that 'Over the years the Welsh Not became and, in much popular memory remains, the ultimate symbol of coercion of the Welsh people by an alien, colonial power intent on the subjugation of a nation's language and, by implication, its soul.'[6]

Political and cultural concerns have thus clouded understandings of the Welsh Not and they were, and remain, a mixture of fact and mythology. The Welsh Not was real and many children were physically and psychologically punished at school for speaking Welsh. This did, in some way, contribute to the fortunes of the language. The state was interested in the question of language in classrooms and it was sometimes contemptuous towards Welsh. However, the detail, nuance, complexity and motives of what happened have been flattened, distorted and lost. Something that happened has been assumed to be ubiquitous. There has been little thought given to questions of when, why and how the Welsh Not was used. Answering those questions, and putting them in the context of education and Welsh society, are the aims of this book. It will show that the Welsh Not was implemented by individual teachers, largely of their own accord and without opposition from parents. How it was used varied, but its direct goal was not to stop children speaking Welsh in their future lives but to help them learn English. However, in this it did not work and the Welsh Not gradually fell out of use over the course of the nineteenth century. Representatives of the state understood its pedagogical limitations and were thus generally supportive of Welsh being used in schools, not out of any love for the language but as a tool to better teach children English.

Remembering the Welsh Not

The Welsh Not is a key part of Wales's collective memory, that vague amorphous sense of the past that people share and which contributes to their sense of identity. Collective memory is rarely quite the same as actual events. It is partial and fragmented, made up of images and ideas rather than coherent narratives. Nor is collective memory static. It is constantly being shaped by and reformed by the present in which the remembering is taking place. Collective memories not only evolve but they also shape and frame the individual memories of people with direct experiences. Indeed, individualised and personalised memories can become almost impossible to discern and separate out from the wider ideas and frameworks that they are remembered within. Although collective memories often seem very certain, scratch the surface and they are often characterised by misunderstanding and error.

This is very much the case with the Welsh Not. Even in the nineteenth century, there was some confusion around it. Few people had a good understanding of how education worked or what actually happened in schools and they might make comments with little evidence or understanding. They might think things must have changed since their schooldays or assumed that things had not. They might think that their experiences were typical and fail to understand just how varied schools were in practice and character.

People's understanding was not helped by the variety of names the practice was known by. More common than the name Welsh Not in the nineteenth century, was the term Welsh Note, with note meaning a sign or token. Edwards himself did not use either word and, instead, used the term 'tocyn' (token). Even in accounts published in the nineteenth century, the different names could be a cause of uncertainty over what exactly was being referred to.[7] In 1893, one children's magazine even printed a correction to say where Welsh Note had been printed Welsh Not was meant.[8] Part of the problem was that the tokens might be marked WN or Welsh N thus leaving open the question of what the final letter stood for. There were linguistic challenges too, when English names were discussed in Welsh. This was evident in an 1880 Welsh-language retrospective account that merged the words to call it 'Welshnot'.[9] It may be that the Not term was originally derived from Note, perhaps through mispronunciation. In Welsh, an 'o' would normally be pronounced in short form and thus the longer 'o' in note could easily have become the shorter o in not. Indeed, one 1924 writer called it the 'Welsh nôt'.[10] Whatever the origins, in the twentieth century, Welsh Not became the standard name used to describe the token. Since the practice centred on stopping people speaking Welsh, 'not' was certainly more powerful and apt.

However, to confuse things further, the practice had also been known by other names. The earliest written record to anything of its sort called it the Welsh Lump, whereas the Blue Books, perhaps the most famous contemporary reference, called it the Welsh Stick. In some places, it was simply known as the 'not'.[11] There is also evidence of it occasionally being known as the Welsh Knot, one isolated reference to it as 'y cwstom' (the custom) and another to it as the 'cribban'.[12] These two stand out because they were in Welsh. But they may be the nicknames used by children rather than the term used in school since it seems unlikely that a teacher punishing children for speaking Welsh would employ a Welsh name. No contemporary Welsh-language accounts made any effort to translate the practice's name. Nor do most nineteenth-century children seem to have come up with a Welsh name for it, despite their own limited English. Thus, as one 1918 writer observed, the term Welsh Not was never translated into Welsh in any context.[13] This remains the case and has added to the idea of it as something alien and imposed from outside.

Whatever it was called, in the late nineteenth and early twentieth centuries, there was a strong sense that the Welsh Not was something from the past.[14] But there was no consistency in understandings of when exactly that past was. An 1895 article described the Welsh Not as the 'way our grandfathers endeavoured to make their boys thorough English speakers'.[15] In contrast, a 1916 discussion of it noted how much had changed since the 'time of our fathers, when the Welsh Knot was used to prevent the Welsh from speaking the language of their mothers'.[16] What there was more certainty about was the idea that the Welsh Not's demise was an example of how education, and thus by implication Wales, had become more progressive.[17] Indeed, some even wrote poetry about the old days of the Welsh Not that declared how much better things were now.[18] In 1888, a speaker at a school prize-giving in Wrexham recounted his experience of the Welsh Note in the 1840s, saying that perhaps those present had 'never heard of that sort of thing'. He wished he had kept one because it could be an example for a museum of 'the educational means used in the Principality in the long, long, time ago, before the colleges or universities were thought of'.[19] In 1879, one writer in a children's magazine claimed that not much had been heard or seen of the Welsh Not for many years but that it had been common forty to fifty years earlier. He concluded children should be thankful that the days of the Welsh Not, the big rod and throwing a ruler at children's heads were now only found in books and traditions.[20] A description of this 'instrument of torture' published in 1897 claimed:

> The methods adopted in certain schools in Wales, not many years ago, to discourage the use of Welsh among the children were little short of barbarous. Happily, better times have since dawned, and scorn and derision are no longer to be heaped upon a Welsh child for conversing in his mother tongue.[21]

Such judgements were framed by the conditions in which they were made. In the late nineteenth century, there was a renaissance in Welsh identity and culture. Led by a prosperous middle class and an active Nonconformist clergy, there was a flowering of Welsh periodicals and newspapers. The National Eisteddfod became a powerful annual celebration of Welshness, while the new national sports teams of football and rugby added a more popular dimension to patriotism. Wales was reborn and this all contributed to the idea that the anti-Welsh-language mindset that the Welsh Not represented was something now gone. A 1904 poem by Gwyneth Vaughan spoke of how a stick and Welsh Note had been used to make children English but how it had not worked and the old Welsh language lived on.[22] Like O. M. Edwards, others proudly recounted stories of resisting the Welsh Not. One from 1894 told of a boy in the past who had refused to speak English and, when asked why by his teacher, replied 'Becos I am a Welshman!', something that earned him four slaps and the promise of a thrashing if he still had the Welsh Not at the end of the day. Yet, in that story, the boy told his father that no one had any business telling him, a Welshman in Wales, not to speak Welsh outside the school. His act of rebellion had been speaking Welsh in the playground rather than in the classroom itself.[23] This sums up how the role of the Welsh language in this renaissance was somewhat contradictory. There was a vibrant press in the language and Welsh also enjoyed considerable cultural capital through its role in Nonconformist religion. But there was also a sense that, while Welsh was the language of home, hearth and heart, it was English that mattered in business and secular matters and thus in education. The boy who took pride in refusing to speak English in the playground seems to have accepted it in the classroom.

This did not change the anger that tellings of the Welsh Not could involve because of its perceived goals and impact on the Welsh language. One 1908 memory of the practice concluded it was 'wicked' and through it 'our beloved mother tongue has been banished from many a hamlet where it had lived and had been loved from times immemorial'.[24] Sometimes such interpretations put the blame (incorrectly) on the state or saw it as an example of England's oppression of Wales.[25] J. Tywi Jones (b.1870) did not make specific reference to the Welsh Not but he did write in 1919 of how Welsh had been 'banned' at his Llandovery school: 'It was at our peril we uttered a word of it. The result was that the majority of us left school with no intelligent grasp of English, and under the impression that it was something low and vulgar to speak Welsh.' He later began to take interest in Welsh literature thanks to the influence of an old miner and began to realise what he had been deprived of: 'We were simply robbed of our birthright by a foreign system of education and its paid servants.'[26] What is significant here is the sense that existed even in the late nineteenth century that there had been a deliberate attempt to, as one 1890s account put it, 'help kill our old language'.[27] Such was the anger that in 1907 one Welsh-language letter writer concluded that 'Wales has not yet forgotten the days of the Welsh Note. The age when the atmosphere of the day schools was pure poison to the old language.'[28]

Such anger owed much to how, by the end of the century, there were real concerns that Welsh was in danger of dying, despite the national revival. Older people were very conscious of how the language had retreated in their own lifetimes. One 1890 reference to the Welsh Not in schools in the past said it was little wonder that Welsh had lost ground when the machinery of the state schools was driving it to perdition.[29] In 1891, a census question was asked for the first time in Wales about what languages people spoke. It revealed that 45 per cent of the population were now unable to speak Welsh. A decade later, the figure had risen to more than 55 per cent. This decline certainly framed memories and assessments of education, and the latter seemed to offer a natural explanation of what was happening. But the anger was not just about the effects on Welsh or any connection with the state. It was also about what it did to children. In 1911, the writer T. Gwynn Jones (b.1871) noted only the 'older generation' now remembered the Welsh Not but other forms of punishing Welsh-speaking, such as being made to stand on a chair, had lasted until 'thirty years ago and even less'. He wrote that such practices were 'admirably calculated to destroy self-respect and to foster duplicity and cowardice'.[30]

In contrast, others used the Welsh Not to make a variety of different points that were more about the present than the past. In 1897, one columnist said the Welsh Not was long gone but Welsh speakers still faced problems in court because proceedings were in English.[31] A 1917 account maintained that the Welsh Not and the slaps he had received for speaking Welsh were not about killing off Welsh but rather helping children who never heard English out of school learn the language. This writer likened the idea that the Welsh Not was an attempt to kill Welsh to how German children were wrongly taught before the ongoing war that everything Britain did was to hurt their country.[32] Another account said:

> A ruder or a more primitive mode of teaching English is hardly conceivable; but it shows that, in those dark and cloudy days, there was some desire to acquire a knowledge of that language which is destined to become the one common medium of international intercourse between the civilised nations of the world.[33]

In this light, the method was wrong but the goal of learning English, and thus joining the modern world, was right. That same year, the *South Wales Echo* published recollections of the 'barbarous' Welsh Notes and the physical punishment they entailed in a South Cardiganshire school in 1868 but concluded 'It would do some of our thin-skinned innocents (?) of the present day an incalculable amount of good to be placed in a school of this type for a day or two every year.'[34] Others understood that the Welsh Not had come from within Wales rather than government policy and used this as an example of self-hurt. In 1916, in the aftermath of the Easter Rising, one writer said that when he remembered the days of the Welsh Not and the arrogance of some Welshmen towards their language, he could understand the sins of the Irish and how they had been misled.[35] The Welsh Not was also invoked in disputes around language and the very name became a byword for attitudes that were deemed anti-Welsh. In 1899, the term Welsh Stick was used to make a point about Welsh-speaking clergy not being promoted in the church.[36] In 1900, when it was reported that Welsh was forbidden inside the new county school at Tregaron to help children's English, a newspaper suggested sarcastically that someone should send the headmaster a 'Welsh note' to help him reach his goal.[37]

After the First World War, invoking education and the Welsh Not to discuss linguistic and national decline intensified. So did the idea that this was the fault of the state or the English more broadly.[38] Sir Ben Bowen Thomas, who worked in adult education before becoming permanent secretary to the Welsh Department at the Ministry of Education in 1945, wrote that education after the 1870 Act that spread its reach was 'designed to obliterate the characteristics of the society which it should have served'. It was geared to making the Welsh 'adaptable to the demands of industry and commerce'. The result was, he said, that people 'gained the whole world' and 'an English soul' but lost a Welsh one.[39] A school textbook from 1938 noted that education after 1870 was 'purely English' but that this 'was not the fault of the English Government'. Instead, it argued that parents had not wanted Welsh taught in day schools so their children could learn English to get on in the world. The result was that they 'grew up with a mongrel dialect and a mongrel patriotism, except where the influence of home and chapel was sufficiently powerful to counteract the Anglicising effect of the school'.[40]

Again, understandings of the Welsh Not were being framed by wider conditions. The 1921 census showed that the proportion of Welsh speakers had fallen to 37.1 per cent and the figure fell again to 36.8 per cent in 1931. The interwar years also saw large-scale migration of young people from Wales as they sought to escape the mass unemployment of home. The idea that the future of Welsh as a living language and culture was in peril intensified, and in 1925 Plaid Genedlaethol Cymru was founded, a political party that aimed to preserve both. The claims of a 'mongrel patriotism' cited above reflected the idea common then in the circles of Plaid Cymru that industrial communities were somehow not properly Welsh. There was even talk that the best thing for Wales would be to deindustrialise and return to agricultural communities that had once dominated the nation and were entirely Welsh-speaking. One of the party's founders was D. J. Williams. In 1959, he wrote that the education system had taught the children of Wales enough English to make them good servants, obedient to government and eager to get good jobs and make money. It had created a colony of tame, rootless and well-behaved people with no national, moral or religious standards. The education system was thus a national murder machine.[41]

The Welsh Not beyond living memory

Williams did not cite the Welsh Not in his attack on education and the Welsh people but, as the practice passed out of living memory, there were new ways that knowledge and thinking about it were perpetuated. In 1939 *How Green Was My Valley* was published, the story of a Welsh mining community in the late Victorian and Edwardian era. It became a global best-seller, with sales being significantly enhanced by a major Hollywood adaption that won the 1941 Oscar for best picture. It was also one of the most influential ways that knowledge and understanding of the Welsh Not was spread, even though author Richard Llewellyn was raised in London and not writing from first-hand knowledge.

The film skirted questions of language, but the novel did not, at least when it came to education. Llewellyn's story has been much criticised for historical inaccuracies but it correctly articulated the difficulty of school for children who spoke Welsh: 'He speaks, reads, writes, and he thinks in Welsh, at home, in the street, and in Chapel, and when he reads English he will understand it in Welsh, and when he speaks English, he will pronounce the words with pain and using crutches.'[42] Where Llewellyn said the blame for this lay reflected the idea that had already emerged in Welsh culture: 'So stupid are the English, who build schools for the Welsh, and insist, on pain of punishment, that English is to be spoken, and yet, for all their insistence, never give one lesson in the pronouncing and enunciation of the spoken word.'[43] However, the novel's picture of the Welsh Not varied a little from the most common tales of a wooden symbol:

> About her neck a piece of new cord, and from the cord, a board that hung to her shins and cut her as she walked. Chalked on the board ... I must not speak Welsh in school ... And the board dragged her down, for she was small, an infant, and the card rasped the flesh of her neck, and there were marks upon her shins where the edge of the board had cut. Loud she cried ... and in her eyes the big tears of a child who is hurt, and has shame, and is frightened.[44]

Huw, the novel's narrator, later discovered that the teacher who implemented this spoke Welsh and is told by him 'Welsh never was a language, but only a crude means of communication between tribes of barbarians stinking of woad ... English. The language of the Queen and all nobility. Welsh. Good God Almighty, the very word is given to robbers on race-courses.'[45] In these passages was the mix of fact and fiction that marked popular understandings of the Welsh Not. Although the system is wrongly blamed on the English, it is rightly shown as being implemented by a teacher who spoke Welsh. Whether the experience of the child and the hatred of the teacher are representative of all those who suffered and used the Welsh Not is less certain.

Understanding precisely how collective memory and understanding develops is impossible. Influences and ideas come from a multitude of places and intertwine, reinforcing each other. But the overwhelming success of *How Green Was My Valley* means it must have had a significant influence. The 1975–6 television adaptation of the novel reinforced this. In it, the headmaster has a strong English accent, criticises the boy's 'atrocious' Welsh accent, and asks the parents to ensure he speaks English at all times and that the school's policy of no Welsh is 'loyally adhered to' at home too. This causes a snigger behind the headmaster's back. In class, his teacher seeks to 'civilise' Huw, who is criticised for his lack of cleanliness and the way he pronounces words. But Huw stands his ground, claiming Welsh is a beautiful language. This adaptation did not include the Welsh Not but it does show Huw hitting the teacher after he had caned another boy for speaking Welsh. The teacher collapses in shame and resorts to cursing in Welsh.[46]

Fourteen years earlier, in 1962, Saunders Lewis made an iconic radio speech on the history and future of the Welsh language. Although he did not mention the Welsh Not, he did perpetuate the idea that education policy had deliberately tried to kill the language. He quoted the 1852 comment of Matthew Arnold, an education inspector, that governments should seek to make nations homogenous, and that the eradication of Welsh would be socially and politically desirable. Lewis concluded that Arnold's 'purpose was to support the recommendations of the Blue Books, and he laid emphasis on the fact that extermination of Welsh was a political policy'.[47] Such interpretations perpetuated the idea that the Welsh Not was part of some wider political campaign and policy to destroy Welsh but they were also rooted in misunderstandings. Arnold, then a newly appointed inspector, was not stating a political policy but his own opinion and it was not one he repeated.

The Blue Books Lewis cited were an official 1847 report into Welsh education that provoked outrage in Wales with its arguments that the Welsh language and Nonconformity were holding the Welsh back from civilisation and some derisive accompanying comments on Welsh morality. The affair became known as 'Brad y Llyfrau Gleision' (Treason of the Blue Books) and a memory of it has lingered, becoming 'an icon for national insult'.[48] It has also become intertwined and confused with the Welsh Not. Indeed, it has sometimes been supposed that the Welsh Not was a direct consequence of the Blue Books. A 2012 popular history of Wales, for example, claimed that the Blue Books stated that 'anyone caught speaking Welsh were to be severely punished'.[49] Even a school textbook could date the Welsh Not to the period after the Blue Books.[50] In fact, the Blue Books argued for Welsh to be used more in schools because its authors understood that English could not be taught to Welsh-monoglot children without the use of their mother tongue. Rather than recommend the use of Welsh Not, the Blue Books criticised it as an example of how misguided schools were being in excluding Welsh from the classroom. The commissioners certainly had no love of Welsh or desire to see the language perpetuated in the medium term; their recommendation that Welsh be used was simply pragmatism. It has also been completely overshadowed in popular memory by their comments on the language more broadly. It was these comments, and the fact that they took place within an official report, that created the idea that it was policy to exterminate Welsh. Thus, in 1919, one columnist in the *Western Mail* wrote that 'studied efforts were being made by "the authorities" to crush out our native tongue; when a policy of repression followed the publication of the libellous report of the Education Commission of 1847'.[51] The occasional voice that pointed out the Welsh Not was not a government imposition made little impression.[52] The reality was, as will be shown in this book, that the aspiration to see Welsh disappear was there in the British state but there were never any direct policies to make this happen and there was a belief that Welsh had to be used in schools if English was to be ever taught effectively.

Understandings of the Welsh Not and the role and aims of the state in education have also been confused by misunderstandings of the 1870 Education Act. This Act is generally regarded as the start of modern state education, but state funding of some schools was already happening and the Act did not make school attendance compulsory nor take over the existing schools run by charities. Instead, it required the creation of elected school boards to establish and run new schools where local provision was not sufficient. It made no reference to the language of instruction. The Act was thus about the provision of education, but it has been interpreted in popular culture and history as creating an anti-Welsh education system that perpetuated or even introduced the Welsh Not. One popular book quite wrongly stated that the 'notorious Education Act of 1870 made it a requirement to hang a board bearing the words "Welsh Not" around the necks of children caught speaking Welsh at school'.[53] Academic books have also made the mistake of linking the Welsh Not to the 1870 Act.[54]

Following Saunders Lewis's lead, Welsh nationalist politicians, whose *raison d'être* was to free Wales from the British state, perpetuated the idea that the Welsh Not and the destruction of Welsh were state policy, although this was often done by discussing the state and the Welsh Not alongside each other rather than saying outright that the practice was state policy. In a 1973 book, Gwynfor Evans, then leader of Plaid Cymru, claimed that after 1870, 'The Welsh language was savagely excluded' from schools, with the Welsh Not being a 'viciously English system'.[55] In a 2018 book, another Plaid Cymru leader, Adam Price, claimed that the Act 'made English compulsory' before going on to discuss the Welsh Not, calling it the 'most telling symbol of all of cultural imperialism in Wales', with the language 'literally beaten out of us'.[56] Such attacks on the British state misunderstand its character. It was never a homogenous body, following single policies. It was dominated by laissez-faire ideals and would only intervene in society where necessary. Yet, even when it did, it did so cautiously and often rather minimally. The growth of state education was slow and piecemeal.

The idea of Welsh being literally beaten out of children was a powerful one and became a widespread explanation for why Welsh-speaking numbers had declined. It was rooted in how widespread a knowledge of the Welsh Not became after the war. This owed much to how the Welsh Not was represented in popular culture in a variety of different settings, particularly during the intensifying of Welsh-language campaigning in the 1970s. A 1976 poem linked the Welsh Not to a desire to break national spirit and concluded that Wales would learn from Africa and Ireland and the school pillory would become the shepherd's sling, hurling stones at the English forehead.[57] In 1979, language-campaigner and singer Dafydd Iwan released 'Baled y Welsh Not', a song seemingly inspired by Owen Edwards's account, where the school is an alien environment with the sun, fresh air and Welsh language shut out.[58] The Welsh Not also featured in later pop songs, novels, travel books and children's stories, most of which emphasised its unfairness and horror.[59] A BBC documentary in 1975 on the history of the language opened with a depiction of the Welsh Not and the teacher saying to the young girl wearing it 'Do you want to grow up as primitive as the black savages in Africa?' The presenter then went on to say that the programme would show how the language had been 'oppressed and beaten out of people. Part of deliberate policy to get rid of and destroy the culture and language of the Welsh. It's a story of a policy that worked too.'[60]

Through such depictions, knowledge of the Welsh Not was kept alive, disseminated and exaggerated. This continued into the twenty-first century, by when there were even small replica Welsh Nots on sale that could be worn as badges. The Welsh Not also became entwined with ideas of imperial shame. In 2019, James Felton published *52 Times Britain was a Bellend*. A chapter entitled 'We beat the shit out of the Welsh for speaking Welsh in Wales' recounted (wrongly) that in the 1800s 'the English' took over schools in Wales and introduced the Welsh Not. He summed up: 'The idea was basically to shame children for being bilingual, encourage a culture of snitching, and make tiny children associate their parents speaking Welsh at home with intense feelings of physical pain.'[61] He was unaware that most children who experienced the Welsh Not were not bilingual at all.

Many accounts of the Welsh Not tried to stir the emotions of readers and viewers. In 1964, Parry-Jones, who did not experience it himself, recorded in a book about children's games:

> The practice would not have been so reprehensible had not the punishment been so brutal and inhuman. It is only those who have been caned on their tender hands who really know how terribly painful it is, and how any child would stoop to involve even his

best friend to escape it, suffering inevitably, I am sure, by this practice of the Welsh Not, some early moral injury.⁶²

Depicting the practice through a picture of a sad-looking child, often a girl, was a powerful way of conveying the emotions. A 1987 documentary on 'Celtic' languages featured a reconstruction of a classroom full of children looking upset, as one of them was given a Welsh Not by a stern teacher.⁶³ Such upset was not always feigned. In the 2014 living history show *Snowdonia 1890*, a child was given it in a classroom reconstruction and brought to tears by the experience. She had to write out 'I must not speak Welsh in School' 100 times but viewers were reminded that in the Victorian period the punishment would have been the cane or belt.⁶⁴ By 1890, detention or similar was actually more common and the irony was furthered by the programme itself being in English. Thus the requirement of the cameras meant the family had to discuss the issue afterwards in a language different to the one they normally spoke at home.

Many children learned about the Welsh Not at school. This was never systematic because there was no national curriculum until 1988 and even after that the curriculum was never specific enough to outline the detail of what was taught. Thus, whether teachers taught about the Welsh Not was down to whether they thought it was important, although they were also influenced by the existence of resources and the guidance passed down. A 1947 handbook for history teachers in Wales stated:

> For many years after the Education Act of 1870, English was the sole medium of instruction in the schools and children were punished for using their native tongue during school hours; reference should be made, for instance, to the 'Welsh Not'. It should be pointed out that as a result very many children ceased to be Welsh speaking.⁶⁵

This wrongly associated the Welsh Not with the 1870 Act and thus the state. It also made a simplistic direct link between it and the decline of Welsh. Other resources also encouraged schools to teach the history of the Welsh Not: for example, in 1978 it was suggested that schools act out the Welsh Not, with children spying on each other.[66] But the majority of Welsh history school textbooks made no mention of the Welsh Not. Perhaps this was because knowledge of the exact details was uncertain. Perhaps it was because there was a desire not to rock the boat. For several decades after the Second World War, the question of language was controversial in Wales. Welsh-medium education was growing slowly but Welsh lessons in other schools could be contentious, often because parents felt it was a waste of time. Further linguistic controversies centred around broadcasting, the availability of public services in Welsh, and real and imagined insinuations that only Welsh speakers were properly Welsh.[67]

Such feelings subsided in the later twentieth century. Defeat in the 1979 devolution referendum and the economic dislocation of the 1980s created a stronger determination to build a more unified Wales. One result was the creation of a Welsh Assembly in 1999 and another was a push for more Welsh history to be taught in schools. Gradually the Welsh Not became a standard reference in accounts of Welsh history for schools. A 2003 book for primary schools told of children not liking school because of how difficult English was for them and celebrated Owen M. Edwards for not passing the Welsh Not on.[68] A children's book in 2007 told readers not to complain about their own teachers and be grateful that they did not attend a Victorian school.[69] Some books did, however, make clear that it was impossible to know how widespread the Welsh Not was and even encouraged readers to question the accuracy of memories of it.[70]

A report in 2021 into history teaching found that visits to museums and the like brought the past alive and were more influential on children's knowledge than lessons.[71] Key here was St Fagan's, the open-air Welsh culture museum opened in 1948 and to which a visit became a ritual of most Welsh children's primary school experiences. In the 1980s, Maestir Board school, built in 1880, was removed from its site near Lampeter and rebuilt at St Fagans. It hosted sessions where children would role play and learn what life was like at a Victorian school and about the Welsh Not.[72] An e-book produced for schools by the museum said although it was not known whether the Welsh Not was used at Maestir, it was used at 'many schools' and linked it to the Blue Books.⁷³ The museum was not incorrect to connect the Welsh Not to schools of the late Victorian period but it did not explain how the practice was unusual by this period, even if lessons did remain in English with Welsh used only as a medium of explanation. Museum staff who ran the sessions noted how children compared their 'Victorian' experiences with their own experiences. This included some second-language children who noted they had to speak Welsh rather than English at school.⁷⁴

St Fagans was also home to two actual Welsh Nots. One was found in a cupboard in Ysgol Pontgarreg (Llangrannog) by a workman painting the blackboard.⁷⁵ The other was found when a chapel at Drefach Felindre was dismantled for re-erection at the museum. One is on permanent display and the present interpretation says the practice was used in 'some schools' (rather than the 'many' stated in the museum's book for schools) and concludes by noting 'Some historians think that the use of the Welsh Not has been exaggerated'. A third Welsh Not is on display at Storiel museum at Bangor. It was discovered under the floorboards of a local school by a teacher who worked there from 1875 to 1897.⁷⁶

Knowledge of the Welsh Not thus permeated post-1945 Welsh society through different routes. As before the war, it was invoked for a variety of different purposes and acted as a generic emblem of prejudices and discriminations towards Wales. Most obviously, it was referred to in cases where there were constraints on people's freedom to speak Welsh. In 1965, for example, Wynn Melville Jones won first prize at Tregaron carnival for dressing up in a suit with a Welsh Not after a local factory had ruled that Welsh was not to be spoken at work.⁷⁷ It was also often cited in support of calls for the expansion of Welsh-medium education. In 1983, for example, children at a protest outside the Welsh Office wore Welsh Nots.⁷⁸ In 2000, a writer claimed that the effect of the Welsh Not was still visible in the mindset of those who believed that success in the world could only be achieved through the medium of English.⁷⁹ It was also referred to in complaints about the census not having a box for Welsh nationality, where flags could be flown, attitudes to accent, and the language of music on local radio.[80] In 2011, Miss Wales was invited by the Wales football manager to help the squad with their anthem's words before playing England in the European championships She decided to tell them what Welsh meant to her and the story of the Welsh Not, concluding 'Your ancestors fought for our language against such oppression. They actually tried to make the language of Wales illegal. What better time, therefore to be able to sing in Welsh than against the English?'[81]

Perhaps it was not surprising that David Davies, a Conservative MP, claimed in 2012 that the Welsh Not was 'largely a myth used to stir up anti-English prejudice'.[82] But Davies too was simplifying the history and using it to make his own political point. Nor was he the only one who began to use the Welsh Not to attack rather than defend Welsh culture. As Welsh-medium education grew, to the exclusion of English-language schools in some communities, the Welsh Not was cited in discussions about the importance of parental choice.[83] Concerns too could arise about whether children in Welsh-medium education were being punished for speaking English in play.[84]

Some recent representations of history have been more been sensitive to the possibility that there is a degree of myth around the Welsh Not. A 2010 documentary on Welsh history said it was difficult to know the level of state intolerance and that 'certain myths have grown up' around the Welsh Not but it did not explain what these were.[85] This, like the object label at St Fagans that notes the possibility of exaggeration, points towards a degree of caution in making assertions around the Welsh Not. This surely explains why it was not included in a book entitled *Wales in 100 Objects* in 2018.[86] The author of *10 Stories from Welsh History that Everyone should Know* (2021) did not want to include it because of the confusion but the publishers insisted and thus it makes a brief appearance with the caveat that it was used in 'a few schools'.[87] In a section entitled 'Making Wales English', *History Grounded*, published with Welsh Government support in 2021, noted how at some schools children were punished for speaking Welsh but made no further comment. Yet a side box showed a photograph of a real Welsh Not and had a drawing of a sad girl wearing one 'to show how it might have felt to have to wear the Welsh Not'. It gave no explanation of what the Welsh Not was.[88]

In 2021, fierce debate erupted amongst Wikipedia editors about how the entry should be framed and presented.[89] The debate suggested that some people had a strong emotional response to their ideas around the Welsh Not being challenged. For Welsh speakers, the language is an integral part of their identity. Its decline has represented an undermining of not just their personal identity but their nation and culture too. The idea that an English government had the language beaten out of people is easier to accept than the idea that it might have been Welsh parents and Welsh teachers who were responsible for what happened in schools. For those who do not speak Welsh, this belief also passes responsibility for the language not being transmitted in their own families to external forces rather than the decisions of their ancestors. But debates have not been helped by those who seek to absolve the British state of responsibility because this detracts from the unequal power balance within the United Kingdom that framed and shaped Welsh people's decisions in the past. In everything from museums to online debates, the complexity of what happened has been lost.

Challenges to the idea of the Welsh Not being universal or government policy are also controversial because they run against family stories. Individuals remembered grandparents who took pride in having worn the Welsh Not in the middle of nineteenth century and never lost their love of Welsh. Such stories mattered to people and could be both inspiring and a source of anger.[90] The social media era has meant such accounts have become far more visible. Many have a ring of authenticity about them and are based on first- and second-hand accounts from relatives who grew up in rural communities at the end of the nineteenth century. Some make links with people's own linguistic position and claim their parents were not taught Welsh by their grandparents because of the latter's experience of the Welsh Not. Some such accounts date these events to the early to mid-twentieth century, periods when there is no written evidence of the Welsh Not still being in use and when use of the Welsh language was positively encouraged by state education policy.[91]

The possibility that understandings of the Welsh Not are ahistorical is not new. In 1925, the Revd J. Vyrnwy Morgan argued that 'violent speeches' and 'acrid articles' had denounced the 'tyrannical effects' of the Welsh Note, 'building up a superstructure of racial and linguistic grievance upon false inferences'. He argued that the Welsh Note had been implemented by teachers who were Welsh and that they were not trying to eliminate Welsh but rather teach English.[92] Similarly, in 1937, scholar W. J. Gruffydd wrote that many people who complained they had suffered under the Welsh Not had gone to schools where it was not used and where teachers spoke Welsh to them. He went on to say that everyone was tired of hearing about the Welsh Not because they knew that it was customary and fashionable to express bitter feeling about it.[93] Such comments point towards how first memories of the practice are not always reliable. Philosopher Maurice Halbwachs argued that memory was something social, constructed by a group rather than an individual.[94] Following this lead, historians of collective memory point to how individuals' recollections of their own lives are influenced by what interests that person and by events and what they have heard about in their subsequent lives. Thus, people can forget experiences that no longer seem relevant or acceptable and overly dwell on what they think impacted on their subsequent lives or what they are reminded of because it resonates with later cultural conditions. Indeed, those later conditions can lead people to misremember or even imagine things that happened to them.[95] As one psychologist put it,

> We recreate or reconstruct our experiences rather than retrieve copies of them. Sometimes in the process of reconstructing we add feelings, beliefs, or even knowledge we obtained after the experience. In other words, we bias our memories of the past by attributing to them emotions or knowledge we acquired after the event.[96]

The ubiquity of the Welsh Not in Welsh popular culture probably led some people to 'remember' being subject to it when what happened was that they attended schools dominated by the English language and where perhaps a teacher hit them for speaking Welsh in the way that same teacher resorted to casual physical punishment for a variety of offences. It could be, too, that people heard stories of English schools from their relatives and later assumed that this referred to the Welsh Not. None of this is to say that all memories and stories of the Welsh Not are wrong but rather that historians have to be careful about accepting any evidence at face value.

Historians and the Welsh Not

Much of the confusion around the Welsh Not comes from the fact that there has never been a scholarly study of the practice. Instead, academic writers have tended to make broad assertions. Educationalist Kevin Smith's brief history of Welsh education saw the Welsh Not as an example of a 'consensual attack' on the Welsh language which 'took many forms and lasted for centuries'. He dates it to the eighteenth and nineteenth centuries and says it was participated in by teachers, administrators and pupils alike. He claims that the punishment was a whipping and that children who informed on those who spoke Welsh in the playground might be rewarded with sweets or similar.[97] Cultural theorist and novelist Raymond Williams claimed in 1975 that, alongside social and economic forces, Welsh was

> also driven back by conscious repression, by penalty and contempt, and in a late phase by a deliberate policy in the schools. You can still see, as carefully preserved [in museums] as the old tools, the little boards, the 'Welsh Nots', which children caught speaking their mother tongue had to hang around their necks, for shame.[98]

Gwyn A. Williams gave no details or dates but called the Welsh Not 'notorious' and claimed that 'Many of the school-teachers in the new schools practised cultural genocide.' He said it was 'not very effective but it enormously reinforced the image of Welsh as an inferior and gutter language'. What it was ineffective at was left unclear.[99] Others have blamed the state more explicitly. Literary specialist Jane Aaron said the Welsh Not was part of a 'systematic government attempt' to make the UK linguistically homogenous.[100]

Despite such assertions, few scholars have produced much evidence of the actual practice itself. Russell Davies argued that 'many schoolteachers adopted the "Welsh Not" to punish Welsh speakers for the use of the language inside the school grounds' but he does not produce any examples of this from the logbooks he widely used in his study of nineteenth-century Carmarthenshire.[101] Robert Phillipson's work on linguistic imperialism wrongly stated that 'the suppression or neglect of other languages was official policy' in Britain. He failed to give any examples of actual policies and simply cited schools' inspector Matthew Arnold saying it would be a good thing if Welsh died. Phillipson thus committed a common mistake of confusing attitudes with actual policies.[102] Historians of education in Wales have also been very critical of the role of the state. W. Gareth Evans wrongly argued that 'every effort was made [by the state] to suppress the Welsh-language in public funded schools'.[103] H. G. Williams argued that nineteenth-century education was one of the state's 'weapons in its war of attrition' against Wales. He went on to argue, incorrectly, that Welsh 'was not even sanctioned as a medium for teaching English more effectively'.[104] Even in sober assessments, there has been a tendency to use emotive language. Ieuan Gwynedd Jones called the education system 'pernicious' and concluded that Welsh was excluded from all schools. He did not discuss how it was excluded or consider whether this was actually feasible in practice.[105] A 1950s study claimed that school inspectors set up a system that was 'genocidal' in character.[106] None of these Welsh accounts claim the Welsh Not as state policy but a reader could easily make that connection.

Genocide is a very powerful word and evidence of how thinking about the history of language in Wales can be very emotional. Chris Williams has thus warned that studies of the decline of Welsh, 'written in an era when so much more political and cultural significance is attached to the survival of that language, run the risk of distorting the socio-historical record if they do not take care to at least suspend current-day attitudes and beliefs'.[107] Other historians have been sensitive to this and the lack of obvious evidence. While not denying that it ever happened, Durkacz said stories of children being beaten for speaking Welsh were largely hearsay.[108] Noting how in 1890 the education department allowed grants for the teaching of Welsh, John Davies's seminal history of Wales noted 'To a certain extent, Welsh had been employed in the elementary schools before 1889; it is unlikely that the use of the "Welsh Note was as widespread as the mythology of the twentieth century maintains.'[109] Russell Grigg's history of the training college at Carmarthen and the lives of its graduates was also sensitive to the complexities. It had a section entitled '"Welsh Not" mythology in schools' but did not actually discuss what that mythology was or the Welsh Not itself in any detail.[110]

A few studies have engaged more directly with the question. Dai Smith argued that the evidence for the Welsh Not 'is oral, impressionistic and, crucially, almost entirely confined to voluntary schools where it was operated by parental desire'. He claims that where it was used in state schools it was 'stamped on by higher authorities immediately'. Pointing to official backing for the teaching of Welsh, he concludes the language 'was not mortally wounded because of schools in the past'.[111] Smith, a historian who does not see the Welsh language as central to modern Welshness, is perhaps being no less political than those who claim the Welsh Not was state policy. He produced no evidence for the higher authorities stamping immediately on it and overstated the reluctant official support for Welsh in schools. Moreover, he, like most historians, failed to distinguish between the different attitudes to the use of Welsh for teaching English and the teaching of Welsh itself. He also repeated the common mistake of drawing a clear distinction between state and voluntary schools, failing to see how the state funded many voluntary schools and had no more control over the schools created by the 1870 Act than it did with those that existed before it. However, Smith is right that education did not mortally wound Welsh.

Such revisionism also shaped the attitudes of those more sympathetic to the idea of Welsh nationalism and difference. Brooks has argued 'The enraged response to the Blue Books is faux nationalism, an attempt in Welsh historiography to blame the English for the understandable decision by the Welsh themselves to abandon their language. For is not the abandonment of disadvantage a form of emancipation?'[112] Jones and Roderick's history of Welsh education argued there was plenty of anecdotal evidence for the use of the Welsh Not but 'not firm statistics as to how widespread it was'. They, wrongly, state there is 'no evidence' it was used in the Board schools created by the 1870 Education Act.[113] Other writers have also expressed some doubt about the Welsh Not, even when they saw it as symbolic of Wales's relationship with England.[114]

The revisionism has also produced a little backlash. Geraint H. Jenkins, for example, argued that the 'widespread use' of the Welsh Not, and similar tools used against other 'Celtic' languages, were 'tangible and painful symbols of the subservient status of all the Celtic tongues'. Nonetheless he still, persuasively, concludes,

> it is arguable that the general pattern of widespread linguistic erosion in all the Celtic heartlands was less attributable to the development of centralised institutions of state and the notion of English (or French in the case of Breton) as a bastion of cultural excellence than to the consequences of depopulation, migration, emigration, urbanization, industrialization, education and the development of communications.[115]

Daniel Williams has argued that it is possible to accept that the Welsh Not was not used as widely as myths suggest 'without losing sight of the fact that where it was in use it laid bare in a particularly graphic and symbolic manner the status and position of Welsh culture within the British state'.[116] This interpretation again wrongly implies a direct connection between the state and the Welsh Not but it is right to argue that the practice does illustrate the Welsh subordinate position within wider British culture.

A handful of writers have offered substantive comments and research on the Welsh Not. David Pretty's study of education in Anglesey identified a number of examples of its use, although he rather oversimplifies the hostility towards Welsh and the complexities of linguistic dynamics in schools.[117] Robert Smith, in a book on Welsh elementary education after 1870, concluded that the Welsh Not was 'a feature of the era before the 1870 Act, rather than a product of the system created' that year. He implied there had been some myth-making happening: 'Reference to the "Welsh Not" has been a necessary ingredient in the comments of those who had grievances against the education system of their childhood, although the numbers who could testify to personal experience of the practice were limited.' Instead, he maintained that the Welsh Not was never a policy of the education department, that its use was 'limited to a minority of schools' and that logbooks show that its use declined after the passing of the 1870 Act. He concluded:

> The 'Welsh Not' may offer an easy explanation of the decline of Welsh, yet to accept that argument would mean discounting the fact that opposition to the Welsh language reflected underlying social attitudes rather than any specific language policy. These attitudes prevented the Welsh language from being given an esteemed place in the education system long after the use of the 'Welsh Not' had been abandoned.[118]

These are reasoned and valid conclusions, but they are asides in a much wider study and Smith does not document the evidence for the Welsh Not from either before or after 1870. As a result, he underplays just how widespread the Welsh Not's use was in the first half of the century.

Tim Williams argued vehemently that the Welsh Not was neither state policy nor responsible for the decline of Welsh. On this he was right, but he overstated the state support for the language and underestimated just how deep the linguistic challenges in education were in areas beyond his Pontypridd focus. He was right that the Welsh Not mostly predated the 1860s but again he underestimated how much hostility to the language endured within many schools.[119] E. G. Millward who, unlike nearly all the other writers, actually outlined a series of examples of its use, also concluded that it predated 1870.[120] Millward's study concluded that the Welsh Not damaged how the language was seen but his study was brief and divorced from the evolving education context that shaped both the use and demise of the Welsh Not. The influence of the revisionism is evident in Rosser's recent study of children's literature; she notes how there was no evidence of the Welsh Not being used consistently or for a long period and that it was never state policy. She argues that young Welsh people turned to English without being compelled to.[121]

This book

Some writers have thus underplayed the extent to which the Welsh Not was part of education; others have exaggerated it or wrongly implied it was sanctioned by the state. Neither side of the argument has focused on the perspective of teachers or pupils. Historians have failed to root the Welsh Not in the context of how education worked, overlooking how children actually learn languages, the practicalities teachers faced, both in instructing and controlling children, and how this all fed into language practices. Moreover, too often, there has been no appreciation that what happened in classrooms was not always in line with what commentators or inspectors wanted. Whatever official policy said, the reality could be quite different. As Bischof concluded, it remains the case that 'Though we have a fairly good sense of how and what teachers were *supposed* to teach, what they *actually* did in the classroom every day remains frustratingly elusive.'[122] This also means thinking about the perspectives of children. How children experienced and reacted to language practices at school should not be judged through a modern lens that is outraged at the Welsh Not but instead understood as just one facet of school life. Historians should remember that children were not only victims, there to be moulded by a system, but were also capable of manipulating and resisting what was done to them. This book attempts to do that. It offers a bottom-up view of the Welsh Not, documenting its scale, rationale and effects. It puts it in an educational and cultural context and explores how language was actually taught, used and experienced in classrooms. It sees the Welsh Not, not as a policy, but as a practice.

The absence of empirical investigations into the Welsh Not is partly rooted in how the historiography of the Welsh language has concentrated more on questions of legal and official status than the dynamics of language in everyday life. This is reflective of a broader situation that led Gallagher to note that 'Historians have been slow to consider language-learning and linguistic competence.'[123] Yet historians have been well aware that other factors beyond education were key to the decline of Welsh. The opening line of the seminal social history of the Welsh language was 'The principal engine of linguistic change in the nineteenth century was demographic growth.'[124] Ieuan Gwynedd Jones, in contrast, sees both the survival and decline of Welsh as being rooted in the consciousness of the people of Wales. He argued that 'the virtually unanimous opinion of the Welsh elite – the educational, religious, commercial and political leaders of Victorian Wales – [was] that the disappearance of the language was inevitable and a good thing'. Yet he also notes how English could be seen as the language of secularism, infidelity and atheism, which Welsh was a defence against. Moreover, the language gave people 'self-confidence and a pride in themselves precisely at the time when all else seemed to conspire to reduce them to the level of slaves'.[125] In considering the impacts of education, this book sets the Welsh Not and schools within these contexts of demographic and cultural influences. It tries to place the Welsh people centre stage, seeing them not just as victims of policies made elsewhere but actors with agency able to resist and shape educational and linguistic practices. It shows how Welsh people took decisions of their own making but not in circumstances of their own making. The book thus tries to understand the Welsh Not and education through the world of those who implemented and experienced it.

Probably the key reason for the absence of any previous study is the complexity of the evidence base. References to the Welsh Not in the written record of the nineteenth century are few and far between and difficult to interpret. Autobiographical writings provide the richest vein of information, but they are far from straightforward sources. They were written later in life and are thus framed by the subsequent dynamics. They also come from people educated or important enough to write their memories and are thus not entirely representative of the wider population, especially those failed by their schooling. Moreover, they are often frustratingly vague in terms of dates, places and explaining how the Welsh Not was used, what language a teacher spoke to the class in, and how a class of Welsh-monoglot children actually understood or learned anything if lessons were held in English. This is evident in the memoirs of politician James Griffiths. He was born to a Welsh-speaking family in Betws near Llanelli in 1890. He attended the village Board school and described the headmaster as a kindly man from Cardiganshire who did not speak Welsh. How Griffiths himself learned English is not explained and he simply records that the teacher nurtured in him a love of reading. The reader is left to guess at how a boy went from not speaking English to loving to read books in that language.[126]

The growing involvement of the state in education generated a wealth of paperwork. As well as the periodic large-scale investigations such as the Blue Books, there are the annual minutes of the government's education department. These contain reports from regional inspectors that are invaluable pictures of local conditions, or at least what inspectors thought was happening or wanted their employers to know. From 1862, schools in receipt of state funding were required to keep logbooks, a daily diary written by the headmaster or mistress.[127] In theory, the logbooks allow for a bottom-up view of what was happening, but teachers took quite different viewpoints of what was required and they vary significantly in character and detail. The historian also faces the challenge of the sheer volume of their number. A regulation that stated 'No reflection or opinions of a general character are to be entered in the log-book' has not helped historians either.[128] Some teachers did reflect on the challenges of running a school, getting children to attend, and local events and customs, but others do little more than record attendance. Too often logbooks allude to things, leaving the historian to read between the lines, something which might mean misinterpreting or guessing at what was happening.[129] Victorian bureaucracy may have counted, observed, recorded and pontificated in capacious scale but its sources are also frustratingly sparse and one-sided.

Unless the Welsh Not is seen through the context of nineteenth-century education rather than the present day, it cannot be understood. But, even then, it is not enough to assess what contemporaries said about it. The historian also needs to explore why people said what they did, whether narratives reflected actual practices and everything that was left unsaid. This requires the use of two different languages. It entails painstaking work across different archives and sources, joining dots, chasing leads, emerging from dead ends, calculating and hypothesising. This book is the result of that work. It is not about debunking myths as such because the Welsh Not was not a myth. Instead, this is a book about how and why children were punished for speaking Welsh at elementary school. It is a book about how language worked in the classroom and how children learned English. It tries to decentre the British state and centre Welsh agency and experiences. It seeks to see the Welsh not just as victims of systems and cultural processes but as living and thinking people who understood the world they lived in. The book tries to step beyond simple dichotomies of people who spoke English or Welsh or both. It demonstrates that in the first half of the nineteenth century, the Welsh Not was relatively common and existed across most of Wales, although it was not used in every elementary school. The Welsh Not became less common as the century progressed as education became more professional and more regulated, but it never disappeared entirely. It also existed in spirit at the end of the century. Although Welsh was being widely used in schools in the 1890s, there were still many children being punished for speaking Welsh but without having to wear any kind of token. Throughout the century, there were teachers who spoke Welsh to their pupils but punished the children if they did the same. Indeed, when this did not happen, children failed to learn much because no one ever explained the new English words to them. In those schools where the Welsh Not meant no Welsh was used at all, the practice was, quite unintentionally, protecting the language because children were not learning English. The injustice of being punished for speaking one's mother tongue was intensified by the failure of many schools to teach English, the very thing parents sent their children to school to learn.

Notes

1. Owen Edwards, *Clych Atgof: Penodau yn Hanes fy Addysg* (Caernarfon, 1906), pp. 15–16, 17–18, 24.
2. Saunders Lewis, 'O. M. Edwards', in *Triwyr Penllyn* (Cardiff, 1956), p. 34.
3. Hazel Davies, *O. M. Edwards* (Cardiff, 1988), pp. 82, 40–1.
4. Gareth Elwyn Jones, 'Edwards, Sir Owen Morgan (1858–1920)', *Oxford Dictionary of National Biography*.
5. John Evans, *O. M. Edwards and the Welsh Not / O. M. Edwards a'r Welsh Not* (Cardiff, 2003).
6. Gareth Elwyn Jones, 'The Welsh language in the Blue Books of 1847', in Geraint H. Jenkins (ed.), *The Welsh Language and its Social Domains, 1801–1911* (Cardiff, 2000), p. 439.
7. 'Notes and queries', *The Welsh Weekly*, 15 January and 12 February 1892.
8. *Dysgedydd y Plant*, June 1893, 2.
9. J. B. Jones, 'Welshnot', *Yr Arweinydd*, 3, 29 (August 1880), 208–10.
10. Ellen Evans, *The Teaching of Welsh* (Cardiff, 1924), p. 75.
11. 'The Welsh Note', *Western Mail*, 30 September 1927, 7.
12. 'Welsh gossip', *South Wales Echo*, 9 March 1897, 2; Dewi Môn, 'Ysgol genedlaethol o'r hen ffasiwn', *Y Geninen*, October 1902, 258–63; Michael Gareth Llewelyn, *Sand in the Glass* (London, 1943), p. 8.
13. 'Yr Hen amser gynt!', *Amman Valley Chronicle and East Carmarthen News*, 27 June 1918, 4.
14. For example, 'John Jones yn yr ysgol', *Yr Ymofynydd*, February 1885, 39–42.
15. 'Gathered from Gwalia', *Western Mail*, 20 May 1895, 5.
16. Translated from John Thomas, 'Addysg yng Nghymru ar ol y rhyfel', *Cymru*, 50 (1916), 253–6, 254.
17. 'Y Welsh Stick', *Y Negesydd*, 16 June 1904, 1; 'Carnarvon council schools', *Carnarvon and Denbigh Herald*, 20 December 1907, 8; J. R. Kilsby Jones, 'Sefyllfa addysg y werinos haner can' mlynedd yn ol, ac yn bresonol', *Y Geninen*, 3, 1 (January 1885), 7; Andronicus, 'Yr ysgol: pennod III: Dim Cymraeg', *Cymru'r Plant*, November 1894, 313–17. Contemporary accounts of the history of English education also had a strong sense of progress, seeing it as part of the evolution of a modern democratic nation. See Christopher Bischof, 'Progress and the people: histories of mass education and conceptions of Britishness, 1870–1914', *History of Education*, 49, 2 (2020), 160–83.
18. 'Ysgolion Cymru Fu', *Tywysydd y Plant*, 4 April 1904, 115.
19. 'Wrexham British Schools', *Wrexham Advertiser*, 17 March 1888, 6.
20. 'Y Welsh Note', *Trysorfa y Plant*, Hydref 1879, 271–2.
21. 'Cambrian gossip', *North Wales Times*, 13 March 1897, 2.

22 Gwyneth Vaughan, 'Bryn Ardudwy a'i bobl', *Yr Haul* (May 1904), 225–30.
23 'John Jones, Junior: sef anturiaethau Cymro ieuangc mewn bywyd cyhoeddus', *Baner ac Amserau Cymru*, 12 December 1894, 12.
24 W. Meredith Morris, *The Renaissance of Welsh Literature* (Maesteg, 1908), p. 262.
25 'Plaid Gymreig', *Y Genedl Gymreig*, 28 October 1885, 6.
26 J. Tywi Jones, 'The gospel of bigotry', *The Welsh Outlook*, 6, 12 (December 1919), 311–312, 311.
27 Andronicus, 'Yr ysgol: pennod III: dim Cymraeg', 314.
28 Translated from 'Cymraeg y Gohebydd', *Y Brython Cymreig*, 18 April 1907, 3.
29 D. Ff. Davis, 'Yr Celt a'r Gymraeg', *Y Celt*, 24 October 1890, 4.
30 T. Gwynn Jones 'Bilingualism in the schools', in *Aberystwyth and District: A Guide Prepared for the Conference of the National Union of Teachers* (Aberystwyth, 1911), p. 249.
31 'Dim Cymrag', *Tarian y Gweithiwr*, 17 June 1897, 1.
32 'Y Welsh note', *Y Clorianydd*, 31 January 1917, 2.
33 'Life and sayings of the Rev. Kilsby Jones', *Herald of Wales and Monmouthshire Recorder*, 25 September 1897, 2.
34 'Welsh gossip', *South Wales Echo*, 12 March 1897, 3.
35 'Y naill beth a'r llall', *Y Darian*, 13 July 1916, 7.
36 'The Welsh stick', *Llangollen Advertiser*, 9 June 1899, 5.
37 'Hyn ar llall', *The London Kelt*, 9 June 1900, 5.
38 For example, *Y Llenor*, 17 (1938), 97.
39 Quoted in Lyn Evans, *Portrait of a Pioneer: A Biography of Howell Thomas Evans* (Llandybïe, 1982), p. 30.
40 Howell T. Evans, *Modern Wales* (Wrexham, 1938), p. 262.
41 D. J. Williams, *Yn Chwech ar Hugain Oed* (Aberystwyth, 1959), p. 228. The phrase 'murder machine' was taken from Irish nationalist Pádraic Pearse's 1916 discussion of education. Pádraic Pearse, *The Murder Machine and Other Essays* (Cork, 1976).
42 Richard Llewellyn, *How Green Was My Valley* (1939; Harmondsworth, 1951), pp. 294–5.
43 Llewellyn, *How Green was My Valley*, pp. 294–5.
44 Llewellyn, *How Green was My Valley*, pp. 295–6.
45 Llewellyn, *How Green was My Valley*, p. 302.
46 How Green Was My Valley, BBC, 1975–6, episodes 3 and 5.
47 Translation from https://morris.cymru/testun/saunders-lewis-fate-of-the-language.html (accessed 25 March 2024).
48 Gareth Elwyn Jones, 'Education and nationhood in Wales: an historiographical analysis', *Journal of Educational Administration and History*, 38, 3 (2006), 263–77, 268. The fullest treatment of the Blue Books is Gwyneth Tyson Roberts, *The Language of the Blue Books: The Perfect Instrument of Empire* (Cardiff, 1998).
49 Terry Breverton, *The Welsh: The Biography* (Stroud, 2012), p. 275.
50 David Evans, *Wales in Industrial Britain, c.1760–c.1914* (London, 1996), p. 50.
51 'A weekly talk on Welsh topics', *Western Mail*, 19 September 1919, 4.

52 David Thomas, 'Brad y llyfrau gleision', *Lleufer Cylchgrawn Cymdeithas Addysg y Gweithwyr yng Nghymru*, 3, 3 (1947), 94–7.
53 Kevin Duffy, *Who were the Celts?* (New York, 1999), p. 216. Also see Julie Brake, *World Cultures: Wales* (London, 2004), p. 31; Frank Delaney, *The Celts* (Boston, 1986), p. 186.
54 Richard B. Baldauf and Robert B. Kaplan, *Language Planning from Practice to Theory* (Clevedon, 1997), p. 56; Emyr Humphreys, *The Taliesin Tradition: The Quest for Welsh Identity* (London, 1983), p. 183.
55 Gwynfor Evans, *Wales can Win* (Llandybïe, 1973), p. 38.
56 Adam Price, *Wales: The First and Final Colony* (Talybont, 2018), p. 34.
57 Brian Morris 'Welsh Not', in *Tide Race: Poems* (Llandysul, 1976), pp. 49–50.
58 *Holl Ganeuon Dafydd Iwan* (Talybont, 1992), p. 21. Also see his song 'Pam fod eira'n wyn', which sees the Welsh Not as a rallying call for political action.
59 For a novel citing it: Carol Jones, *Late in the Day* (London, 1983), p. 114. For a children's story: Wendy White, *Three Cheers for Wales* (Llandysul, 2015). In 1995, the iconic Welsh band Anrhefn used the Blue Books' description of the practice as the lyrics to the song 'Welsh Not' on their album *Hen Wlad fy Nhadau* (Sain, 1995). An account in a guide to pub walks in Snowdonia concluded: 'That's how the English tried to destroy the Welsh language': Laurence Main, *Pub Walks in Snowdonia* (Wilmslow, 1993), p. 74.
60 *Let's Look at Wales: The Welsh Not Part 1*. Transmitted: 10 November 1975, 21 November 1975, 14 January 1980.
61 James Felton, *52 Times Britain was a Bellend: The History You Didn't Get Taught at School* (Sphere, 2019).
62 D. Parry-Jones, *Welsh Children's Games and Pastimes* (Denbigh, 1964), p. 150.
63 *The Celts*, BBC2, 11 June 1987.
64 *Snowdonia 1890*, BBC2 Wales, 9 June 2014.
65 Irene Myrddin Davies, *Welsh History: A Handbook for Teachers* (Cardiff, 1947).
66 *Yr Ysgol: Nodiadau Athrawon* (Llandysul, 1978).
67 For the language in this period, see Martin Johnes, *Wales since 1939* (Manchester, 2012), ch. 7.
68 John Evans, *O. M. Edwards a'r Welsh Not* (Cardiff, 2003).
69 Catrin Stevens, *Oes Ofnadwy Victoria* (Llandysul, 2007), p. 51.
70 Richard Carter and Walter Jones, *Ysgol yng Nghymru tua Diwedd Oes Victoria* (Llandysul, 1994), pp. 39–40.
71 Estyn, *The Teaching of Welsh History including Black, Asian and Minority Ethnic History, Identity and Culture* (2021).
72 Gerallt D. Nash, *Victorian School-days in Wales* (Cardiff, 1991), p. 1.
73 See *https://shared.kotobee.com/#/book/49374/reader/chapter/6* (accessed 25 March 2024).
74 Matthew Davies, 'Perfformio Hanes: cyfryngu, dehongli ac ysgrifennu'r gorffennol mewn perfformiad Cymreig'. Paper given at Imagining History: Wales in Fiction and Fact conference (2021).
75 Jon Meirion Jones, *Ôl Troed T. Llew: Deg Taith lenyddol* (Llandysul, 2011), p. 15.

76 See *https://collections.storiel.cymru/collections/getrecord/BANBM_B-2244* (accessed 25 March 2024).
77 Wynn Melville Jones, *Wyn Mel: Y fi a Mistar Urdd a'r Cwmni Da* (Talybont, 2010), p. 41.
78 Catrin Stevens, *Stori'r Gymraeg* (Llandysul, 2009), p. 26. Also see, for example, 'The teenagers on Merthyr's Gurnos Estate who love learning Welsh', *Wales Online*, 22 December 2021, *https://nation.cymru/opinion/teaching-children-welsh-isnt-forcing-it-on-them-but-giving-them-a-choice-of-two-languages/* (accessed 25 March 2024).
79 Fiona G. H. Wells, 'Addysg Gymraeg: achubydd yr iaith?', *Y Traethodydd*, 155 (2000), 94–105, 93.
80 Letters, 'Welsh Not', *Western Mail*, 26 February 2001, 10; 'Letter: A New Welsh Not', *Daily Post*, 9 April 2003, 8; 'The Welsh Not; Our nation's accents lack prestige', *Daily Post*, 17 January 2005, 3; '"Welsh-Not" claim sparks musical demo against radio station', *Western Mail*, 15 September 2004, 7.
81 Courtney Hamilton, *Tu ôl i'r Tiara: Bywyd Miss Cymru* (Talybont, 2012), pp. 59–60.
82 'MP finds no evidence that "Welsh Not" punishment was imposed by British Government on pupils', *Western Mail*, 17 November 2012, 19.
83 For example, 'Form of racism', *Weekly Worker*, 464 (23 January 2003), 3.
84 See the debates and comments at *https://www.iwa.wales/agenda/2014/11/the-trouble-with-bilingual-education-the-ever-increasing-gap-between-research-policy-and-practice/* and *https://www.leaderlive.co.uk/news/15936590.school-tells-pupils-speak-welsh-or-else/* (accessed 25 March 2024).
85 *Wales and the History of the World: Ideas*, BBC 2 Wales, 2010.
86 Andrew Green, *Wales in 100 Objects* (Llandysul, 2018).
87 Ifan Morgan Jones, *10 Stories from Welsh History That Everyone Should Know* (Caerphilly, 2021). Similarly, it is not covered in Tanwen Haf, *Y Teithwyr Amser: Llyfr Gweithgareddau Hanes Cymru* (Caerphilly, 2021).
88 Elin Jones, *History Grounded: Looking for the History of Wales* (Llanrwst, 2021), pp. 161–2.
89 See *https://en.wikipedia.org/wiki/Talk:Welsh_Not#Request_for_comment_on_including_a_computer-generated_image* (accessed 25 March 2024).
90 Beti Rhys, 'Ein iaith a'n huniaeth', *Cristion*, 62 (February 1994), 19. One author said he had met many people whose grandparents had been punished in school for speaking Welsh and 'who still shudder whenever this type of punishment is recalled by them. Some of these grandparents had refused to pass on the "Welsh Not" to other children, preferring to be the only ones punished for speaking Welsh': Bud B. Khleif, *Language, Ethnicity, and Education in Wales* (1980; De Gruyter, 2019), p. 114.
91 Such accounts are easy to find by searching for the term Welsh Not or #WelshNot on social-media platforms.
92 J. Vyrnwy Morgan, *The Welsh Mind in Evolution* (London, 1925), pp. 130–3.
93 W. J. Gruffydd, *Owen Morgan Edwards: Cofiant. Cyfrol 1, 1858–1883* (Aberystwyth, 1937), p. 99.

94 Maurice Halbwachs, *On Collective Memory* (1925; London, 1992).
95 Michael Roper, 'Re-remembering the soldier hero: the psychic and social construction of memory in personal narratives of the Great War', *History Workshop Journal*, 50 (2000), 181–204; Anna Green, 'Individual remembering and "collective memory": theoretical presuppositions and contemporary debates', *Oral History*, 32, 2 (2004), 35–42; Alistair Thomson, 'Anzac memories: putting popular memory theory into practice in Australia', *Oral History*, 18, 1 (1990), 25–31.
96 D. Schacter quoted in Jay Winter, *Remembering War: The Great War between Memory and History in the Twentieth Century* (London, 2006), p. 4.
97 Kevin Smith, *Curriculum, Culture and Citizenship Education in Wales* (London, 2016), p. 20.
98 Raymond Williams, 'Welsh Culture' (1975), reproduced in Daniel G. Williams (ed.), *Raymond Williams: Who Speaks for Wales? Nation, Culture, Identity* (Cardiff, 2021), p. 54.
99 Gwyn A. Williams, *When was Wales? A History of the Welsh* (Harmondsworth, 1985), p. 246.
100 Jane Aaron, *Welsh Gothic* (Cardiff, 2013), p. 53.
101 Russell Davies, *Secret Sins: Sex, Violence and Society in Carmarthenshire 1870–1920* (Cardiff, 1996), p. 84.
102 Robert Phillipson, *Linguistic Imperialism* (Oxford, 1992), p. 18.
103 W. Gareth Evans, 'The British state and Welsh-language education 1850–1914', in Gareth H. Jenkins (ed.), *The Welsh Language and its Social Domains, 1801–1911* (Cardiff, 2000), p. 459.
104 H. G. Williams, 'Nation State versus National Identity: State and Inspectorate in Mid-Victorian Wales', *History of Education Quarterly*, 40, 2 (2000), 145–168, 146, 167.
105 Ieuan Gwynedd Jones, 'Language and community in Nineteenth Century Wales', in David Smith (ed.), *A People and a Proletariat: Essays in the History of Wales, 1780–1980* (London, 1980), pp. 47–71, 62.
106 E. D. Jones, 'The Journal of William Roberts ("Nefydd")', *National Library of Wales Journal*, 8, 2 (1953), 205.
107 Chris Williams, '"Going underground"? The future of coalfield history revisited', *Morgannwg*, 42 (1998), 41–58, 51.
108 Victor Edward Durkacz, *The Decline of the Celtic Languages* (Edinburgh, 1983), p. 224.
109 John Davies, *A History of Wales* (Harmondsworth, 1993), pp. 455–6.
110 Russell Grigg, *History of Trinity College Carmarthen, 1848–1998* (Cardiff, 1998), p. 125.
111 Dai Smith, *Wales! Wales?* (London, 1984), p. 161.
112 Simon Brooks, *Why Wales Never Was? The Failure of Welsh Nationalism* (Cardiff, 2017), p. 80.
113 Gareth Elwyn Jones and Gordon Wynne Roderick, *A History of Education in Wales* (Cardiff, 2003), p. 84.

114 Anthony Crockett, 'Hawliau lleiafrifoedd a diwylliannol ac ieithyddol: yr apêl at gyfiawnder', *Efrydiau Athronyddol*, 57 (1994), 50–60, 51.
115 Geraint H. Jenkins, 'Introduction', in Geraint H. Jenkins (ed.), *Language and Community in the Nineteenth Century* (Cardiff, 1998), pp. 1–20, 16.
116 Williams (ed.), *Raymond Williams*, p. 20.
117 David A. Pretty, *Two Centuries of Anglesey Schools, 1700–1902* (Llangefni, 1977). This book was invaluable to me in helping focus my research within the large number of school logbooks from the island.
118 Robert Smith, *Schools, Politics and Society: Elementary Education in Wales, 1870–1902* (Cardiff, 1999), pp. 182–3.
119 Tim Williams, 'Language, Identity and Education in a Liberal State: The Anglicisation of Pontypridd, 1818–1920' (unpublished PhD thesis, University of Wales, Cardiff, 1989); cf. Tim Williams, 'Language, religion, culture', in Trevor Herbert and Gareth E. Jones (eds), *Wales 1880–1914* (Cardiff, 1988), pp. 73–105.
120 E. G. Millward, *Cenedl o Bobl Ddewrion: Agweddau ar Lenyddiaeth Oes Victoria* (Llandysul, 1991), pp. 183–9.
121 Siwan M. Rosser, *Darllen y Dychymyg: Creu Ystyron Newydd i Blant a Phlentyndod yn Llenyddiaeth y Bedwaredd Ganrif ar Bymtheg* (Cardiff, 2020), pp. 186–7.
122 Christopher Bischof, *Teaching Britain: Elementary Teachers and the State of the Everyday, 1846–1906* (Oxford, 2019), p. 158.
123 John Gallagher, *Learning Languages in Early Modern England* (Oxford, 2019), p. 3.
124 Jenkins, 'Introduction', pp. 1–20, 1.
125 Jones, 'Language and community', pp. 48, 64, 68, 69.
126 James Griffiths, *Pages from Memory* (London, 1969), p. 6.
127 Pamela Horn, 'School Log Books', in K. M. Thompson (ed.), *Short Guides to Records, Second Series* (London, 1997).
128 *Minute of the Committee of the Privy Council on Education establishing a Revised Code of Regulations* (1861), p. 10.
129 Susannah Wright, 'Teachers, family and community in urban elementary school: evidence from English school log books c.1880–1918', *History of Education*, 41, 2 (2012), 155–73, 160.

2
THE AGE OF THE WELSH NOT: LANGUAGE AND PUNISHMENT BEFORE 1862

In 1800, Wales was on the cusp of an industrial and demographic revolution. Merthyr and the valleys of Monmouthshire had become one of the most important iron-producing districts in the world. Making metal required heat and coal mines were springing up to feed the ironworks. In the 1830s and 1840s, the coal industry outgrew this role, expanded its markets, and became the heart of the Welsh economy. In the north-east, another industrial zone emerged, again with metal and coal at its heart. This spectacular growth of industry caused a population explosion. In 1801, 587,000 people lived in Wales. Fifty year later, the figure had doubled. The growth was concentrated in the south and, by 1851, a third of the Welsh people lived in Glamorgan and Monmouthshire. That population increase was fuelled partly by migration from rural counties where life was characterised by poverty and graft. In both rural and industrial districts, most working-class people lived their lives entirely through the Welsh language in the first half of the century. Only in the borders, south Pembrokeshire and Gower was English commonly heard, although migration from England into the industrial zones was beginning to change that.

These facts shaped and drove the educational context. The middle and landed classes wanted to see the English language spread to help further open Wales's economy and to avert the danger of a workforce that spoke a different language to many employers and landlords. The workers themselves wanted to be able to speak English because they saw it as a route out of the poverty and grind of manual work. Teaching English was thus the primary goal of nineteenth-century working-class education. Indeed, for much of the century, most schools taught little else beyond arithmetic, and reading and writing in English, the 3Rs. This was not a matter of controversy. There was no substantive agitation for anything else because of the perceived importance of English to people's life chances and because Sunday schools existed to teach Welsh. This reflected a widespread belief that the two languages had different spheres. Welsh was the language of religion and home, while English was the language of secular public matters.

Teaching English did not have to mean excluding Welsh from the classroom but that is what often happened. In 1887, the school inspector Dan Isaac Davies, giving evidence to an inquiry on education, described the situation in Wales half a century earlier:

> I do not know whether any other witness has explained the very strange traditional arrangements in Wales, which are something of this kind. The idea is that if you shut Welsh out of the schoolroom and the playground, you are in that way likely to teach English better. There is a plan by which if a boy is heard to speak a word of Welsh, a piece of stick or board, about a finger's length, is taken out of the master's desk, with the letters W.N. on it, meaning 'Welsh Note'. This is handed to the child, and the meaning of that is that the child, if he has it in his possession at the close of the school, is to be punished. This child is not now thinking of his lesson; he is very anxious to find somebody who speaks Welsh, in order to hand the W.N. on to him; so that he attends to right and left, to somebody before or behind him who is likely to speak Welsh, and as soon as he hears a Welsh word, he hands it over; and that goes on, and at last the final culprit is brought up and punished.[1]

This chapter explores that practice and why Welsh was excluded from classrooms before a significant change to how the state funded schools in 1862.

The first schools and teachers

The Welsh Not was the product of a patchwork education context that was rudimentary, ill-developed and often brutal. There were Madame Bevan's 'circulating' schools, remnants of an eighteenth-century charity movement where a teacher briefly set up in a rural parish to instruct local people how to read.[2] This movement had once concentrated on teaching Welsh but, in response to local demand, it now focused far more on the English language. In many isolated parishes, these temporary schools were the only education provision on offer. In other areas, there were charitable schools run through the support and endowments of the local gentry and religious bodies. Such support was partly paternal, but it was also about minimising social tensions. The Bridgend Society for the Education of the Poor argued in 1821 that its education had helped children find good jobs and gave them 'sound principles and moral habits'. It maintained its work had encouraged the 'higher classes' to be 'interested' in the lower classes, while the latter had gained an attachment and respect for the former. This, it felt, had been 'in no inconsiderable degree to the moral improvement of both'.[3] Most schools, however, were not charitable but private enterprises, funded by fees of a few pence a week. Amongst the most common were the so-called dame schools that were run by working-class women, often in their own kitchen. As well as literacy, they might teach skills such as knitting and handcrafts, but some were run by illiterate women and primarily about looking after young children whose parents were at work.

These schools all varied very significantly in character and size. Some only ran in the summer and others only in winter, especially in rural areas where agriculture created other demands on children's time. They might be held in chapels, barns or outhouses. Mud floors, leaking roofs, inadequate light, poor ventilation and a lack of heating were common problems. The Blue Books, an 1847 investigation into education across Wales, was full of descriptions of such conditions. At Llanwenog, it found eighteen children learning in a cold and wet converted cowshed, no bigger than ten by sixteen foot.[4] The Blue Books became notorious for its prejudices towards Wales but its observations on the condition of schools seem accurate and are confirmed by the memories of attendees. W. Carnero Harries recalled the school he attended in Llanelli in the 1840s. It was held in a small room 'with one low door, a small window, without any apparatus to open and close ... The floor was of dark, damp earth; a low and rotten roof, leaking in torrents on a rainy day. In fact, it was nothing but an unhealthy and deadly hole.' There were no desks and children sat on benches that were planks with crude legs or balanced on stones. Writing meant sitting on the floor and using the bench as a desk. Such conditions were not only uncomfortable and unhealthy; they were also far from conducive to concentration and learning.[5]

Thanks to employers' patronage and, sometimes, enforced deductions from workers' wages, schools in industrial areas were often better funded. This enabled 'industrial schools' to afford more and better teachers and resources. The Guest schools in Dowlais had plentiful books, a piano and a chemical laboratory; it was as advanced as any working-class school in Britain.[6] But, in general, the impact and reach of such schools was stymied by the speed with which the population was growing in industrial districts and the fact that most children left education by age ten to join the workforce.[7] This was evident in Merthyr in the 1840s. A report from 1846 claimed there were 6,857 children living there but only 1,313 attending schools. It concluded the town and area had 'no proper infant schools; no good juvenile schools, two only middling; most of the teachers being illiterate, two of them not able to write'.[8] Another investigation of the area argued that its schools were 'utterly incompetent and insufficient, and the wonder really is, how and where the labouring classes who were bred in this district obtained so much knowledge, not to say learning, as they possess'.[9] In many ways industrialisation had set back the cause of education because it created jobs for children. While the idea of children as young as six in a colliery might seem horrific to modern sensibilities, it did increase the income of working-class families, whereas sending children to school involved the financial sacrifice of both paying fees and losing wages.

Teachers in most schools had rarely undergone any training. Many were disabled and had turned to teaching only because they were unable to undertake manual work. Some were not even literate and only able to attract scholars because there was no alternative school in the locality. Yet parents' fees were rarely enough to offer much of a living and some teachers had occupations that they pursued alongside and even at their schools. Such financial precarity affected the stability of schools and many only lasted a few years thus further disrupting the education of those in attendance. Such problems were not unique to Wales. One 1914 history of education described teachers in private schools before state intervention as 'the refuse of every other profession, the lazy, the economic misfit, the decrepit, and the unemployed, as well as others who combined the office of teacher with such occupations as cobbling, tinkering, engraving, and in the case of women washing and shopkeeping'.[10]

In Wales, the main qualification of many for teaching was that they knew some English. One of the Blue Books commissioners concluded that in some places 'any person who is supposed to understand the English language better than his neighbours is encouraged to undertake the office of schoolmaster'.[11] A teacher's knowledge of English might have come through travelling, working in a trade that involved contact with the English or upper classes, or serving in the army. Yet, in areas where the language was not often heard, it was difficult for parents to judge the linguistic skills of the teacher they paid. Some teachers had very poor English and the Blue Books commissioners found themselves having to use interpreters with some masters who were supposed to be teaching English.[12] At Llanwenog, a small private school was kept by 'a poor half-starved looking man' who greeted the commissioner and his assistant 'rod in hand'. His English was limited and the commissioners concluded that he knew little more than his scholars.[13] At a school in Pembrey, the teacher was even recorded as 'illiterate'.[14] In the dame schools, things could be worse. The commissioner for north Wales thought them 'utterly worthless', with teachers 'Wholly unprepared for their calling, and ignorant of English.'[15] In such situations, much teaching seems to have been limited to writing down and repeating words read out by the teacher, with little heed to what they meant or how to pronounce them correctly. One commissioner recorded that he 'not unfrequently heard masters set the children wrong when they were right'.[16]

Despite the criticisms of the Blue Books, education provision in Wales was improving. Fearing growing Nonconformist influence on education in England, a National Society for Promoting the Education of the Poor in the Principles of the Established Church had been founded in 1811. The society began to set up its own schools on the principle that 'the national religion should be made the foundation of national education, and should be the first and chief thing taught to the poor'.[17] This was particularly important in Wales, where Anglicanism was floundering against the rising tide of Nonconformity. But the society also shared broader beliefs in the intellectual and moral value of education and reports from its schools stressed how they were improving the conduct and morals of local children. Wales's first National schools, as institutions under the society's jurisdiction were known, were founded in Penley (Flint) and Bridgend in 1812. Using the church's influence, networks and resources, the society grew, often superseding the less organised and poorer private and charitable schools. By 1839, there were 177 National schools in Wales.[18] Some were in purpose-built buildings, but others were in churches, cottages and outhouses. Indeed, conditions were not always any better than the private day schools.[19]

National schools, and others run by Anglicans, were controversial in Wales. Children were usually taught the catechism, a summary of the key tenets of the Anglican faith, which upset some dissenters who correctly perceived church schools as an attempt to undermine Nonconformism. In England, such concerns led to the formation of what became known as the British and Foreign School Society to promote non-denominational education. By the 1840s, there were around thirty 'British schools' in Wales, a fraction of the number run by Anglicans.[20]

Creating a school required money but both the National and British societies had limited funds. It was not until the state began offering financial support in the 1830s that either society began to have a significant impact on education provision. Ever since the French Revolution, there had been some unease about Britain's stability; economic problems and demands for an expansion of the electorate in the early 1830s intensified those concerns. Industrialisation and urbanisation were breaking traditional social bonds and creating new communities that were removed from the traditional structures and relationships that had helped keep people in their places. In 1830, there were agrarian disturbances in southern England and an armed riot in Merthyr in 1831. To remove any potential bourgeois leadership from the unrest, the Great Reform Act gave the middle classes the vote in 1832. In 1834, the poor law was reformed to remove the worst consequences of poverty. Educating the masses seemed to be another way of fighting disaffection. For those who believed this, the thinking was that if people were able to read the Bible, they would understand and accept the social hierarchy.[21]

In 1833, Parliament voted to give £20,000 towards providing schoolhouses for the poorer classes. But this was a drop in the ocean and, in 1839, R. A. Slanley, the MP for Shrewsbury, warned the Commons that 'if they did not give the humbler classes of society the means of obtaining a good practical education, in a short time it would be found that those people were not to be ruled by any Government'.[22] A state education department, technically known as the Committee of the Privy Council on Education, was formed in 1839. It had a budget of £30,000, which, to put it into context, was £40,000 less than the sum the House of Commons allocated for the repair of the Windsor Castle stables that same year.[23] Nonetheless, this marked the beginning of the state taking a permanent and recurring responsibility for education. Yet it had no machinery to distribute funds and thus relied on the two religious charities who were given the right to apply for grants. To ensure money was not wasted, inspectors were appointed to visit schools in receipt of public funds.

As well as annual payments from the state, there were grants to cover the cost of building schools but at least half the cost had to be met by other means. The National Society was far quicker in making use of such grants and had the advantage of the church's resources and its cultural capital with the local gentry and aristocracy in raising match funding. In contrast, without the support of local gentry, Nonconformist communities struggled to raise a share of the costs. Moreover, Nonconformists were also very suspicious of state aid, fearing that it, and the required inspection, was a means of forcing Anglicanism on people.[24] But the advances of the National schools encouraged a more pragmatic approach. In 1843, Hugh Owen, a clerk with the Poor Law Commission, published a *Letter to the Welsh People*, which called for a system of British schools to be established in Wales. This, he argued, would avoid the 'oppressive yoke' of an Anglican education being placed on the necks of districts.[25] The letter led to the appointment of a British Society agent for north Wales who travelled around, working with local communities to establish schools. From then on, Nonconformist influence on education started to rival that of the Anglicans.

Teaching in state-funded British and National schools was not necessarily any better than their private counterparts. In 1863, an editorial in the *Cardiff Times* recalled the early days of British and National schools of Merthyr a generation before. Teachers were 'bores of the worst kind', who were hated and employed the 'rule and birch' to punish children.[26] A man born in 1836 who attended a National school at Bodedern remembered his teacher drank, read the paper and snoozed in the afternoon, shouting 'Silence' if the pupils woke him up. He left most of the teaching to the older children.[27] In 1889, Reverend T. Levi of Aberystwyth described a Welsh schoolmaster of fifty years earlier who 'frequently got drunk in the afternoon' and then slept on the classroom floor.[28] In Daniel Owen's 1885 novel *Rhys Lewis*, set in the author's hometown of Mold, the author gives an account of a school earlier in the century run by an old soldier who was stupid, lazy, hypocritical and cruel. The narrator recounts:

> The most important part of his job, in the view of the soldier, was to take our pennies. His next care was to break at least one stout cane on our backs or hands. Our parents knew about his rough ways, but they believed it contributed to our improvement. ... No one was interested in learning, and our teacher was the least

interested of all. It gave him more pleasure to see us fail to learn, than to help us succeed.[29]

That account might be from a novel, but similar descriptions can also be found in a variety of other sources, not least the Blue Books. This 1847 education inquiry became infamous for the picture it painted of an immoral, backwards and untrustworthy people. It claimed drunkenness, unchastity and dishonesty were particular problems and much of the general blame was, directly and indirectly, laid at the feet of Nonconformity and the Welsh language. The reports were not written for a public audience but rather the education department. Nor did they contain much that had not been said before in official documents.[30] Nonetheless, there was outrage in parts of Wales. Public meetings were held, there was considerable discussion in papers and periodicals, and the reports were translated into Welsh to ensure a wider audience. They were deemed to be a judgement on the whole of Wales, 'a libel upon the national character' as one contemporary commentator put it.[31] What was not debated was its scathing portrayal of education. Having visited well over a thousand schools, the commissioners outlined their criticisms in meticulous detail. British, National, Bevan and private schools were all blasted for the quality of the buildings, staff and teaching. Moreover, most children were not attending school at all. The Blue Books only made passing reference to the Welsh Not but the crude schools it described – private, British and National – were where the instrument was used and the unsophisticated teachers it criticised were the people responsible for its use.

The Welsh Not, Note, Lump and Stick

At Llandyrnog (Denbighshire), one of the Blue Books commissioners recorded:

> My attention was attracted to a piece of wood, suspended by a string round a boy's neck, and on the wood were the words, 'Welsh

stick.' This, I was told, was a stigma for speaking Welsh. But, in fact, his only alternative was to speak Welsh or to say nothing. He did not understand English, and there is no systematic exercise in interpretation.[32]

Elsewhere, his report expanded on how it was used:

> The *Welsh stick*, or *Welsh*, as it is sometimes called, is given to any pupil who is overheard speaking Welsh, and may be transferred by him to any school-fellow whom he hears committing a similar offence. It is thus passed from one to another until the close of the week, when the pupil in whose possession the Welsh is found is punished by flogging. Among other injurious effects, this custom has been found to lead children to visit stealthily the houses of their school-fellows for the purpose of detecting those who speak Welsh to their parents, and transferring to them the punishment due to themselves.

This was said to be 'a custom which has been invented in the hope of promoting a knowledge of English'.[33]

The first mention of any practice of this sort appears to come from the 1790s. Noting how English was replacing the Welsh language in Flintshire, the Reverend Richard Warner of Bath recorded in 1798:

> One great object of education, it seems, in the schools (both of boys and girls) of North-Wales, is to give the children a perfect knowledge of the *English* tongue; the masters not only having the exercises performed in this language, but obliging the children to *converse* in it also. In order to effect this, some *coercion* is necessary, as the *little Britons* have a considerable aversion to the Saxon vocabulary; if, therefore in the colloquial intercourse of the scholars, one of them be detected in speaking a Welsh word, he is immediately degraded with *the Welsh lump*, a large piece of lead fastened to a string and, suspended round the neck of the offender. This mark of ignominy has had the desired effect; all the children

of Flintshire speak English very well, and were it not for a little curl, or elevation of the voice, at the conclusion of the sentence, (which has a pleasing effect) one should perceive no difference in this respect between the North-Walians and the natives of England.[34]

Other evidence of similar practices in the eighteenth century is very limited. After the Blue Books' Welsh Stick account was republished in the *Morning Post*, the newspaper was told by an anonymous reader that he remembered the practice sixty years before. It reported that their informant was often the last to possess the token: 'Being of a rather hasty temperament, when anything was said to provoke him, his mother tongue would out, despite ... the pains and penalties of the awful *Welsh stick*'. The article was vague on detail but the punishment seems to have been being kept behind after school.[35] The earliest first-hand named memory of the practice is also from the late eighteenth century. Lewis Powell, who was born in 1788 at Defynnog (Breconshire), recorded that at his school the token was named the Welsh Note and was called for at the end of every afternoon. He remembered it was hated by the children and would bring them to tears, although they also tried to trick each another into speaking Welsh and would laugh at the bearer and his weeping.[36] A Welsh Stick also seems to have been used at Friars Grammar School in Bangor in the eighteenth century. A story was later published of a bishop visiting the school in 1805 and seeing the son of the solicitor-general for Ireland with it. Although the boy could not speak Welsh, he had been tricked into saying some words by another pupil. The master explained to the bishop that giving the boy the stick was a 'gross misapplication' of the object's purpose which was 'to restrain the native Welsh boys from continually chattering and clattering their *Cymraeg*' and to ensure they practised their English. The bishop took the stick and put it on a table. It was never used again.[37]

Most of the evidence for the use of a physical object to punish speaking Welsh at school dates from the early to mid-nineteenth century. By then, it was more commonly known as the Welsh Not or Welsh Note. One description of the practice from 1851 described the symbol as 'a square piece of wood, about an inch thick and three inches long, with the letters W and N, either burnt into it, or else cut with a knife, and then inked'.[38] However, its size and engraving were not consistent. One man remembered it in Llanddewi Brefi being just an inch-and-a-half long, whereas at a Llandysul school in the 1830s, the Welsh Not was two-foot long.[39] Goronwy Jones, born in Bala in 1849, also recalled a big stick but this time with 'NO WELSH' written on it.[40] A retrospective account from 1911 said that in some schools the token had written upon it: 'Welsh Note, a slap for every time you speak Welsh'.[41] Elsewhere, it just had 'Welsh' engraved on it.[42] In contrast, in another account it was a tied handkerchief called the Welsh Knot.[43] These physical variations undermine the image commonly held today of it being something hung around the neck. Certainly, some memories fit that picture.[44] But others suggest it was something to be placed on a desk, in a pocket, or even that it was the instrument itself used to hit children.

How it was administered varied too. In 1843, the vicar of Cilymaenllwyd (Carmarthenshire) gave the inquiry that followed the Rebecca Riots an account that was probably quite typical:

> The schoolmaster in my parish, for instance, amongst the common Welsh people has a little toy on a little bit of wood, and on the wood is written 'Welsh not;' that is to say, they must not speak Welsh; it is a mark, and they pass this mark one to another. The rule of the school is, that there is no Welsh to be spoken in the school; if anybody speaks a word of Welsh he is to have the Welsh mark, which he to carry about his neck, or to hold it in his hand. There is the greatest anxiety to catch one another speaking Welsh, and there is a cry out immediately, 'Welsh not.'[45]

But practice was more varied than this. In some schools, it was given out at the start of the day to a child whose job it would be to listen out for someone speaking Welsh to pass it on to.[46] In one memory of Llandysul in the 1830s, it seems only to have been used at playtime.[47] In other places, there were multiple Welsh Nots in circulation at the same time.⁴⁸ The most common memories point to only the last child holding the Welsh Not being punished but this was not universal. In 1885, one old man recalling his youth in Llanddewi Brefi wrote that the Welsh Not was called for at the end of the morning and the end of the day and everyone who had held it was hit, with whoever had not passed it on being struck the hardest.⁴⁹ An account of 1850s New Quay also noted every holder would be given a swipe of the cane on the hand, although the punishment was on the backside for those who had had the Welsh Not in their possession more than others.⁵⁰

An account from Llanwinio described the punishment as a 'hearty slap'.⁵¹ In other accounts the violence was described in much sterner terms. One 1851 retrospective and generalised description of the practice recorded:

> The penalty for having this stick in one's possession at noon, or in the evening, was to have the palm of the hand hit as hard with the thick end of a stout birch-rod, as the master was able. And, to do the masters justice, they laid it on with unmistakable emphasis.⁵²

After speaking Welsh at school, David Lloyd George's uncle, Richard Lloyd (b.1834), was hit so hard on one ear that he was partially deaf for the rest of his life.⁵³ A man born in 1832 remembered the 'blessing' of the Welsh Note was to be hit on the backside until you bled. But he said the worst punishment for holding it was having to stand on one leg with your head up the chimney and the other boys laughing at you.⁵⁴

That account demonstrates how not all punishments were physical. Alternative penalties included learning passages from the Bible, not being allowed out for playtime or having to write lines.⁵⁵ In 1879, one man remembered seeing a Welsh Stick in a cupboard at Llanarmon Dyffryn Ceiriog at some unspecified date. He was told the bearer had to stand in the corner on one leg with the stick in his mouth.⁵⁶ In at least one school, monetary fines were used, but this obviously had limited use in poor districts.⁵⁷ The poet Eben Fardd (b.1802), who himself later employed the Welsh Not as a teacher, was reputed to have been made to drink his own urine at school for speaking Welsh.⁵⁸ One man remembered that at Nantglyn (Denbighshire) in 1853–4, the Welsh stick was six inches long. The victim was identified by other pupils who shouted 'John Hughes talk Welsh'. The pupil who had it at the end of the day had to stay behind on their own to complete a task. This frightened the children because they thought the school was haunted.[59]

Such examples show how psychology and humiliation were integral to the Welsh Not. A memory from Cardiganshire in the 1860s stressed the public nature of the punishments:

> Behind the door, hanging on a nail, was a small board, the breadth of hand, and written on it was 'Welsh not'. Welsh was not allowed inside or outside the walls of the school from 9 o'clock in the morning until 4 o'clock in the afternoon. And if a word of Welsh was spoken (which was done often) the Welsh not was thrown around the offender's neck at once, and he would have to carry it to his great shame. But if he heard anyone else speaking Welsh he had the right to transfer it to the new offender. At the end of the day, the one with the Welsh not went to the teacher's desk to receive his punishment before the whole school, and the punishment was the rod four times on the offender's two hands.[60]

Part of the public nature of the punishment was the physicality of the object itself. Emotions can be affected and prompted by objects and memories might focus as much on the Welsh Not itself as on its consequences.[61] In 1943, one writer recounted what he had been told by his father:

> The 'Welsh Not' was a piece of flat wood about four inches long, upon which were carved the words WELSH NOT. At the end of it a small hole had been bored through which a loop of thick string had been threaded. This enabled the unfortunate holder to suspend the hated article from his wrist. Generations of children who had worn it thus in the village school had made the string dark and greasy and the piece of wood black as bog oak.[62]

There was thus an element of display around the punishment. Indeed, sometimes the only punishment was being made to wear the board around the neck.[63] The Welsh Not was an object of shame, something that spoke not just to the offender, but to the whole school. It put one's transgression on display in a sustained way that a quick slap or caning did not. The token itself may have been small but the emotions it might generate were not.

It is difficult to be sure of how widely employed the Welsh Not was. Education inquiries offered no clear statements, while the autobiographical writings are too unsystematic to offer any conclusive evidence of patterns or certainty about its frequency. Many writings do not mention it but that might be because it had little impact on them or was too commonplace to make an issue of. The Blue Books were the most comprehensive survey of Welsh education ever conducted but they only contain one mention of it. This might suggest it was not widespread, but the commissioners' school visits were fleeting and intrusive and thus they did not always witness a normal day in the classroom. Other mentions of the practice are vague in detail and difficult to interpret. Some writers from the middle of the century felt the need to describe the practice, suggesting they did not expect their readers to know what it was. They also normally use the past tense suggesting they thought it was no longer in use.[64] One man in 1879, on coming across a reference, was perplexed enough to write to a newspaper to ask if anyone else had heard of it.[65] A 1927 letter to the *Western Mail* from a man in Narberth who attended two schools between 1857 and 1863 recalled that teachers spoke English to the pupils but 'neither showed the least desire to make us speak English to one another'. He said he had never heard of the Welsh Note until many years later.[66]

All this suggests that it was not in universal use in the early and middle of the century. However, some contemporary writers did think it had been very prevalent.[67] There are certainly enough mentions of the practice in the first half or so of the nineteenth century, if only in retrospect, to suggest that it was far from uncommon. Moreover, the references from early in the century can be found across nearly all Wales, although less so frequently in Glamorgan and Monmouthshire where

English was more prevalent and thus there was less pressing need to discourage Welsh-speaking.[68]

Some people in the early twentieth century who made oral enquiries also got the sense that it had been quite general.[69] The Welsh Not may not have been universal but it was not something only employed in a handful of schools. From the sheer range of references to it, in both private schools and those run by the British and National societies, it does seem reasonable to conclude that the Welsh Not was widely used in the first half of the century, even if it did vary in name, form and practice. Moreover, even in schools where it was not used, English was still the dominant language and children could still be hit for speaking Welsh even if they did not have to wear the Welsh Not. As the Blue Books showed in great detail, English was the primary medium of education in Wales.

A culture of punishment

Stopping children from speaking Welsh did not have to require any form of physical punishment. However, in most schools in the first half of the century discipline was very strict. At Madam Bevan's circulating schools, the rules stated that every morning teachers should inspect children to ensure their hands and face were clean and that their hair was combed. Any child found to be dirty was to be sent out of school 'in disgrace to rectify the negligence'. A pupil caught thieving, lying or swearing was to be 'exemplarily degraded and punished' for the first offence, and expelled for a second.[70] Strict discipline was thus part of the culture of the schools and education in general. It was used not just to punish children but to control them by acting as a frightening deterrent. Indeed, it was so common that drawings of teachers often showed them holding some form of rod or birch. It had a religious justification too in the biblical proverb 13.24: 'He that spareth his rod hateth his son, but he that loveth him chastenth him betimes.'[71] One professor of education even claimed in 1856, with a touch of sarcasm, that it was widely believed that 'a competent knowledge of Greek and Latin can only be secured to a boy by *flogging it into him*'.[72] In this context, the horror of the Welsh Not was just another part of the general tenor of schooling.

Memories of harsh punishments fill many autobiographical writings about the early nineteenth century. Henry Jones, who attended a school in Llangernyw (Denbighshire) in the 1850s, remembered that his teacher was 'very cruel' and would hit children for speaking Welsh but also anything from whispering, getting sums wrong, to turning around in class.[73] As well as a Welsh Not, Gwilym Wyn recalled that at Cwmllynfell British school in the 1850s being late could lead a child to be locked in the 'black hole' under the floorboard, while fighting could see a child hung from the wall on a nail.[74] A man who attended a chapel school at Llandysul in the 1830s said his teacher enjoyed punishing the children more than anything – except a drink. They would be hit until their 'blood flowed' and their 'skulls cracked'.[75]

Henry Morton Stanley (b.1841) remembered his teacher at St Asaph workhouse as a vicious, bad-tempered man who would fling children to the floor, hit or kick them for being noisy or making mistakes in their lessons:

> The ready back-slap in the face, the stunning clout over the ear, the strong blow with the open palm on alternate cheeks, which knocked our senses into confusion, were so frequent that it is a marvel we ever recovered them again. Whatever might be the nature of the offence, or merely because his irritable mood required vent, our poor heads were cuffed, and slapped, and pounded, until we lay speechless and streaming with blood. But though a tremendously rough and reckless striker with his fist or hand, such blows were preferable to deliberate punishment with the birch, ruler or cane, which, with cool malice, he inflicted.

Those who made a series of errors were hit 'until he was exhausted, or our lacerated bodies could bear no more'. Stanley concluded that he and his classmates lived every hour 'in mortal fear of the cruel hand and blighting glare of one so easily frenzied'.[76] This was an extreme example. As a workhouse school, the teacher did not have to be mindful of losing the fees of unhappy parents, but it nonetheless illustrates just how vicious schools could be. Children being beaten for speaking Welsh thus has to be viewed in the context that the children experienced it. They were often getting beaten for any misdemeanour or indeed things well beyond their control. In 1889, Reverend Thomas Levi described a Welsh school of fifty years earlier: 'The boys did not get the cane in those days. It was a long birch rod, and the Welsh note was so strictly applied that a child got the birch rod almost if he coughed. They had to speak English even if they knew nothing but Welsh.'[77] This was deeply unfair but so was much of school life.

The Welsh Not involved emotional as well as physical pain since it was something where the offender was put on show and had to endure the shame of wearing or holding a token that reminded all of the crime and the punishment to come. But here, too, it was not unique and humiliating or scaring children was a common method of punishment. An 1808 book on education contained a sermon by a chaplain who maintained that children would be motivated more by the fear of disgrace than physical pain.[78] Some schools had a wooden Last Note, engraved with LN, which put those last to school on show.[79] Others employed dunce or fool's hats to shame those whose learning did not meet expectations.[80] In some schools, children who broke a rule were made to stand on one leg on a bench or table, holding a Bible above their head. Another child might be put on watch to hit the culprit if they put a foot down.[81] Dewi Môn (b.1836) went to Bodedern National school and remembered a child who repeatedly failed to learn his or her lessons had to stand on a bench in the middle of the room wearing a pointed paper hat. The rest of the pupils would then point their fingers at the offender and loudly shout 'Fool'. No one, he said, who underwent this wanted to experience it again. But the worst punishment at the school, although not often used, was to be locked in what they called the black hole, a disused cupboard which would terrify children. The rumour amongst the children was that after a boy had kicked the door, it had been covered in lime dust so that anyone who did it again would choke.[82] In Abergele, one child was made to confess to a theft, while the master held a rope as a reminder of how thieves were hanged.[83] The psychological trauma inflicted by the Welsh Not was thus not something that happened in isolation.

Some contemporary commentators thought violence in schools was the result of how untrained many teachers were.[84] Without training, they were simply unaware that there were other ways of maintaining discipline. A Blue Books commissioner wrote of a Church school in Anglesey:

> The conduct of the master was wantonly severe. He was in the habit of striking the children in the face with a large rod, boys and girls indiscriminately, and without regard to merit or demerit. In this manner I saw him strike one little girl, who had committed no kind of offence, a blow which deprived her of sight during the remainder of my visit. Yet he did not appear to be naturally ill-natured, but was ignorant of any better system of discipline.[85]

Similarly, an 1837 select committee recorded:

> I have been in schools, for instance, where the mistress, who has been speaking to me, has said to the children, 'Hold your tongues, you little deviles', and burst out into a violent fit of passion, striking the child nearest to her; not perhaps the one that most deserved it; and none of them seemed to have any idea of treating the children in any other way than by punishment. Rewards are, with them, out of the question; their means will not afford it, and, therefore, punishment is the only mode left.[86]

But it might be that the violence was rooted in teachers' personal failings too. One witness to an 1830s education inquiry claimed that the adverse circumstances, such as infirmity or misfortune, that forced individuals into teaching influenced their tempers and made them unfit for an occupation that required patience and kindness.[87] Similarly, Henry Morton Stanley remembered his teacher at Asaph workhouse school 'was soured by misfortune, brutal of temper, and callous of heart'.[88] There certainly seems to be a degree of sadism involved. A woman born in 1852 remembered that her teacher, who employed the Welsh Not, would sleep a lot, leaving the children with their Reading Made Easy books. If they made a noise and woke him, he would push his thumb into their ribs. Her next teacher broke sticks on children's backs and thick rulers on their hands. The sound of the 'wailing of the children', she recalled, would fill the schoolyard.[89] A book from 1893 told the tale of a dame school where a teacher known as 'Nana the Lane' would heat a large appliance resembling tongues in the fire until it was red hot. She would hold it open on either side of a naughty boy's head, leaving him unable to move for fear of being burned. The poor victim then had to promise to be good.[90] Even allowing for some exaggeration in the telling, it is difficult not to think that the teachers responsible for such acts had brutal or vicious personalities. A more sympathetic interpretation might point to the pain and isolation suffered by teachers outside mainstream society, or coping with physical disabilities; but even if the Welsh Not was not rooted in teachers' sadistic personalities or personal frustrations, it still reveals how limited their classroom skills were.

Yet there was some rationale to the use of violence. Punishments were not just about control and discipline: they instilled and symbolised the authority of the master and the requirement that pupils do what they were told. Developing obedience was itself an important goal of education for many patrons of schools given the wider political concerns about the impact of urbanisation, the legacy of the French Revolution and the rise of Chartism.[91] The teacher had more practical concerns and for them the rod or birch itself had a symbolic role signifying their authority.[92] This was also why, in some nineteenth-century schools, it was hung on the wall where it would remind children of the consequences of not following the master's rules. The Blue Books commissioner for north Wales concluded that corporal punishment was employed in the majority of schools but 'I have seldom seen it actually administered except by ignorant and petulant teachers'. He felt that, instead, the pupils were 'habitually governed by fear' of the possibility of punishment.[93] Adults certainly remember the pain and humiliation they endured when at school, but they were less adept at remembering that these things were not always daily accounts. Only in the worst schools was violence routine. In many more, it was the threat of it that mattered far more. Indeed, the rules of Llantwit National school in 1831 declared explicitly that corporal punishment would only be used when all other modes of punishment had failed.[94]

In the Middle Ages it was thought that rods and birches were controlling mechanisms that restrained a master's 'own potential for rash aggression'. The use of a stick meant the pain was inflicted on the hands or behind, where less damage would be done than by punching or kicking in the heat of the moment. As Parsons argued, contemporary thinking was that through using a rod or stick, 'the master can guarantee that beating is properly calibrated, and that he is not acting spontaneously and unthinkingly'.[95] For more reflective teachers, the use of symbols in language teaching may have had the same purpose. They ensured the punishment was controlled, rationalised and delayed. They ritualised the whole process, removing the possibility of teachers acting in anger, spite or dislike of a particular child. They also helped ensure that children had time to think about the offence rather than just the outcome.[96] By focusing the punishment on the last child to hold it, the amount of punishment handed out was also curtailed. Across different periods, educationalists were aware that physical punishment was only effective at regulating behaviour when it was used sparingly. The Welsh Not was an example of that in practice.

Thus, despite the fact that it was rooted in schools' harsh punishment cultures and used by untrained and sometimes cruel teachers, there was some pedagogical rationale behind the Welsh Not. This is central to why it was far more widespread than just the worst and severest schools. The use of a physical symbol that would be passed around by the children was part of a culture where pupils did not just learn but helped run schools too. This was something encouraged and theorised by the educational thinkers of the time, such as Joseph Lancaster and Alexander Bell.[97] Teachers trying to instruct and control classes of different ages all at once faced practical problems. Lancaster and Bell had thus developed systems of class monitors where older children taught and supervised younger ones. But, even then, it was difficult to ensure that everyone was doing what they were meant to be. Engaging all the children in enforcing the rules made things easier. This was a form of surveillance, where the children were watched from all directions, making the likelihood of being caught greater, something key to changing behaviours.[98] The passing around of the Welsh Not, and only punishing the last child to hold it, therefore made enforcing no Welsh rules easier for a teacher by uniting all the pupils in its operation and ensuring anyone already caught still had motivation to behave and seek other culprits. Indeed, keeping children active and alert in this way also helped stop them from getting distracted.

Requiring children not to speak Welsh had the further advantage for teachers of keeping them quiet. As one victim recalled, to prevent Welsh-monoglot children from speaking Welsh was to prevent them speaking at all.[99] With limited staff and furniture to keep the often large number of children in place and focused, schools had the potential to be very busy and noisy places. Silence was seen as important because it was a symbol of order, discipline and hard work; it might even be somewhat democratising for pupils because it, at least temporarily, detracted from children's different linguistic skills.[100] Thus the purpose of the Welsh Not may have been as much about enforcing silence as the prevention of Welsh. The rules of Llantwit National school, opened in 1831, declared that no child was allowed to speak during school hours.[101] One man remembered that at his school the last child to hold the Welsh Not had to write out 'I must not disturb the order of the school' fifty or a hundred times.[102] A school in Hebron in Pembrokeshire had both a Welsh Not and a similar Talk Not, engraved with the letters TN.[103]

The Welsh Not's origins

The Welsh Not was perpetuated by the rudimentary nature of education and the punishment culture within it. But that does not explain where the idea originated in the first place. Punishing pupils for speaking their mother tongue when learning another does have a long history. English was used to teach Latin to younger children in medieval England, but older ones were expected to speak Latin and not always just in the classroom. Thus, in the 1460s, choristers at Wells were told if they wanted anything at mealtime, they had to ask for it in Latin not English. This did not mean the complete exclusion of English: translating back and forth was a common teaching method and it was used as a means of explanation.[104] But those who spoke English where it was not allowed might expect to be punished. In medieval Europe, there was a belief that physical punishment helped 'engrave the memory' and that recollection was something physiological. Pain thus helped people remember.[105] This meant that the use of physical punishment in schools was both widespread and seen as something pedagogical. A set of thirteenth-century directives from the choristers' schools at Westminster Abbey stated, 'whoever is with a classmate, or with any student, if he presumes to speak in English or in French when he understands Latin, for each word he will sustain a blow with the rod'. The key point here is that punishment was inflicted only when boys were able to speak their new language. Beatings in medieval education may have been common but they were moderated and rationalised, not indiscriminate.[106]

The learning of Latin remained the goal of formal education and, in many sixteenth- and seventeenth-century grammar schools, boys were not allowed to speak English. In the 1570s, pupils at Southampton Grammar School were obliged to speak French at mealtimes, with anyone who spoke a sentence of English made to wear a fool's cap and watch the others eat. Some scholars have doubted the practicalities of such rules and argued they were aspirations or only referred to certain times of the day rather than being 'an absolute prohibition'.[107] An observer in 1612 also noted how such practices were problematic. Monitors set to watch out for the speaking of English were said to often give more attention to this task than to their own learning, while the accused might deny their offence or become discouraged in their lessons. He concluded that the resistance of the children, the time wasted and quarrels that arose meant that the benefits of excluding English were lost.[108]

Pupils were not just assumed to be able to absorb Latin and such schools also used English and translation exercises to ensure pupils developed their skills and understanding in the language they were learning.[109] Indeed, across Britain and mainland Europe, Latin and other languages were seldom taught by just banishing the mother tongue and instead translation exercises were common, with the vernacular used until boys had a good grasp of Latin grammar and syntax.[110] The 1657 charter of King James Grammar School in Knaresborough, Yorkshire noted that anyone who spoke English in class or on the playground would be beaten, but this only applied to those who had been at school for three years and thus could be expected to have some skills in Latin.[111]

Grammar schools in Wales in the sixteenth and seventeenth centuries were influenced by these practices but had the added complication of the Welsh language. Welsh did not have the social or educational status of either English or Latin and it was common for these schools to employ teachers from England. In teaching, they largely eschewed Welsh, instead using English with younger pupils and Latin with older ones. Statutes introduced at Ruthin in 1590 stated, 'if in one of the upper classes he speaks English and if in one of the lower Classes he speaks Welsh he shall be deemed faulty and an Imposition [punishment] given to him'. However, Welsh was not entirely absent from such schools, partly because there were sympathetic masters but also just for the practical issue of communication with those pupils who spoke little else.[112]

Whether punishments for speaking Welsh in early modern grammar schools involved a token or symbol is unrecorded but it is likely that the Welsh Not had its roots in grammar school practices. None of the British medieval or early modern evidence seems to mention the use of a physical token but evidence from England and other countries in these periods shows that shame was used against those who failed to conform or learn.[113] Moreover, the fact that similar practices to the Welsh Not were also found in nineteenth-century language teaching outside Wales suggests a common root in pre-modern education where the teaching of Latin was a challenge shared across Europe. One such example comes from an 1832 story about a school for young ladies set two or three decades earlier. French was the school language and those caught speaking English were presented with 'an oval piece of wood, with "ENGLISH", in large capitals, engraved on its front, suspended by a riband from the neck'. It was passed form lady to lady as they were caught and then called for three times a day, with the possessor fined threepence.[114] The parallels with the Welsh Not are obvious.

Symbols of shame were used across nineteenth-century France when children spoke their local language at school. These included cardboard tickets, wooden planks, bars, sticks, pegs, clogs, ribbons, and metal objects. Weber has claimed the idea was inherited from the Jesuits who used it to teach Latin to French children.[115] In Ireland, some children were given a tally stick (in Irish the *bataí scóir*), which was hung around their necks with notches for each time they spoke Irish. The punishment they would receive at the end of the day corresponded with the number of notches.[116] There is even evidence of parents helping to implement the system and adding a notch when their child spoke Irish at home.[117] In Scotland, the practice was called *maide-crochaidh*, or in English the hanging or punishment stick. The first-hand evidence for it is sketchy but there are suggestions that it went further than anything that happened in Wales. In 1881, a letter to the *Scottish-American Journal* claimed that children who spoke Gaelic at his school had to wear a horse skull around their neck.[118] In 1926, a man was told by an elderly neighbour that the punishment for speaking Gaelic at his school in around 1850 was to have a human skull hung around the neck for the rest of the day.[119] In at least one place, the practice was more similar to the Welsh Not. A folklorist was told memories of a school in Urquhart from the end of the eighteenth and start of the nineteenth century, where there was a small wooden token with a Latin name *tessera*. It would be passed around by all who were heard speaking Gaelic, with every holder of it being 'severely flogged' at the end of the day. That school also had other punishments more humiliating than anything in Wales. The teacher put a fool's cap, a smelly fox skin and a necklace of old bones on children being punished for different offences. Sometimes, wearing all three, a child would be made to stand outside to be jeered at by passers-by or in the middle of the class where the other pupils would spit on them.[120] The research of a curator at the National Museum of Antiquities of Scotland led him to conclude that this school's practices were not general.[121]

What all these contexts had in common was not just the use of humiliation and a physical token but a belief that excluding the mother tongue helped children learn another language. Contemporaries remarked on how, in the words of J. D. Morell, the inspector for British schools in north Wales, 'the whole organ of communication' in day schools was 'almost exclusively English'.[122] This was a kind of immersion technique based on an assumption that forcing children to use the new language helped their skills in it. Today, the Welsh Not is thought about in terms of stopping children from speaking Welsh but, for people at the time, it was much more about teaching them English. The Society for Utilizing the Welsh Language summed up that it was a 'cardinal principal of education' that the proscription of Welsh was 'the readiest means of ensuring the acquirement' of English.[123] An 1894 retrospective description of a school, put it more simply: to make the children practice their English, the teacher had a Welsh Note.[124] Quite plainly, wherever it came from, the Welsh Not was regarded as a mode of instruction.

The influence of training schools

The idea of the Welsh Not may also have owed something to emerging theories in the world of education. In response to concerns about incompetent teachers in England, there was a push for the development of training schools in the early nineteenth century. The pioneer was Joseph Lancaster (1778–1838), who ran an innovative school at Borough Road in London. The monitor system he employed, where older children taught younger ones, and his suggestions for how a school should be physically arranged, were highly influential and in 1817 the Borough Road school became a formal training establishment for the British Society.[125] Other colleges followed in its wake and in 1839 the state extended its nascent funding of education to training colleges. The emerging belief in the need for teachers to be selected and trained was rooted in genuine concern that too many schools were run by uneducated and ill-suited people. But it was also perhaps partly prejudice and snobbery, a sense that untrained and sometimes disabled working-class people could not teach.¹²⁶ Training schools were also a way for the state to influence education without having to take control of it. Through inspections and requirements of what training colleges should teach in return for grants, the education department hoped to shape the nation's schools. The funding of training colleges was thus, in the words of one historian, an attempt at 'centralisation by stealth'.¹²⁷

Whatever the motive, the furore around the Blue Books intensified the already identified need for similar institutions in Wales. The National Society had been relying on two 'organising masters' who went around Wales to help develop teaching and organisational methods.¹²⁸ The British Society, meanwhile, was sponsoring Welshmen to attend Borough Road but few stayed long because of the cost. Some struggled too with their own poor English and they do not seem to have been taught anything about how to deal with children's own lack of the same language. The Blue Books noted the young master at Rhosymedre British school had trained there but he was not able to speak English correctly. He was criticised for not giving any systematic interpretation of English lessons to his largely Welsh-monoglot pupils.¹²⁹ An 1840 report on elementary education in Merthyr and mining parishes in Monmouthshire found that just ten teachers in the forty-seven schools investigated had received any kind of training.¹³⁰ In north Wales, the Blue Books recorded that only sixty-five of the 643 teachers observed were trained, with the average time spent at a training college being just six months.¹³¹

The first training college in Wales was opened by Nonconformists in Brecon in 1846. However, it struggled financially, and relocated to Swansea in 1849, before closing in 1851. More successful was the South Wales and Monmouthshire Training College, which opened in Carmarthen in 1848 and the North Wales Training College which opened in Caernarfon in 1849.¹³² Both were Anglican institutions and were more stable thanks to government grants and the support of the local elite hoping to strengthen the hold of the church on Welsh education. The British Society was slower to respond and at first believed teachers that were better off at Borough Road in London where their English could improve.¹³³ However, the advances made by the National

Society, and the difficulty in finding suitable teachers for British schools, encouraged a change of attitude and the British Society opened Normal College in Bangor in 1858. Training institutions became routes to social mobility for working-class students able to scrape together the fees or lucky enough to win a scholarship. They gradually ensured schools across Wales were run by teachers with some training in their management and operation. But the transition was a very slow one. By 1859, there were still only sixty-three female and 245 male certified teachers working in Wales.[134]

The growth of training may also have been partly responsible for the Welsh Not. Joseph Lancaster, founder of the British Society's first training school, devised and published an elaborate system of punishments, many of which were based around humiliation rather than physical punishment. Boys who were dirty could be washed by a girl in front of the whole school. Older pupils working as monitors had a series of cards with statements such as 'I have seen this boy talking' or 'I have seen this boy idle', which would be given to a child to mark their offence. Lancaster wrote:

> When a boy is disobedient to his parents, profane in his language, or has committed any offence against morality, or is remarkable for slovenliness, it is usual for him to be dressed up with labels, describing his offence, and a tin or paper crown on his head. In that manner he walks round the school, two boys preceding him, and proclaiming his fault; varying the proclamation according to the different offences.

Truants, meanwhile, would have 'a large card' tied around their neck with 'TRUANT' written on it. Lancaster explained that, for repeat or frequent offenders, a heavy log could be put around their neck that restricted their ability to move. Frequent offenders could also be shackled or tied together with a wooden yoke and made to walk backwards around the school. Children could also be put in a sack or basket and suspended to the roof, where the other pupils would smile at the 'birds in the cage'. The latter was thought too terrible to use often.[135]

Despite how callous such techniques now seem, Lancaster's aim was to change pupils' habits rather than terrorise them. It is unclear how widely these punishments were actually used, either at Lancaster's school or at schools run by those trained under his system. Certainly, a school opened in Usk contained an elaborate list of similar punishments in its first set of rules.[136] But it may be that these punishments were more deterrents or for extreme cases. Lancaster himself noted that any single kind of punishment used constantly 'becomes familiar, and loses its effect'.[137] Nonetheless, the parallels with the Welsh Not are very clear. The earliest examples of the Welsh Not predate Lancaster, who published his ideas in 1803, and he cannot be deemed as the main inspiration behind it. But he, and the number of Welsh teachers who attended his London training school, do seem to have contributed to the idea that shame and visual symbols of an offence were effective methods of regulating and influencing children's behaviour. Lancaster may thus be the reason why the object used in punishments for speaking Welsh changed from simply being a token, as in the Welsh lump noted in the 1790s, to something with the offence written on it, as was so common in the nineteenth century. There is no evidence that the training schools in Wales taught students Lancaster's system of punishments but that does not mean they were not discussed, and his book was widely disseminated. People would not even have had to have read it or attended his training school to be influenced by his ideas. As some teachers introduced them, knowledge would spread through word of mouth and teachers' own experience of having been subject to them in their schooling.

Lancaster's ideas also encouraged teachers not to rely on physical punishments. In this, the training schools reflected a gradual shift in public opinion as opposition to the birch and its like grew. Even early in the century, there had been some concern around corporal punishment in education and this grew in the middle of the century, led by literary depictions of cruel teachers such as in Dickens's *Nicholas Nickleby* (1839). Such concerns extended beyond education too. Pillories and whippings were already no longer in use and the armed forces controlled floggings from 1859.[138] Transportation ended in 1853 and the last public execution took place in Britain in 1868. Legislation outlawing cruelty to animals was passed in 1835. The emergence of more humane ideas in education was evident in a report of Cardiff Infant School's 1843 annual general meeting. It stated that 'Kind looks, and the gentle voice of woman, now do the business of that very formidable abstraction – the schoolmaster – and the change is for the better.' It noted a 'gentle caress' was a good substitute for the cat-o-nine-tails which 'in the olden time, were mercilessly applied to quicken dull parts'.[139] Longueville Jones, a Welsh schools inspector, reported in 1850, 'I have met with some lingering traces of the old system of bodily punishment; but, in general, I have found the teachers able to maintain discipline by milder methods, and an excellent feeling seemed to prevail between the masters and the mistresses and their pupils.'[140] Books about teaching cautioned against the excessive use of corporal punishment.[141] By 1859, one pamphlet proclaimed that there was now a tendency to do away with the rod, although practice varied greatly.[142] The slow and gradual shift in public opinion was further encouraged by the 1860 conviction of an English public-schoolteacher for manslaughter after the death of a child that he punished. This established a legal test that punishment must be 'moderate and reasonable'.[143]

Not all teachers listened to or were even aware of such debates and cases and the violent imposition of the Welsh Not continued. But they do seem to have had some effect in muting and lessening its use from the middle of the century. From the 1850s, memories of or references to violent punishments for speaking Welsh decline. Yet they do not disappear. Nor do mentions of the Welsh Not. Indeed, what the debates around corporal punishment and the ideas of Lancaster may have done is change rather undermine the Welsh Not. Where it survived, the Welsh Not slowly became associated with detention and lines and the like. In nineteenth-century USA, being encouraged not to hit children had prompted teachers to employ shaming techniques instead.[144] Something similar may have happened in Wales and the Welsh Not could still inflict a powerful punishment without being followed by a beating or caning.

Conclusion

This shift occurred in a decade of significant change for Welsh education. In the wake of the Blue Books, both the British and National societies made major strides forward in utilising state funding to open new schools and extending modern education delivered by trained teachers. Whereas at the start of the 1850s, maybe 70 per cent of Welsh children were not attending day schools, by a decade or so later the figure had fallen to around 52 per cent.[145] Progress was hampered by rivalries between the two societies, the difficulty of raising the funds required to match the state grants on offer, and, according to one inspector, the indifference and parsimony of the local gentry.[146] Even in the mid-1860s, only a quarter of Welsh parishes were in receipt of government grants to support schools.[147] Nonetheless, the 1861 Newcastle Commission concluded that the character of education had 'undergone considerable improvement within the past ten or a dozen years'. However, it also noted that this was not universal, and Wales continued to have a complex and varied education system made of quite different kinds of schools.[148] The old-style private schools, run by untrained teachers and free from state inspection, continued to be common. Some parishes had adequate or even too many places at British and National schools but in other places there were no such schools at all. Even within British and National schools, there was considerable variety in standards and methods. The charities that helped fund them did not dictate classroom practices, which instead were left in the hands of local teachers and managers. The state may have inspected such schools in return for its annual grants but it too made no demands over how subjects should be taught. Thus, in both private- and publicly funded schools, it was teachers who were the key influence on methods in the classroom.

This variety shaped the Welsh Not in the first half or so of the nineteenth century. It was never found in every school and there were not universal methods of instructing and controlling children. However, as thousands of children knew, the Welsh Not was used across Wales, even if it did vary in what it was called, its form and how it was used. In places it was a product of a sometimes cruel and violent classroom culture, created and perpetuated by teachers who appeared to know no other way of controlling children. Such cultures gradually faded, as teaching grew more professional and religious charities started to rival private schools as providers of education. But the Welsh Not could be found in such schools too, partly because many relied on untrained schools but also because the use of shaming punishments fitted with the training schools' discouragement of physical punishment and were actively promoted by the leading educational theorists of the day. Moreover, there was always some rationale behind it. Some teachers, consciously or otherwise, saw it as a way of keeping children quiet and involving all in a shared venture to keep Welsh out of the school. All teachers who employed it believed it helped children learn and develop their English. Yet, as the next chapter explores, the Welsh Not actually achieved quite the opposite.

Notes

1. *Third Report of the Royal Commission appointed to inquire into the Working of Elementary Education Acts, England and Wales* (London, 1887), p. 7 [hereafter Cross Commission].
2. On the earlier movement see M. G. Jones, *The Charity School Movement: A Study of Eighteenth Century Puritanism in Action* (Cambridge, 1938), ch. 8 and W. T. R. Pryce, 'The diffusion of the "Welch Circulating Charity Schools" in Eighteenth-Century Wales', *Welsh History Review*, 25 (2011), 486–519.
3. GA, Bridgend Society for the Education of the Poor, 3 October 1821. Paternalism was central to the ethos of the aristocracy. See Matthew Cragoe, *An Anglican Aristocracy: The Moral Economy of the Landed Estate in Carmarthenshire, 1832–1895* (Oxford, 1996), pp. 1–2.
4. *Reports of the Commissioners of Inquiry into the State of Education in Wales. Part II* (London, 1847), p. 169 [hereafter Blue Books].
5. 'A glimpse of old Llanelly', *Llanelly and County Guardian and South Wales Advertiser*, 15 July 1897, 4. On the impact of physical conditions on learning see Catherine Burke, Peter Cunningham and Ian Grosvenor, '"Putting education in its place": space, place and materialities in the history of education', *History of Education*, 39, 6 (2010), 677–80.
6. Leslie Wynne Evans, 'Sir John and Lady Charlotte Guest's educational scheme at Dowlais in the mid-nineteenth century', *National Library of Wales Journal*, 9, 3 (1956), 265–86.

7   Leslie Wynne Evans, *Education in Industrial Wales, 1700–1900* (Cardiff, 1971), p. 335.
8   G. S. Kenrick, 'Statistics of Merthyr Tydvil', *Journal of the Statistical Society of London*, 9 (1846), 14–21, 20.
9   Reproduced in Jules Ginswick (ed.), *Labour and the Poor in England and Wales, 1849–51: Vol. III The Mining and Manufacturing Districts of South Wales and North Wales* (London, 1983), p. 79.
10 C. Birchenough, *History of Elementary Education in England from 1800 to the Present Day* (London, 1914), p. 4. On teachers in this era see Phil Gardner, *The Lost Elementary Schools of Victorian England* (London, 1984), ch. 4.
11 Blue Books, Part III, pp. 12, 29–30. Also see 'Report of Mr Seymour Tremenheere on the State of Elementary Education in the Mining district of South Wales', published in CCE, *Minutes, Part II, 1839–40*, pp. 208–18, 210. For memories of such teachers see Richard Jones, 'Asiedydd', *Heddyw*, 1, 3 (March 1897), 67–8.
12 For examples see Blue Books, Part III, p. 12.
13 Blue Books, Part II, p. 169.
14 Blue Books, Part I, p. 216.
15 Blue Books, Part III, p. 54.
16 Blue Books, Part II, p. 34.
17 Quoted in Birchenough, *History of Elementary Education*, p. 50.
18 H. G. Williams, 'Learning suitable to the situation of the poorest classes: the National Society and Wales 1811–1839', *Welsh History Review*, 19, 3 (1999), 425–52; Shelia M. Owen-Jones, 'Religious influence and educational progress in Glamorgan, 1800–33', *Welsh History Review*, 13 (1986), 72–86; Tudor Powell Jones, 'The contribution of the established church to Welsh education (1811–1846)', in Jac L. Williams and Gwilym Rees (eds), *The History of Education in Wales* (Swansea, 1978), pp. 105–26.
19 Williams, 'Learning suitable', 443–4.
20 On the early history of the British Society see A. L. Trott, 'The British School movement in Wales, 1806–1846', in Jac L. Williams and Gwilym Rees Hughes (eds), *The History of Education in Wales* (Swansea, 1978), pp. 83–104 and Idwal Jones, 'The voluntary system at work: a history of the British School Society', *Transactions of the Honourable Society of Cymmrodorion* (1931–2), 72–164.
21 Although others feared that if the masses were too educated they would become disaffected. Gwyneth Tyson Roberts, *The Language of the Blue Books: The Perfect Instrument of Empire* (Cardiff, 1998), pp. 21, 32.
22 *House of Commons Debate*, 14 June 1839, vol. 48 c. 298.
23 John Hurt, *Education in Evolution: Church, State, Society and Popular Education 1800–1870* (London, 1971), p. 11.
24 Hurt, *Education in Evolution*, p. 19; D. Eryl Davies, *Christian Schools: Christianity and Education in Mid-Nineteenth-Century Wales and Its Relevance for Today* (Bridgend, 1978).
25 The letter is reproduced in Evans, *Education in Industrial Wales, 1700–1900*, pp. 223–4. On Owen see B. L. Davies, 'Sir Hugh Owen and education in Wales',

Transactions of the Honourable Society of Cymmrodorion, Part 2 (1971), 191–223.
26 'Records and Recollections of Merthyr Tydfil', *Cardiff Times*, 6 February 1863, 6.
27 Dewi Môn, 'Ysgol genedlaethol o'r hen ffasiwn', *Y Geninen*, 20, 4 (October 1902), 258–63.
28 *Cambrian News*, 7 June 1889, 10.
29 Daniel Owen, *Rhys Lewis: The Autobiography of the Minister of Bethel*, trans. Robert Lomas (1885; 2017), ch. 9.
30 The inquiry into the Rebecca Riots had, for example, concluded the 'ignorance of the English language which pervades so large a portion of the country' was 'a great drawback upon the advancement of the community, and a serious impediment to the removal of those evils which most require correction': *Report of the Commissioners of Inquiry for Turnpike Roads, South Wales* (London, 1844), p. 36.
31 'The Blue Books, in Welsh', *The Principality*, 13 April 1849, 6.
32 Blue Books, Part III, appendix A, p. 60.
33 Blue Books, Part III, p. 19.
34 *A Second Walk through Wales by the Revd. Richard Warner, of Bath, in August and September 1798*, 4th edn (London, 1813), pp. 262–3.
35 'The Welsh stick', *Morning Post*, 21 January 1848, 3.
36 Lewis Powell, *Hanes Bywyd y Parch. Lewis Powell* (Cardiff, 1860), pp. 8–9. For another memory from the eighteenth century see Carnhuanawc, 'Ysgolion Cymreig', *Seren Gomer*, April 1824, 114.
37 'Bangor school and the Welsh stick', *North Wales Chronicle*, 9 November 1850, 5.
38 Revd James Rhys Jones (Kilsby), 'A Lecture on the educational state of Wales' (1851), reproduced in *Mid Wales Herald*, supplement no. 1 (1860).
39 Evan Evans, 'Adgofion pedwar ugain mlynedd', *Cyfaill Yr Aelwyd*, 5, 4 (1885), 101–3; J. B. Jones, 'Welshnot', *Yr Arweinydd Annibynol*, 3, 29 (August 1880), 208–9.
40 'Goronwy ar grwydr', *Y Negesydd*, 16 June 1904, 1.
41 Jonathan Ceredig Davies, *Folk-Lore of West and Mid-Wales* (Aberystwyth, 1911), p. 87.
42 Samuel Owen, 'Cwmwd cysylltau yn nechreu y ganrif ddidweddaf', *Y Traethodydd*, 75 (1920), 181–92, 190.
43 Evan Jones, *John Jones yn yr Ysgol: Ffug-hanesyn, yn Rhoddi Darluniad o Ysgolion Gwledig Cynru, oddeutu'r Flwyddyn 1840*, 2nd edn (Lampeter, 1904), p. 61.
44 'Addysg Plant Cymru ddoe a heddyw', *Tywysydd y Plant*, 73, 4 (April 1910), 109; Watcyn Wyn, 'Haner cant o flynyddau', *Y Diwygiwr* (September 1894), 263.
45 *Report of the Commissioners of Inquiry for Turnpike Roads, South Wales* (London, 1844), p. 102.
46 W. Jones, 'Talybont a'r gymydogaeth haner can' mlynedd yn ol', *Y Negesydd*, 3 January 1896, 1.
47 J. B. Jones, 'Welshnot', *Yr Arweinydd Annibynol*, 3, 29 (August 1880), 208–9.

48 Andronicus, 'Yr ysgol: pennod III: dim Cymraeg', *Cymru'r Plant*, November 1894, 313–17.
49 Evan Evans, 'Adgofion pedwar ugain mlynedd', *Cyfaill Yr Aelwyd*, 5, 4 (1885), 101–3.
50 Myra Evans, *Atgofion Ceinewydd* (Aberystwyth, 1961), p. 48.
51 Nathan Dyved, 'Cymru-Vu', *Cardiff Times*, 1 December 1888, 1.
52 Jones, 'A Lecture on the educational state of Wales'.
53 William George, *My Brother and I* (London, 1958), p. 55.
54 'Hanes hynod, ond gwir', *Tarian y Gweithiwr*, 30 August 1888, 3.
55 Sir Henry Jones, *Old Memories* (London, 1922), p. 33; 'Hen Scwlmistir', *Cymru*, 37 (1909), 121.
56 'The Welsh Lump', *Bye-gones relating to Wales and the Border Counties*, April 1879, 196.
57 Jones, 'A Lecture on the educational state of Wales'.
58 W. C. Elvet Thomas, *Tyfu'n Gymro* (Llandysul, 1972), p. 18.
59 'Ysgol Nantglyn yn 1953–4', *Baner ac Amserau Cymru*, 25 September 1915, 11.
60 Translated from Isfryn, 'Pan oeddym ni yn blant yn yr ysgol', *Perl y Plant*, April 1900, 125–6.
61 Sally Holloway, Stephanie Downes and Sarah Randles (eds), *Feeling Things: Objects and Emotions through History* (Oxford, 2018).
62 Michael Gareth Llewelyn, *Sand in the Glass* (London, 1943), p. 8.
63 *North Wales Times*, 24 July 1909, 2.
64 Jones, 'A Lecture on the educational state of Wales'; 'Yr ysgolfeister foel y bu yn Nghymru', *Yr Adolygydd*, 1 (June 1850), 35–47; Henry Griffiths, 'Addysgiaeth', *Y Traethodydd* (October 1849), 416–46, 442.
65 'The Welsh lump', *Bye-gones relating to Wales and the Border Counties*, March 1879, 188–9. For similar uncertainty see 'John Jones, Junior', 12.
66 'The Welsh Note', *Western Mail*, 28 September 1927, 11.
67 'Prifysgol i Gymru', *Cronicl y Cymdeithasau Crefyddol*, January 1873, 25.
68 One Glamorgan example comes from a 1901 writer who says his mother had attended Pant-yr-Eisteddfa school in the Rhondda around 1840 or earlier where the Welsh Note hung around the neck of the 'Kawl' who spoke Welsh. 'Doleni yn hanes y Rhondda', *Tarian y Gweithiwr*, 19 December 1901, 2.
69 The letter refers to it being 'quite general' in West Glamorgan and East Carmarthenshire: 'The Welsh Note', *Western Mail*, 30 September 1927, 7.
70 *Report of the Commissioners [charity] 32, part III* (London, 1838), p. 487.
71 Philip Greven, *Spare the Child: The Religious Roots of Punishment and the Psychological Impact of Physical Abuse* (New York, 1991).
72 James Pillans, *Contributions to the Cause of Education* (London, 1856), p. 339.
73 Jones, *Old Memories*, pp. 32–3.
74 Quoted in Hywel Gwyn Evans, *Pum Ysgol: Ardal Cwmllynfell* (Llandysul, 2003), p. 14.
75 J. B. Jones, 'Welshnot', *Yr Arweinydd Annibynol*, 3, 29 (August 1880), 208–9.
76 Henry M. Stanley, *The Autobiography of Sir Henry Morton Stanley* (Boston, 1909), pp. 12–13, 14.

77 *Cambrian News,* 7 June 1889, 10.
78 Andrew Bell, *The Madras School, or Elements of Tuition* (London, 1808), p. 271.
79 'Yr ysgolfeister foel y bu yn Nghymru', *Yr Adolygydd,* 1 (June 1850), 35–47; 'Hen Scwlmistir', 121; Jones, *John Jones yn yr Ysgol,* pp. 18, 20.
80 'Roby Fach dan y cap drwg', *Trysorfa y Plant,* January 1901, 4; 'Clywed y gog', *Perl y Plant,* May 1910, 151–2. Dunce caps date back to the medieval period. See Peter N. Stearns and Clio Stearns, 'American schools and the uses of shame: an ambiguous history', *History of Education,* 46, 1 (2017), 58–75, 65 and Heather A. Weaver, 'Object lessons: a cultural genealogy of the dunce cap and the apple as visual tropes of American education, *Paedagogica Historica,* 48, 2 (2012), 215–41.
81 Richard Jones, 'Trallodion a gofidiau: gadael yr ysgol', *Yr Haul,* May 1890, 145–7; Jones, 'A Lecture on the educational state of Wales'.
82 Môn, 'Ysgol genedlaethol o'r hen ffasiwn'.
83 D. Parry-Jones, *Welsh Children's Games & Pastimes* (Denbigh, 1964), p. 152.
84 Jacob Middleton, 'Thomas Hopley and mid-Victorian attitude to corporal punishment', *History of Education,* 34, 6 (2005), 599–615, 602.
85 Blue Books, Part III, p. 25.
86 Minutes of Evidence, *Select Committee on Education of Poorer Classes in England and Wales* (London, 1837–8), p. 116.
87 Minutes of Evidence, *Select Committee on Education of Poorer Classes in England and Wales,* p. 125.
88 Stanley, *The Autobiography,* p. 12.
89 Gwyneth Vaughan, 'Bryn Ardudwy a'i bobl: ein hysgolfeistri', *Yr Haul,* 6, 65 (May 1904), 225–30.
90 Marie Trevelyan, *Glimpses of Welsh Life and Character* (London, 1893), p. 22.
91 P. W. Musgrove, *Society and Education in England since 1800* (London, 1968), p. 20; James Walvin, *A Child's World: A Social History of English Childhood, 1800–1914* (Harmondsworth, 1982), p. 47.
92 Ben Parsons, *Punishment and Medieval Education* (Woodbridge, 2018), pp. 78–90.
93 Blue Books, Part III, p. 25.
94 GA, Rules of the Llantwit Major National school, est. 1831.
95 Parsons, *Punishment and Medieval Education,* pp. 97–8.
96 For similar arguments about the use of the birch see Parsons, *Punishment and Medieval Education,* p. 106.
97 Andrew Bell, *The Madras School, or Elements of Tuition* (London, 1808), ch. 4; David Hogan, 'The market revolution and disciplinary power: Joseph Lancaster and the psychology of the early classroom system', *History of Education Quarterly,* 29, 3 (1981), 381–417.
98 On surveillance as discipline see Joakim Landahl, 'The eye of power(-lessness): on the emergence of the panoptical and synoptical classroom', *History of Education,* 42, 6 (2013), 803–21.
99 Môn, 'Ysgol genedlaethol o'r hen ffasiwn'.

100 Peter Verstraete and Josephine Hoegaerts, 'Educational soundscapes: tuning in to sounds and silences in the history of education', *Paedagogica Historica*, 53, 5 (2017), 491–7.
101 GA, Rules of the Llantwit Major National school.
102 Bangor University archives: Letter from J. Ll. Evans to Ifor Williams, 10 February 1955.
103 'Y gwehydd ddaeth yn Faer', *Y Tyst*, 30 August 1895, 5; 6 September 1895, 3. Also see 'Welsh gossip', *South Wales Echo*, 12 March 1897, 3.
104 Nicholas Orme, *English Schools in the Middle Ages* (London, 1973), p. 101; Nicholas Orme, 'Schools and languages in medieval England', in Mary Carruthers (ed.), *Language in Medieval Britain: Networks and Exchanges* (Donington, 2015), pp. 152–67; Michael Van Cleave Alexander, *The Growth of English Education, 1348–1648* (London, 1990), p. 81; Matthew Adams, *Teaching Classics in English Schools, 1500–1840* (Cambridge, 2016), ch. 3.
105 Mary Carruthers, *The Craft of Thought: Meditation, Rhetoric, and the Making of Images, 400–1200* (Cambridge, 1998), pp. 8, 106–8.
106 Parsons, *Punishment and Medieval Education*, p. 60, ch. 2.
107 Adams, *Teaching Classics*, p. 37; Eric W. Hawkins, *Modern Languages in the Curriculum* (Cambridge, 1981), p. 100.
108 E. T. Campagnac (ed.), *John Brinsley, Ludus Literarius or the Grammar Schoole (1612)* (London, 1917), pp. 217–20.
109 The rule of Friars School (Bangor), 1568, which state that pupils should speak Latin in and outside school but also outline some of the translation exercises: Henry Barber and Henry Lewis, *The History of Friars School Bangor* (Bangor, 1901), pp. 145–7.
110 Henry Wingate, 'The natural method of teaching Latin: its origins, rationale, and prospects', *The Classical World*, 106, 3 (2013), 493–504, 494–6. On translation as a method of learning in European schools see Andrea Bruschi, 'Learning vernaculars, learning in vernaculars: the role of modern languages in Nicolas Le Gras's noble academy and in teaching practices for the nobility (France, 1640–c.1750)', in Vladislav Rjéoutski and Willem Frijhoff (eds), *Language Choice in Enlightenment Europe. Education, Sociability, and Governance* (Amsterdam, 2018), pp. 15–38, 24–6.
111 Hawkins, *Modern Languages in the Curriculum*, p. 101.
112 William P. Griffith, 'Schooling and society', in J. Gwynfor Jones (ed.), *Class, Community and Culture in Tudor Wales* (Cardiff, 1989), pp. 79–119, 93, 107–8; William P. Griffith, 'Humanist learning, education and the Welsh language, 1536–1630', in Geraint H. Jenkins (ed.), *The Welsh Language Before the Industrial Revolution* (Cardiff, 1997), pp. 289–315, 98–9, 307–8; Glanmor Williams, 'Education and culture down to the sixteenth century', in Jac L. Williams (ed.), *The History of Education in Wales* (Swansea, 1978), pp. 9–27, 25; L. Stanley Knight, *Welsh Independent Grammar Schools to 1600* (Newtown, n.d.), p. 4.
113 Adams, *Teaching Classics*, p. 40; Stearns and Stearns, 'American schools and the uses of shame', 60–1.

114 Mary Russell Mitford, 'Caroline Cleveland: a School-day Anecdote', in Ackermann's Juvenile Forget Me Not (London, 1832), pp. 81–92.
115 Eugen Weber, *Peasants into Frenchmen: The Modernization of Rural France, 1870–1914* (Stanford, 1976), p. 313.
116 Aidan Doyle, *A History of the Irish Language* (Oxford, 2015), pp. 132–3. The exclusion of the home language led to similar complaints in Ireland that Irish-speaking children were 'practically' being taught 'nothing': 'The Gaelic in the National Schools', *The Gaelic Journal*, 3 , 1 (1883), 98. For evidence see *https://gript.ie/an-bata-scoir-a-first-hand-account-of-beating-the-language-out-of-people/* (accessed 25 March 2024).
117 William Wilde, *Irish Popular Superstitions* (Dublin, 1852), p. 27.
118 Eoghann MacColla (Evan MacColl), letter to editor of *The Scottish-American Journal*, 13 January 1881. Quoted at: *https://web.archive.org/web/20210616170117/https://www.patreon.com/posts/31967127* (accessed 25 March 2024).
119 James Robertson, 'Memories of Rannoch' (1926). Published in *Transactions of the Gaelic Society of Inverness*, 51 (1979–80), 199–208, 204, 208. The article notes some confusion over which school it was used at but maintains that the key point was the skull was utilised.
120 William Mackay, *Urquhart and Glenmoriston: Olden Times in a Highland Parish*, 2nd edn (Inverness, 1914), pp. 403–4.
121 St Fagans archives: Stuart Maxwell to Iorwerth Peate, 19 June 1953.
122 *Minutes of the CCE, 1855–56*, p. 458.
123 Society for Utilizing the Welsh Language, *Scheme of Instruction for Use in Elementary Schools in Wales* (Caernarfon, 1893), p. 3.
124 'John Jones, Junior', 12.
125 For an analysis of Lancaster's methods see David Hogan, 'The market revolution and disciplinary power: Joseph Lancaster and the psychology of the early classroom system', *History of Education Quarterly*, 29, 3 (1981), 381–417. Also see Carl F. Kaestle (ed.), *Joseph Lancaster and the Monitorial School Movement: A Documentary History* (New York, 1973). For Welsh memories of studying there see D. Evans, 'Athrofa y Boro' Road yn Llundain, neu Y Normal School', *Y Drysorfa*, 158 (February 1844), 59–60.
126 Richard Johnson, 'Educational policy and social control in early Victorian England,' *Past & Present*, 49, 1 (1970), 96–119, 114; Jonathan Franklin, 'Disability panic: the making of the normal school teacher', *Victorian Studies*, 62, 4 (2020), 644–67.
127 Anne Digby and Peter Searby, *Children, School and Society in Nineteenth-Century England* (London, 1981), p. 8.
128 L. M. Rees, 'A Critical Examination of Teacher Training in Wales, 1846–1898' (unpublished PhD thesis, University of Wales, Bangor, 1968), 34.
129 Blue Books, Part III, p. 74.
130 'Report of Mr Seymour Tremenheere on the state of elementary education in the mining district of South Wales', published in *CCE: Minutes, Part II, 1839–40*, p. 210.

131 Blue Books, Part III, p. 27.
132 R. Meredith, 'Early history of the North Wales Training College', *Transaction of the Caernarvonshire History Society*, 7 (1946), 64–87.
133 Rees, *A Critical Examination of Teacher Training*, pp. 53–6.
134 *Report of the CCE, 1859–60*, p. xxxv.
135 Joseph Lancaster, *Improvements in Education as it Respects the Industrious Classes of the Community*, 3rd edn (London, 1805), pp. 100–3, 113–14.
136 E. T. Davies, *Monmouthshire Schools and Education to 1870* (Newport, 1957), pp. 67–70.
137 Lancaster, *Improvements in Education*, p. 104.
138 Middleton, 'Thomas Hopley', 602.
139 'Cardiff infant school', *Glamorgan, Monmouth & Brecon Gazette*, 2 December 1843, 3.
140 *Minutes of the CCE, 1848–59–50*, vol. 2 (London 1850), p. 209.
141 For example, Pillans, *Contributions to the Cause of Education*.
142 Alfred Jones, *The Philosophy of Corporal Punishment: An Investigation into the Policy and Morality of School Coercion* (Edinburgh, 1859), p. 8.
143 For an account of the case and its impact see Middleton, 'Thomas Hopley'.
144 Stearns and Stearns, 'American schools and the uses of shame', 66.
145 See the calculations in Neil J. Smelser, *Social Paralysis and Social Change: British Working-Class Education in the Nineteenth Century* (Berkley, 1991), pp. 160–5.
146 *Minutes of the CCE, 1852–3*, p. 558; *Minutes of the CCE, 1855–56*, p. 462.
147 *Report of the CCE, 1867–68*, p. 505.
148 *Reports of Assistant Commissioners appointed to inquire into State of Popular Education in England*, vol. II (1861), pp. 542–3.

3
LEARNING WITHOUT UNDERSTANDING: THE PROBLEMS OF EDUCATION BEFORE 1862

A Blue Books commissioner noted the case of an untrained teacher in Aberffraw with the reputation of being a good scholar. In his school, none of the pupils could 'read with ease':

> They understand nothing of what they read in English, and are unable to translate the simplest English words into Welsh. The master assured me that they knew nothing of the meaning of what they read; that it was impossible for them to do so, considering that at home they never heard a word spoken in English ... He does not attempt to assist them by any system of interpretation *vivâ voce*, or by any kind of explanation in Welsh of what is read or learned. Under such circumstances it is difficult to comprehend how any ideas can be communicated between a master and his scholars.

The commissioner, Henry Vaughan Johnson, argued that it was rare to find a teacher 'who has ever thought of the importance of explaining or interpreting English to his scholars'.[1]

The exclusion of Welsh from classrooms made no sense pedagogically. In such circumstances, it was very difficult for children to learn anything useful. They could learn how to read and say words by copying their teacher but if Welsh was not used to explain those words then the child would be clueless as to what anything meant. Children were thus learning to read English without understanding it. They could recite English phrases but not say the simplest thing in their own words. Moreover, if Welsh was never used, then children's understanding could not be tested by quizzing them in their own tongue. Nor could children ask anything, or understand instructions from the teacher, be they educational or practical. Former-teacher Beriah Gwynfe Evans gave an inquiry in the 1880s an example of the confusion not using Welsh could lead to. When an 11-year-old was asked to explain why he was late, he told Evans it was because he was dead. In subsequent retellings of this story, Evans was reported to have burned the Welsh Not on the spot.[2]

This was not an unknown problem. Griffith Jones, founder of the circulating schools of the eighteenth century, had said that to run his schools in English would be 'the same as setting up French charity schools for the poor in England. It is absurd, in the very reason and nature of the thing, to set about instructing the people in religion in any other language but such as they understand.'[3] Others made similar points. In 1843, a man wrote to a local newspaper saying that a country and, indeed, the whole world, would be better off if it had just one language but this was not the case and thus Welsh should be used in schools. The fact that it was not made little sense he argued:

> What would be thought of the philosopher who should propose to impart scientific information to the bulk of the English people through the medium of French? What would be thought of a Protestant bishop who should propose that public worship should be conducted and the gospel preached in England in a language other than the vernacular language of the people?[4]

Yet this, as this chapter explores, is what happened in many Welsh schools. It was not, however, universal practice and the realisation of the limitations of not employing Welsh meant the language did slowly find a place in classrooms. Indeed, it was probably never quite as absent as many observers thought.

Learning without understanding

As some schools started to accept government grants in the 1840s, they had to open themselves up to state inspectors. Some made it clear that many children were not actually learning English. An inspection report on Llandovery workhouse school noted of the children, 'They think and talk in Welsh, and read English without understanding it.'[5] In 1846, another inspector complained that Welsh children were being taught to read and pronounce words 'without any conception of their meaning whatever'.[6] But it was the Blue Books that first emphasised the real stupidity of the failure to employ Welsh in teaching children who spoke no other language. Henry Vaughan Johnson, the commissioner for north Wales, described how the 'very limited' English of pupils at Ruthin workhouse school was not likely to increase,

> for no kind of interpretation is adopted; not a word is allowed to be spoken in Welsh, either by the master of the scholars. It is difficult to conceive how any progress can be made when their language – the only medium through which the mind receives instruction – is taken from them, and none given in its stead.[7]

More broadly he reported,

> I have found no class of schools in which an attempt has been made to remove the first difficulty which occurs to a Welsh child at the very beginning of his course of instruction in consequence of his ignorance of the English language. Every book in the school is written in English; every word he speaks is to be spoken in English; every subject of instruction must be studied in English; and every addition to his stock of knowledge in grammar, geography, history, or arithmetic must be communicated in English words; yet he is furnished with no single help for acquiring a knowledge of English ... The promoters of schools appear unconscious of the difficulty, and the teachers of the possibility of its removal. In the mean time it is difficult to conceive an employment more discouraging than

> that of the scholars, compelled as they are to employ six hours daily in reading and reciting chapter and formularies in a tongue which they cannot understand, and which neither their books nor their teachers can explain.[8]

Similarly, Ralph Robert Wheeler Lingen's report on Carmarthen, Glamorgan and Pembroke stated it was 'impossible to exaggerate the difficulties' presented by the fact that schoolbooks were not in the language spoken by the children. He worried that if a teacher stuck to English then his words were not understood but if he employed Welsh he was undermining the most important point of the lessons, which was to teach English. The answer, this commissioner felt, was to use Welsh as a scaffolding in lessons but to leave no trace of it in the finished building, with the mother tongue 'if not lost, at least stowed away'. He concluded that as long as the children were only familiar with Welsh 'they must be educated to a considerable extent through the medium of it', even though superseding the language was 'the most important part of their education'.[9] Jelinger C. Symons, the final commissioner, noted:

> In 45 schools out of 72 in Welsh districts, I found not the slightest attempt made to question the children, or to inform them on the subject on which they read, or even of the meaning of words: in each school they were grossly ignorant of it, and only a very few children in each were able to give the Welsh for ordinary English words. In these schools they were uttering the words of the Scriptures in English without the most remote conception of their meaning, any more than if they had been reading Greek.[10]

He concluded that it was 'fallacious' to infer that children were learning English, just because schools were trying to teach it.[11] Thus, despite their antipathy towards the language, the commissioners understood that Welsh had to be used in schools if children were going to learn anything. They argued that English could not replace Welsh as the language of Wales unless the latter was used to teach the former.

The Welsh section of the Newcastle Commission into education, conducted between 1859 and 1861, came to similar conclusions. It was written by John Jenkins, a barrister and minister who had been a teacher. He seems to have spoken Welsh but thought it a language of the past and that its 'final extinction' was inevitable.[12] But he also thought that those who 'think they are aiding the dissemination of English by repressing the use of Welsh' and forbidding its use in schools did not understand how employing Welsh would actually help children learn English.[13] He was highly critical of the results of excluding it from the classroom:

> one of the principal defects in reading which I met in most of the schools that I visited was want of knowledge of the meaning of words ... To Welsh scholars especially, nothing is more necessary than explanation of the meaning of the terms which they meet in reading English books, as in the most simple lessons the majority of the principal words are unknown to them, and yet, in both public and private schools, particularly in South Wales, no department of school teaching is more ill-charged or more frequently omitted than this.[14]

Elsewhere, the report concluded of teaching through a language which a pupil does not understand:

> Its patent absurdity scarcely merits confutation. Without a knowledge of English the child may, indeed, learn to put sounds together, but he evidently can have no understanding of the things they represent. What would be thought of the attempt to teach even an adult through the medium of a language of which he is entirely ignorant? Yet this is the practice generally adopted in schools in the district of Wales, where Welsh is the language in use by the scholars beyond the walls of the schoolroom, in which they speak to and are addressed by their parents at home, which they use for all the ordinary purposes of life.[15]

Jenkins concluded, 'Under the circumstances it is surprising that many of the schools in the country districts of Wales accomplish as much as they do.' For him, the 'remedy' was obvious: adopting the Welsh language as the medium of instruction would 'accelerate the progress of English' throughout Wales.[16]

Learning without understanding was not unknown in England too. There, too, there were observations that working-class children struggled with the arcane language some schoolbooks were written in and that teachers often did not explain to children what they were reading.[17] In 1838, a select committee on education for the poorer classes heard evidence from Birmingham that 'the main truths of religion' were not communicated to any great extent because 'the language employed is generally unintelligible to the children ... I find many are considered quite proficient who are totally ignorant of a great proportion of the words employed'.[18] But in Wales the problem ran far deeper, not least because children were not always even being taught to say words correctly. English was rarely heard in many communities and children were dependent on what they learned at school. Thus, if the teacher did not know how to pronounce words correctly, they would pass that on to the pupils.[19] Some people recalled they had problems with English in later life because they had learned to pronounce letters the Welsh rather English way.[20] Even in schools with teachers with good English, children might still struggle with pronunciation, especially if they were simultaneously learning to read Welsh at Sunday school. Adults sometimes called the English language *yr iaith fain* (the thin language) because of the mildness of its consonants. Children thus had to learn a completely different way of saying words and pronouncing letters to their native language. As the Newcastle Commission reported: 'In reading and spelling, not only the words but the very sounds of the letters are strange to the scholar', and learning either was not easy when children were not taught their meanings. Unsurprisingly, it reported that reading was better in the south where children heard more English outside school.[21]

Learning English was exactly why many were sent to school but many were being denied what their parents were paying for.[22] One man recalled in 1885 how, fifty years earlier, children at his school could recite grammar books to their teacher without forgetting a single line but also without understanding a single word of what they said.[23] Another person remembered that not more than one in a dozen pupils at their school could put together a dozen English words correctly.[24] Not understanding what was going on also made school extremely boring. An account of Llangollen National school made this clear. The teacher there spoke little Welsh and the children no English. The result was the children were sleepy and monotonous, and the teacher was unable to draw their attention to anything to enliven lessons or to wake them up.[25]

The practical challenges of teaching

Why such a situation could develop owed much to the practical challenges of delivering education. In the case above from Llangollen, the language of the classroom was exclusively English because that was the only language the teacher spoke. This was not uncommon because, in the first half or so of the century, there were school managers and patrons who believed that employing a teacher from England was the best way to ensure children learned English. Inspector Joseph Fletcher noted in 1846, 'that in places not far removed from the English border, there is a considerable inclination, in both patrons and parents, to have English masters, who do not understand Welsh at all'.[26] The 1861 Newcastle Commission's examination of schools in Corwen, Dolgellau, Bala, Ffestiniog, Neath and Merthyr Tydfil found that in a majority of schools most pupils could not speak English and most teachers could not speak Welsh.[27]

Such teachers hampered the effectiveness of education, not just because they were unable to properly teach English but also because they endangered parents' confidence in the whole school, something that mattered when attendance was entirely voluntary. In 1847, the inspector Revd H. W. Bellairs noted how in Monmouthshire many teachers were 'unaccustomed to the habits of the people' and therefore liable to offend. He suspected there were 'few Englishmen with sufficient tact or sympathy to find their way into a Welshman's heart' and thus be able to induce the parental 'confidence and affection' that was necessary for the success of a school.[28] In 1865, Joseph Bowstead, an inspector who looked at British schools in the south, reported his belief that English teachers were unsuitable for work in rural Wales. This was, he felt, down to more than language and he noted that some English-monoglot teachers from Pembrokeshire had done well in Welsh-speaking areas because they understood local customs and manners. In contrast:

> an English youth, fresh from a London normal school, when transported into a remote corner of the principality, is apt to regard the people around him as semi-barbarians, and himself as the only person in the locality who has any real pretensions to civilization. He soon lets this feeling appear in his intercourse with his scholars, and the remarks which he drops from time to time are carried with the speed of wind to every fireside within reach of his school.

This would, he argued, cause attendance levels to fall away. Although Bowstead argued that there were exceptions, he maintained that in Welsh-speaking areas, schools could not succeed unless teachers spoke Welsh and that this was so widely accepted that the services of those who could not were 'seldom desired by the managers of country schools'.[29]

Some schools employed teachers from England, not to keep Welsh out of the classroom but because they had little choice. Before 1870, a shortage of trained teachers meant that rural school committees often had to rely on the British and National societies to find them staff. This was not always possible and instead some schools had to employ whoever they could get. The 1861 Newcastle Commission argued that untrained teachers in rural districts were generally incompetent: they were small tradesmen, farm lads who could read a bit, or young men hoping to move on to some other calling such as the ministry.[30] Even much later in the century, when there were more training school graduates, schools still might have to appoint teachers without meeting them and were thus not always sure what they were getting.[31] Many schools did want Welsh-speaking staff but the training colleges simply did not produce enough to meet demand. This was partly because getting into a training college was not easy for a Welsh pupil who had received a substandard education and thus found it difficult to pass the scholarship exam. Some Welsh graduates preferred to work in England, where wages were often higher and perhaps because securing a job there seemed a sign of social elevation.[32] By 1859, a third of teachers trained in Wales had left the country, while fifty-two of the 163 certified teachers in Church of England schools in Wales were trained in England. Yet recruiting from England was not easy either, because wages in rural schools were low and potential candidates might know the considerable challenges they would face there.[33] Thus teachers willing to come to rural Wales were frequently those unable to find work in England. They were often inexperienced and sometimes even unaware of the fact that their pupils would not speak English. This explains not just why some teachers did not fully understand the problems of excluding Welsh but also why it happened.

On the surface, the idea of employing a teacher unable to speak his or her pupils' language seems absurd. Yet there were contemporaries who thought this did not matter. In 1849, the report for a school at Ystradgynlais noted that children read fairly, could translate English into Welsh and understood what they read. This has been achieved, he noted, without the master understanding Welsh himself.[34] Other inspectors were also not against the employment of teachers from England. Shadrach Pryce, the most vehement opponent within the inspectorate of Welsh in schools, used the examples of Llanboidy and Penrhyn Coch in Carmarthenshire, which he said were both in a 'very satisfactory condition', to argue that English-monoglot teachers were not a problem.[35] Ultimately, such judgements show how rudimentary education could be, both in practice and ambition. At the start of the century, Joseph Lancaster recommended short clear commands such 'Front' or 'Clean slates'.[36] Teachers who followed this must have overcome their lack of Welsh by repeating the short instructions and physically demonstrating what was meant so pupils would come to understand the simple orders. If reading was just a matter of repeating rather than understanding what the teacher said, then it too could be taught by example and repetition.

But this severely limited what a school could achieve. An English-monoglot teacher's problems must have been particularly acute when it came to explaining moral and behaviour issues, interacting with parents, or, indeed, dealing with anything out of the ordinary.[37] While some inspectors just accepted such situations, others were well aware of the challenges and even the ludicrousness of teacher and pupils not speaking the same language. In 1849 one bemoaned teachers unaccustomed with Welsh and local habits: he recorded a 'most amusingly ridiculous, though rather provoking' day he had spent at a school 'where two-thirds of the children knew no word of English, and the master had not troubled himself by any vain endeavours to learn Welsh'. He described teachers not having sympathies in common with the communities they served as an 'evil'.[38]

One solution was to enlist the help of bigger children. If there were older pupils with enough English to understand the teacher, they could translate and explain things to the pupils. Joseph Lancaster's monitor system was important here, but monitors were not much older than the other pupils and thus did not always have better English. Concerns about whether monitors made effective teachers led the state to introduce a system of pupil teachers in 1846. These were five-year teaching apprenticeships for teenagers who had finished school. They would teach younger children during the day and then receive their own education from the school's teacher after hours. At the end of five years, they could apply for a scholarship to a training college. Some inspectors made it clear in their annual reports that such positions were 'essential' in Welsh schools because of language difficulties.[39] In 1847, one inspector said these 'native children' would form a valuable 'link between the master and his scholars'. Another said their ability to explain things in Welsh avoided the 'tyrannous and idealess drudgery which has heretofore characterised the learning of English in the Welsh schools'.[40] But this was all fraught with difficulty because it relied on pupil teachers and monitors having a reasonable level of English. A monitor or pupil teacher might not be able to tell a child how to pronounce a word, let alone what it meant. At the National school in Brymbo, the Blue Books noted that the English-monoglot teacher had

> great difficulty in conveying ideas to her pupils. She employs a child to explain to the class an English word by a Welsh one, but is unable to detect whether the Welsh interpretation is correct; and so little English is known by any of her pupils that this is seldom the case.[41]

The blind were leading the blind.

Monitors and pupil teachers also added to the violent culture in some schools. Some monitors were given canes to give them authority and a means of controlling their fellow pupils. At a Church school in Ruthin, a Blue Books commissioner observed 'One or two monitors amused themselves by wandering about, striking the younger boys, but indiscriminately, and with no useful object in view.'[42] In some schools, they were the ones responsible for giving out the Welsh Not and some set out to trick younger children into saying Welsh words.[43] Pupil teachers were also learning a trade and, if they were apprenticed under a teacher that employed the Welsh Not, they too might use it when they had their own school. This was probably one of the chief ways the practice was able to continue in some places late into the century. But the pupil teachers and monitors were also children themselves. At the British school in Llandudno, the Blue Books reported that the monitors were 'rude, undisciplined, and ignorant, and neither able to teach nor to maintain discipline'.[44] They were thus another ingredient in what made education so ineffective.

Many schools relied on monitors and pupil teachers because of their size. Schools varied hugely from the tens to the hundreds and many had just one or two adult teachers. One master might thus have 200 pupils to teach, with only the help of designated older children. The Blue Books noted that a single 21-year-old master and his monitors ran Rhosllannerchrugog British school with its 267 children.[45] Such situations meant that children were often left to work on their own for much of the time. They might be called to appear before the master occasionally to demonstrate what they had been working on. Whole classes periodically recited their reading or their sums aloud but the noise this generated made it difficult for the other children to concentrate on what they had been left to do.[46] The frequent reliance on classes reading together also made it difficult for a teacher to identify those who were struggling and thus needed correction. Amidst such challenges, younger pupils were particularly likely to be marginalised by teachers and left to monitors and pupil teachers whose own English might not be much better than those they were teaching.[47]

Perhaps the biggest problem education faced was the irregularity and brevity of many children's attendance. Some started at five but others not until they were ten. Few stayed for much more than four or five years and some only attended for a few months. Nor did most children attend continuously. Attendance dropped off significantly in the summer because children were working in the harvest, tending livestock or even at sea. Indeed, some children were only sent to school during the winter and thus said to receive a 'quarter' of school.[48] Some schools closed altogether for three or four months because of this. In industrial districts, children might come late, leave early or not attend at all so they could take food to family members in the works.[49] In rural areas with dispersed populations, many children had to walk anything up to a few miles down muddy lanes or across fields to reach school. This meant younger children were not sent until they were old enough to make the walk and children of all ages stayed away when the weather was bad.[50] One rural teacher told the Newcastle Commission irregular attendance 'renders valueless a great portion of our labours'.[51] Many children did not attend school at all. They were often kept away by money. Not only did parents have to pay fees but they might also have to buy slates, copy books and even coal for the schoolroom. Or there might not be a school in their district, especially if they lived in a remote rural area. In 1855–6, one inspector estimated that while in England 40 to 50 per cent of children aged between five and fifteen attended school, in Wales it was 30 per cent, of which roughly one-third were in private schools and two-thirds in schools receiving state funds.[52] Some of those not then at school would have attended at other times in their childhood, but the fact remains that education was a sporadic experience for the majority.

This all mitigated against effective teaching and the spread of English and exacerbated the problems caused by the Welsh Not. So too did the frequent use of the Bible to teach English, something that happened because of the religious ideals of education sponsors, the cost of children's books and the physical prevalence of Bibles in communities. The Bible was not a suitable text for learning to read, especially in a foreign language. When a Blue Book commissioner visited a school in Trawsnant (Cardiganshire), the class was reading the 38th chapter of Genesis. The first passage of the King James version reads:

> And it came to pass at that time, that Judah went down from his brethren, and turned in to a certain Adullamite, whose name was Hirah. And Judah saw there a daughter of a certain Canaanite, whose name was Shuah; and he took her, and went in unto her.

The commissioner reported:

> The reading was very imperfect; and in questioning the class upon what was read, I found that scarcely a single word was understood and the master told me that he was not in the habit of asking them any questions, nor using any means to make the scholars understand what they read and spelt.

However, when asked general questions on the scriptures in Welsh, the children answered 'tolerably well'.[53] The Revd Robert Williams, vicar of Gwernaffield (Mold), told a Blue Books commissioner that the use of the Bible was 'injurious' in both a religious and intellectual sense because it associated the book with 'tasks and punishments' and limited children's English to 'phrases employed in Scripture, which are inadequate for the purposes of daily life'.[54]

Welsh in the classroom

The problems of attendance were well known to teachers but the difficulties of understanding less so. Those who believed that Welsh should never be used in school, or were unable to speak it themselves, did not test children by asking them to explain things in their own language and words. Such teachers may not have fully comprehended just how little their pupils understood. Thus, without using Welsh, the problems of not using it would not be fully revealed. But teachers must have had some sense of the difficulty by how little children could say in English. Indeed, the situation of not using Welsh was so absurd that it cannot have been as common as the commissioners and inspectors thought. It is probable that some teachers were telling and showing the inspectors and commissioners what they thought the investigators wanted to hear. On the day of a visit, they might refrain from using Welsh because they assumed this is what the grand English visitor would be impressed by. The Blue Books commissioners might have reflected more on their own repeated criticisms that many teachers had very poor English and whether this made it realistic for them to banish the only language they spoke well. In contrast, in 1852 the inspector Matthew Arnold noted that since masters often did not know English well, they did not employ it with their scholars 'by any means so much as they should'.[55]

There were very real practical reasons for teachers to use Welsh. Running a school was never an easy task anywhere but doing it in a foreign language would have been near impossible. Robert Roberts recalled his first day as one of fifty pupils in a new school in 1840s rural Denbighshire:

> In age we ranged from six to twenty and upwards; stalwart young farmers and grown up girls stood side by side with the small urchin just breeched. But, however, unequal we were in size, we were pretty equal in ignorance. Some half-a-dozen could read, indifferently, and in a phonetic Welsh ways, words of one syllable, and could make lame attempts at forming letters. None understood the

simplest sentence in English – we must be addressed in Welsh if we were to understand at all.[56]

Without Welsh being used, children could not easily understand when to fetch things, shut doors or get out their slates. As the curate of Llanfachreth told an inquiry, 'Welsh, to some extent, would be decidedly necessary in the schools in this part of the country, as the people do not know a word of English.'[57] Thus, even if children were prevented from speaking Welsh, it is likely that many teachers spoke Welsh to them for the simple purpose of telling them what to do. Indeed, it is difficult to see how any school could be run smoothly if this did not happen.

Other masters and mistresses, like their monitors and pupil teachers, did use Welsh as a means of explanation. The extensive research of the Blue Books found that while English was the medium of instruction in most schools, this was not universal. The three commissioners did not collect statistics in quite the same way but collectively their reports suggest that 318 out of 1,657 day schools seen were offering bilingual instruction.[58] The nature of this instruction varied and in some schools individual words were being explained in Welsh but not whole passages. In others, translation exercises were set and the two languages were employed alongside each other.[59] The exact approach came down to the master or mistress. This meant there was no consistency within areas or even within specific schools if there was more than one teacher there. Moreover, the whole approach of a school could change when its teacher did.[60]

These varying approaches, along with the probable uncertainty of teachers in what they should tell or show outsiders about their practice, produced some confusing evidence about the extent to which Welsh was used. This was evident in the seemingly contradictory statement in the Blue Books that in Carmarthen, Glamorgan and Pembroke teachers 'employ Welsh for all colloquial or explanatory purposes (if any)'.[61] The 1861 Newcastle Commission's widespread investigations led to the conclusion that in the north more attention was paid to the 'interpretation of English into Welsh', and in a few 'rare' cases teachers systematically taught children to translate from one language to another.

In contrast, in the south, 'I could not discover the remotest approach to systematic aid to the scholars in public schools, in overcoming this difficulty resulting from the scholars being ignorant of the language through which they received instruction.'[62] In contrast, according to the Blue Books 60 per cent of schools in Carmarthenshire were offering bilingual instruction, by far the highest proportion anywhere in Wales.[63] Meanwhile, in 1849 Longueville Jones, who inspected schools in the south, wrote that he 'commonly found the teachers accustomed to give explanations and to put questions in Welsh whenever necessary'.[64] Jones was very sympathetic to Welsh and it may be that he was witnessing the genuine practice, while other visitors witnessed less Welsh because teachers felt using the language would suggest their efforts to teach English were not working.

A growing realisation that excluding Welsh from the classroom made teaching English ineffective was probably the key reason why the Welsh Not was never universal and why it gradually became less common. Excluding Welsh entirely meant no questions could be asked and no explanations or clarifications could be given. Children might pick up or work out for themselves the odd word or phrase from its repetition, the actions of teachers or pictures in books, but this was not going to give them even a basic understanding of the language. What was happening in such schools was akin to sitting a modern pupil in front of a television broadcasting in a language that they never heard anywhere else and expecting the poor child to somehow become fluent in that language. Worse, the Welsh Not did not even encourage them to try and work out what was going on. As one woman schooled in Felinheli in the 1830s recalled, the Welsh Not was a barrier rather than a help to learning because, rather than concentrating on the lesson, the children watched it being passed around the class and devoted their energies to eavesdropping in order to get rid of it.[65]

Such realities meant that the use of the Welsh Not probably did not mean the complete exclusion of the language from the classroom. One memory of the practice in Llandysul added that children could speak Welsh if they prefaced it by saying 'can't say English'.[66] Probably more often teachers forbade children from speaking Welsh but used it themselves to communicate instructions to pupils about what was required of them, in lessons, discipline and practical help. This may not feature in autobiographical accounts, but it is very unlikely that adults would remember the details of how they were taught. They would remember not being allowed to speak Welsh, because that seemed unnatural and unfair, but the things said that they did understand were unlikely to become imprinted on their memories.

The picture is further complicated by the fact that even in schools that used the Welsh Not, there could be a variety of creative techniques used to teach English vocabulary. Rhymes were one example:

> Hearth is aelwyd, fire is tân,
> Cloth is brethyn, wool is gwlan,
> Ash is onen, oak is derwen,
> Holly tree is pren cerdynen,
> House is ty, and mill is melin,
> Fiddle is crwyth, and harp is telyn,
> River is afon, brook is nant.
> Twenty is ugain, hundred is cant.[67]

Common in autobiographical accounts are memories of vocabulary games. Children might be given lists of English words to learn (and a rod to the hand if they forgot). Sometimes this was called 'How do you call' (shortened by the children to 'Howdigal') since the teacher would ask a child 'How do you call' and then give the Welsh word he wanted translated. One man remembered he would go through the words he was given to learn all night, seeing them in his sleep.[68] Many schools used a weekly game called 'poso' or 'posio' (from to pose) or 'capo' (from to cap) where children lined up in two teams and asked someone from the other side to translate a Welsh word, again often using the phrase 'How do you call'. If they could not do it, they had to sit down.[69] This played on children's competitiveness and one recollection of the game described how the winning side would shout 'Welsh Blockheads' at the losers and the whole thing could end in blows.[70] Another writer recalled the winner getting a homemade rosette which they would wear as proudly as a poet who had won an eisteddfod.[71] Yet such games could only go so far since they were another form of rote learning, teaching vocabulary rather than grammar and not how to actually use the words. One Blue Books commissioner complained that children were asked to translate into Welsh specific words from their reading but not whole sentences. The result was that 'children are constantly found, who can read whole chapters with comparative fluency, and give the Welsh for single words, yet have not the remotest idea of what they are reading about'.[72] The brightest children made some effort to work things out for themselves but others must have just given up. In 1888, one man recalled being given a list of English words to learn was called 'Inglishwrs' in his school. The day after being given the words, children would have to write them on a slate when given the Welsh equivalent. There was a physical punishment for getting one wrong. The Welsh Not was also in operation in his school with the punishment being a 'hearty slap'. With no way of learning the language beyond the vocabulary lists, he concluded that 'our English, being learnt by rote, was of little use to us in understanding our lessons!'[73]

Things were easier in schools that moved away from using the Bible and adopted books designed for teaching reading.[74] Early private schools could not always afford these but British and National schools had better resources. Typical was *New Reading Made Easy*, published by Routledge in 1856. It contained lists of words for spelling and a series of illustrated readings that began with letters and simple one-syllable words and evolved into short passages with moral and educational messages on topics such as the dog, the cow, work and truth.[75] The lists of words to be learned in such books, which were there to teach spelling, had the added advantage in Wales of being useful to teach vocabulary.[76] Although children could have their interest stirred and employ some guesswork thanks to the pictures, the lists and simple reading passages still only worked effectively if the meaning of words was given to children in Welsh – something which was plainly not always happening.[77] The effectiveness of such books was also hampered by schools not being able to afford enough copies or different versions. This left some schools resorting to books that they knew were too hard. Other children were left reading the same book again and again, which must have been boring. In such cases, understanding what was being read probably made this worse.[78] Some lucky schools had a much-treasured Welsh-English dictionary.[79] But others had no access to reading books at all.

Welsh also had a place in the classroom because not all teachers were the incompetent monsters of so many popular memories and contemporary investigations. In 1853, an Anglesey Church Schoolmasters' Association was formed to exchange ideas and good practice. Two years later, the chairman told its annual meeting that it was a mistake to exclude Welsh from school and the language should be used to ensure children understood what they read.[80] In contrast to the Blue Books, school inspectors tended to offer more praise than condemnation, although they only saw schools in receipt of government monies, which were, in theory at least, better resourced and more professional. Longueville Jones, an inspector who was partly trying to refute the image generated by the Blue Books, was particularly complimentary about many teachers, stressing their intelligence, standing in their communities and achievements in adverse circumstances.[81] In Meidrim, an 1849 inspection recorded that good discipline was maintained through kindness and the children were in good humour. It noted that as 'the younger children left the school they each came to the master; he kissed them on the lips; they then each put their arms around his neck and kissed him on the cheek'.[82] An 1850 report for the same school noted that the teaching methods were 'Old-fashioned, but employed with great judgment and kindness, and producing a good result ... [The master] is one of the old school, but a worthy man, and producing a most happy effect upon the children's minds.'[83] It is difficult to imagine such teachers hitting children for speaking a language when they knew no other. Even those teachers who were far sterner might still care about their pupils. Some gave out books or food to poor children, paid for from their own pockets.[84] Certainly some people remembered their teachers fondly. One man recalled that his teacher at an 1840s school in Llanelli was an 'unpretentious and meek man' with poor health. His English was limited, mispronounced and mixed in with Welsh. When he lost his temper, he would 'thrash unmercifully' but he still stimulated the pupils' 'intellect' and the writer was very grateful for how the teaching had awoken ideas in him.[85] Similarly, Owen M. Edwards wrote that he would never forget his love for his second teacher. English was the language of the school but the teacher came to their homes, spoke Welsh to them, lent them Welsh books and raised in them a 'passionate desire for knowledge'.[86] Likewise, E. Herber Evans (b.1836) attended Llechryd British school from the ages of eleven to fifteen. The teacher there encouraged the children to excel by placing their examination results on the wall for all to see. He stopped boys from quarrelling by kneeling among them and praying. Evans recalled that this school gave him 'a taste for learning and knowledge'. He made no mention of language difficulties.[87]

It thus does seem that Welsh gradually found more of a place in classrooms before 1862. The growth of trained teachers improved education standards, although there is no direct evidence that they had radically different attitudes to language from their untrained peers. But trained teachers were more reflective about their teaching and aware that there was a method to it. This was clear in the evidence given to the Newcastle Commission. A teacher in Llwyn-y-gell took children aged seven but found that they could not work without interpretation into Welsh until they were about ten and then it was another two years before they understood English tolerably. A teacher in Bala felt that translation could never be wholly dispensed with and was important as lessons got harder. Other teachers felt two to five years were needed get children to understand English.[88] It was these reflective teachers that were explaining things in Welsh, using it to ask questions to check pupils' understanding and setting translation tasks.[89] Thanks to a greater use of Welsh and some talented and persistent teachers, some children did learn some English, and it would be wrong to argue schools were universally poor or to not acknowledge that teaching methods could be better than external observers acknowledged. Indeed, some contemporaries thought schools provided a good education.[90] An 1843 report of a public examination from the National schools in the Bangor area claimed that the children 'read the scriptures fluently, and for the most part very articulately'; they answered every question given to them and gave proof, presumably in Welsh, that they understood what they read.[91]

Neither the British nor National societies were enthusiastic about employing the Welsh language, but they were more likely to have trained teachers than private schools and they were also concerned about the religious dimensions of education. Not using Welsh would have undermined the religious goals of education because children would not understand what they were reading in the Bible. The British Society worried less about this because it knew the chapels and Sunday schools that dominated Welsh society offered children religious knowledge it approved of. For Anglicans, National schools were key to instructing people in their ways and tempting the next generation into the churches. Thus, in some National schools, pupils were taught the catechism in both Welsh and English to ensure they understood it. They might also be expected to be able to translate scripture passages into Welsh to show their comprehension.[92]

A few schools went much further and were teaching children to read Welsh, often at the behest of its patron or the charitable legacy left to pay for it. For example, an 1810s school at Gellifelen (Monmouthshire), paid for by Thomas Price, a patriotic vicar and historian, was conducted 'chiefly' in Welsh, 'In conformity with the requirements of the people.'[93] Similarly, a charity based on a 1722 bequest paid for a school to teach the poor children of Betws-yn-Rhos religious principles and to read Welsh. But such cases were becoming less common and there were more far more charitable bequests that specified that children should be taught to read English.[94] This was a product of the long-term anglicisation of the Welsh gentry and how they often shared English prejudices towards the Welsh language. They also felt the practical challenges of having tenants that spoke a different language.[95] The Blue Books recorded that just three out of 1,657 schools it saw were teaching Welsh rather than English.[96] In 1858, the south Wales agent for the British Society recorded that a school in Aber-carn was the only one he knew where Welsh was taught. His diaries show he appreciated the value of Welsh-speaking teachers, but he thought Aber-carn 'scarcely worth' being called a school given 'the amount of information acquired by the children.'[97]

Sunday schools and popular literacy

There was very little pressure for schools to teach Welsh because that was happening in Sunday schools. These were run from within communities and were part of the democratic Nonconformist tradition that had taken root across the country; they took place in chapels, churches, farmhouses and homes, and could be led by anyone confident, clever or literate. They educated both children and adults and an education census held in 1851 counted 2,771 Sunday schools in Wales, with 269,378 pupils. In Anglesey that year, there were forty-seven weekday schools but 115 Sunday schools.[98] For some pupils, they supplemented what was learned in weekday schools but for others it was their only education. This might be because there was no other education provision in their community, but it could also be because Sunday schools did not compete with paid employment by virtue of being held on the Sabbath. Their emphasis was on teaching reading and religious knowledge in Welsh, but some taught music, general knowledge and English too.[99] According to the Blue Books, 71 per cent of Sunday schools in north Wales were held in Welsh and 21 per cent were bilingual.[100] Whatever language they taught in, Sunday schools were important in developing literacy, creating an interest in reading and feeding a wider desire for wider education.[101] They were also places of empowerment, as they built people's sense of confidence and put individuals in a position of authority for the first time.[102]

Sunday schools are thus important correctives to the picture of education painted by the Blue Books. The commissioners did recognise their achievements in spreading religious knowledge but because Sunday schools were generally in Welsh such institutions never got the credit from English contemporaries that they deserved.[103] However, it is important not to exaggerate their reach or their impact on Welsh literacy levels, especially since many only taught reading rather than writing. This is evident from an 1839 investigation in a mining district that focused on what it thought were seventeen typical families. Thirteen of the families owned Welsh Bibles but none had any other books. Four husbands could read Welsh well, six imperfectly and seven not at all.

None could write. Only four of their wives could read Welsh, although another said she could read but not understand. Just fourteen of the twenty-three children in the sample went to Sunday school. While this was significantly higher than the two who went to a weekday school, it is a reminder that many children were not going to Sunday school either.[104]

Another yardstick of literacy levels is marriage registers. In 1845, 46.3 per cent of men and 69.5 per cent of women who got married in Wales signed with a cross rather than writing their name. The advances made in education were clear in 1865 when the figures had fallen to 35.5 per cent for men and 50.5 per cent for women.[105] It does thus seem that education, whether in weekday or Sunday schools, was having an impact, although less so for girls since parents were less likely to send them to school. But these are crude measures. Some people probably learned to write their name without being able to write or read. More commonly, others, thanks to Sunday schools placing an emphasis on understanding the Bible over writing, may have learned to read but not write their name. The ability to sign a register thus indicates little about reading or comprehension skills, but nor does the inability to sign one's name indicate a lack of reading ability.[106] What the statistics do show is how literacy levels in Wales were far behind England. In 1855, just 46 per cent of Welsh brides and grooms were able to sign their names in marriage registers, whereas the figure for England and Wales combined was 65 per cent; in Scotland it was as high as 83 per cent.[107] Wales was the least literate part of Britain and the failure of schools to employ Welsh was one key reason for that.

Conclusion

Middleton has argued that historians can fall into the trap of concentrating on the violence of schools and thus 'indulging in the same prurience that provided the sensation news of the mid-Victorian era'.[108] It is important that the Welsh Not is not only put into the context of the wider violence of schools but also the less dramatic context of how teaching actually worked and the practicalities of running a school. In most Welsh communities, any teacher who wanted children to understand basic instructions had to speak Welsh to their pupils, or get a monitor or pupil teacher to do so. If they wanted children to understand what they were learning, Welsh was essential. This meant that Welsh was probably never as excluded from classrooms as some commentators thought and it gradually found a more open place in classrooms, just as investigators said it should. This was part of a broader shift in education where purpose-built schools were erected, teachers were increasingly trained and assisted by apprentice pupil teachers, corporal punishment became less routine, and the state helped pay for everything and carried out inspections to advise and ensure its money was not wasted. In 1862, one writer thus spoke of the cruel days of the Welsh Not in the past tense and said teachers were now not afraid to admit to speaking Welsh and to use it when needed. He wondered if there had ever been a nation that had made such a fool of itself and its children as Wales did when it kept Welsh out of its schools.[109] But the sheer variety of schools and the variety of approaches followed by teachers meant there were still schools both doing that and punishing children for speaking Welsh. Indeed, that was happening in some schools where teachers freely used Welsh to try to ensure children understood their lessons. There was thus no consistent practice. In some schools Welsh was not allowed at all. In others, it was widely used to teach English. In most, the reality lay somewhere in-between.

This meant education was never quite as bad as many investigators thought. Indeed, across Britain, there was a tendency in education inquiries to highlight the problems rather than positive features. As a 1914 history of education noted, 'Investigators, apparently without any deliberate intention to be unfair, were led in their zeal for better things to emphasise the bad, and rarely gave equal importance to the good work that was being done.'[110] In the very best schools, geography, history, algebra and even chemistry, astronomy or maritime or agricultural knowledge were being taught.[111] Grigg has thus pointed to how some private schools in Wales met local needs by teaching topics such as maritime knowledge or sewing, and providing Nonconformist parents with an alternative to church-based education.[112] But for that to be effective in most regions Welsh had to be used. Some contemporaries also thought education was having some impact on the only thing they thought really mattered, the ability to speak English. In 1849, Longueville Jones, inspector for Anglican schools in Wales, argued that some Welsh children were picking up 'a good knowledge of English in an exceedingly short period'.[113] A decade later, he wrote that 'One proof of the increased efficiency of schools in Wales is to be found in the greater diffusion of the English language.'[114] Even those who attended schools that used the Welsh Not could later still feel the limited education provided had helped.[115] Indeed, the fact they were writing at all shows they had made a success of their lives.

In considering education's effectiveness, the 1861 Newcastle Commission surveyed children at eleven north Wales schools and found significant variations in linguistic abilities within similar communities. Of 429 children over ten looked at, 239 spoke English well, 244 spoke it imperfectly and 74 not at all. But there were significant variations that were surely rooted in the different qualities and methods of instruction. In Beddgelert British school almost half the children spoke Welsh only, whereas at Bala British school all spoke English either well or imperfectly. In Dolgellau, a quarter of children over ten at the National school spoke Welsh only, but in the British school none did. It also examined south Wales where some success in teaching English was even clearer. Whereas nearly 43 per cent of those under ten in the five schools examined spoke only Welsh, just 8 per cent of those over ten did.[116] But the report did not define what it meant by speaking English well or how it had assessed this. It seems likely that these figures exaggerated children's skills in English somewhat. Being able to speak some prepared words or tasks in a classroom was very different to speaking it freely outside. When children had to use English outside school, they tended to express themselves in unidiomatic terms and struggle with their limited vocabulary.[117]

The Welsh Not and the exclusion of Welsh from schools was common enough to have a significant detrimental effect on the teaching of English. In 1869, a schoolmaster at Llanrhaeadr described the poor state of education:

> Welsh children may at this age (9 or 10) be able to read fairly, but they cannot understand what they read; they may be able to work the first rules of arithmetic, but they cannot comprehend them so as to be able to apply them to common and domestic purposes; they may also be able to write a neat handwriting, but they cannot spell very well.[118]

Thus, whether they had to wear the Welsh Not or not, education failed many children. Too many were, in the words of one Blue Books commissioner, just left to pick up English 'as best as they can'.[119] Some theories of second-language acquisition do think children have innate abilities to learn languages, but more often they emphasise the impact of teaching methods and the environment children are in.[120] Since children were not encountering English outside school, there was little to reinforce lessons let alone the 'intensive and extensive exposure' that linguists argue is key to learning a new language effectively.[121] Early and mid-nineteenth-century schools were assuming children would just pick up a second language in the way they learned their first – through being immersed in it – but school did not replicate the same conditions that babies and toddlers learned to speak in. It was only the teacher speaking English and children's exposure to the language was only during school hours. Moreover, much of the English they were being immersed in was on the page only rather than something freely spoken. It was of a formal type and not accompanied by actions that could convey meaning. Above all, the formal school environment meant there was not the interaction and back and forth that is so important in language learning. Repetition of what the teacher said could only get a child so far.

The utilisation of Welsh to help children learn would have overcome much of this but its omission was not the only issue. This is clear when comparisons are made with England. The Newcastle Commission thought that even in the best English schools two-thirds of children left without the standard of education they needed, unable to check a shop bill or write a legible letter to their mother.[122] It blamed poor instruction and a lack of attendance. However, unlike their peers in schools where Welsh was forbidden, children in England could at least understand the basics and the instructions of their teachers. In Wales, the result of the complete or partial exclusion of Welsh was not just that school became a boring and frustrating experience, but also that English itself failed to take root in many communities. What the Welsh Not did was not spread English but prevent that from happening. The irony of the Welsh Not is that what it achieved is exactly the opposite of what many people today think happened. Welsh was not beaten out of children. That could not happen if children did not learn another language. Instead, many children were just beaten.

Notes

1 *Reports of the Commissioners of Inquiry into the State of Education in Wales. Part III: North Wales* (London, 1847), p. 17 [hereafter Blue Books].
2 *Third Report of the Royal Commission appointed to inquire into the Working of Elementary Education Acts, England and Wales* (London, 1887), p. 3 [hereafter Cross Commission]; 'Welsh gossip', *South Wales Echo*, 9 March 1897, 2; Beriah Gwynfe Evans, 'Addysg plant Cymru: ddoe a heddyw', *Tywysydd y Plant*, 73, 4 (1910), 108–11.
3 Griffith Jones, report for 1744 reproduced in Thomas Phillips, *Wales: The Language, Social Condition, Moral Character, and Religious Opinions of the People* (London, 1849), p. 283.
4 'The Welsh language', *Glamorgan Monmouth and Brecon Gazette and Merthyr Guardian*, 7 October 1843, 4. Also see 'Addysg yn Nghymru', *Y Cronicl*, March 1846, 40–2 and 'At athrawon yr Ysgolion Brutanaidd', *Y Cronicl*, October 1847, 309–11, 310.
5 *Minutes of the CCE, 1847–48–49: Schools of Parochial Unions* (London, 1849), p. 312.
6 *Minutes of the CCE, 1846*, p. 305.
7 Blue Books, Part III, p. 44.
8 Blue Books, Part III, p. 11.
9 Blue Books, Part I, pp. 31, 7.
10 Blue Books, Part II, p. 25.
11 Blue Books, Part II, p. 34.
12 *Reports of Assistant Commissioners appointed to inquire into State of Popular Education in England*, vol. II (1861), pp. 449, 453 [hereafter Newcastle Commission].
13 Newcastle Commission, vol. II, p. 456.

14 Newcastle Commission, vol. II, p. 550. Public schools referred to those in receipt of state grants rather than elite private schools.
15 Newcastle Commission, vol. II, p. 567.
16 Reports of Assistant Commissioners, pp, 567, 571. Similarly, a commission on the employment of children in agriculture noted that 'It is simply impossible for a child who hears English spoken only at school, and who is often unable to attach any meaning to the sounds which he hears, and whose school lessons in English are learned merely by rote, to have acquired any practical use of such a language': *Commission on the Employment of Children, Young Persons, and Women in Agriculture (1867): Third Report of the Commissioners* (London, 1870), p. 56.
17 John Hurt, *Education in Evolution: Church, State and Popular Education, 1800–1870* (London, 1971), p. 80; James Pillans, *Contributions to the Cause of Education* (London, 1856), p. 8.
18 *Select Committee on Education of Poorer Classes in England and Wales* (London, 1837–8), p. 125.
19 Blue Books, Part II, p. 34.
20 Glaslyn, 'Adgofion bore oes', *Cymru*, 15 October 1904, 149–54.
21 Newcastle Commission, vol. II, pp. 566, 550.
22 John Owen Jones, *Cofiant a Gweithiau Parch Robert Ellis, Ysgoldy Arfon* (Caernarfon, 1883), p. 17.
23 J. R. Kilsby Jones, 'Sefyllfa addysg y werinos haner can' mlynedd yn ol, ac yn bresonol', *Y Geninen*, 3, 1 (January 1885), 1–8, 7.
24 'Y Welsh Note', *Trysorfa y Plant*, October 1879, 271–2.
25 'The Welsh stick', *Llangollen Advertiser*, 9 June 1899, 5.
26 *Minutes of the CCE, 1846*, p. 305. Also see 'John Jones, Junior: sef anturiaethau Cymro ieuangc mewn bywyd cyhoeddus', *Baner ac Amserau Cymru*, 12 December 1894, 12.
27 Newcastle Commission, vol. II, p. 450.
28 *Minutes of the CCE, 1847–48*, p. 61.
29 *Report of the CCE, 1864–65*, pp. 157–8.
30 Newcastle Commission, vol. II, p. 532.
31 J. Lloyd Williams, *Atgofion Tri Chwarter Canrif, cyf. IV* (London, 1945), p. 79.
32 *Minutes of the CCE, 1854–55*, p. 604; *Report of the CCE, 1864–65*, p. 332. Evidence of Evan Davies, former principal of Brecon Training College, in *Report from the Select Committee on Education* (London, 1866), p. 524. For an example of a school unable to secure a Welsh-speaking teacher see the comments of the British Society agent in his diary of 13 March 1856, published in E. D. Jones, 'The Journal of William Roberts ('Nefydd')', *National Library of Wales Journal*, 9, 1 (1955), 93–104.
33 *Report of the CCE, 1859–60*, p. 296; *Minutes of CCE, 1855–56*, pp. 451–2.
34 *Minutes of the CCE, 1848–49–50*, vol. II (London, 1850), p. 250.
35 *Report of the CCE, 1868–69*, p. 164. Also see *Report of the CCE, 1872–3*, p. 237.

36 Joseph Lancaster, *The British System of Education: Epitome of Joseph Lancaster's Inventions and Improvements in Education Practised at the Royal Free Schools, Borough-Road, Southwark* (London, 1810), p. 40.
37 On problems in dealing with Welsh-speaking parents see William E. Marsden, *An Anglo-Welsh Teaching Dynasty: The Adams Family from the 1840s to the 1930s* (London, 1997), p. 71.
38 *Minutes of the CCE, 1848–49–50*, vol. I, pp. 313–14.
39 *Minutes of the CCE, 1848–49–50*, vol. II, pp. 293–4.
40 *Minutes of the CCE, 1847–48*, pp. 61, 300.
41 Blue Books, Part III, p. 18.
42 Blue Books, Part III, p. 25.
43 Andronicus, 'Yr ysgol: pennod III: dim Cymraeg', *Cymru'r Plant*, November 1894, 313–17.
44 Blue Books, Part III, p. 27.
45 Blue Books, Part III, p. 29.
46 *Report of the CCE, 1859–60*, p. 154; *Minutes of the CCE, 1848–49–50*, vol. 2, p. 294; *Report of the CCE, 1875–6*, p. 392; 'A glimpse of old Llanelly', *Llanelly and County Guardian and South Wales Advertiser*, 15 July 1897, 4; Newcastle Commission, vol. II, p. 531.
47 'The Welsh stick', *Llangollen Advertiser*, 9 June 1899, 5; Newcastle commission, vol. II (1861), p. 564; Frank Smith, *A History of English Elementary Education, 1760–1902* (London, 1931), p. 231.
48 *Commission on the Employment of Children, Young Persons and Women in Agriculture: Third Report of the Commissioners* (1870), p. 7; Beriah Gwynfe Evans, 'Addysg plant Cymru ddoe a heddyw', *Tywysydd y Plant*, 73, 4 (April 1910), 109. For later complaints of the continuation of this tradition see PA, Llidiart-y-waun school, 29 March 1873. For attendance patterns more broadly see David C. James and Brian Davies, 'Patterns of and influences on elementary school attendance in early Victorian industrial Monmouthshire 1839–1865', *History of Education*, 46, 3 (2017), 290–305.
49 Newcastle Commission, vol. II, pp. 463–4, 507.
50 *Minutes of the CCE, 1855–56*, p. 448.
51 Newcastle Commission, vol. II, p. 464.
52 *Minutes of the CCE, 1855–56*, p. 457.
53 Blue Books, Part II, p. 169.
54 Blue Books, Part III, p. 11; Part II, p. 34.
55 *Minutes of the CCE, 1852–53*, vol. 1, p. 675. For memories of a teacher with poor English see Watcyn Wyn, 'Haner cant o flynyddau', *Y Diwygiwr*, September 1894, 261–7.
56 Robert Roberts, *A Wandering Scholar: The Life and Opinions of Robert Roberts* (Cardiff, 1991), p. 106.
57 Revd Osborne Williams in Newcastle Commission, vol. II, p. 583.
58 Dot Jones, *Statistical Evidence Relating to the Welsh Language, 1801–1911* (Cardiff, 1998), p. 356.

59 Blue Books, Part II, p. 25. For an example of positive remarks on children learning bilingually see the comments on Llanddeusant in *Minutes of the CCE: Reports by Her Majesty's Inspectors of Schools, 1850–51, vol. II.*
60 For example, Glaslyn, 'Adgofion bore oes', *Cymru*, 15 October 1904, 149–54.
61 Blue Books, Part I, p. 32.
62 Newcastle Commission, pp. 566, 570–1.
63 Jones, *Statistical Evidence*, p. 356.
64 *Minutes of the CCE, 1848–49–50*, vol. II, p. 206.
65 Bob Ty'n Brynog, 'Adgof mam am ei hen ysgol-feistr', *Cymru'r Plant*, November 1893, 296–7. For similar memories see Gwyneth Vaughan, 'Bryn Ardudwy a'i bobl: ein hysgolfeistri', *Yr Haul*, 6, 65 (May 1904), 225–30.
66 J. B. Jones, 'Welshnot', *Yr Arweinydd Annibynol*, August 1880, 208–9.
67 Jonathan Ceredig Davies, *Folk-Lore of West and Mid-Wales* (Aberystwyth, 1911), p. 87. Also see John Jones, 'Yn yr ysgol', *Yr Ymofynydd*, February 1885, 39–42.
68 Wactyn Wyn, 'Trem yn ol', *Y Geninen*, 22, 3 (1904), 181–5, 182.
69 *Y Clorianydd*, 11 August 1910, 3; Cross Commission, third report, p. 4; 'Mr D. Williams, Prif-athraw coleg ysgolfeistresi, Abertawe', *Tywysydd y Plant*, December 1891, 314–18; James Rhys Jones, 'A Lecture on the educational state of Wales' (1851), *Mid Wales Herald*, supplement no. 1 (1860).
70 D. Parry-Jones, *Welsh Children's Games and Pastimes* (Denbigh, 1964), pp. 16–17.
71 Jones, 'Sefyllfa addysg y werinos haner can' mlynedd yn ol, ac yn bresonol', 7.
72 Blue Books, Part I, p. 32.
73 Nathan Dyved, 'Cymru-Vu', *Cardiff Times*, 1 December 1888, 1.
74 Michael, Ian, *The Teaching of English from the Sixteenth Century to 1870* (Cambridge, 1987), pp. 384–5.
75 Anne Bowman, *Routledge's New Reading Made Easy: A First Book of Lessons in One and Two Syllables* (London, 1856).
76 Richard Jones, 'Trallodion a gofidiau: gadael yr ysgol', *Yr Haul*, May 1890, 145–7.
77 On the importance of pictures in such books see Phil Gardener, *The Lost Elementary Schools of Victorian England* (London, 1984), p. 175.
78 Newcastle Commission, vol. II, p. 561.
79 Sarah Janes Rees, 'Hunan-gofiant', *Y Frythones*, 6, 4 (1884), 119–20.
80 'Holyhead', *Carnarvon and Denbigh Herald*, 19 May 1855, 5. It may be indicative of how much this went against the grain of received opinion that in other reports of the same meeting the advice was not mentioned. 'Anglesey Church Schoolmasters' Association', *North Wales Chronicle*, 19 May 1855, 8.
81 See his reports on individual schools in *Minutes of the CCE, 1848–49–50*, vol. II.
82 *Minutes of the CCE, 1848–49–50*, vol. II, p. 245.
83 *Minutes of the CCE, 1850–51*, vol. II, p. 544.
84 For example, see Sir Thomas Phillips, *Life of James Davies: A Village Schoolmaster* (London, 1850).

85 'A glimpse of old Llanelly', 4.
86 Owen Edwards, *Cylch Adgof: Penodau yn Hanes fy Addysg* (Caernarfon, 1906), p. 36.
87 H. Elvet Lewis, *The Life of E. Herber Evans, DD. From his Letters, Journals etc* (London, 1900), pp. 27–8.
88 Newcastle Commission, vol. II, p. 632.
89 For example, the Blue Books (Part I, pp. 54, 57) noted that at the ironworks schools at Blaengwrach and Hirwaun there were only English books but that Welsh was used to explain them to the children.
90 For example, MT, 'Aberporth ac addusg', *Yr Haul*, December 1868, 389.
91 'Bangor national school', *North Wales Chronicle and Advertiser for the Principality*, 8 August 1843, 3.
92 H. G. Williams, 'Learning suitable to the situation of the poorest classes: the National Society and Wales 1811–1839', *Welsh History Review*, 19, 3 (1999), 425–52, 448; Roberts, *Wandering Scholar*, pp. 288–9; 'Examination of the children attending the Bangor National schools', *North Wales Chronicle & Advertiser for the Principality*, 13 August 1829, 3.
93 Thomas Price and Jane Williams, *The Literary Remains of the Rev. Thomas Price, Carnhuanawc*, vol. 2 (Llandovery, 1854), p. 74.
94 *Report of the Commissioners [charity] 32 part III* (London, 1838), pp. 50, 107, 112, 151, 160.
95 *Report of the Commissioners of Inquiry for Turnpike Roads, South Wales* (London, 1844), p. 239.
96 Jones, *Statistical Evidence*, p. 356.
97 Jones, 'Journal of William Roberts', 218.
98 *Census of Great Britain, 1851. Education. England and Wales* (London, 1854), pp. clxxxvi, 212.
99 'Report of Mr Seymour Tremenheere on the State of elementary education in the mining district of South Wales', published in CCE, *Minutes, Part II*, 1839–40, p. 217. For a vivid description of a Sunday school see Roberts, *Wandering Scholar*, pp. 18–21.
100 Blue Books, Part III, p. 58.
101 Newcastle Commission, vol. II, pp. 460–1.
102 Emma Griffin, *Liberty's Dawn: A People's History of the Industrial Revolution* (New Haven, 2013), p. 183.
103 Blue Books, Part III, p. 55.
104 'State of elementary education in the mining district of south Wales', pp. 208–18. For later claims of widespread literacy in Welsh see Newcastle Commission, vol. II, p. 495.
105 Jones, *Statistical Evidence*, p. 346.
106 Barry Reay, 'The context and meaning of popular literacy: some evidence from nineteenth century rural England', *Past and Present*, 131 (1991), 89–129, 129.
107 Gareth Elwyn Jones and Gordon Wynne Roderick, *A History of Education in Wales* (Cardiff, 2003), p. 51. For literacy patterns more broadly see W. B.

Stephens, *Education, Literacy and Society, 1830–70: The Geography of Diversity in Provincial England* (Manchester, 1987).
108 Jacob Middleton, 'Thomas Hopley and mid-Victorian attitude to corporal punishment', *History of Education*, 34, 6 (2005), 599–615, 612.
109 'Yr ysgolion ddyddiol yn Nghymru', *Baner ac Amserau Cymru*, 4 June 1862, 1.
110 C. Birchenough, *History of Elementary Education in England and Wales* (London, 1914), p. 100.
111 Newcastle Commission, vol. II, p. 543; Evans, *Education in Industrial Wales*, pp. 288–9; Ginswick, *Labour and the Poor in England and Wales*, p. 78; 'Ross British School', *Monmouthshire Merlin*, 29 April 1843, 4.
112 G. R. Grigg, '"Nurseries of ignorance"? Private adventure and dame schools for the working classes in nineteenth-century Wales', *History of Education*, 34, 3 (2005), 243–62, 249, 258.
113 *Minutes of the CCE, 1848–49–50*, vol. II (London 1850), p. 207.
114 *Report of the CCE, 1859–60*, p. 154.
115 R. Richards, 'Trawsfynydd', *Yr Haul*, September 1896, 283–6.
116 Newcastle Commission, vol. II, p. 631.
117 Evidence of Evan Davies, teacher: *Schools Inquiry Commission, Col. V: Minutes of Evidence taken before the Commissioners Part II* (1868), pp. 347–8.
118 *Commission on the Employment of Children, Young Persons, and Women in Agriculture (1867)*, p. 95.
119 Blue Books, Part I, p. 32.
120 Norbahira Mohamad Nor and Radzuwan Ab Rashid, 'A review of theoretical perspectives on language learning and acquisition', *Kasetsart Journal of Social Sciences*, 39, 1 (2018), 161–7.
121 Victoria Fromkin and Robert Rodman, *An Introduction to Language*, 4th edn (Toronto, 1988), p. 391.
122 Newcastle Commission, vol. I, pp. 242–4.

4
THE WELSH NOT'S AFTERLIFE: PUNISHING WELSH-SPEAKING AFTER THE 1862 REVISED CODE

With many children leaving school illiterate, the 1861 Newcastle Commission into education expressed concern that the state's investment had not produced the desired results. From that inquiry came major reform in how schools were financed. A Revised Code of regulations was published in 1862, creating what became known as a payment by results system. Annual state grants to schools were now determined by attendance levels and pupils' performance in reading, writing and arithmetic when examined by an inspector. The grant went to school managers who often linked teachers' salaries to it thus creating a financial pressure on them to ensure children passed. The system was intended to ensure that education would only be expensive for the state if it produced children with the required literacy and numeracy skills.

The Revised Code was very controversial. The curriculum narrowed in some schools to just the grant-earning-3Rs, although this had always been the primary focus of most. There was now little incentive to keep children beyond the age of twelve since older pupils could not earn any grants. To ensure children passed their examination, many schools concentrated on a minimum number of books, which would be gone over again and again until they could be read with a sound of fluency. Whether a child understood what they read was immaterial; so too was how easily they could read any text not being examined.[1]

The Revised Code made no mention of the Welsh language but its examinations were in English, which created a sense that Wales was being treated unfairly. Before the code's implementation, the board of Caernarfon's National school wrote to the government, saying Welsh schools would be placed 'under great and serious disadvantage' because the great majority of pupils entered them 'entirely ignorant of the English language in which they would be examined'.[2] Two years later, the master of the town's British school wrote that the standards expected were 'generally very hard for Welsh children' given that they did not speak English.[3]

Although there were revisions to the code over the following years, it remained controversial. The problems were summed up in an 1889 novel by former teacher T. Marchant Williams (1845–1916). In it, a Welsh mistress bemoaned how it was impossible to reconcile 'the rigid requirements of the Code with the principles of true Education'. She wanted to teach ideas, whereas the code wanted their heads crammed with words. The novel's other teachers concentrated on what would earn them grants and saw no reason to extend the education offered. They taught children to read mechanically with no enthusiasm or imagination. In the novel's laments, the question of language did not arise.[4] As a teacher himself, Williams had used Welsh extensively with lower classes and to a lesser extent with older children to ensure they understood lessons.[5] He thus knew that the Revised Code did not prevent the use of Welsh in classrooms. But he also shared the idea that the primary function of education in Wales was to teach children English. This was simply not a controversial perspective. The question was always how much Welsh should be used to achieve that.

The period from 1862 to 1900 saw a considerable but gradual expansion of education. The 1860s witnessed significant advances in the numbers of British and National schools. The rivalries between the two societies meant some larger communities had both types of schools. In the town of Beddgelert, the National and British schools were within 160 yards of each other.[6] But rural areas remained poorly served because it was difficult for small communities to raise the money to build and run a school, even with state grants available. By the end of the decade, there were still only around 60 per cent of the school places that were needed in Wales.[7] England was little better off, and this was a matter of real concern to the state. It worried about falling behind other nations, especially after Prussia and the northern states of the USA, both with more advanced education systems, won wars in the 1860s. An expansion of the electorate in 1867 furthered concerns about how informed and educated the working class was.[8] The result was the 1870 Education Act, the first state intervention towards ensuring all children received an education. Under it, school boards had to be created in areas where there were insufficient schools. Existing schools, however, were not taken into public control and the Act was, in its architect's own words, to 'fill up gaps' in the existing patchwork of provision.[9] It did lead to new schools being built across rural and industrial communities and the number of funded schools in Wales and England increased from 5,141 in 1860 to 17,614 in 1880.[10] The new boards had the power to enforce attendance but this was not required; it was not until 1880 that legislation required children to go to school, and then only between the ages of five and ten.[11] The minimum leaving age was raised to eleven in 1893 and then twelve in 1899, although many children still stayed until thirteen because they had not achieved the required standard. The energy and effort put into enforcing these rules varied significantly from area to area and, in rural areas especially, child employment remained a constant threat to education levels. School boards could also enforce local taxes to cover some of their costs and this led some British schools to gradually move to their control. But, whether they were run by the National or British societies or a local board, schools continued to charge fees until these were replaced by further state funding in 1891.

Free and compulsory state education arrived in the 1890s, but it was still provided by a patchwork of different agencies. This meant that it continued to be plagued by religious controversies and tensions.[12] The old private schools had sunk into decline but had not disappeared. Numbers of untrained teachers had fallen but they continued to be found across the sector, while the quality and approach of those who were trained varied significantly. There was no regulation of classroom methods and individual teachers had considerable freedom in how they taught and enforced discipline. Quite simply, uniformity in education was an ideal rather than a reality.

The complexity of provision means it is misleading to talk of a late Victorian education system and very difficult to make confident generalisations, although that is what many historians have done. In particular, the 1870 Act has been seen as integral to the anglicisation of Wales.[13] It certainly made no provision for the Welsh language, but its significance is overstated. It was important in laying the basis of the expansion of elementary education to reach every child, but it led to no change in how or what children were taught, or the treatment of Welsh in schools. Educational historians maintain that the Revised Code was more significant for Welsh than the 1870 Act. W. Gareth Evans argued that the code reinforced negative attitudes towards the language and ensured teachers concentrated on teaching their pupils to pass English exams:

> The Revised Code led to the more widespread use of the Welsh Not by Welsh and non-Welsh-speaking headteachers and an increase in rote-learning in the English language as Her Majesty's Inspectors rigorously scrutinized its implementation. To a considerable degree, the elementary school became an alien institution for generations of pupils in Victorian Wales.[14]

B. L. Davies called the Revised Code 'the most insidious edict ever imposed upon the Welsh language in our schools'.[15] Such claims go back to the historical section of a 1927 inquiry which claimed that the code:

> was fatal to the use of Welsh in the schools. The grip of the State now became a strangle-hold, and as Welsh was not mentioned in the Code, it was effectively choked out of every school in the land ... every schoolmaster was henceforth for a generation and more directly, pecuniarily interested in boycotting the language, and in cramming his pupils for the annual examinations.[16]

However, there is no contemporary evidence of people saying that the code had led to an increased exclusion of Welsh. That interpretation seems to have come about later through not understanding just how English schools were before 1862. Historians' claims are thus simplifications and overestimate the changes the Revised Code brought about. It did not marginalise Welsh: that had already happened and there is no evidence at all to support assertions that use of the Welsh Not increased after its implementation.

Claims that the Revised Code exacerbated the subordination of Welsh also misunderstand how it was implemented and underestimate the professionalism and common sense of some teachers and inspectors. While some teachers certainly continued the old hostilities to Welsh, others knew perfectly well that the language had to be used if schools were to be run efficiently and pupils were going to understand anything. The code itself may have encouraged a narrow focus on learning the books and exercises required to pass examinations but teachers and inspectors knew that education was supposed to be about more than that, and they tried to expand their pupils' horizons within the confines of the system. Moreover, while the code decided what the outcomes of education should be, how that was achieved remained in the hands of teachers. The prescription of the Revised Code masked the variety of practice within schools.

This chapter, and the one that follows it, argue that the gradual abandonment of the Welsh Not and the growing use of Welsh as a medium of instruction continued after the Revised Code. It was not a uniform process and, at many schools, children continued to be punished for speaking Welsh, even if this involved physical chastisement and a wooden token on a lesser scale. Encouraged by the professionalism of teachers and the advice of inspectors and teaching manuals, schools became better places of learning, which further brought Welsh into the classroom to help the children learn and understand English and their lessons. Again, it was not a uniform process, but rather than see the period after the Revised Code as one where the needs of Welsh children were ignored, this and the following chapter argue that they were gradually addressed.

The professionalisation of teaching

As significant as the changes to how schools were financed was the continuing evolution of a sense of professionalism amongst teachers. As early as 1853, an Anglesey Church Schoolmasters' Association was formed to exchange information and 'elevate the profession from the disrepute into which it had too generally fallen'.[17] This sense of professionalism gathered pace after 1862 and began to characterise how teachers worked. Inspection, the growing number of British and National schools, and the 1870 Act slowly killed the old private schools and with them teachers who were employed because of their inability to find other work or simply because they could speak English. Teachers did not need to have attended training schools to win grants under the Revised Code but this gradually became the norm, and inspectors could also certificate untrained teachers if they felt his or her work was up to scratch.

The sense of being a profession encouraged teachers to reflect on their practice and work; it created ideals about the emancipatory and moral potential of education and a disdain for older methods that taught nothing but memorised facts.[18] This process began at training school, but there it was often something that students managed among themselves: the institutions themselves seem to have paid surprisingly little attention to the theory and practice of teaching.[19] Instead, colleges spent most of their time providing working-class students with a punishing schedule of fact-based lectures to give them the secondary education most had missed. One former student later recalled he had learned a little about a lot of things, without having learned a lot about anything.[20] Another wrote that he did not remember getting any advice on how to improve his teaching practice at Bangor Normal College in the 1870s. Instead, he taught himself such things from books.[21]

Early in the century, training colleges may have been a way that Lancaster's ideas around shaming pupils gained popularity but his influence faded quickly. The colleges seem to have given little attention to the question of how to deal with the Welsh language. This makes it unlikely that they were a forum where the Welsh Not was encouraged officially. A student at Bangor Normal College in the 1870s later claimed that in his two years there he did not hear an official word about Wales or the Welsh language.[22] The result of such neglect was that graduates of Welsh training colleges who did not speak the language, and had thus not encountered difficulties in their own schooling, were rather naive when it came to challenges they would face. William Adams was from an anglicised part of Pembrokeshire and studied at Bangor. In 1866, he and his wife were appointed to a school in Merthyr but, after just eight months, they were looking for new jobs. Adams wrote to the British Society saying that they found not speaking Welsh 'a great drawback to our complete success as teachers' and 'had we formed any idea of the drawbacks consequent on this, we should never have accepted the appointment'.[23]

However, training colleges might have played an indirect role in encouraging the continued use of the Welsh Not. In a PhD thesis from 1968, L. M. Rees claimed that students at the colleges were 'cut off from their native culture' and language and thus left with 'neither the inclination nor the capacity to contribute to the revivification of their native culture'.[24] English was the formal language of the colleges, the language that students were going to need and use in their profession, and the one that carried wider status as the medium of law, state and officialdom. Lecturers must have conveyed this to future teachers. The inspectors who visited the colleges certainly did. They were not used to working in Wales and thus more prejudiced than those inspectors who looked after schools. Some of their reports imply that the purpose of the training schools was to anglicise their students and celebrate those who overcame 'Welsh difficulties in accent, pronunciation, and grammar'.[25] Such reports must have rubbed off on the ethos of the colleges and their students too. Thus, even if the colleges did not teach students to use the Welsh Not, they were contributing to the mindset that led teachers to employ it.

But the idea of training colleges as essentially English institutions is misleading. The National Society was well aware that effective teachers needed Welsh and it had insisted that the first vice-principal of its Carmarthen training college was Welsh-speaking. At the college's opening, the lawyer and educational campaigner Sir Thomas Phillips declared,

> We intend to make no crusade against the Welsh language, and on the other hand it is not our intention to extend it ... Masters will however be provided to teach the Welsh language for the benefit of those who may choose to avail themselves of the privilege.

In the admissions process, preference was given to students resident in Wales and the college sought to train teachers 'who shall be possessed of competent knowledge of the Welsh and English languages'.[26] In 1866, the principal of the training college at Bangor told a select committee, 'we find that in order to be successful in Wales, the teachers should understand the language of the natives'.[27] Welsh was also used with pupils by the headmaster at Bangor's model school where students practised their teaching skills and could witness the benefits of employing children's mother tongue.[28]

Moreover, the training schools themselves had to employ Welsh in their own teaching because, thanks to the failings of their own elementary education, not all students were fluent in English.[29] The 1864 report on Caernarfon noted its students were 'generally young Welshmen whose knowledge of English is so small that they require peculiar treatment'.[30] Of the twenty-eight students at Bangor Normal College in 1870, three spoke English only, one was bilingual and the other twenty-four Welsh only.[31] In such climates, students spoke Welsh amongst themselves when not in class and probably also reflected on the linguistic challenges they faced in their own learning and in their practise schools.[32] Even if the colleges were failing to teach future teachers how to deal with questions of language, students might develop their own ideas regarding this. It may be that in these discussions students passed on knowledge of the Welsh Not and the idea that it helped teach English. But equally they also probably shared stories and experiences of how ineffective the instrument was in teaching anything much.

Thus, the growing professionalism of teaching sowed seeds to address the 'learning without understanding' criticisms of the Blue Books and Newcastle Commission by encouraging teachers to move beyond rote learning and to see the potential of schools for enlightening and developing pupils. This might mean the use of Welsh in the classroom in order to better teach English. However, the training schools failed to encourage this in any systematic manner and left teachers to work out their own ways of navigating the challenges, including, if they so chose, to exclude Welsh as so many of their predecessors had. And that is what some trained teachers decided to do.

The Welsh Not after 1862

There is no contemporary evidence of people thinking the Revised Code led to an increased use of the Welsh Not. As chapter 1 argued, there was instead a sense late in the century that the Welsh Not was something of the past. However, there is evidence that it was still in use in some places. Published accounts of the Welsh Not that use the present tense are rare but they do exist. In 1874, one writer called it a sign of the times that schools were disregarding Welsh and using the Welsh Stick to punish the children.[33] Another present-tense account comes from an 1889 drama about the need for Welsh to be used in schools to explain English terms. It included one character complaining that his daughter had been given the Welsh Note and beaten by a teacher, but another calling this is a splendid medicine for teaching children English, likening it to jumping into water to learn to swim.[34] The continued use of the Welsh Not in the late nineteenth century is also clear from early twentieth-century accounts that spoke of the practice as being in recent living memory.[35] In 1919, a JP in Solva gave his account of school life fifty years earlier when 'the greatest brand of disgrace in an elementary school was the wearing of the "Welsh note"'.[36] In 1901 one account claimed that most readers would be familiar with the Welsh Not.[37] In contrast, Evan Jones (1850–1928), an amateur antiquarian who asked older people for stories and information about it, declared that few knew about the Welsh Not and even fewer had seen it at school. He concluded it died out in the 1860s.[38] Nonetheless, the Welsh Not did exist throughout the forty or so years that followed the Revised Code. One reason for its continuation was how slow change in education was. The old private schools run by untrained teachers continued in some communities late into the century. Even in schools funded by the state, there were still many untrained teachers. In rural areas, schools struggled to recruit staff and thus often relied on inexperienced staff who could be as naive in their practice as the old teachers lambasted in the Blue Books.

The continued use of the Welsh Not in some schools is confirmed by the logbooks that schools in receipt of public funds after 1862 were required to keep. Most were fairly mundane and dominated by daily reports of attendance and the weather. They often offer no or little clue as to how Welsh was treated. Indeed, many read as if the school was in England, with no mention that lessons were in a foreign tongue for many children. But others do contain reflections on teaching methods and linguistic challenges. Sometimes this was because the teacher was concerned but it could also be because they wanted to communicate certain messages to the school managers and inspectors who read the logbooks. Yet even these reflections are frustratingly vague and, as historical sources, school logbooks offer the historian the twin challenge of being simultaneously long and voluminous, whilst also sketchy and uninformative.

Some previous researchers have failed to find evidence of the Welsh Not in their delves into logbooks.[39] This in itself does not signify anything about its prevalence use since most logbook entries do not routinely record anything much about discipline. When logbooks do occasionally make references to punishing children, it is impossible to know if these represent the only occurrences in that school or were just examples that the teacher decided to record for some unknown reason. There is evidence of the Welsh Not existing in schools that did not record it in their logbooks. In a 1927 letter to the *Western Mail*, a former pupil recalled that the Welsh Note was 'much in evidence, and considered one of the most serious sections of the day's curriculum' at the Board school he attended in the Gwaun valley from 1883 to 1887.[40] Yet the school's logbook contains no evidence of the Welsh Not or similar punishments and instead is a running lament of how the low attendance made it impossible to make any progress with the pupils.[41]

Nonetheless, the Welsh Not does appear, under a variety of names, in a number of logbooks from rural areas. In 1876, a logbook entry at Llanfihangel National school read: 'Welsh-notes given to the different classes. Find it answers very well.' Two weeks later, the master recorded that 'Several had to be punished for speaking Welsh.'[42] In 1875, the logbook at Aberffraw noted the introduction of square '"woods" ... worn by a string on the breast ... to check Welsh speaking, which is very prevalent in the play ground'.[43] The following year, the Rowen logbook stated 'Introduced the Welsh Note both in the school and in the playground in order to check Welsh speaking.'[44] At Llannerch-y-medd British school, children who erred were given a 'Welsh ticket', with the last holder in the morning kept in for half an hour, while the afternoon punishment was to sweep the school.[45] At Llanllyfni British school, the master recorded in 1870 'Silent work under the command of the Welsh sticks which prove a good cure to the defects in discipline and English.' This statement implies that their use was common in the school but it was 1872 before the topic was recorded again, this time with an entry that simply read 'Speaking Welsh in school punished.'[46]

Whether these passing mentions of the Welsh Not were recorded on a whim or because its use was unusual is impossible to know. Some do clearly imply that its use was inconsistent. Vaughan's charity school opened at Llangynog in 1872 and in the following year logbook entries read that the Welsh Notes had been distributed 'for the purpose of preventing Welsh talking'. Some months later, an entry read:

> First class were deprived of a part of their midday leisure for carelessness in setting down their arithmetic exercises. Others found themselves in trouble for indulging rather too freely in their mother's tongue. The Welsh Notes have been abolished as they tended to create animosity and unpleasantness during leisure times. The teacher goes out among them at intervals and those caught transgressing are punished by being compelled to furnish their memory with a few additional English sentences.

Not until 1876 is the practice mentioned again when an entry read 'Welsh notes were again distributed to prevent Welsh speaking among the higher classes', while in 1882 another isolated entry noted their use.[47] Such sporadic entries probably do not record the only times the Welsh Not was employed in schools but they do point to how its use was inconsistent, both within specific schools and across Wales. Where it was used, it was down to the initiative of individual teachers rather than any universal culture.

Far more common than specific mentions of the Welsh Not are sporadic or concentrated references to preventing the speaking of Welsh in more general terms. In 1865, for example, there was a group of logbook references at Bodedern National school to punishing children for 'talking Welsh'.[48] References to such actions and explicit no-Welsh rules are particularly common in the first months of a new school or teacher. Two days after Capel Evan British school opened, the logbook read: 'Gave orders that there should be no Welsh spoken by the children during school hours.'[49] Two months after opening, an 1864 entry at Brawdy simply read 'Caution against talking Welsh in school'.[50] A new teacher at Llangeinwen recorded 'The Welsh language is strictly prohibited in school.'[51] At Felinheli, an 1878 entry read:

> The boundary wall of the school having been built we have made a rule to the effect that no Welsh is to be spoken within the school grounds. We find it very difficult to impose the rule but by constant care we hope to reap the benefits hereafter.[52]

The logbooks did not record how, or even if, these rules were enforced.

Logbooks do show how teachers could become periodically vexed by different specific issues.[53] Addressing Welsh-speaking could be an example of this and sometimes no-Welsh rules were introduced by established teachers in response to what they perceived as a growing or suddenly noticeable problem. At Corris British school, for example, the logbook recorded in 1870, 'Chequed Welsh talking which is these days gaining ground rather.'[54] That same year, the master at Llangefni British school recorded he had made a new rule that children should only speak

English in school and in the playground because they were 'in the habit of carrying on all their conversations in Welsh'.⁵⁵ In 1880, the master at Dyserth National school noted that 'nearly all the children have for some time past talked Welsh, even inside School with the [Pupil] Teacher'. He set two older pupils to listen all morning and report the Welsh speakers at lunch time. Twenty-two pupils were kept in to write twenty-five lines each, with the threat of 100 lines if they did it again. The next day, one boy found himself given that task and kept at school until 6.30 p.m. to finish it.⁵⁶ At Esgairdawe in 1887, the logbook simply declared: 'Today the teacher informed the scholars that no more Welsh is to be spoken in school hours within the school premises. The regulation is to come into force on 1st November.'⁵⁷

The way Welsh was often periodically rather than systematically suppressed was very evident at Llangefni National. It was under the same teacher from 1860 to 1897 and his logbooks were sprinkled with intermittent comments about Welsh-speaking and his 'little schemes' to stop it. He tried the cane, detention, putting offenders' names on the wall, informing parents, and even allowing those who spoke English to play a game where they could bite an apple on a string. He sometimes noted his satisfaction that more English was being spoken in class and the playground but this was never sustained. In 1884, he recorded 'I find it very difficult to get the children to speak English habitually. I have tried every plan with but very little success.' Indeed, in later years, he felt that less rather than more English was being spoken, something he attributed to a growth in the number of pupils from outside the town. But it was also notable that some of his periodic complaints and schemes were about getting children to 'endeavour' to speak English. This was an admission that children who knew little English could not be stopped from making some use of their mother tongue.⁵⁸

For teachers, such situations could be very frustrating because both the Revised Code's examinations and the expectations of parents and managers centred on children learning English. When the teacher's salary was linked to examinations, the frustration could be even greater. At Caio, the master summed up that it was 'impossible' to carry on until the children were familiar with English.[59] In 1874, the master of Llandysul National school recorded:

> Children learn to think and express their thoughts in Welsh, consequently take no interest whatever in the many interesting reading lessons contained in their books. English is to them – completely a foreign tongue, and it is quite disheartening to witness their apathy owing to the fore mentioned cause during an interesting lesson in reading or arithmetic.[60]

The bans on Welsh were attempts to remedy such situations by making the children practise their English. At Llechryd, a new teacher recorded in 1882 that the children's 'want of English' was the greatest obstacle to progress. After a few days in the job, he decided to prohibit the speaking of Welsh in school, something which he periodically recorded detaining older children for.[61] In 1871, the logbook from Cwm Penmachno National illustrated both how the Welsh Not was no longer standard practice but also how it could come back into use because of the frustrations around children's English. It stated, 'Find great difficulty in getting the children to speak English. Thus I introduced the old system of Welsh Sticks which seems to answer the purpose.'[62] Of course, often, to stop children speaking Welsh was to stop them speaking at all; a child could not simply start speaking a new language without being taught it. The best teachers knew this but others, in their hurry to progress children, seemed to have forgotten or become desperate.

Although no examples of post-1862 'no Welsh' rules and punishments have been found in logbooks from industrial districts, language could still be a challenge in such places. Welsh was dominant in many industrial communities in the west throughout the period, as it was further east in the middle of the century. In Rhymney, a mining community in Monmouthshire, an 1868 logbook entry noted 'Find the Welsh language a hinderance to their progress in English as it is Welsh in the home, in society, and in the chapel.'[63] In Bryncethin, a mining village near Bridgend, the master of a new National school complained in 1870 that 'scarcely any' of the children understood a word of English.

He continued to bemoan this was a barrier to their progress and in 1874 recorded:

> very few of the children having any sort of English Reading book at home makes it very difficult for the children to read a language which they cannot speak in a way that will be satisfactory for an Inspector who knows nothing about this benighted district.[64]

These complaints were not dissimilar to rural areas, but they were less common because migration was changing the linguistic make-up of many industrial communities. There was probably no need to punish Welsh-speaking because children were using English more and more of their own accord, either because they spoke it at home or because their linguistic skills were developing by playing with the children of migrants (see chapter 8). Not all migration, however, was from England. In the mining community of Troed-y-rhiw, a teacher recorded in 1883 that several new children had joined the schools 'who can hardly speak a word of English having come from the country schools in N. Wales'.[65] But such children probably quickly learned English because it was all around them and, unlike in the countryside, not just in the classroom. In Ferndale in 1885, an inspector contrasted the poor reading of younger pupils with the excellent results of older ones. The former was attributed to children starting school late and being 'ignorant' of English, while the latter was put down to the effect of excellent teaching. It may well have been an excellent school but the inspector should also have realised that children's advances in English were far from just conditioned by what was happening at school.[66]

Clampdowns on Welsh might also be driven by frustration at the general noise in schools. As education grew and attendance was enforced, large schools became more common and it was not unusual to have 100 children in a single room. Even when a classroom was partitioned, it might be with curtains rather than a proper wall.[67] In such conditions, quiet was deemed important. Indeed, one Welsh inspector recommended teachers observe 'the utmost silence' in all schools.[68] This would allow children to concentrate and the master to hear the reading of the section whose turn it was to have his attention. Thus, as before the Revised Code, banning Welsh could be as much about reducing noise as linguistic concerns. In 1886, the master of Pennant National school complained, 'I find that the children are too much addicted to talking, especially Welsh, during school hours.'[69] At Llandegfan, the master recorded in 1864 that he had established 'a system to secure silence and to prevent the children talking Welsh either in or out of school'.[70] At Llanddona, after five months in post, a master introduced a Welsh Note and recorded that it had 'done away' with talking amongst the older children.[71] With no reference to language, a new master at Llangeitho complained in 1869 that hitherto the children had been allowed to talk excessively and he was determined to suppress it.[72] As with controlling Welsh more generally, the methods used to secure silence varied. At Sarn National school, a girl was made to write the word 'Talking' 500 times after school, although it was not clear in which language she had spoken.[73] Benjamin Jones, born in 1903, remembered a two-inch 'Talk Not', inscribed with the letters TN, in use at his Cardiganshire school.[74]

The explicit introduction of bans on Welsh imply that the language had been allowed, or at least tolerated, beforehand. This was partly pragmatic, and many logbooks contain evidence of the great difficulty of enforcing no Welsh when children spoke so little English. In Abergwili, the headmaster recorded: 'The rules of the school forbid the speaking of Welsh, and still no rule is more often violated, even by the [pupil] teachers themselves.'[75] At Aberaeron British school, the master recorded in 1880: 'Cannot get the children from the habit of talking in Welsh; the school as a whole is backward in English.'[76] A response to such challenges was to only have no-Welsh rules for older children who could be expected to have better English. In 1884, the school logbook for Bryngwran recorded:

> The children of this school have been of late too much in the practice of speaking Welsh. To-day a rule was laid down that no child in the three upper standards was to speak Welsh during school hours, and that any violator of this rule was to be duly punished. The culprit was found out by means of a 'Welsh mark'.

In a short time it is to be hoped that this rule can be extended to the III & II standards, without causing too much severity.[77]

Other schools expected even younger children to refrain from Welsh but still graduated their rules. After a poor inspection in 1872, Llanllyfni British school introduced new rules where Infants and Standards I and II were not allowed to speak Welsh in the school, Standards III and IV were also not allowed to speak it in the playground, while Standards V and VI, the oldest children, were not allowed to speak it on the road to school either. There was no mention of how this was to be enforced.[78] At Llanfrothen National school, the master wrote in 1866 that: 'Welsh is not allowed to be spoken in the 1st class [the oldest children] during school hours.' Yet, within a couple of months, he was recording that Welsh was often spoken despite the rule against it being 'strictly attended and enforced'. He may have used the Welsh Not in his efforts because he later recorded that at his evening school, attended by older boys working in quarries, there were fines for speaking Welsh with half the sum being paid by the holder of the 'Welshnote' at dismissal.[79]

In the face of the challenges, some teachers probably did give up trying to stop children speaking Welsh. The rules outlined at a start of a teacher's tenure may not have lasted, being quietly dropped or adapted as their instigator realised how difficult it was to actually enforce restrictions on Welsh. At some schools, logbooks contain repeated mentions of the introductions of no-Welsh rules suggesting they were not maintained.[80] Certainly, logbook references to both the Welsh Not and bans on Welsh-speaking seem to have become less common in logbooks after the 1870s. In particular, attempts to restrict the language's use in the playground fell away and by the 1880s there was a claim that in the north-west Welsh was 'the universal language of the playground'.[81] Josiah Jones (b.1890) remembered of his education in Cwmllynfell that speaking Welsh in the classroom led to a clout but in the yard the children all played in Welsh.[82] The abandonment of rules against using the language in the playground reflected an older belief that speaking Welsh mattered less there. At one school in the Gwaun valley in the 1860s, those who spoke Welsh in the playground received a 'severe cut' (swipe of the cane) on each palm but those who did so inside the school were given 'a severer cut on the back of each hand'.[83] But the changes were also just pragmatism. As the master of Menai Bridge British school told the Cross Commission, children universally played in Welsh: 'it is almost impossible to get them to speak English when at play'.[84]

Rather than try to enforce rules outlawing Welsh, some teachers turned to persuasion. When a new school opened at Blaen-ffos in 1879, the teacher recorded: 'The children show a great desire for learning. Spoke to them about attempting to speak English at play.'[85] At Marianglas, an entry read: 'I tried to persuade the children to speak English together, especially during school hours; also some punishment was inflicted on those that refused to do so.'[86] After a new master took over Caernarfon British school in 1867, he recorded: 'Speaking Welsh being prevalent by the children I cautioned them against that habit.'[87] Such cautions could be part of general attempts to improve pupils' conduct, morals and behaviour. At Y Ferwig in 1876, the teacher gave children a warning not to swear, use nicknames or speak Welsh.[88] In 1880, the master at Swyddffynnon cautioned children against speaking Welsh in and outside school but also about knocking on doors, not taking their caps off inside and mocking a local disabled man.[89]

Such lectures were part of a wider trend where teachers might appeal to children's sense of reasonability and morals rather than punish them. At Bethel in 1865, for example, a teacher asked pupils about their view of truancy. He concluded: 'They agree all that I ought to punish severely whoever will accustom such habits henceforth.'[90] When it came to speaking Welsh some teachers found they needed to repeat their entreaties over time. In 1877, the master at Trecastell recorded that he had given pupils 'several addresses' on punctuality and 'their duty to speak English to each other while in school'. The elder pupils were asked to help 'carry this into practice among the country children and lower standards'. In 1881, he spoke to pupils about 'the habit of talking Welsh too freely' in the playground and school. The following week the teacher again spoke on the issue but this time 'very strictly'. Later these appeals turned into a rule that 'strictly prohibited' Welsh on the playground, but even then two weeks later the pupils were again being spoken to on the issue.[91] After it had been open for around eight months, the master of Llanaelhaearn Board school recorded: 'Children cautioned about talking Welsh in and about the school, this is one of the most difficult things I find to put a check to amongst them. A plan tried with hoping it will answer the purpose.' What the plan was he did not record but if it was the Welsh Not the early ambitions became more muted. The following year, the logbook read: 'This week the children's attention was drawn to their speaking too much Welsh. The biggest children were strictly cautioned for this, whereby they all promised to alter.'[92] The strict caution, of course, encouraged compliance but it is still notable that the teacher appealed to the children to comply and that the complaint was of too much Welsh rather than any at all.

Noting how common frustration was in logbooks, Bischof argues this might be seen 'as a subtle request for sympathy from the school inspector because of both the factors that were out of the teacher's control and the emotional toll which teaching took'.[93] That might be true, but it was also a genuine feeling. Logbooks are a litany of complaints about the slow progress of children, poor facilities and resources, and, in particular, low attendance caused by the weather, the needs of local agriculture, fairs and festivals, and lax enforcement by parents. Language was just one more challenge to face and the exasperation of teachers was undoubtedly very real. It was also intensified by just how difficult it was to get children to stop speaking Welsh. This mattered to teachers because it was a sign that their efforts to teach English were failing, something which undermined their sense of professional achievement. In these circumstances, the bans on Welsh were more the result of desperation than any hostility to the language. This also explains why the known examples of explicit no-Welsh rules are concentrated in rural communities. It was there that it was hardest to teach English because the language was so rarely heard outside school. It was there that teachers believed that stopping children from speaking Welsh would overcome this, whether that meant permanent and sustained bans or periodic attempts.

This was all evident at Tywyn in Meirionnydd where the headmaster was unusual in recording his struggles with the language in some detail.

Table 4.1. Tywyn school logbook entries detailing attempts to stop children speaking Welsh (MRO)

14 Aug. 1863	I feel at a loss to know the best method to adopt in order to prevent the children generally from speaking Welsh. Today, I have introduced a 'Welsh stick' into each of the classes, and the child who has it last is to be kept in half an hour after school hours.
14 Oct. 1863	The children will not be prevented from speaking Welsh during school hours.
16 Oct. 1863	Welsh stick was rather effective this afternoon.
9 Nov. 1863	I cannot prevent the children from speaking Welsh. Today found many.
23 Nov. 1863	Welsh is spoken. Let me do what I can.
23 Jun. 1864	Much Welsh spoken in the playground. Kept several in for their speaking Welsh during school hours.
5 July 1864	Several of the children not knowing English and which have been of late admitted have caused considerable trouble in preventing Welsh being spoken.
20 July 1864	Was obliged to punish ... several for speaking Welsh
3 Aug. 1864	William Martin kept in was talking Welsh continually
9 Aug. 1864	By continual application and diligence I have prevailed at last as regarding Welsh speaking during school time. I am happy to report a great improvement in this point
30 Sep. 1864	Was obliged to keep in several in for speaking Welsh during play-time.
11 Nov. 1864	Much Welsh spoken these days in the playground and punished several.
1 Dec. 1864	Punished several boys of the third class for their speaking Welsh. I have too much of it even in the schoolroom though I try my best to get them all to speak English.
3 Jan. 1865	Their speaking Welsh at home and in the streets is a great drawback.

9 Mar. 1865	Was much troubled today with the Welsh speaking which is continued impediment in our Welsh schools. I have tried all imaginable plans but have totally failed in the case of many children. Nothing will cause them to yield. I must consult HM Inspector.
21 Mar. 1865	The Welsh speaking seems to be on the increase again amongst the younger children.
26 May 1865	Was obliged to punish several boys for their speaking Welsh.
1 June 1865	Gave out xtra Exercise to several boys for having caught them conversing in Welsh in the playground. I am determined to stop this practice – which is a barrier to their progress.
12 July 1865	I have to complain much of the practice of the children in speaking Welsh. I find that I am unable to stop it. But I shall not give it up. Today I was tormented a great deal by it. I have tried a great many cures, but nothing seems to prevail. The parents complain that their children do not learn to speak English and I am left in an awkward position.
25 July 1865	Must do something to get the children to speak English.
Nov. 1865	Much trouble is given me by the continual practice of some of the children in speaking Welsh in the playground and even in the schoolroom. It is very difficult to discover a just punishment for the crime. I find that, in most cases, persuasion is by far the best plan. I must confess, however, that they are much better now than they used to be six or seven months back.
12 July 1866	Welsh is spoken too freely in and without the school. Have had occasion to refer this great draw back and cannot invent a suitable process of punishment to get rid of the evil. Most of my younger children know no English.

| 30 July 1866 | Am still troubled with the frequency of Welsh speaking both in the Playground and in the Schoolroom. Were I to get the children to try to convey their thoughts in English I should find it much easier to get through a greater amount of words. I myself am forced to break the rule which I make forbidding the speaking of Welsh during school hours, in order to get the younger ones to understand anything I have to teach them. Consequently I lose a great deal of the influence which I ought to command on that account |

Here we see a situation that was probably common across rural Wales after the Revised Code. The teacher's struggle with Welsh was daily but the punishments were not. They seem to have been given to pupils who continually spoke Welsh rather than the odd word. The Welsh Not was not the only method used and punishments might be given for speaking Welsh in either the playground or classroom. But above all we see, regardless of the punishment, that the Welsh Not, and attempts to suppress Welsh more generally, simply did not work in stopping children speaking Welsh. And they did not stop the teacher himself employing Welsh to help children understand what was being taught.

Punishments for speaking Welsh

The Tywyn account is also notable for worrying about what the most just and effective punishment for speaking Welsh was. There are relatively few references in logbooks to physical punishments for speaking Welsh but it can be assumed that those that did not specify a specific punishment did involve the cane or similar, even if this was a last resort. For example, a teacher at Swyddffynnon recorded in 1883 that he had punished three boys for speaking Welsh in school after being 'frequently warned about it'.[94] More explicit was an 1881 entry at Abergwili that said, 'Talking Welsh' was the 'most serious fault prevalent in the school' and that 'Spasmodic and at times, violent efforts, have been made to minimise the evil.' Yet, it noted, that 'a short time' after punishments 'the mischief is as widespread as ever'.[95] There is also autobiographical evidence of children being hit in this era for speaking Welsh. T. Gwynn Jones (b.1871), for example, went to a school where there was no Welsh Not but where children who spoke Welsh were made to stand on a bench. They could get down if they heard someone else speaking Welsh and the person there at lunchtime was caned. But, after Jones had kicked out at the teacher for caning him, there were no more physical punishments for speaking Welsh at that school.[96]

This teacher had his own reason for abandoning physical punishment, but he was in line with a wider trend already in train before the 1860s and gathering pace as the century progressed. In 1857, John Gill's influential *Introductory Text-book to School Education, Method and School Management* was published. In the following twenty-five years, it sold 50,000 copies and was influential in discouraging corporal punishment in schools.[97] Gill saw discipline as something used to enforce the 'right conduct' amongst children but stressed how it was rooted in the character of the master and what he inspired: 'It depends more on the *man* than on his means.' He stressed that teachers should be patient, earnest, cheerful and considerate, and inspire love in pupils. They should not 'needlessly give pain, raise a blush, or excite a laugh, by unnecessary exposure of ignorance, error or mistake ... A teacher should never bluster, never bully, never scold.' Gill did concede that punishment that deprived some pleasure or inflicted some pain was necessary and that the aim was to 'associate pain with wrong doing'. But he stressed the punishment had to be fair. Rebuke and tasks were recommended, with corporal punishment only used cautiously and when a parent would.[98] Training schools also discouraged the excessive or routine use of corporal punishment. For example, students from Bangor Normal College were criticised by their model school's headmaster not just for hitting children but also for speaking harshly and not trying to get children to like them.[99] In 1882, inspectors were told to make clear to schools that 'the more thoroughly a teacher is qualified for his position by skill, character and personal influence, the less necessary is it for him to resort to corporal chastisement'.[100] This was all part of what Judith Rowbotham called a 'new repugnance for "gratuitous" violence' in the second half of the nineteenth century. Executions were no longer public after 1868 and there was less use of corporal punishment against adults, with floggings in the military abolished entirely in 1881. It also contributed to changes in the domestic sphere. Parents were becoming less likely to employ physical punishment as an everyday strategy to control children, although this change was less common amongst the working classes.[101]

This wider climate was reinforced by teachers' own practical experiences. They came to think that if corporal punishment was felt unfair by children then it was resisted and resented, and that it also had no effect if used fairly but too frequently. Thus, many teachers started to think corporal punishment should be a matter of last resort.[102] This helps explain why the Welsh Not was not in consistent use in all schools where it was employed: any punishment or rule that was commonplace was unlikely to focus children's minds on its intended purpose.

A reluctance to employ corporal punishment is clear in many logbooks. In 1863, the master of Forden National school recorded after much disorder that he would see whether keeping scholars behind after school would be more effective than the rod.[103] At Llanfrothen National school, the teacher recorded in 1870 that he found keeping latecomers in after school was more effective than corporal punishment.[104] In 1873, the master of a new school at Llidiart-y-waun recorded proudly that he not used corporal punishment once in its first year. He claimed, 'firmness and kindness combined will always ensure good discipline, while the children will certainly become more gentle and amiable than if corporal punishment were resorted to'.[105] Caning in a fit of temper was particularly frowned upon and, when in 1865 the master of Caernarfon British school recorded that he had punished two offenders for disobedience and using dirty language, he stressed he did so 'not in a passion but from a sense of duty'.[106] Even if teachers were inclined to cane, their employers might not like it. At Aberdaron, a teacher shied away from using physical punishment after being chastised by his managers for it.[107] Llanfihangel-y-Creuddyn Lower school board even dismissed an assistant mistress because of her 'undue severity' in punishing children 'as to cause injury'.[108] By the early twentieth century, some schools began to keep punishment books which showed how caning had become far from a daily occurrence. At Cilcennin, for example, there were just seven entries for 1901 and nineteen for 1902. Most just got one stroke and their crimes were lateness, inattention, carelessness, truancy, collusion, disobedience, disrespect, talking and laughing in class.[109]

One reason for the decline in physical punishments was the growth of women teachers. The first training institution in Wales for women had been opened by the British Society in Swansea in 1872. One of its goals was to increase the number of Welsh-speaking teachers but it was also driven by the fact that women could be paid less, something which patrons hoped might make the expansion of schools required by the 1870 Act more achievable.[110] Women teachers were certainly not unknown to use corporal punishment but they also sometimes had more sympathetic outlooks and were maybe reluctant to physically punish the bigger boys. It could thus be that their growing number contributed to more humane attitudes to Welsh in schools.

At first, the move away from physical punishments did not undermine the Welsh Not since the chastisement it offered was always as much emotional as it was physical. Indeed, it might have even encouraged use of the Welsh Not as teachers sought alternatives to corporal punishment. In some places, the penalty for speaking Welsh was to stand in the corner of the room wearing the Welsh Not.[111] In other places the holder of the Welsh Not still received an additional punishment. In 1870 at Llanon, for example, the teacher recorded 'Endeavoured to compel the children to converse in English by means of a piece of wood. Offenders to be shut in after school hours.'[112] An account from 1927 claimed the Welsh Not had died out in about 1880 but that in its later years the punishment had been to stand on one leg or to hold up a slate.[113] One man recalled that in around 1870 the punishment for speaking Welsh at Newmarket (Flint) was to wear a hoop around the neck.[114] Welsh was not the only 'offence' punished with such public humiliation. In 1869, the headmaster at Caio Board school (Llanwrda) recorded that he sought to 'imitate and ridicule' pupils who could not read properly. He put the names of those who had not recited their home lessons correctly on the classroom wall for a week.[115]

However, teaching manuals and the general professionalisation of teaching discouraged humiliation as a disciplinary technique. An 1864 handbook for Welsh teachers suggested praising the 'humblest attempts' at speaking English and never ridiculing the children's efforts.[116] This movement against humiliation as a teaching method meant the Welsh Not gradually fell out of use at most schools as a means of checking Welsh-speaking. As already noted, by late in the century there was a strong sense in the press that the Welsh Not was something from a generation or more before.[117] These writers were not entirely correct that the practice had come to an end, but the general trend is further evidenced by the paucity of published memories of receiving the Welsh Not late in the century. Indeed, there were people who wrote that their older siblings had received it but that when they were at school they were just slapped for speaking Welsh.[118]

Instead of corporal punishment and humiliation, detention and educational tasks gradually became the standard punishments used where Welsh-speaking was penalised. The pattern was evident in the memories of a man who recalled holding up slates as the punishment for speaking Welsh in the 1880s, but this was replaced by staying behind after school to practise spellings.[119] Logbooks illustrate the typical punishments. At Llandybïe, the teacher recorded in 1866 that: 'I have made it a rule from this day that no Welsh is to be spoken by the 1st and 2nd classes [the oldest children] once they are on school premises.' Two days later, he gave two boys twenty lines for speaking Welsh.[120] At Llanddeusant in 1870, a boy and girl were made to write fifty lines each for speaking Welsh.[121] In Flintshire, one master made anyone caught saying something in Welsh write it out in English twenty times.[122] Even with these non-physical punishments, logbooks show that the punishment for speaking Welsh might be a last resort after several warnings.[123] At Llanllyfni, a teacher came up with an elaborate system where pupils were given a Welsh card. Every time they spoke Welsh a mark was entered on the card and they were fined half a penny for every twelve marks. The fines were awarded to the child with the fewest marks.[124]

The tempering of punishments does not necessarily mean a tempering of the hostility towards Welsh. It was, after all, still being punished. David Samuel (b.1856 in Aberystwyth) said he had never seen the Welsh Note but remembered that the children at his school were not allowed to speak Welsh and that his teacher had ridiculed the language and anyone who spoke it. He translated Welsh idioms into English to make fun of them.[125] J. Lloyd Williams, remembering his time as a pupil teacher in the late 1860s and early 1870s, claimed that even acknowledging the existence of Welsh had been an unforgivable sin.[126]

Moreover, physical punishments never disappeared. One reason for this was the continued importance of monitors and pupil teachers. Being children themselves, they were not generally supposed to use corporal punishment but the size of schools meant they were often not closely observed. One man recalled that as a pupil teacher in the Rhondda in the early 1890s he ended up fighting with the older boys because they were 'not prepared to obey me unless I could hit them down'.[127] Some pupil teachers seem to have enjoyed their new authority and logbooks are full of teachers admonishing their apprentices for striking pupils or to be kinder to the children.[128] Thus some of the physical punishments for speaking Welsh may have come from pupil teachers asserting their authority and resorting to means their masters might not approve of.

At some schools, the headmasters themselves still regularly employed the cane for disobedience, being late, swearing, stealing, causing trouble, education failings and speaking Welsh. Few teachers were willing to completely abandon their right to use it.[129] Indeed, most educational comment did support corporal punishment, seeing it as a disagreeable necessity because working-class children could be difficult to control otherwise. It was accepted as a means of deterrent and punishment, as long as it was fair and appropriate and not done out of temper or spite.[130] The idea of it as a last resort was evident in the words of the master of Abergwili National school who recorded that if 'moral influence' failed to get children to do their homework then 'physical may, as usual, be more successful'.[131] Indeed, oral and autobiographical sources suggest physical punishments were far more common than both educational thinking and logbooks indicate.[132] Abel Jones, who was at school in the Rhondda in the 1880s, remembered canings for talking in class and getting sums wrong. When the headmaster whistled, everyone was expected to be silent and those who were not immediately still or quiet were physically punished.[133] Frank Richard, born in 1883 and raised in industrial Blaina by his tinplate worker uncle, recalled that he and his cousin 'used to keep count of the number of hidings we had from my Uncle and the number of canings we had from the schoolmaster'.[134] William George (b.1865) described Llanystumdwy National school as an austere place:

> I never remember the headmaster raising a laugh or cracking a joke. He always kept a rod within reach, and he would fling it with great dexterity from one end of a room to another. The silence, that followed the dropping of the rod in front of the class of which the offender was a member, was broken by the announcement by the headmaster of the name of the culprit who thereupon had to pick up the rod and carry it along to the place of judgment like a doomed slave, carrying his halter to the scene of execution.[135]

Such evidence has led one historian to conclude: 'The impression emerges from autobiographies that most teachers caned almost automatically, without special vindictiveness; the cane was a symbol of office.'[136] But adults remember the pain they endured as children and not the times it was not inflicted. Nor would they be aware of how corporal punishment was no longer as acceptable as it once was. That shift was evident in how the law became involved in some cases. Occasionally, the Bench decided the punishment was not excessive and that teachers had the right to administer corporal punishment – even where parents did not like it – if it was not cruel or unreasonable.[137] But there were other examples of teachers being convicted. In 1889, a master at the Ynysybwl Board school was found guilty of assault on an 11-year-old boy. The pupil had used a 'dirty term' in speaking to a girl monitor and was caned twice and then punched on the back three or four times by the teacher. He cut his cheek on a desk on being knocked down. A fine of 20s. was imposed.[138] When such things happened, it is not surprising that those children who spoke Welsh contrary to school rules could find themselves formally caned or informally hit. Such cases may have become gradually less common but they continued to happen.

Teaching: 'a very hard occupation'

Violence in classrooms meant there were always concerns about the quality of people employed in the profession. In the early 1880s, only around half of teachers in England and Wales had studied at training colleges.[139] As late as 1900, 28 per cent of male teachers and 51 per cent of female teachers in England and Wales had not attended a training college.[140] But training did not necessarily mean quality. Teaching was never a well-paid job and there were apprehensions that it was consequently not attracting people of the right quality. Low pay also encouraged teachers to concentrate on getting children through grant-earning exams; many simply could not afford the pay cut that children failing might entail. Pay was lowest in rural areas where schools were smaller and thus earned less income from fees and the Revised Code; the result being that these schools struggled to recruit staff and often had to turn to inexperienced or even untrained teachers, both of whom might have unsound pedagogical practices. Thus, in the Welsh-speaking countryside, where the challenges of teaching English ran deepest, those given the task were often those least equipped for it.

This is at the root of why many teachers continued to believe that excluding Welsh helped children learn English. The Newcastle Commission argued objections to the use of Welsh were 'a confusion of thought' that showed the matter of how to teach English had received little attention from teachers and those with an interest in education. It concluded that the idea that excluding Welsh helped children learn required 'no very profound analysis to perceive' that it was 'founded on an entire misapprehension'.[141] Yet this misapprehension continued throughout the period amongst some teachers. In 1882, for example, a new teacher at Llechryd recorded: 'the greatest difficulty to a good progress being made is the want of the knowledge of English, Welsh being the language of the scholars both in and out of schools'. But his solution was to prohibit children from talking 'any Welsh in school', and to give detention to older children who broke this rule.[142] A new teacher at Cwm British school near Swansea recorded in 1863: 'Feel very discouraged by finding the majority of children ignorant of the English language but made a resolution not to speak a word of the Welsh language to the children.' It did not work because after a new teacher took over a few years later the logbook read: 'The children all speak Welsh to each other and do understand me when I ask them their names.'[143] A former teacher told the 1887 Cross Commission that children had an 'intuitive, or almost instinctive, power of learning a language' and thus, while teaching them in English might be complicated, it had advantages. When asked if he would recommend that arithmetic be taught in Greek or Latin in an English school, he replied he would if it was as important 'for an Englishman to learn Latin or Greek, as it is for a Welshman to learn English'.[144] Some teachers appeared to not even realise that their pupils were facing challenges. An 1868 education enquiry reported that some teachers interpreted children's 'apparent dullness' as being down to 'natural deficiency' rather than 'an imperfect knowledge of English'.[145] Logbooks often contain complaints that blamed their pupils for their lack of English, using words like backwards, stupid, dull, slow and unintelligent.[146] Given such blinkered attitudes, it is unsurprising that some could claim that there was no language problem in Welsh schools.[147]

Such viewpoints cannot be put down to teachers' inexperience and naivety alone. They were also products of how teaching was, in the words of the master of Caernarfon British school, a 'very hard occupation'.[148] Even with monitors or pupil teachers to help, there were just too many children in many single-teacher schools, and they all had to be taught at once, despite their different ages and abilities. All schools also struggled with a lack of books and equipment and the constant battle to get children to attend, even after attendance was made compulsory.[149] Classrooms were often uncomfortable because of the cold or the heat.[150] There could be interfering parents and clergy to deal with, while any local resident unhappy with children's behaviour outside schools might blame the teacher too.[151] After the Revised Code, there were new administrative burdens such as keeping registers and logbooks, as well as the stresses of the annual examination and inspections. One inspector in England claimed that the system discouraged pioneering and enterprise amongst teachers.[152] The code certainly made teaching in elementary schools a highly pressurised occupation, where both a sense of professional success and wages were vulnerable to the whims of an inspector and structural forces well beyond the teacher's control.[153] Inspection reports that criticised teachers' lack of energy and vigour must have been disheartening.[154] The knowledge that these were seen by managers surely made this worse. Hugh Morris, a teacher at Bwlch-y-Sarnau (Radnorshire), probably spoke for many when he wrote in 1890: 'I feel heartless in trying to continue with such irregular attendance, and such discouraging report from the Inspector is enough to eat the very life out of a poor fellow.'[155] Poor inspection reports could lead to teachers quitting or losing their jobs; one master heard this was to happen to him from local rumours rather than from his manager.[156]

In response to these challenges, some teachers found solace in drink.[157] Others left the profession looking for easier lives. In 1890, the master of Swyddffynnon recorded:

> I have decided, after much hesitation and consideration, to send in my resignation of the school. It is utterly impossible to feel contented and happy at one's work when it is done in such adverse circumstances. The examination is close at hand and yet there are children whom I have not seen for many months. In some cases their absence is excusable but when the inspection takes place their parents, the B[oar]d and the Inspectors will expect to see them 'pass' and if not the schoolmaster will suffer in pocket and reputation although he has really had no opportunity of doing anything to improve the children.

He decided to give up the profession and go into business.[158] A consequence of all this was that rural schools could have a very rapid turnover in staff. A new teacher at Trefriw recorded: 'I find it very hard work because nearly all the children cannot understand English'; he left after just one week in post.[159] A small school at Pennant had as many as nineteen headteachers in twenty-six years.[160] Such instability would not have helped the children but there were far worse tragedies. The most extreme cases could result in suicide.[161]

In Welsh-speaking areas, all teachers had to deal with children who were often from very impoverished backgrounds and thrown into an environment dominated by a language that they did not understand and that they rarely heard outside school. Teachers from England could not turn to Welsh to help them or even communicate with their parents. Moreover, living in a small Welsh-speaking community where very few spoke English must have been an isolating experience for such staff. In 1894, there were reports that a school in Cardiganshire had four different teachers in a single year. All were English and one said he had been misled in taking the job, thinking all the children would be able to speak English. He left, saying it was impossible for him to teach them anything.[162] Others employed from England did not even take up their post. In 1875, the Henllan Board school at Denbigh was having great difficulty in appointing a master. Three had accepted the position but then resigned before starting. A local newspaper thought the salary was good so 'we imagine it must be the locality'.[163]

Most teachers struggled on, but the swathe of practical challenges surely helps explain why some did not give much thought to pedagogy, or perhaps carried on regardless with techniques that they knew did not work. They also explain why so many teachers fell back upon the cane to punish any perceived 'wrongdoing', including speaking Welsh. Some of the teachers still making free use of the cane or rod were probably older men whose formative years in the profession were early in the century when violence and the Welsh Not were normal practice. Others were trained but had little imagination about how to control children or what was fair. Howell Roberts, the master at Llanllyfni British school who used the Welsh Not, recorded in 1872 the children were 'more active and obedient, the strict discipline kept making them more comfortable and happy than usual'.[164] The master at Glanwydden recorded of a boy who was being obstinate: 'a taste of the stick soon convinced that obedience was the best policy for him to pursue'.¹⁶⁵ For many teachers, physical punishment probably seemed to be the only way to control and influence children in challenging conditions that denied them the time or patience to try something else. Those teachers that hit children for speaking Welsh were not necessarily even thinking much about what they did but were instead resorting to a method to which they had become inured and reliant on.¹⁶⁶ Indeed, this might be done in temper rather than intention. A teacher who did not use the cane might still deliver a passing slap or blow, something that was not generally regarded as corporal punishment.¹⁶⁷ Yet because this was unexpected and uncontrolled, it might actually be worse than the controlled blow of a formal caning.¹⁶⁸

We should, perhaps, be wary of criticising those teachers who punished children for speaking Welsh. W. J. Gruffydd (b.1881) who went to school in Bethel remembered a teacher who insulted the children and even kicked one boy around on the floor because he could not do his sums. But Gruffydd thought him a sincere and responsible man who was caught in a 'fiendish system devised by English snobs'.¹⁶⁹ Certainly the system was unrelenting in its demands on teachers. Many suffered while trying to get children to attend, behave, learn and pass the annual examinations, whilst at the same time dealing with inspectors, managers and parents, some of whom interfered too much and others not enough. Teachers could be as much victims of how education worked as the pupils themselves.

Caring power and Welshness

It would be wrong to think that the exclusion and punishment of Welsh-speaking was simply a product of frustration, a lack of training and the failures of the professionalisation of teaching. In some ways, the duty of care that professionalism created perpetuated the attempts to stop children speaking Welsh. Most teachers in Wales came from the same kind of working-class backgrounds as their pupils, but many had a strong sense that part of their role was to tame and improve their charges. This was evident in their reminders to pupils to be kind to each other, the less fortunate and to animals.[170] At Cwmcothi in the late 1870s, the master made multiple logbooks entries such as: 'The children in order to conduct and behave themselves properly were this afternoon duly cautioned in habits of punctuality, of good manners and language and cleanliness, of obedience to duty, of consideration and respect for others, and of honour and truthfulness in word and act.'[171] Such cautions were given because many teachers felt their pupils were ill mannered, dirty, disrespectful and naughty. Some went further and, even accounting for the different ways Victorians employed language, seemed to think their pupils were stupid. At Llidiart-y-waun, a teacher recorded: 'seldom I have witnessed so many children that are so wanting in mental capacity as in this neighbourhood'.[172] It was common to blame the parents. After the opening of Llangian National school in 1873, the new master recorded: 'The children are exceedingly dull, undisciplined and for the most part entirely untaught. Having been utterly neglected by the parents.' Later that month, he was again complaining about their dullness and the 'utter neglect of discipline at home'.[173] Yet such aloofness did not undermine the fact that teachers wanted to save children from such conditions.

Susannah Wright has argued that teachers operated a form of 'caring power' as they sought to raise the moral and physical character of children.[174] This was something encouraged by the professionalisation of teaching because it meant that schools were thought of as not just delivering basic literacy but as something integral to both the good of society and the individual. Teaching English to children was another part of this caring power. The language was both a sign of modernity and civilisation, and thus exactly the kind of thing that education was supposed to impart. Like the attempts to make children cleaner, more polite and better behaved, this was not only to shape them but to help them. Since speaking English had clear practical advantages in life, the teachers that sought to ensure children had that skill were doing what they thought best, something their professional sense of duty encouraged. Indeed, some dipped into own pockets to achieve this.

A master at Trecastell British school bought *The Children's Friend* to improve pupils' English. He said they seemed very fond of the magazine and that it had increased their taste for reading.[175]

It was educational naivety that led teachers to believe that excluding Welsh helped children and it was their sense of duty that encouraged them to put this into practice.[176] Yet that is not how teachers who prevented children from speaking Welsh came to be remembered. Gwyneth Vaughan (b.1852) maintained in 1904 that teachers' aim in using the Welsh Not had been for every baby born in Wales to grow up to be English, to forget their language, their nationality and their own country as soon as they could.[177] That was going too far but some teachers clearly did expect children to stop speaking Welsh outside school. The son of a Welsh-speaking teacher at Ruthin recalled that since school was meant to help children master English, his father spoke that language at home too. The only Welsh his children thus learned was in the community.[178] Some teachers might have developed such outlooks through their own experiences of being looked down upon. The principal of the training school at Culham wrote of a Welsh student there: 'after all the time he has been here, [he] is yet so utterly provincial that he would be unfit for any school out of Wales. Rather given to smoking & not wanting in cleverness – but very uncouth & rustic.'[179] It is surely not impossible that such teachers returned to Wales seeking to erase in their pupils the very Welshness that they themselves had suffered for.

But such cases were probably in a minority. Teachers lived in and were part of the communities where they taught. Many were very active in local religious, cultural and political activities.[180] They might help adults too by running evening classes and Sunday schools or even by writing letters for those unable to.[181] This all gave them some local influence and status, but it depended on them being able to speak Welsh to parents, neighbours, worshippers and others. Even if they discouraged it at school, many teachers in Welsh-speaking communities brought up their own children in that language. Under the headmastership of John Davies, Welsh was rarely heard at Hermon Board school in Pembrokeshire but the 1901 census recorded his wife and three children as Welsh monoglots, showing how different his home life was.[182] If such teachers did not exclude Welsh from their own homes, it seems unlikely that they were trying to stop children from speaking Welsh outside school when they prohibited it in the classroom. Moreover, since most teachers cared about their pupils, they also would have known perfectly well that Welsh was a skill that mattered in Welsh-speaking communities; those teachers living isolated lives because of their own lack of Welsh knew this better than most.

Some teachers were deeply committed to Wales and Welsh culture. One in Carmarthenshire told the Honourable Society of Cymmrodorion that the introduction of Welsh as a specific subject was desirable because it would encourage children 'to cast off the English yoke' and help 'regain our former position among the nations of the world'.[183] Mary Edmunds, who taught at British schools in Ruthin and Bangor, was patriotic enough to write poems about her love for 'Dear Cambria!'[184] In 1871, the master of Llangeitho British school proudly wrote into his logbook a poem in Welsh he had received from a pupil.[185] Some schools were teaching children to sing Welsh-language songs. At Esgairdawe, Welsh was prohibited from 1887 but eighteen months later the children were being taught 'Hen Wlad fy Nhadau'.[186] At Trefdraeth in 1878, children were even taught 'Gwadu'r Iaith Gymraeg', a song which said English was the language of thieves and betrayal, and implored people to be great Welshmen and proud of their own language.[187] In 1888, the National Union of Elementary Teachers decided against changing its name to the National Union of English Teachers after objections from teachers in Wales. In opposing the suggestion, the secretary of the north Cardiganshire Teachers' Association wrote that it was important to show 'that the Welsh are a nation as real and distinct as the English'.[188] Some teachers brought such outlooks into what they taught. Even in the 1860s, there were teachers choosing to give lessons on topics like 'the birds of Wales'.[189] In 1895, the master at Trecastell recorded that he was not going to begin geography in the usual way by learning the capes of England, saying he thought it better to start with their own county and then Wales more broadly.[190] Such cases show how teachers were not simply agents of the state, enacting a foreign system upon hapless pupils.

Bischof has argued that teachers were rather a point of contact between the state and communities, helping both understand each other. Indeed, their logbook entries and conversations with inspectors about the difficulties of teaching in Welsh-speaking communities were probably part of the reason why many inspectors understood the need for Welsh to be employed (see chapter 6). As Bischof argues, teachers 'humanized poor, working-class, and colonial and foreign subjects in the eyes of the state'.[191]

'Of course we all love the old tongue, but school life is not a matter of sentiment, but a serious preparation for the battle of life' wrote one Anglesey teacher in 1885.[192] Even when they were committed to Wales and Welsh culture, there was still a general view that classrooms should be as English in language as much as possible in order to develop children's skills in that language. Percy Watkins, born in Montgomeryshire in 1871, remembered of his school 'we never heard of a word of Welsh, although "Master" was a thoroughly good Welsh-speaking Welshman' who preached in Welsh at chapel.[193] John Evans, who taught in Llanegryn, was remembered as believing 'in the best cultural traditions of Wales. He brought up his children in the literature of their country, teaching them to sing and write verse even as small children. Their character was grounded in Welsh culture.' But the author of a book on the school where he taught noted that there was no evidence he had done the same for his pupils.[194] Teachers who promoted Welsh culture in the classroom could still punish their pupils for speaking the language. At Aberffraw in 1875, a new teacher introduced a system to 'cure' Welsh-speaking, where the last child 'guilty of it' every morning and afternoon was given detention; yet two weeks later he was teaching the school 'Land of my Fathers' and 'Men of Harlech'.[195] In such cases, punishments for speaking Welsh were probably being given from a sincere belief that it would help the children learn English and thus improve their lives.

Whatever the intention, the exclusion and punishment of Welsh was not fair on children and possibly a betrayal of Wales itself. Some teachers came to think this after going through their own personal epiphany. In his campaign to make Welsh part of the curriculum, Beriah Gwynfe Evans told the Cross Commission:

I never permitted a word of Welsh to be spoken under any circumstances inside the schoolroom or even on the playground. I am to this date ashamed to own that I as a schoolmaster did what was at one time an universal custom, and caned my boys for using in my hearing their mother toIe ... I shall regret it to my dying day.[196]

Another teacher who later embraced his Welshness more intensely was Howell Roberts. He used the Welsh Not in Llanllyfni in the early 1870s, but he left teaching and became a Welsh Calvinist Methodist minister and gained some fame as a Welsh poet. By the 1891 census, he had changed his name to Hywel and claimed that he and his entire family did not speak English.[197]

Conclusion

After 1862, the variety of schools gradually narrowed but teachers continued to have significant freedom in how they managed their classrooms. Despite the influence of inspectors, parents, and school boards or managers, the teachers were the only adults in school every day and they drew upon their instincts, prejudices and experiences in deciding what and how to instruct and discipline children. This shaped how they treated the Welsh language. Although they received advice and sometimes instructions around the place of Welsh at school (see chapter 6), their practices were ultimately something personal, which meant there was considerable variation between and even within schools. When teachers chose to punish those who spoke Welsh, it was a product of old-fashioned thinking, a culture of punishment, or frustration at the challenge of teaching a language to children who had no contact with it outside school and whose attendance was very often patchy. Ultimately, punishing Welsh was seen as a way of teaching English. As the logbook of Rhydypennau Board school recorded in 1877, 'the children were forbidden to talk Welsh in school and in the playground, which was enforced in order that they might be brought to pay more attention to English'.[198]

It is impossible to be precise about how widespread punishments for speaking Welsh, physical or otherwise, were after 1862. As in the earlier period, the evidential base is fragmented and complex. A large number of logbooks from rural schools do make occasional references to attempts to suppress Welsh-speaking. But such defiant statements are not a guide to day-to-day practice, especially as teachers realised how difficult it was to make Welsh-monoglot children speak English. There is no evidence at all of contemporaries saying the Revised Code had made the Welsh Not more common but there is a wide number of people saying it was something of the past, even if they were unsure when exactly that past was. Indeed, it is clear that late in the century not everyone had heard of the Welsh Not. At an 1882 education meeting of the Cymmrodorion Society, the Welsh Not came up in discussion but no one seemed to have any knowledge of it. A reporter on the meeting, however, remembered it being in 'extensive use' in Meirionnydd 'not twenty years ago'.[199] There is also evidence that in some schools children were allowed to speak Welsh. The writer T. Gwynn Jones remembered that discipline was poor and no one was punished for speaking Welsh in his rural Church school in Denbighshire. He speculated that this may have been because the shy teacher was afraid of the bigger boys in schools, who were as old as eighteen and there to learn 'a bit of English'.[200] Some autobiographical writings in Welsh made no mention of language issues at school at all, suggesting they encountered no such problems.[201] A pupil at Llandybïe from 1894 noted that he knew no English at all when he started school and it was rarely heard in the village but stated, 'I cannot recollect, however, experiencing any particular linguistic difficulty after entering school.'[202] Such memories must have been partly because Welsh was used but also that the Revised Code did not make too taxing demands on children's comprehension. They could just muddle through.

In 1892, J. E. Southall, an advocate for Welsh, described the Welsh Note as the invention of 'two or three generations past' and said that it was 'nearly, if not quite obsolete'.[203] Dan Isaac Davies, an inspector working in Glamorgan and parts of Brecon, told the 1880s Cross

Commission that the Welsh Not did not exist extensively any more but 'the spirit which resulted in that arrangement 50 years ago still remains, and marks the system'.[204] Both of these comments were correct. The Welsh Not had not completely vanished by the end of the century. It may have just been there in schools, no longer in use, but on display as a visible reminder to children not to speak Welsh.[205] Persistent offenders might still be given it, or beaten without it, if they refused to follow no Welsh rules. More importantly, what the Welsh Not represented was still very common. English was the dominant language of the classroom and children freely speaking Welsh, at least in the classroom, was widely frowned upon, even if not always forbidden or actively suppressed. There remained a strong sense that this was for children's own good.

Nonetheless, it is likely that an increasing number of schools allowed children to speak Welsh to each other as they recognised it was impossible to stop them doing this. The fairness of rules and punishments was increasingly regarded as important and excluding Welsh was unfair because children, especially younger ones, had limited English. Moreover, caning was frequently seen as ineffective, harsh and a poor reflection upon the teacher. Discarding a child's first language also did not fit the growing trend to understand and celebrate childhood. Cruelty of all kinds was increasingly frowned upon and banishing a child's mother tongue started to be seen as such. There was also more attention given, in education and popular culture more broadly, to indulging and encouraging children's intellectual and imaginative needs.[206] As the next chapter demonstrates, that meant making greater use of children's mother tongue.

Notes

1   C. Birchenough, *History of Elementary Education in England and Wales* (London, 1914), pp. 114–18; Huriya Jabbar, 'The case of "payment-by-results": re-examining the effects of an incentive programme in nineteenth-century English schools', *Journal of Educational Administration and History*, 45, 3 (2013), 220–43; A. J. Marcham, 'The Revised Code of education, 1862: reinterpretations and misinterpretations', *History of Education*, 10, 2 (1981), 81–99.
2   CRO, Caernarfon National school minute book, 12 March 1862.
3   CRO, Caernarfon British school, 18 April 1864.
4   T. Marchant Williams, *The Land of my Fathers* (London, 1889), pp. 114–15.

5 *Third Report of the Royal Commission appointed to inquire into the Working of Elementary Education Acts, England and Wales* (London, 1887), pp. 26–7 [hereafter Cross Commission].
6 *Report from the Select Committee on Education* (1866), p. 201.
7 Robert Smith, *Schools, Politics and Society: Elementary Education in Wales, 1870–1902* (Cardiff, 1999), p. 53.
8 Gareth Elwyn Jones and Gordon Wynne Roderick, *A History of Education in Wales* (Cardiff, 2003), p. 78.
9 William Forster, *Hansard*, vol. 199, c. 443, 17 February 1870.
10 Cross Commission, 1st Report, p. 518.
11 Gary McCulloch, 'Compulsory school attendance and the elementary education act of 1870', *British Journal of Educational Studies*, 68, 5 (2020), 523–40.
12 W. Gareth Evans, 'Free education and the quest for popular control, unsectarianism and efficiency: Wales and the Free Elementary Education Act, 1891', *Transactions of the Honourable Society of Cymmrodorion* (1991), 203–31.
13 For a political view of this see D. J. Williams, *Yn Chwech ar Hugain Oed* (Aberystwyth, 1959), p. 189. For an academic view see Janet Davies, *The Welsh Language* (Cardiff, 1993), p. 49.
14 W. Gareth Evans, 'The British state and Welsh-language education, 1850–1914', in Geraint H. Jenkins (ed.), *The Welsh Language and its Social Dimensions, 1801–1911* (Cardiff, 2000), p. 471.
15 B. L. Davies, 'The right to a bilingual education in nineteenth-century Wales', *Transactions of the Honourable Society of Cymmrodorion* (1988), 133–51, 135.
16 *Welsh in Education and Life* (London, 1927), p. 60.
17 'The Anglesey Church Schoolmasters' Association', *North Wales Chronicle*, 13 May 1853, 3.
18 On teaching as a profession see Asher Tropp, *The School Teachers: The Growth of the Teaching Profession in England and Wales from 1800 to the Present Day* (London, 1977).
19 Pamela Horn, *Education in Rural England, 1800–1914* (Dublin, 1978), pp. 108–9; *Minutes of the CCE, 1856–57*, p. 50; H. G. Williams, 'Elementary Education in Caernarvonshire, 1839–1902' (unpublished PhD thesis, University of Wales, Bangor, 1981), 371.
20 G. R. Hughes, 'Ein hathrofeydd a'n hysgolion: Coleg Athrawol Bangor', *Cymru*, 2, 15 June 1892, 248–51, 250.
21 J. Lloyd Williams, *Atgofion Tri Chwarter Canrif, cyf. IV* (London, 1945), pp. 72–4.
22 Williams, *Atgofion Tri Chwarter Canrif*, p. 75.
23 Quoted in William E. Marsden, *An Anglo-Welsh Teaching Dynasty: The Adams Family from the 1840s to the 1930s* (London, 1997), p. 71.
24 L. M. Rees, 'A Critical Examination of Teacher Training in Wales, 1846–1898' (unpublished PhD thesis, University of Wales, Bangor, 1968), 87.
25 *Report of the CCE, 1866–67*, p. 496.

26 Russell Grigg, *History of Trinity College Carmarthen, 1848–1998* (Cardiff, 1998), pp. 182–4; W. Gareth Evans, 'The "bilingual difficulty": the inspectorate and the failure of a Welsh language teacher-training experiment in Victorian Wales', *National Library of Wales Journal*, 28, 3 (1994), 325–33, 326.
27 Report from the Select Committee on Education [Pakington Committee] (1866), p. 129.
28 Cross Commission, 3rd Report, p. 27.
29 *Minutes of the CCE, 1852–53*, p. 376.
30 *Minutes of the CCE, 1864–65*, p. 330.
31 *Report of the CCE, 1870–71*, p. 392.
32 On students talking Welsh to each other see Cross Commission, 1st Report, p. 168.
33 'Y Gymraeg yn marw', *Cronicl y Cymdeithasau Crefyddol*, October 1874, 278–9.
34 H. Howell, 'Y cyfarfod adloniadol: Cymraeg yn yr ysgolion ddyddiol', *Cyfaill yr Aelwyd*, January 1889, 20–2.
35 'Twyllo Cymru', *Y Cymro*, 16 November 1905, 4.
36 'New education act', *Haverfordwest & Milford Haven Telegraph*, 15 October 1919, 2.
37 'Welsh box', *Bye-gones relating to Wales and the Border Counties*, 22 May 1901, 109.
38 Herbert Hughes, *Cymru Evan Jones: Detholiad o Bapurau Evan Jones (1850–1928)* (Llandysul, 2009), p. 221.
39 Griffith G. Davies, 'Addysg elfennol yn Sir Aberteifi, 1870–1920', *Ceredigion*, 4, 4 (1963), 367; A. Bailey Williams, 'Education in Montgomeryshire in the late nineteenth century', *Montgomeryshire Collections Relating to Montgomeryshire and its Borders*, 52 (1952), 83–106.
40 Arnold Lewis, 'The Welsh Note', *Western Mail*, 7 October 1927.
41 For a discussion of this school see: https://martinjohnes.com/2019/08/01/trawling-through-the-past-and-unexpected-emotions-in-the-archives/ (accessed 25 March 2024).
42 CA, Llanfihangel National, 24 January, 7 February 1876.
43 AA, Aberffraw,, week ending 6 March 1875.
44 CwyA, Rowen, week ending 27 May 1876.
45 AA, Llannerch-y-medd British, 31 March 1870.
46 CRO, Llanllyfni British, 18 September 1870, 3 January 1872.
47 CmA, Llangunnock Vaughan's charity, 24 April, 3 July and 22 December 1873, 13 October 1876, 21 July 1882.
48 AA, Bodedern National, 26 April, 3 May, 11 May 1865.
49 CmA, Capel Evan British, 4 January 1866.
50 PbA, Brawdy, 1 March 1864.
51 AA, Llangeinwen National, 15 April 1873.
52 CRO, Port Dinorwic (Felinheli) British, 3 May 1878.
53 For explicit recognition of this see the discipline drive in CA, Llandysul National, 29 July 1887.
54 MRO, Corris British, 17 August 1870.

55 AA, Llangefni British, 17 February 1870.
56 NEWAR, Dyserth National, 19, 20 February 1880.
57 CmA, Esgairdawe, 10 October 1887.
58 AA, Llangefni National, 24 June, 6 October 1863, 27 April 1865, 28 April 1865, 1 August, 13 December 1866, 28 June 1870, 18 October 1871, 5 June 1883, 18 June 1886.
59 CmA, Caio, 5 August 1869.
60 Llandysul National school, 4 June 1874. Quoted in Grigg, *Trinity College*, p. 127.
61 CA, Llechryd, 25 November 1865, 27 January 1882.
62 CwyA, Cwm Penmachno, 4–8 September 1871. The limitations of this teacher's approach were evident in his report that year which stated, 'Efforts must be continually made to make them understand what they read.'
63 Quoted in Thomas Jones, *Rhymney Memories* (1938; Llandysul, 1970), p. 51.
64 GA, Bryncethin National, 12 July 1870, 2 February 1871, 7 April 1871, 13 March 1874.
65 GA, Troed-y-rhiw Mixed, 21 June 1883.
66 GA, Ferndale Board, 1885 report.
67 For example, CRO, Ffestiniog British, review of 1885–6.
68 *Report of the CCE, 1872–3*, p. 224. When a new school opened in Aberaman in 1866, a teacher found himself in charge of more than 500 pupils with just two pupil teachers to help. He threatened to expel some children if they were not quiet. GA, Aberaman Boys school, 18 and 21 June 1866. On the value of minimising noise see P. W. Joyce, *A Hand-Book of School Management and Methods of Teaching* (Dublin, 1863), pp. 74–6.
69 PA, Pennant National, 26 November 1883.
70 AA, Llandegfan National, 20 January 1864.
71 AA, Llanddona British, 20 September to 4 October 1872.
72 CA, Llangeitho British, 13 January 1869.
73 PA, Sarn National, 9 February 1865.
74 NLW, Benjamin Jones oral interview.
75 CmA, Abergwili, 30 July 1881.
76 CA, Aberaeron British, 5 November 1880.
77 AA, Bryngwran, 17 September 1884.
78 CRO, Llanllyfni British, 20 December 1872.
79 MRO, Llanfrothen National, 24 August 1866, 7 November 1866, 13 April 1869.
80 For example, AA, Llandegfan, 20 January 1864, 6 November 1866.
81 Evidence of Edward Roberts, assistant inspector, in Honourable Society of Cymmrodorion, *Preliminary Report upon the Use of the Welsh Language in Elementary Schools in Welsh-Speaking Districts* (London, 1884), p. 9; MRO, Letter from Revd R. R. William to William Pryce Williams, 4 November 1904.
82 South Wales Miners' Library, Josiah Jones interview (1972).
83 W. Meredith Morris, *The Renaissance of Welsh Literature* (Maesteg, 1908), p. 262.

84 Cross Commission, 2nd Report, p. 288.
85 PbA, Blaen-ffos, 2–6 June 1879; Similarly see PbA, Solva British, 17 February 1868.
86 Quoted in Williams, 'Education in Montgomeryshire'.
87 CRO, Caernarfon British, 8 April 1867.
88 CA, Y Ferwig, 12 April 1876.
89 CA, Swyddffynnon, 19 March, 14 May, 9 July, 1 October 1880.
90 MRO, Bethel, 28 March 1865.
91 PA, Trecastell British, 19 January 1877, 14, 18 March 1881, 16 September 1881, 2 October 1881.
92 CRO, Llanaelhaearn Board, 30 October 1874, 12 February 1875.
93 Christopher Bischof, *Teaching Britain: Elementary Teachers and the State of the Everyday, 1846–1906* (Oxford, 2019), p. 168.
94 CA, Swyddffynnon, 18 May 1883. For another example of physical punishment see PbA, Dinas, 6 September 1870.
95 CmA, Abergwili, 30 July 1881.
96 T. Gwynn Jones, *Brithgofion* (Llandybïe, 1944), p. 34.
97 John White, 'Philosophy and teacher education in England: the long view', *British Journal of Educational Studies*, 67, 2 (2019), 187–200.
98 John Gill, *Introductory Text-book to School Education, Method and School Management* (London, 1876 edn), pp. 85, 87–8, 114–15. Gill was not alone: an 1856 teaching manual recommended that corporal punishment only be used for moral failing and turpitude and not minor offences such as not preparing, getting questions wrong, being late or inattentive, talking or teasing other pupils. James Pillans, *Contributions to the Cause of Education* (London, 1856), p. 343.
99 CRO, Garth Board (Bangor), 18 May 1881, 7 October 1881, 12 October 1892.
100 *Report of the CCE, 1882–3*, p. 159.
101 Judith Rowbotham, 'When to spare the rod? Legal reactions and popular attitudes towards the (in)appropriate chastisement of children, 1850–1910', *Law, Crime and History*, 7, 1 (2017), 98–125.
102 Jacob Middleton, 'The experience of corporal punishment in schools, 1890–1940', *History of Education*, 37, 2 (2008), 253–75.
103 PA, Forden National, 13 March 1863.
104 MRO, Llanfrothen National, 11 October 1870.
105 PA, Llidiart-y-waun, 30 September 1873.
106 CRO, Caernarfon British, 16 May 1865.
107 MRO, Aberdaron Deunant Board, 12 and 15 December 1882.
108 CA, Llanfihangel-y-Creuddyn Lower school board minute book, 14 January 1890.
109 CA, Cilcennin punishment book.
110 'Training college for School-mistresses in Wales', *Carnarvon and Denbigh Herald*, 17 April 1875, 3; W. Gareth Evans, *Education and Female Emancipation: The Welsh Experience, 1847–1914* (Cardiff, 1990), ch. 4; British & Foreign School Society, *Swansea Training College 1872–1913* (Swansea, 1913).

111 Jacob Davies, *Hanes Pedair Ysgol* (Llandysul, 1975), p. 61; 'Y Gol. Oddicartref', *Y Brython*, 6 November 1919, 4.
112 CA, Llanon National, 8 February 1870.
113 'The Welsh Note', *Western Mail*, 30 September 1927, 7.
114 St Fagans Archives, Note by John Griffiths (1925), St Fagans 2933.
115 CmA, Caio, 18 October 1869 and 5–9 July 1871.
116 James Jones, *A Few Plain Hints and Suggestions on Teaching English in Welsh Country Schools, with Directions for Self-Instruction* (Bala, 1864), p. 30.
117 *Ye Brython Cymreig*, 27 July 1900, 2; 'The teaching of Welsh in day schools', *Rhyl Record*, 30 November 1895, 7; J. R. Kilsby Jones, 'Sefyllfa addysg y werinos haner can' mlynedd yn ol, ac yn bresonol', *Y Geninen*, 3, 1 (January 1885), 1–8; 'Wales day by day', *Western Mail*, 20 May 1895, 5; W. Llewelyn Williams, 'Yr Iaith Gymraeg', *Y Llenor*, April 1896, 77–94, 86; 'Hanes John Parry', *Dysgedydd y Plant*, May 1893, 117–18, 118.
118 'Y Welsh note', *Y Clorianydd*, 31 January 1917, 2.
119 St Fagan's oral history collection, Mr Jones, Y Tymbl.
120 Bryn Thomas, *The Good Old Days: Notes and Jottings on Llandybie, Llandeilo, Fair Fach and the Amman Valley* (Llandybïe, 1973), p. 23. For memories of half an hour detention for speaking Welsh which involved writing out spelling words, see St Fagans oral history collection, Mr Jones, Y Tymbl.
121 AA, Llanddeusant National, 15 December 1870.
122 'Some old school log-books', *Welsh Outlook*, 18, 3 (1931), 62–5.
123 CA, Llechryd, 24 February 1882.
124 *A Catalogue of an Exhibition on the History of Education in Caernarvonshire, held at the Normal College, Bangor, 5–9 May 1978* (Caernarvonshire County Records Committee, 1970), p. 33.
125 'St David's Day', *Welsh Gazette and West Wales Advertiser*, 3 March 1910, 8; David Samuel, 'Adfywiad y Gymraeg', *The Grail*, 2, 6 (1909), 117–19.
126 J. Lloyd Williams, *Atgofion Tri Chwarter Canrif, cyf. II* (London, 1942), p. 12.
127 Abel J. Jones, *I was Privileged* (Cardiff, 1943), p. 12. For memories of the challenges of being a pupil teacher see Michael Gareth Llewelyn, *Sand in the Glass* (London, 1943), pp. 166–8.
128 For example, MRO, Bala British, 1 July 1863; CRO, Caernarfon British, 17 October 1864; CA, Llanon British, 15 October 1869; GA, Pentrebach Infants, 4 January, 16 February 1877.
129 Philip Gardner, 'The giant at the front: young teachers and corporal punishment in inter-war elementary schools', *History of Education*, 25, 2 (1996), 141–63, 162.
130 Rowbotham, 'When to spare the rod?'; Middleton, 'Experience of corporal punishment in schools'.
131 CmA, Abergwili, 16 September 1863.
132 Middleton, 'Experience of corporal punishment', 274; Paul Thompson, *The Edwardians: The Remaking of British Society*, 2nd edn (London, 1992), p. 73.
133 Jones, *I was Privileged*, p. 7.
134 Frank Richards, *Old Soldier Sahib* (1936; Cardigan, 2016), p. 2.

135 William George, *My Brother and I* (London, 1958), pp. 48–9.
136 John Burnett (ed.), *Destiny Obscure: Autobiographies of Childhood, Education and Family from the 1820s to the 1920s* (London, 1982), p. 149.
137 'Alleged assault by a schoolmaster: what is legitimate punishment at school', *North Wales Chronicle & Advertiser for the Principality*, 25 November 1899, 6; 'Alleged assault by a schoolmaster', *Evening Express*, 29 July 1898, 3.
138 'Assault by a school teacher at Ynysybwyl', *Pontypridd Chronicle and Workman's News*, 28 June 1889, 5.
139 Bischof, *Teaching Britain*, pp. 70–1.
140 *Report of the Board of Education, 1900–01*, vol. I, p. 27.
141 Newcastle Commission, vol. II, pp. 569, 570, 566.
142 CA, Llechryd, 27 January 1882.
143 WGA, Cwm British, 12 February 1863, 14 May 1867.
144 Cross Commission, 3rd Report, p. 323.
145 Schools Inquiry Commission. *General Reports by Assistant Commissioners. Vol VIII: Midland Countries and Northumberland* (London, 1868), p. 7.
146 PA, Trecastell British, 1 December 1882, 18 June 1886; CmA, Bryn British, 29 November 1869, 28 January 1870; AA, Llangristiolus, 15 June 1870.
147 Cross Commission, 1st Report, p. 168. Also see comments of the headmaster of Talybont elementary school in *Cambrian News*, 7 June 1889, 9.
148 CRO, Caernarfon British school, 28 February 1865.
149 *Report of the CCE, 1872–3*, p. 238.
150 For an example of how a new building could lift the spirits of a teacher see Bangor University Archives, Diary of David Griffith, 16 September 1868.
151 See the 1893 entries for an interfering clergyman at NEWAR, Ruabon Boys National; NLW, Diary of Harry Thomas, Llanmaes, 10 May 1859.
152 Edmond Holmes, *In Quest of an Ideal: An Autobiography* (London, 1920), p. 68.
153 Bischof, *Teaching Britain*, pp. 34–6, 52–3.
154 For example, MRO, Brithdir 1887 annual report, which criticised the teacher and proclaimed the school 'extremely unsatisfactory'.
155 Quoted in H. L. V. Fletcher, *Portrait of the Wye Valley* (London, 1968), p. 55.
156 CRO, Llanllyfni British, 14 October 1874.
157 For example, MRO, Llanfrothen National, 27 October 1871.
158 CA, Swyddffynnon, 29 August 1890. Cf. *Minutes of the CCE, 1848–49–50*, vol. II, p. 290.
159 CwyA, Trefriw, 10–14 January 1876.
160 Williams, 'Elementary Education in Caernarvonshire, 1839–1902', 378; *Report of the CCE, 1870–71*, p. 273.
161 'Suicide of a Montgomeryshire teacher', *The Aberystwith Observer*, 12 October 1889, 4.
162 *Ye Brython Cymreig*, 27 July 1894, 3.
163 'Schoolmaster wanted', *Wrexham Guardian*, 4 May 1878, 6.
164 CRO, Llanllyfni British, 28 January 1872.
165 CwyA, Glanwydden, 24 October 1888.

166 On teachers' reliance on the cane out of frustration and their dispassion about it see Gardner, 'The giant at the front', and R. J. Selleck, *The New Education: Background 1870–1914* (1968), pp. 52–3.
167 Rowbotham, 'When to spare the rod?', 116.
168 Edmund Stonelake, *The Autobiography of Edmund Stonelake* (Bridgend, 1981), p. 47.
169 W. J. Gruffydd, *The Years of the Locust*, trans. D. Myrddin Lloyd (Gomer, 1976), pp. 89–90.
170 For example, CA, Llanon British, 15 November 1866.
171 CmA, Cwmcothi, 12 December 1877. Similarly see the entries for 3 and 20 February 1878.
172 Quoted in M. J. Evans, 'Elementary education in Montgomeryshire 1850–1900', *The Montgomeryshire Collections*, 63, 1 (1973), 1–46, 9.
173 CRO, Llangian National, 10 and 31 March 1873.
174 Susannah Wright, 'Teachers, family and community in urban elementary school: evidence from English school log books *c.*1880–1918', *History of Education*, 41, 2 (2012), 155–73.
175 PA, Trecastell British, 9 March 1877, 2 November 1877.
176 W. Edwards, *The Direct Method of Language Teaching: A Suggestion in the Education of Wales* (Newport, 1900), pp. 4–5.
177 Gwyneth Vaughan, 'Bryn Ardudwy a'i bobl: ein hysgolfeistri', *Yr Haul*, 6, 65 (May 1904), 225–30.
178 J. D. Jones, *Three Scores Years and Ten* (London, 1940), p. 17.
179 Student record quoted in Horn, *Education in Rural England*, p. 219.
180 Smith, *Schools, Politics and Society*, pp. 240–2.
181 Abel Jones, *From an Inspector's Bag*, p. 109; Williams, *Atgofion Tri Chwarter Canrif, cyf. IV*, pp. 229–30.
182 For memories of the school see Hefin Wyn, *Ar Drywydd Niclas Y Glais: Comiwnydd Rhonc a Christion Gloyw* (Talybont, 2017), p. 34.
183 Honourable Society of Cymmrodorion, *Report of the committee appointed to inquire into the advisability of the introduction of the Welsh language into the course of elementary education in Wales: the introduction of Welsh as a specific subject. Appendix* (Aberdare, 1885), p. 14.
184 Lewis Edwards, *Yr Athrawes o Ddifrif* (Caernarfon, 1859), pp. 52–3.
185 CA, Llangeitho British, 13 February 1871.
186 CmA, Esgairdawe, 10 October 1887, 24 April 1889.
187 AA, Trefdraeth National, 17 October 1878; 'Gwadu'r Iaith Gymraeg', *Dysgedydd y Plant*, May 1885, 124.
188 *The Schoolmaster*, 23 June 1888, 866; 30 June 1888, 896.
189 CA, Newgate British, 1 August 1864.
190 PA, Trecastell British, 1 November 1895.
191 Bischof, *Teaching Britain*, p. 2.
192 Honourable Society of Cymmrodorion, *Report of the Committee appointed into the Advisability of the Introduction of the Welsh Language Appendix*, p. 3.
193 Sir Percy E. Watkins, *A Welshman Remembers* (Cardiff, 1944), p. 11.

194 Gwilym Prys Davies, *Ysgol Llanegryn: Amlinelliad o'i Hanes* (Talybont, 2009), p. 86.
195 AA, Aberffraw, 15, 29 January 1875.
196 Cross Commission, 3rd Report, p. 3.
197 Various census entries and G. A. Jones, 'Roberts, Howell ('Hywel Tudur'; 1840 – 1922)', *Dictionary of Welsh Biography* (2001).
198 Quoted in W. Gareth Evans, 'Education in Cardiganshire, 1700–1974', in Geraint H. Jenkins and Ieuan Gwynedd Jones (eds), *Cardiganshire County History, vol. 3* (Cardiff, 1998), pp. 540–69, 556.
199 'Teaching English in Wales', *Bye-Gones relating to Wales and the Border Countries*, February 1882, 12–14.
200 Jones, *Brithgofion*, p. 33.
201 For example, S. Gwilly Davies, *Wedi Croesi'r Pedwar-Ugain* (Llandysul, 1967), ch. 3.
202 T. H. Lewis, *A Short History of Llandebie National School, 1851–1951* (1951), p. 27.
203 J. E. Southall, *Wales and her Language* (Newport, 1892), pp. 106, 386.
204 Cross Commission, 3rd Report, p. 7.
205 Smith, *Schools, Politics and Society*, p. 183.
206 Harry Hendrick, *Children, Childhood and English Society 1880–1990* (Cambridge, 1997).

5
THE EMPLOYMENT OF WELSH IN SCHOOLS AFTER THE 1862 REVISED CODE

The continued exclusion of Welsh and the emphasis on passing examinations curtailed what children were learning. The old problem of reading without understanding, that had so shocked the Blue Books commissioners, was still there. Beriah Gwynfe Evans, who began teaching in the 1860s and became a campaigner for Welsh in schools, told the 1887 Cross Commission that in Welsh schools:

> Children learn a number of English words, but these words convey no ideas to their minds ... The child reads his book, his pronunciation of words may be correct, he may give an English synonym for any given word, but he actually knows nothing of it ... To the ordinary English child his reading book contains stories in simple language which amuse and interest him; to the ordinary Welsh child, on the contrary, most of his books are sealed books ... the words are mere dry symbols, presenting no idea to his mind.[1]

At first, the Revised Code did nothing to challenge this longstanding problem. Teaching under the code often involved little more than a master reading a passage, perhaps a few words at a time, with the pupils then repeating it.[2] This technique dated back to Joseph Lancaster's ideas that children were imitative creatures but it was cemented by the way the Revised Code was assessed because its examinations did not require what was read and recited to be understood.[3] Schools went over the same book again and again so that children could read it well enough to impress the inspector. Those teachers who refused to speak Welsh did not explain what anything meant and, because children did not understand the words, the emphasis in their reading was on each individual word rather than the important parts of the sentence. Moreover, children practised passages so often that many were reciting from memory, and not reading from the page. An inspector in Monmouth described much of the reading he heard as 'jerking out each word like a pellet from a pop gun'.[4] In England, there were similar problems when children encountered words or ideas they did not already know. An inspector working there claimed that the Revised Code was making children passive, with no need to think, reason or do anything for themselves.[5]

However, the code did evolve with inspectors encouraged to ask questions rather than just listen. This in turn encouraged teachers to think about whether pupils understood what they were doing. The evidence presented to the Cross Commission by Evans and others was exaggerated because the witnesses were trying to win recognition of the need for Welsh in the classroom. In fact, despite the continuing punishment of children who spoke Welsh, the language was widely used in a growing number of schools, including those that disciplined children for speaking it. This chapter explores how Welsh was used after the Revised Code. More than a century on, it is very difficult to know exactly what teachers were doing since inspectors rarely saw an ordinary day in the classroom and teachers themselves controlled what they decided to record in their logbooks. But it does seem that, contrary to assertions about the Englishness of the system, there was more and more Welsh in classrooms.

Using Welsh in the classroom

As the previous chapter explained, training and professionalism in teaching helped diminish corporal punishment but its effects went far beyond that. Most teachers took their responsibility to instruct and improve pupils seriously and they wanted to improve the lives of those under their charge, even if they were not always very good at their job. The code may have only required a mechanical examination, but good teachers wanted to go beyond pupils being able to simply remember and recite facts and words. Their professional literature encouraged this too. Gill's seminal teaching manual said that reading 'without giving the sense' was very common but stressed the importance of connecting meaning with the words.[6] Methods of motivating children grew more sophisticated. Incentives started to replace punishments. Treats, prizes and outings were offered to improve attendance and learning, with teachers often paying for these out of their own pockets.[7] At Llangefni British school, the master even started giving prizes in 1873 to those who 'abstained' from speaking Welsh.[8] In 1881, the master of Bethel recorded that his new system of marks for merit and deductions for bad conduct was influencing children for the better.[9] In 1876, the headmaster at Merthyr Tydfil British school introduced a spelling bee and tickets for regular and punctual attendance, cleanliness and good behaviour, all of which could lead to monetary prizes.[10] At Troed-y-rhiw, the teacher built up a school library of over 200 books through local donations and children were allowed to borrow them in reward for 'full attendance, cleanliness, neatness of personal appearance, punctuality and obedience'. The master recorded that this was having an effect and the children were anxious to access the books.[11] That particular teacher regularly gave physical punishment and even confessed to kicking a boy crying on the floor but, more generally, the use of rewards was a symptom of how examples of caring teachers were becoming common. When J. W. Jones, a teacher who employed Welsh but never the cane, left Newgate British school in 1865, he gave a parting lecture and wrote in the logbook: 'The children and myself are much affected. I am very fond of them, and they of me.'[12] Employer testimonials for William Pryce Williams, who ran a school in Brithdir, noted how happy his pupils were and how they loved as well as obeyed him.[13] A master in Tregroes was remembered as having a tender heart, sitting younger children on his knee to read and being upset when boys had to be caned.[14]

There were signs too of more professional and reflective approaches to teaching English. In 1864, James Jones, the master of Bala free school, published *A Few Plain Hints and Suggestions on Teaching English in Welsh Country Schools*.[15] Jones was opposed both to all education being in Welsh, stressing this did not give children enough time or encouragement to develop their skills in English, and to everything being in English, which he said was 'quite at variance with the principles and rules of modern teaching'. Instead, his book was a practical guide to a method between the two extremes, where Welsh was used to help children learn and understand English. His goal was not to just to better teach children English but also to awaken their intelligence and desire to learn and read for pleasure. The book stressed the importance of translation work, teaching vocabulary and explaining things to children in Welsh, but did not advocate the free use of the language. It envisaged Welsh being employed less and less as the children grew older and better acquainted with English. This would involve giving older children English synonyms for new words rather than their Welsh equivalent. It is impossible to know how widely the book was read or its influence on training schools but one inspector recommended it in his 1866 report.[16]

The influence of its ideas, however, was clear in how commentators began to note that Welsh was finding a pedagogical use in schools. In the late 1860s a diocesan inspector noted how Welsh was now used more, which meant education was 'not nearly as mechanical as it used to be'.[17] In the 1880s, a teacher from Llanberis stated that he did not understand how any instruction could happen in rural districts without 'copious' use of Welsh.[18] Logbooks are also full of allusions and explicit references to Welsh being employed to explain readings. In 1870, for example, the master at Solva British school recorded that he gave a reading class on London and 'thoroughly' explained the words and terms to the children who were 'much interested'.[19] At Cross Inn British school, the teacher complained that composition and paraphrasing was 'miserably done' because of the pupils' poor English, even though he always took 'particular care' to explain to the children everything they read.[20] At Cwmcothi, the master recorded that with older children the most difficult words in a passage were written on the board for children to practise spelling and pronouncing before going on to reading the whole thing. After the reading, the subject was explained and then it was read again, with questions asked at the end, although it was not clear in which language these were.[21] Perhaps out of embarrassment, such entries did not actually state that the explanations were in Welsh but some logbooks were more explicit on this. As one headmaster put it, 'I find that to teach them in Welsh is the most intelligible and beneficial way'.[22] In 1891, a new teacher at Penwaun recorded that pupils' reading was mechanical but he hoped to advance 'by making every word understood in each of the lessons in their Readers. This is certain to be slow work at first, but the time spent will be amply repaid in the future.'[23] At Blaen-ffos too, the teacher noted how working with new books could be a painstaking process. He recorded that it required, 'a great deal of tact and teaching power to make the lessons really attractive and of benefit as the simplest words have to be explained before the meaning of the different passages can be understood owing the children being deficient in their knowledge of English.'[24] At Crickhowell, the teacher read passages so pupils could copy his tone and style. Difficult words were put on the blackboard, with their meaning and pronunciation explained. Children were made to read sentences again and again until they could do so without a mistake.[25]

As well as explanations in Welsh, translation exercises were used in many schools. At their most basic, this just involved children giving the Welsh equivalents for English words in their reading. At Garn-swllt, for example, a teacher recorded in 1894: 'The children never hear a single word [of English] other than that used in school. So that each simple word in the reading lesson has to be translated into Welsh.'[26] But translation exercises might also involve children giving a Welsh explanation of the English, either for single words or whole passages; occasionally, children had to write down the Welsh equivalent for English nouns.[27] In 1887, the master of the British school at Menai Bridge described to the Cross Commission how he taught in Standard I (the stage reached at the age of around seven): 'The first thing that I do is to read sentence by sentence and for the children to follow; then I ask them sometimes what are the meanings of the words; and they have to explain them in Welsh, and afterwards as well as they can in English.' After that, he explained the meaning of passage as a whole in Welsh and asked the children to do the same in both Welsh and English.[28] At Felinfach Board school in the 1870s, the teacher not only made sure he explained readings to the children, he also got pupils to explain their reading in their own English words, and translate words and passages into Welsh. He also had them look at texts that were not their regular class books 'with the view of cultivating intelligence'.[29] In 1886, the master of Tynyfelin Board school was using extensive translation exercises with children and had given them English-Welsh vocabulary books. He noted, 'so little do they know of the English language that not one of the whole school can converse in that language. It is exactly like teaching a Foreign Language.'[30]

The growing care shown for children and the desire to ensure their education was useful and character building also brought Welsh into classrooms. Logbooks never make clear the language of the frequent lectures on cleanliness, morality and the need to be kind to each other, animals and vulnerable local people, but it is difficult to believe that they were in English if teachers wanted them to be effective. Similarly, the religious aspirations of National schools meant the catechism and prayers might be taught and read in Welsh to ensure children understood them, even in schools that punished children for speaking the same language.[31] But more than this, a more caring and less hostile environment also helped children develop their English in other ways: sociolinguists have shown that nurturing and non-threatening environments support people's success in learning a second language.[32] Simply speaking Welsh to a child made the school environment less intimidating and thus probably made it easier for them to relax and learn.

Even schools that used the Welsh Not or stopped children speaking Welsh could still employ the language as a mean of instruction. In 1870 to 1871, the master at Corris British school was stopping the children speaking Welsh but also teaching infants to count in Welsh, setting older ones tasks where they had to translate given passages and sentences into English and teaching the geography of Wales.[33] At Trecastell British school in the early 1880s, the teacher was using Welsh to explain things in the classroom but still made one logbook entry that read: 'Cautioned them not to talk Welsh on the playground as they are so liable to carry on with their games in their mother tongue.'[34] At Llangunnock, the teacher used the Welsh Not but also noted that 'much time is taken to render reading intelligible'.[35] At Dyffryn British school, an isolated logbook entry in 1863 read, 'John Roberts Shop fined for Welsh speaking', but the following year the same teacher recorded he was setting translation exercises.[36] In 1884, the master of Llanilar, where Welsh was prohibited in school and on the playground, recorded that he found it 'a good plan' to allow children Welsh summaries of each chapter in their geography readers.[37] That same year, the teacher at Ystumtuen was giving bilingual object lessons and explaining readings and arithmetic in Welsh but children were not allowed to use the language at all in the classroom or playground.[38] It thus seems it was relatively common for children to be prevented from speaking Welsh at the same time that their teachers used it to ensure pupils developed the required skills in English. This was not at odds with some of the professional advice. Jones's handbook on teaching English in Welsh schools was critical of the lack of opportunities children had to speak English and argued teachers should make efforts to ensure the language's introduction to the classroom, playground, roads, fields and homes. 'Let them be trained', Jones wrote, 'to cultivate a habit of speaking English.'[39]

Some of the use of Welsh was not the result of the professionalisation of teaching but mere pragmatism. When Nantlle Board school opened in 1874, its master recorded that only three of the forty-eight children could understand English.[40] In such a situation, he had to speak Welsh to his new school if they were going to know what to do. Similarly, on the first day of Llangeitho British school in 1869, the master recorded:

'The English language seemed to be an unknown tongue, and I was compelled to speak exclusively in Welsh in order to make myself understood.'[41] New children could enrol at a school at any time during the year and thus many rural schools had a constant influx of Welsh monoglots. Moreover, at least in the early years of the Revised Code, there were teachers too whose own English was not perfect and thus might struggle with the reading and doing everything in that language.[42] The Revised Code also required girls to be taught sewing. This could be a way of improving English when it involved sewing 'samplers' of the alphabet or simple phrases.[43] But, in schools run by men, it usually required the employment of local women, many of whom were not fluent in English and some did not speak it at all.[44] At Crai Board school, the headmaster recorded in 1875 that he could not get the girls to stop speaking Welsh because the sewing mistress always 'speaks WELSH to them'.[45] In all these cases, completely excluding Welsh entirely from a school was impossible.

Monitors and pupil teachers were another way Welsh found a place in the classroom. The Revised Code had ended direct state funding for pupil teachers and schools instead had to pay for them from their general school grant. This meant some schools were less able to afford to take them on. Nor was it easy for schools to find suitable candidates. In industrial areas, many teenagers preferred to take better paid manual work. This left many schools reliant on monitors, who might still be paid but who were generally younger than the teenage pupil teachers and thus less able in both English and teaching. In Ruabon in 1892, the master complained that the monitors, all younger than thirteen, were continually talking and playing with the pupils rather than working.[46] Nonetheless, however old they were, pupil teachers and monitors always had a central role in education provision since they were more closely involved in supervising and instructing individual children than the master or mistress who had to oversee a whole school or section.

As chapter 3 noted, when the pupil teacher system had been created in the 1840s, some inspectors had thought it would help the efficiency of schools with monoglot English teachers by ensuring there was someone with authority to translate instructions for the younger pupils. One inspector working in the north-west claimed in 1884 that where English-monoglot teachers were employed, younger children were mostly left in the charge of Welsh-speaking monitors and pupil teachers.[47] There were also schools where a Welsh-speaking teacher did not use the language but allowed the pupil teachers to do so to ensure children understood their lessons.[48] In contrast, it is clear from logbooks that some pupil teachers spoke Welsh to their charges against the wishes of the master.[49] This might be an act of rebellion or just because it felt more natural. At Abergwili in 1880, the headmaster condemned 'most severely' the pupil teachers' 'continual chattering of Welsh'. He accepted that it might be needed with the infants but he felt he must stop them speaking Welsh to older children and each other and thus recorded that he would punish them for this in future. Yet, in the same entry, he also criticised the pupil teachers for not asking the children to translate English words into Welsh thus developing their understanding of the meaning of what they read. This might be down to their inexperience as teachers but pupil teachers' and monitors' use of Welsh with each other and classes could be because their own English was limited. The following year, the same master at Abergwili said the pupil teachers' constant use of Welsh was holding back their improvements in English and that lessons they were giving could be brought to a standstill by the 'loss of a common English word'.[50] The 1874 report of the training college at Caernarfon claimed that the majority of pupil teachers had 'such a very slender acquaintance with any but their native tongue, that they seldom or never speak or write a word of English by choice'.[51] At the 1891 census, four of the eleven pupil teachers living in Tregaron were recorded as Welsh monolinguals.[52] Yet these same pupil teachers were responsible for teaching younger children English.

In contrast, there was the ongoing issue of English-monoglot teachers. In the last decade of the century, around three quarters of teachers working in Wales were born in the country. This suggests a fairly sizable minority of schools had teachers who were unable to speak Welsh, even in the rural west.

Table 5.1: Percentage of school masters, mistresses and teachers born in Wales, 1891 and 1901 censuses[53]

	1891	1901
Glamorgan	76	79
Monmouth	62	66
Anglesey	64	86
Caernarfon	69	66
Meirionnydd	82	86
Cardigan	84	86
Carmarthen	84	87
Pembroke	66	68
Montgomery	50	58
Brecon	63	75
Radnor	50	41
Denbigh	63	64
Flint	66	67
Total	71	74

Some inspectors thought English-monoglot teachers could succeed in Wales but it is evident from logbooks that, even with the help of monitors or pupil teachers, a master or mistress unable to speak Welsh faced significant practical challenges.[54] In 1896, at the end of his first week in Uwchygarreg, the new master recorded: 'A very fair week's work has been got thro' but I find a very great difficulty in consequence of the scholars' scanty knowledge of English and my worse knowledge of Welsh.'[55] Similarly, a new teacher at Staylittle Board school in 1884 wrote: 'I find great difficulty to make myself understood not being able to speak Welsh.' A few months later, her first inspection report stated that the school was in a 'deplorably backward condition'.[56] Some six months after taking over Nevern school, the master recorded that his school's grant had fallen. He explained his lack of success by pointing to how he had no assistant and was 'unable to speak any Welsh'.[57] It was exactly these kinds of challenges that meant that Welsh-speaking teachers did often use the language. Yet logbooks also suggest that not all English teachers fully comprehended what was, or was not, happening. In 1869, the master of Llanon British school, who was from Middlesex, complained how difficult it was to teach because of the children's lack of English. And still he gave a lesson to older boys on the principles of cleanliness, health and fresh air. The following year, he gave a lesson on the feudal system and chivalry but noted that the explanation was 'necessarily a very short one and extremely incomplete'.[58] It is difficult not to wonder whether children understood anything of such lessons.

A few teachers learned Welsh to overcome such challenges.[59] Even those teachers who did not speak Welsh must surely have picked up some basic skills in the language, if only for the practical purpose of issuing simple instructions. A notable example was John Crowther (b.1847), who was from Lancashire but attended Bangor Normal College. His first school was at Rhydlewis in Cardiganshire. A few months into his teaching career, he had tried to stop older children speaking English in the playground but found they would not.[60] Such experiences seem to have been key to him learning Welsh while at the school and using translation exercises in his teaching. He was later described as one of the most successful teachers in Wales and 'a fervent supporter of everything Welsh'. He even went on to publish poetry in the language and in Bethesda helped run the local children's eisteddfod.[61] Yet his conversion to Welsh in both his professional and private lives should not be exaggerated. The census suggests that he and his Welsh wife spoke English to their children.[62] A pupil who attended Cefnfaes British school at Bethesda, which Crowther ran from 1890, claimed that it was not until he had left that he knew that his teacher could speak Welsh.[63] Crowther is evidence that the growing use of Welsh did not change how English dominated classrooms. As one inspector put it in 1886, 'it is the rule in all Welsh schools that the teachers must not use Welsh *more than they can help*'.[64] The master of the British school at Menai Bridge summed up what was probably the dominant attitude when he told the Cross Commission that he disapproved of Welsh being the general language of a school. Welsh, he thought, should be used for explaining things but English should be the language that was generally spoken.⁶⁵ The headmaster of Carneddi British school had a similar approach. At his school, pupils were not allowed to speak Welsh during school hours without specific permission and the language was only used by teachers where necessary for explaining readings, arithmetic processes and geographical terms and the like. English was 'the medium of communication', and he claimed:

> The intelligent teacher is careful as to how and when to resort to Welsh in the course of a lesson, for he knows that its too frequent use will slacken the pace, and ultimately prove detrimental, and be a barrier to the success and efficiency of the scholars under his care.⁶⁶

Ongoing challenges and the evolution of the curriculum

The criticisms of the Revised Code led it to evolving away from its emphasis on mechanical examinations of the 3Rs. This both encouraged the use of Welsh but also presented new challenges. Singing was encouraged from the early 1870s and some teachers enthusiastically adopted this. On the very first day of Alma Board school, the children learned 'Twinkle, Twinkle Little Star'.⁶⁷ Yet teaching songs was not easy when children did not understand the words, although some schools did use Welsh to develop and test children's understanding of the lyrics.⁶⁸ A revision to the code in 1875 allowed inspectors to ask children to explain their reading in Welsh to see if it was understood.⁶⁹ This, in turn, laid down an example to teachers that using Welsh with the children was acceptable. Another change introduced in 1875 was a move away from relying on dictation to test writing. Now older children had to write the substance of a story from memory at Standard V and a letter or short essay at Standard VI. Such tasks were very difficult for children with little English. Thus, at Mynachlog-ddu, the teacher recorded in 1896: 'I find it very difficult to teach composition as the pupils are so very backward in English.'[70] At Rhiwhiriaeth Board school Standards III and IV were asked to write a letter to a friend describing the mountain system of England and most were 'were quite at a loss to know how to express themselves. With a little encouragement they wrote a few lines.'[71] Such challenges again made it more important that children could understand and employ English rather than just read and write down words that they had practised. To challenge children and ensure they were not just learning reading passages by heart, another change to the code in 1882 required the use of three books a year for Standards III to VII. This was a lot to learn for pupils still struggling with English. With more books to cover, some teachers seem to have been discouraged from spending time on explaining and translating. It was thus a backwards step in some schools and one teacher felt it left some pupils hating reading.[72] Another recorded that the requirement was far too much work 'in such Welshy places as this'.[73]

The code also evolved to allow schools to earn grants for subjects beyond the 3Rs if they so wished. From 1867, there were new grants available for older scholars who passed exams in additional 'specific subjects', while from 1875 'class subjects' for younger pupils could earn grants, this time assessed on the proficiency of the whole class rather than on specific children. Geography was the most popular of these subjects and involved understanding and drawing maps, and then gaining knowledge first of the county, and then Britain, Europe and finally the globe. It, like history, tended to be taught through special reading books and thus had the benefit of developing literacy skills too. There were claims in Wales that these subjects had made school less tedious for pupils and teachers.[74] However, history and geography required schools to have access to relevant books and apparatus, for children to have the linguistic skills to understand them, and staff the time to teach the subjects. The latter was a particular challenge given how much time was spent on linguistic skills and explaining reading at the best schools. In 1873, the new master at Solva recorded he was giving up extra subjects because of the 'backward condition' of children in the main subjects.[75] In 1881, the master at Bethel complained that the recommended method of teaching geography through reading books was not working because of the children's lack of English. He stated it was hard to make the subject interesting for them and they found it more a burden than a pleasure. It was not clear whether he was explaining things to them in Welsh but his logbook entries do show efforts to improve children's English. The problem may have been more how much pupils were left to read on their own rather than with the teacher who could then explain the subject and words as they went along. In all schools, it was common to leave children to work through their tasks quietly on their own but this was particularly common in rural schools with small teaching staffs. At Bethel, there were around 120 children in regular attendance but just two teachers and a monitor. An inspector ended up recommending the school stop teaching additional class subjects.[76]

The content of geography and history books did not help since they were often about things beyond children's experience. In 1865, the master of Gwenddwr recorded: 'I find it difficult to make children retain in their memory the meaning of words: I believe that the reason of this is that they are not acquainted with the things they read about.'[77] Combatting this meant explanation had to go into the subject matter broadly; narratives had to be explained and not just individual words, something which one inspector complained rarely happened.[78] Yet ascertaining how much the children understood was not easy unless a master was willing to both ask questions in Welsh and have the children answer in this language. In 1888, the master at Staylittle does not seem to have been willing to let children answer in Welsh and was thus perplexed about the outcomes of his lessons. He recorded that he spent considerable time trying to ensure the children understood their lessons but found they could not 'express even the little they do know. It leaves a very uncomfortable impression that they know nothing at all of what they read.' In his struggles to get the older children to understand their history book, he got them to master small amounts of text at once and to give substitutes for words. He recorded that unless they understood it, the reading was of no benefit to a pupil.[79] Yet that was exactly what happened in many schools. The result was that geography and history turned into children learning facts about things they did not comprehend if Welsh was not used enough to ensure a full understanding of the topic rather than just individual words. As an example of this, the chief inspector in Wales pointed to children being able to name cotton towns in Lancashire but not anything made from cotton.[80]

The persistent exclusion of Welsh in some schools does suggest serious deficiencies in teachers' abilities and imagination. Some logbooks suggest that teachers assumed that somehow the pupils would just absorb English. At Llanwenog, a new teacher noted the difficulty of doing dictation with the first class, who seemed to be deaf and needed each word repeated three or four times.[81] The fact that they might not understand the words did not seem to have occurred to him. In Llanrug, the master recorded in 1878: 'The third Standard was examined in solving problems. Few of them show intelligence. I find that when the question is translated to Welsh, they understand it better.'[82] Was the teacher really unable to see that this was not a sign of a lack of intelligence or was he trying to defend his use of Welsh to the logbook readers? Other teachers also wrongly perceived their pupils as dim-witted because they were slow to answer as they tried to translate what they were told into Welsh in their heads. A different problem was teachers not perceiving how little pupils understood because their understanding was never tested in Welsh. Some failed to appreciate how much was being done by children through practise rather than knowledge or ability. Children might, for example, develop very good accents when reading because they were copying what they heard from a teacher and this masked their lack of understanding and fluency.[83] One inspector remarked:

> they read with a fluency that ... used to amaze me, knowing, as I did, that they knew very little English; till I found by greater experience that they knew the two books by heart, and could go on equally well if the book fell on the ground.[84]

When teachers recorded that they were sorry that pupils were not able to understand their readers and thus took little interest in them, it is difficult to wonder why they did not just explain things in Welsh in the way other teachers did.[85] Some teachers did claim that turning to Welsh was not straightforward. At Llangristiolus, the teacher complained in 1881 that some of his pupils were 'the most stupid children that ever I tried to teach. It is impossible to get them to understand even by talking in Welsh with them.'[86] In Solva, in 1875, the master complained of the difficulty of teaching children the meaning of readings. He recorded: 'When I explain to them in Welsh what they read I find that their Welsh is so limited that it is with difficulty I can make them understand me.' It was not clear whether this was down to a lack of practice, his own Welsh or the children's mother tongue being rooted in dialects and colloquialisms. Later he lamented, 'How the meaning of words are to be learned, to those that can hardly understand what you speak, is difficult to divine.'[87]

Others blamed a lack of time for not using Welsh. Passing the examinations was always a teacher's priority since it affected their reputation and often their salary. While some inspectors did test children's understanding and thus encourage the use of Welsh, not all did, and children could still pass without comprehending the meaning of what they wrote and read. Thus, it was never the priority and with children's attendance often haphazard or infrequent, teachers might feel they did not have the time to ensure children understood their lessons.[88] In 1882, the master of Cwmcothi Board school said he was devoting more attention to explaining reading than usual but that it required 'more attention than we can afford to give especially in a Welsh district like ours'.[89] National schools particularly struggled with time because they were also expected by their sponsors to teach scriptural knowledge, as well as everything required by the Revised Code.[90]

In his report for 1863, W. Scoltock, an inspector looking at British schools in north Wales, noted the excellence and intelligence of teaching at some schools and how children understood what they read. He compared this with cases where teachers put 'forward the Welsh language as an excuse for the bad state of a school'. In making these comparisons he concluded that the fault rested more 'with the teacher than with the taught'.[91] He was not alone. Inspector Shadrach Pryce argued that some teachers were 'too hopeless or rather too careless and indolent' to teach the children English, with the language used as 'an excuse' for their own failings.[92] Certainly there were bad teachers throughout the second half of the century, some of whom were trained and some were not. Some teachers were just conservative, sticking to what they knew, uninterested in learning about classroom management or the techniques taught at training colleges. Too many felt their job was to just to get the children to pass the exams and nothing more. While some of their peers were reflecting on how to improve, they objected to new ideas or doing anything more than was required.[93] Nor did they all have the right temperament or skills. Some lacked patience. Others were violent. Spelling mistakes in logbooks show that even late in the century there were teachers with far from perfect English.[94]

In 1881, the master of Tregroes lamented that the younger children did not understand anything they read and were thus not excited by it but that they made much greater progress in arithmetic.[95] In those schools where Welsh was not much used, basic arithmetic could be a respite from the challenges of reading.[96] Counting, adding and subtracting did not require language skills once the basic numbers were known. This was something that might be taught at home too but some schools were also teaching counting in both Welsh and English.[97] Fingers and abacuses made the task easier, although inspectors discouraged the use of the former. But once the basics were mastered then language did become an issue in arithmetic. Teachers noted the difficulties of explaining addition, subtraction, multiplication and division, although they could have turned to Welsh to overcome this.[98] Another problem was that the tasks required of older children were often based around problems which asked children to work out how money, flour and the like might be shared and calculated. This was a challenge because children did not always understand the vocabulary in the problem set.[99] And even if the English was understood, there was the arcane system of English money to grapple with. In 1866, the master at Caernarfon British school noted in his logbook how much easier things would if money was decimalised.[100]

Most teachers were well aware that their youngest pupils might not speak any English when they first came to school and thus punishments for speaking Welsh were often concentrated on older children. Yet many schools made little effort to ensure infants (those under seven) learned English. There does not seem to have been any knowledge of how, if there is consistent and prolonged exposure to it, learning any new language can be easier at a young age.[101] In too many schools, the infants were an afterthought since they did not undertake grant paying exams. At smaller schools, their instruction might be mostly left to pupil teachers, while the master concentrated on those who would be examined. The historian litterateur R. T. Jenkins remembered of his time at Bala Board school that infant lessons were shouting the multiplication tables, reading at the top of their voices and spelling difficult words.[102] Not all young children experienced this. Despite the growth in the number of schools, some children still lived some distance from one and a walk of two or three miles meant they might not be sent there until they were seven or so. Once at school, teachers were impatient for such children to catch up so they were ready for examination. Teachers might thus 'hurry over the rudiments to the detriment of their real progress'.[103] In this, we again see the real harmful effects of the Revised Code. It was not that it encouraged the exclusion of Welsh but rather that it undermined efforts to teach English properly.

There was, however, a growing recognition in education that the youngest pupils had specific needs. Inspectors and education manuals encouraged the use of object lessons, where pupils in Standard III and below would learn about, and discuss the origins and uses of everyday items, animals and plants in order to develop their thinking, language and observation skills.[104] That was the theory at least; in England, inspectors complained object lessons were often dull, mechanical and a repetition of facts.[105] One inspector's book stressed the importance of teaching infants in 'plain, homely' language, to explain the things they did not understand and to bring object lessons to life with anecdotes or stories.[106] Yet that was impossible if Welsh was not used, something the more backwards teachers were not willing to do. A master in Mynachlog-ddu recorded on 9 July 1897: 'I find it difficult to teach object lessons as the children are so very backward in English. They do not know the names of common objects in English.' Elsewhere, the logbook recorded: 'Gave a lesson on the horse to the infants. It is difficult to teach object lessons as the children scarcely know a word of English.'[107] The 1896 inspection report on Llanrhystid noted that object lessons were given in language 'quite beyond the comprehension of the children'.[108]

The solution was, of course, to employ Welsh and the better schools used the language extensively with infants.[109] Object lessons were found to be a useful way to teach English vocabulary, although one inspector said this technique meant not much could thus be expected in terms of 'interesting and intelligent lessons'.[110] In contrast, inspector Shadrach Pryce, who was opposed to Welsh in the classroom, said he could not 'speak too highly' of the beneficial effects of the greater use of object lesson and other appropriate tasks in infants schools.[111] Vocabulary was taught to younger children outside object lessons too. In 1886, children at Swyddffynnon were learning the English names of parts of the body, common animals, and things in the house, schoolroom, field and farm.[112] In schools with more than one adult teacher, the youngest children often had a dedicated member of staff, increasingly a woman. This helped nurture and acclimatise them to school rather than just being thrown into the bewildering deep end of a school in a foreign language ruled over by the cane.

There were plenty of other challenges for children in learning English, even in schools where Welsh was used. Books and reading cards were often in short supply, whether the school supplied them or asked parents to.[113] Reading books were also designed for English children and they often lacked the pictures and suitable vocabulary needed to help Welsh children understand them. Standard I books included words like saw, teach and stalk, when Welsh readers were still struggling with rat, mat and made.[114] Some schools' stock of books were so old they had come apart and had parts missing.[115] Children who had already mastered a title might have to go over it again, not for the exam but because there was nothing else in the school to read.[116] Even if children did come to understand a book, too many were dry and uninteresting.[117] Writing skills, meanwhile, were held back by both schools and parents being unable to afford slates, paper and ink. At Llanon, the teacher was told by an inspector to do more writing in exercise books but not all parents could supply them. When he sent one boy home to get one, the boy was withdrawn from the school.[118] Shadrach Pryce said teachers often complained to him that young children learning to read Welsh at Sunday school interfered with their progress in English because the letters were pronounced differently. John Rhŷs, who had been a teacher in Cardiganshire and was an inspector in Flint and Denbigh from 1871 to 1881, also felt children mixed up Welsh and English in their spelling.[119] But Welsh children did have the advantage in spelling that they learned words from reading rather than knowing them already and thus spelling the teacher's dictations phonetically.[120] A good range of maps was another problem. So too was the building itself, even if it was new. They might be too hot or too cold. They were often cramped.[121] Schools might be more comfortable than the impoverished homes many children came from but they were still far from ideal learning environments.

The best teachers gave struggling pupils individual attention.[122] But this was not always possible. Schools were understaffed and had pupils that might range from as young as three to eighteen or even older. At Bethel, where the average attendance was 117, the headmaster recorded that Standard I was 'so numerous' that it required all of the assistant mistress's attention. His monitor could not teach beyond Standard II, which left him teaching standards III to IV by himself. He concluded that the idea that the classes he taught could make any real progress considering how little time he could give them individually was 'utter absurdity'.[123] In such situations, children were often left to find their way through their books and tasks on their own, overseen by a pupil teacher or monitor, often not that much older than them, sometimes younger and occasionally just as bad at English.[124] The best pupils managed this but were then left with nothing to do; the weakest pupils were left to flounder.

Too much of the teaching was about passing the exam and traditional grammar, identifying nouns, adjectives and verbs, rather than learning to speak English. Reading was often done aloud and as a class, thus allowing children to practise saying words, but masking in the general din the weaknesses of individual children. The reliance on books to teach English also meant children struggled to develop vocabularies beyond words in those texts.[125] With many teachers not inclined to ask children questions, the school system did not give pupils many formal opportunities to develop conversational skills in English. The result was the Newcastle Commission's finding that in rural districts 'questions which could not be answered in English were very intelligently replied to in Welsh'.[126] Such evidence suggests that children's understanding was ahead of their oral skills in speaking English. Teachers noted this too. In 1890, the master of Trewen recorded:

> The children take a great deal of interest in agriculture but cannot express themselves either in Welsh or English, even after it had been explained to them in the most simple language and yet it is evident that they understand different passages in the Book from the lively interest they take in the subject.[127]

The very best teachers realised the need to learn to speak rather than just read and understand. Rather than just relying on the reading needed to pass the exam, they asked questions of children in Welsh to test their understanding and in English to develop their oral skills. In 1883, at the new Bryncroes Board school, the master, already doing a 'great deal of explanation of words', recorded he had introduced conversation lessons to 'get the children to speak English'. He also gave translation exercises and tested children's English vocabulary. His annual inspection report concluded: 'This little school is intelligently conducted and is likely to do well.'[128] Garth Board school, a training school for Bangor Normal College was congratulated in its 1897 inspection report for making children answer questions in full sentences.[129]

The pronunciation of English words was a particular challenge in areas where even the sound of English was not familiar. Children might overemphasise consonants or pronounce vowels in the Welsh rather than English ways. John Rhŷs, an inspector who later became a professor of Celtic at Oxford, was particularly concerned with the issue of pronunciation. Welsh children, he said, were placing too much emphasis on endings, unable to pronounce 'sh' and saying the short English 'i' as the longer Welsh 'u'. He also despaired of the influence of

Cheshire English on border communities and how this meant 'h's were being dropped.[130] Such issues frustrated some teachers but one recalled that he only corrected the biggest mispronunciations because it was more important to teach the children some basic English.[131]

Others had much greater ambitions and wanted to do away with the children's Welsh accents. At Bethel, the master complained in 1880, 'It is disheartening to find that, notwithstanding all efforts to the contrary, the children continue to be very Welshy in their talk.'[132] In most schools changing accents would have been impossible since children were learning through imitating their teacher, most of whom were Welsh and thus no doubt spoke that way. Those teachers who did seek to kill their pupils' Welsh accents were probably being snobbish but also trying to help the children. Accents rarely stop people understanding what is being said but they do convey things about the speaker. As Lynda Mugglestone has shown, accent was 'regarded as a marker of social acceptability, facilitating or impeding social advance; it could secure deference or disrespect, acting as an image of "worth"'.[133] A Welsh person speaking his or her second language was never going to find it easy to live up to the standards that had emerged of standard pronunciation in England. Thus, even when schooling did give children reasonable proficiency in English, if they spoke with a strong Welsh accent, the social capital gained was muted and teachers surely knew this. Their desire to change their pupils' accent could also be down to their own experience of suffering disadvantage when working in England because of how Welsh they sounded.[134] The prejudices that existed around accent also mean some caution has to be exercised around the claims from inspectors and investigators that many children were leaving school unable to speak English. Those from upper middle-class backgrounds often had strong opinions that there was a right way of speaking English and thus might be highly critical of those who spoke English in different ways to them.

One historian summed up of this period, 'If a nation can be stupefied by its schools then the Revised Code came near to the point of stupefying children between 1862 and 1890.'[135] Such conclusions overstate the case, not least because of how poor, narrow and uninspiring so many schools were before the code. They also miss just how much education, and the code itself, evolved after its introduction. So, too, did attitudes to Welsh in the classroom. It seems to have been used very generally with younger children, if only for the practical reason that in many areas they knew no English at all. With older children, it was increasingly used to translate the meaning of reading and lessons, as well as sometimes in general communication. This did not preclude children from being prevented from, and punished for, speaking Welsh. But both, and particularly the latter, were at odds with the growing ethos that schools should nurture children and that teachers should develop their minds and not just the memories. Engaging children meant speaking and listening to them in the language they were most capable of, even if only occasionally. But no matter how far the general picture had developed, in both the best and worst schools, many children in Welsh-speaking areas still failed to become fluent in English. As the chief inspector in Wales conceded in 1888, in the purely Welsh-speaking districts, despite the pass rates, children's 'real command of the English language for the purpose of conversation or composition is generally meagre and imperfect'.[136] The primary goal of education in such areas was to teach English. It often failed and it was those schools that were excluding Welsh that were the worst culprits.

The formal recognition of Welsh

In the history of Welsh, the rector of Benfleet in Exeter is an unlikely hero but the Revd D. Jones Davies's paper, 'The Necessity of Teaching English through the Medium of Welsh in Elementary Schools in Welsh Spoken Districts', from 1882 was a key spark in promoting debate and a movement to bring about change. He argued that not using Welsh was hurting children's acquisition of English and thus their social mobility. He placed the blame not on teachers but the 'system', which he claimed did not exist through malevolence or indifference from the 'powers that be' or from any desire to make Welsh extinct. Instead, he said the situation was 'mainly if not entirely due to the expressed wishes of Welshmen themselves a generation ago'. His goal was not to promote the teaching of Welsh but its use, which he felt should be the medium of instruction until the age of seven.[137]

From this prompt, a movement emerged to secure a better place for Welsh in schools, not only as a means to teach English but as a subject in its own right. In 1885, the Society for Utilizing the Welsh Language was formed. It was not a large organisation but it gained some influence thanks to the hard work and status of its members, many of who had prominent positions in universities and religious bodies.[138] Its key breakthrough came with the Cross Commission set up in 1886. The Welsh representative on the commission, Henry Richard, Merthyr's Liberal MP, was lobbied by the society and he helped ensure the question of language was considered. Members of the society gave evidence to the commission, stressing they were not trying to replace English or hinder its teaching.[139]

In some sense, the campaigners were pushing at an open door. The commission was a product of concerns that the 1870 Act had not created an effective education system.[140] There were already moves from within both schools and the education department to make learning more effective, humane and in line with what children and the nation needed. The encouragement of crafts, singing, drill, drawing and poetry and even flowers in the classroom were all part of this but so too was moving away from the rote learning that had so long characterised parts of education.[141] Thus, in 1884, an inspector in Montgomeryshire said it was necessary for inspectors to 'discourage the tendency to mechanical routine' and encourage 'the cultivation of life, spirit, and intelligence in the schools'.[142] Payment by results itself was abolished for the 3Rs in 1890, and for other subjects in 1897. The use of Welsh was entirely line with such aspiration.

It was also in line with a wider growing appreciation in Westminster that Wales had distinct needs. This was rooted in the influence of the Welsh Liberal Party and a cultural renaissance where a vibrant press and prosperous middle class was pushing an interest in Welsh religion, culture and history. The 1881 Sunday Closing (Wales) Act was one product of this, the first piece of modern legislation to treat Wales differently to England. The second was the 1889 Welsh Intermediate Education Act which led to the creation of nearly 100 state secondary schools, well before similar schools were sanctioned in England in 1902.[143] Welsh was not widely taught in those schools but, in 1887, while the Cross Commission was still in process, Welsh was made into a specific subject in elementary schools. This meant those schools who wanted to teach it to older children could earn grants for doing so if individual pupils passed an annual examination in the subject.[144]

Out of the society's lobbying and the Cross Commission's 1888 report came a series of changes that went further and recognised that Welsh was a useful means of teaching English and other subjects. In 1889, a new code was issued that allowed the use of bilingual books and translation exercises instead of dictation in examinations.[145] These things already happened in some schools but further changes were to come. From 1891, Welsh was allowed as a grant-earning optional subject for higher classes. From 1893, it was allowed as a class subject, which meant it could be taught throughout the whole school. In 'Welsh districts', that year's code also allowed the teaching of Welsh songs and poetry, required arithmetic problems for younger children to be in English and Welsh, and for history and geography to include a focus on Wales. In these districts, English was to be taught bilingually and in inspectors' assessments additional credit was to be given for utilising the children's knowledge of Welsh for the acquisition of English or the fuller understanding of lessons in English. Finally, Welsh was added to the languages that could be taken in training school examinations.[146] The revised instructions for inspectors stated: 'It is desirable that the attention of teachers should be called to this question [of the advantages of utilising Welsh], and that inspectors should encourage the practice of bilingual teaching by themselves making use of Welsh in testing children's intelligence.'[147]

Historian B. L. Davies argued this meant 'The ban of using the Welsh language in the schools had been lifted, the era of the "Welsh Not" was at an end.'[148] However, this ban had never existed as such and some of the changes, such as the use of Welsh songs, were already in practice in some schools. Moreover, an increased use of Welsh by the teacher could still co-exist with bans on the children doing the same.

Indeed, despite its complaints about the moral effects of bans on Welsh, the Society for Utilizing the Welsh Language itself said it 'did not in any way' recommend ending the 'salutary custom of enforcing the conversational use' of English during school hours, because making pupils practise developed their oral skills.[149] Nonetheless, there was some celebration in Wales. The *South Wales Daily Post* described the 1893 code as revolutionary, saying it 'will do more to keep alive our Nationalism than all the legislation in the world; for it will teach our children the language and history of their country, and will link the Wales of the past to the Wales that is to be'. It went on to contrast this with the past where 'everything' was done to banish Welsh from all aspects of life except the chapels and homes. It maintained that Welsh had been degraded as an inferior language belonging to the vulgar and ignorant, not worthy of study and cultivation. Moreover, 'Even in times that are within the memory of living men, a child who used his native language was punished by having the "Welsh Note" transferred to him ... Welsh children have been taught to be ashamed of their language.'[150] But the paper had also earlier claimed that the recognition of Welsh was 'somewhat niggardly', with the language tolerated rather than sanctioned or encouraged.[151] It was, indeed, not some moment of government largesse or revolution but a concession made somewhat reluctantly because it would help the learning of English. Sir William Hart Dyke, the education department's vice president from 1887 to 1892, wrote that Welsh must not be encouraged at the expense of English but instead used for 'the sounder and more rapid acquisition of English'.[152] His successors were willing to go further and embrace Welsh for its own sake. In 1900, the education department declared that Welsh should be 'freely' used as medium of instruction with younger children in districts where it was the home language. However, it stated in English lessons instruction should be, 'as far as possible' in that language, although Welsh 'should be used for purposes of necessary explanation'.[153]

Rules only went so far when there was little determination to ensure they were enacted. As always, what actually happened in schools ultimately came down to teachers and many were very conservative when it came to language. The Welsh Not, with a punishment of detention, was still in use in Aberffraw in 1894.[154] Inspectors noted in the late 1890s that Welsh was now in greater use in classrooms but also that this was not universal in Welsh-speaking districts.[155] Far less successful was the idea of teaching Welsh as a subject itself. There were claims that, where Welsh was taught as a subject, children were stimulated and their English improved, but this was not enough to change many teachers' minds, whatever codes, inspectors and campaigners said.[156] When the London-based Honourable Society of Cymmrodorion had surveyed teachers in 1885 about introducing Welsh as a specific subject, 339 responses were positive and 257 negative. One of the negative responses from Anglesey said they were already compelled to use Welsh 'too extensively' because of how little English was spoken in the district and that introducing Welsh formally would rashly open the door further. 'Welsh is very nice in London', the reply said, 'but our cry in Anglesey and Carnarvonshire is "*more English*"'.[157] Divisions were clear at a local level too. In 1893, a motion to a teachers' association in the Rhondda and Pontypridd asking the education department not to interfere in the linguistic medium of schools was only defeated narrowly.[158] There was a concern that teaching Welsh would add to workloads.[159] Some teachers feared their own Welsh was not good enough to teach the language, having never formally learned its grammar.[160] Others did not like the formal Welsh of bilingual books.[161] In 1903, a school manager in Caernarfonshire claimed that boards had passed resolutions that Welsh should be taught but teachers were not acting on them.[162]

There was more enthusiasm in the industrial south where some boards made significant efforts to promote the teaching of Welsh in response to the growing anglicisation of their districts.[163] In 1902, Merthyr Board school, for example, introduced Welsh reading books and devoted two hours a week to teaching Welsh.[164] Such moves were not just down to national sentiment. In 1893 the chairman of the Swansea school board, in deciding to introduce Welsh as a subject into some schools, declared it was 'their duty to keep it alive as long as possible, if only for the teaching of the Gospel'.[165] But aspirations were not always turned into realities. In 1897, Welsh was made compulsory in all infant schools in the Rhondda but implementing this proved difficult because not all teachers spoke Welsh. That year, just thirty-nine schools in all of Wales were offering Welsh as a specific subject.[166]

Thus in many schools very little changed and the old complaints about how the exclusion of Welsh was hindering the acquisition of English continued.[167] In 1895, one writer said Welsh was rarely heard in schools and claimed that a little of the Welsh Note of old days was rerising when a child spoke Welsh in trying to explain something.[168] Another man recalled that at his school in a Welsh-speaking industrial community at the end of the century the language of the playground was mostly Welsh, but in school itself, 'never a word of Welsh was heard from any of the teachers and only in whispers between one child and another. The mother tongue of the majority of us did not count for anything in that house of learning.'[169] So engrained was the Englishness of some schools that Welsh was being taught to children through the medium of English, as if Welsh was a foreign language rather than their mother tongue.[170]

One reason for the lack of reform was how educational thinking on language teaching was beginning to change by 1900. On the Continent, languages were increasingly taught by what was known as the 'direct method'. This involved immersion in the new language and its use as a medium of instruction rather than just the end goal of lessons. This approach began to influence thinking on language teaching in the UK but it ran contrary to all the recent pressures in Wales. Influenced by ideas of the 'direct method', a new Welsh Language Society was formed at the turn of the century. It advocated in Welsh-speaking areas that children should be taught in Welsh, but when it came to learning English they should be taught in that language. In English-speaking areas, it similarly recommended that children be taught Welsh through the medium of that language. This, in effect, was a call to return to some of the old ideas of language teaching.[171] The education department was similarly influenced. In 1904, inspector Thomas Darlington said English lessons in Wales 'should be as English as possible in atmosphere', and he recognised in calling for this the Board of Education 'was really returning to the principle which was very common and well recognised in Wales several generations ago and was embodied in the institution known as the Welsh note'. Although it had become very 'unpopular' and had been 'ridiculed', he argued the Welsh Note could be 'justified as an educational instrument' in the teaching of English. Nonetheless, he was careful to stress the importance of giving Welsh a place of dignity in schools and argued that it should be used to teach subjects other than English in places where it was the language best understood by children.[172]

Such debates must have caused a degree of confusion over what was best to do, and again encouraged teachers to rely on what they thought worked well. Driven by a sense that there was still much to do, a Welsh Department of the Board of Education was created in 1907. Under its regulations, Welsh was strongly encouraged and all subjects were allowed to be taught in it.[173] The board's chief inspector was Owen M. Edwards, a prominent cultural nationalist and victim of the Welsh Not. Edwards was somewhat self-congratulatory, arguing: 'The bilingual difficulty is now at an end. The two languages are taught in the schools, and as living languages.'[174] But the reality could be quite different and the hostility of teachers and communities still constrained state desires. There were new concerns in Welsh-speaking areas that too much Welsh was being used in schools.[175] Such worries owed something to parents themselves feeling hampered by their own lack of English and thus thinking that ensuring their children's fluency was what mattered in education.[176] The continued belief that teaching in Welsh held back the acquisition of English meant that as late as 1928, a professor of education could write: 'Until recently, and even to-day in backward schools and areas, the Welsh child has to cope with the difficulty of learning a subject combined with the extra difficulty of learning that subject in a tongue that is unfamiliar.'[177]

Thus the opposition to Welsh in schools continued into the twentieth century. There is some evidence that suggests the Welsh Not was still being used in some schools that late. This is unsurprising given how slow change could be in corners of the education system and the considerable freedom teachers enjoyed in how they operated. A woman born in 1892 remembers a Welsh Not at her school in Felin-wen, which was engraved with the words 'Don't Speak Welsh'. The punishment was a caning.[178] Another woman who went to school in Llanfihangel-y-Creuddyn from around 1910 remembered the Welsh Not as a large hat that had to be worn, although it stopped being used while she was there and was hung on a nail instead.[179] A man born in 1903 recalled his own school was very Welsh in atmosphere but said he heard the Welsh Not was in use in nearby Llangernyw and that one girl moved to his school because of this.[180] These sources are oral and no published autobiography or contemporary commentary dates the Welsh Not to the twentieth century. This, like the official support for both the use and teaching of Welsh, suggests any use of the Welsh Not after 1900 was very unusual. However, state policy and local practice are very different things. An unpublished autobiography recalled a no Welsh rule being introduced for older children in the Carmarthenshire mining village of Tymbl in the Edwardian period, although it noted most children ignored this and the rule was discontinued.[181] The challenges of teaching and the persistence of anti-Welsh prejudices meant it was probably not uncommon for some early twentieth-century teachers to casually hit children for speaking Welsh out of frustration or temper. Indeed, the fallibility of teachers means there are people who can remember being hit for speaking Welsh at school in the 1950s.[182] These incidents might not have been formal, systematic or sanctioned but they happened nonetheless.

Conclusion

By 1900, there was widespread pride amongst the Welsh intelligentsia about the state of Welsh education from elementary schools to the national university. In 1901, the *Western Mail* claimed that there was no country in Europe where education had 'made greater strides within such a short space of time as in Wales'. It maintained there was now nowhere in Wales where 'the schoolmaster is not standing witness to mental development and culture, not a valley, however remote, without its temple of learning'.[183] On the surface at least this meant that the spectres of the Blue Books and the Welsh Not had been laid to rest.

In 1890, one Welsh-language writer wondered if readers remembered the sad days of the Welsh Not, which had been useless both to teach English or hinder Welsh. He compared them with the present when the government paid for people to learn Welsh.[184]

But self-congratulation obscured continuing problems in some schools. There were still bad and violent teachers, a concentration on teaching facts rather than skills, unsuitable and overcrowded buildings, apathetic parents and irregular attendance. Moreover, in many schools Welsh was still seen only as a tool to help teach English rather than something important and valuable in itself. And there were still a few teachers punishing children for speaking it. The best teachers understood, that, to quote one Caernarfonshire teacher, 'nothing but a parrot-like knowledge of English can possibly be imparted to scholars in Welsh-spoken districts ... without freely using the Welsh language'. Thus, as another from Flintshire put it, 'The most successful teachers use it [Welsh] freely.'[185] But those teachers who spoke Welsh to their pupils might still discourage or prevent their pupils from speaking the language, at least in the classroom. The old beliefs that excluding Welsh was the best way to improve English had not died out.

Quite how widespread Welsh was used after 1862 is impossible to know. One historian has suggested that the use of Welsh was surreptitious and almost subversive.[186] Some teachers may have hidden their use of the language from inspectors during visits and kept it out of the logbooks from an assumption it would be disapproved of. Certainly, inspectors had different ideas on how common the language was in classrooms. In response to enquiries from Ireland at the end of the 1870s, Revd E. Watts wrote that teachers 'frequently resort to Welsh as a medium of explanation'. In contrast, the reply of William Williams stated that three-quarters of schools he inspected were in Welsh-speaking areas but Welsh was not used to convey instructions and only sometimes to explain words or phrases to 'young or backward' children.[187] The next two decades does seem to have seen considerably more Welsh used as a means of explanation, but much was down to individual teachers and thus a change of leadership at a specific school could also see a move away or towards the use of Welsh. The variety of attitudes were evident in logbook comments on pupil teachers: some were criticised for not explaining difficult words but at other schools they were criticised for using too much Welsh.[188]

The variety of approaches, temperament and thinking amongst teachers was a key characteristic of education throughout the century. This was hardly surprising given the size of the profession. By 1891, there were more than 9,000 elementary teachers in Wales.[189] Some were preoccupied by the morality, behaviour or cleanliness of their pupils; a few by the language the children spoke. Some teachers wrote in their logbooks in ways that conveyed their pride in and care for their children; others seem to treat the children as an enemy to be overcome. But all were worried about how the children would do in their annual exam because their own reputation, sense of achievement and often pay depended upon it. For many, passing the exam was more important than whether the children understood anything. Some teachers had no choice because they did not speak Welsh and were thus unable to explain anything. Others surely knew the limitations of their practice but concentrated on the exam out of desperation rather than choice. But teachers were also becoming more and more professional and such apathy towards pupils' levels of understanding was in gradual decline.

It was this variety in teachers, as well as the considerable professional freedom they had, that explains why there were so many different approaches to Welsh in the classroom. One 1896 writer put teachers into three categories – those that thought it was best to use Welsh, those who thought it had to be used to teach English, which would then lead to Welsh disappearing, and those who thought English should be the language of the day schools, with Welsh being for Sunday schools.[190] This variety of practice was the product of how the state's regulation concentrated on outcomes rather than methods and the diversity of teachers' own backgrounds and approaches. But it was an inconsistent position since some teachers changed their own views and experimented with different methods.

One thing they could all agree on was that teaching was challenging. In 1885 an executive of the National Union of Elementary Teachers was applauded at a union meeting at Caernarfon for pointing out the difficulties faced by children in Wales and saying the code was scandalous for ignoring Welsh. There were complaints at the meeting about the 'drudgery and wrong' entailed by both teachers and scholars in trying to meet the standards of efficiency required by the code and that teachers were insecure in their posts, subject to wage reductions and religious prejudices if they belonged to the wrong sect.[191] However professional they were, teaching was never an easy job in any circumstances. In communities where English was little known it was even more difficult. Of course, Welsh-medium education would have solved that but that was not what anyone wanted. Learning English was what parents, teachers and the state thought education was for.

Notes

1 *Third Report of the Royal Commission appointed to inquire into the Working of the Elementary Education Acts, England and Wales* (London, 1887), p. 3 [hereafter Cross Commission].
2 R. Robinson, *A Manual of Method and Organisation* (London, 1863); Cross Commission, 2nd report, p. 289.
3 Joseph Lancaster, *The British System of Education: Epitome of Joseph Lancaster's Inventions and Improvements in Education Practised at the Royal Free Schools, Borough-Road, Southwark* (London, 1810), p. 40.
4 *Report of the CCE, 1886–87*, p. 353.
5 Edmund Holmes, *In Quest of an Ideal: An Autobiography* (London, 1920), pp. 67–8.
6 John Gill, *Introductory Text-book to School Education, Method and School Management* (London, 1876 edn), p. 156.
7 For example, PA, Trecastell British, 10 December 1886; MRO, Brithdir, 1 June 1900.
8 AA, Llangefni British, 5, 11 July 1873.
9 MRO: Bethel, 18 November 1881.
10 GA, Merthyr Tydfil British, 21 January 1876.
11 GA, Troed-y-rhiw Mixed, 30 January, 15 February 1885. On his physical punishments and kicking see 5 June 1886, 11 July 1895.
12 CA, Newgate (Rhydlewis) British, 17 February 1865.
13 Testimonials from 1904 in MRO, W. Pryce Williams papers.
14 Kate Davies and T. Llew Jones, *Canrif o Addysg Gynradd: Ysgol Tregroes, 1878–1978* (Llandysul, 1978), p. 5.
15 James Jones, *A Few Plain Hints and Suggestions on Teaching English in Welsh Country Schools* (Bala, 1864).
16 *Report of the CCE, 1865–6*, p. 66.

17 *Commission on the Employment of Children, Young Persons, and Women in Agriculture (1867): Third Report of the Commissioners* (London, 1870), p. 89.
18 Honourable Society of Cymmrodorion, *Preliminary Report upon the Use of the Welsh Language in Elementary Schools in Welsh-Speaking Districts* (London, 1884), p. 12.
19 PbA, Solva British school, 4 August 1870.
20 CmA, Ammanford Junior (formerly Cross Inn British school), 8 March 1865, 15 September 1865.
21 CmA, Cwmcothi, 21 November 1877.
22 Owen Thomas, 'Log books of Cardiganshire Schools, 1860–1880', *Transaction and Archaeological Record of the Cardiganshire Antiquarian Society*, 13 (1938), 56–69.
23 Reproduced in J. Towyn Jones, *Ysgol Penwaun Cofnodion Canrif 1880–1980* (Bangor, 1981), pp. 25–6.
24 PbA, Blaen-ffos, 28 November–2 December 1881.
25 PA, Crickhowell British, 22 November 1867, 19 February 1868, 27 February 1868.
26 WGA, Garn-swllt, 20 April 1894.
27 PA, Staylittle Board, 12 June 1876; CA, Newgate (Rhydlewis) British, 23 September, 18 October 1864; PA, Rhiwhiriaeth Board, 26 May 1876; CA, Llanon British, 2 October 1875.
28 Cross Commission, 2nd report, p. 289.
29 CA, Felinfach Board, 29 September 1876, 4 May 1877, 15 February 1878, 14 October 1878.
30 NEWAR, Tynyfelin Board, 30 April 1886.
31 For example, NEWAH, Rhuddlan Boys National, 14 April 1863, 3 February 1868, 31 July 1870; AA, Llangristiolus, 17 November 1863, 7 March 1864.
32 Norbahira Mohamad Nor and Radzuwan Ab Rashid, 'A review of theoretical perspectives on language learning and acquisition', *Kasetsart Journal of Social Sciences*, 39, 1 (2018), 161–7.
33 MRO, Corris British, 19 July 1869, 2 March, 17 August, 25 November 1870, 23 January, 23 February 1871.
34 PA, Trecastell British, 7 December 1883.
35 CmA, Llangunnock Vaughan's charity school, 8 December 1875.
36 MRO, Dyffryn British, 19 August 1863, 5 October 1864.
37 CA, Llanilar, 14 November 1884.
38 Honourable Society of Cymmrodorion, *Report of the Committee appointed into the Advisability of the Introduction of the Welsh Language into the Course of Elementary Education in Wales: The Introduction of Welsh as a Specific Subject* (Aberdare, 1885), p. 5.
39 Jones, *A Few Plain Hints and Suggestions on Teaching English*, p. 29.
40 MRO, Nantlle Board, 12 January 1874.
41 CA, Llangeitho British, 11 January 1869.
42 See the account in O. L. Roberts, *Cofiant Y Parch O. R. Owen, Glandwr a Lerpwl* (Liverpool, 1909), p. 23.

43 Iorwerth C. Peate, 'Diwylliant gwerin', *Transactions of the Honourable Society of Cymmrodorion* (1937), 241–50, 247.
44 Elizabeth Williams, *Brethyn Cartref* (Llandysul, 1951), p. 51.
45 Quoted in Glenville Powell, 'Hanes plwyf Crai: VI addysg yng Nghrai', *Brycheiniog*, 10 (1964), 39–68, 49. In contrast, at Dinas, the woman who came in to teach sewing repeatedly complained to the master that the girls were speaking Welsh. On one occasion this led to two of them being made to write out the word 'English' 100 times; on another several were caned. PbA, Dinas, 31 March, 3, 19 May 1870, 21 March, 11 May, 7 November 1871.
46 NEWAR, Ruabon Boys National, 20 October 1893.
47 Honourable Society of Cymmrodorion, *Preliminary Report upon the Use of the Welsh Language*, p. 11; Dan Isaac Davies, 'Cymru ddwyieithog', *Y Geninen*, July 1885, 206–12, 211.
48 See the memory of Aberdare British school in Cross Commission, 3rd report, p. 26.
49 For example, PbA, Solva British, 16 November 1877; CRO, Llanystumdwy National, 14 January 1873.
50 CmA, Abergwili, 10 December 1880, 30 July 1881.
51 Quoted in L. M. Rees, 'A Critical Examination of the Teacher Training in Wales, 1846–1898' (unpublished PhD thesis, University of Wales, Bangor, 1968), 292.
52 Gwenfair Parry, 'Tregaron', in Gwenfair Parry and Mari A. Williams (eds), *The Welsh Language and the 1891 Census* (Cardiff, 1991), p. 291. For complaints of a PT's poor English see CRO, Cefnfaes British, 20 March 1893.
53 Calculated from coded data on Integrated Census Microdata, http://icem.data-archive.ac.uk/ (accessed 25 March 2024). The figures include teachers at intermediate, grammar and private schools. This, along with coding errors, mean these figures are more indicative than exact.
54 William Williams, chief inspector, in Honourable Society of Cymmrodorion, *Preliminary Report upon the Use of the Welsh*, p. 28.
55 PA, Uwchygarreg National, 10 January 1896.
56 PA, Staylittle Board, 27 June 1884.
57 PbA, Nevern, 20 January 1879, June 1878. He recorded a case where these language problems had led to parents removing a pupil from his school.
58 CA, Llanon British, 29 September 1869, 23 November 1869, 7 July 1870.
59 *Commission on the Employment of Children, Young Persons, and Women in Agriculture (1867)*, pp. 56, 129.
60 CA, Newgate (Rhydlewis) British, 27 May and 12 June 1867.
61 Roberts, *Cofiant Y Parch O. R. Owen*, p. 24; Abel J. Jones, *From an Inspector's Bag* (Cardiff, 1944), p. 106.
62 His nine children of school age were all recorded as bilingual in 1891 but the two youngest children, aged two and three and not old enough to have picked up Welsh in the community, were English monoglots. Crowther family 1891 census entry, 15 Ogwen Terrace, Llanllechid.
63 J. Elwyn Hughes and André Lomozi, *Canmlwyddiant Ysgol y Cefnfaes Bethesda ynghyd â hanes Canolfan Gymdeithasol y Cefnfaes* (Bethesda, 2007).

64 Cross Commission, 1st Report, p. 168; my emphasis.
65 Cross Commission, 2nd Report, pp. 281, 284, 285.
66 Honourable Society of Cymmrodorion, *Preliminary Report upon the Use of the Welsh Language*, p. 16.
67 CmA, Alma Board, 1 February 1876.
68 PbA, Solva British, 14 June 1878; PA, Trecastell Board, 12 March 1882.
69 Education Department, *1875. New Code of Regulations* (London, 1875), p. 7.
70 PbA, Mynachlog-ddu, 17 January 1896.
71 PA, Rhiwhiriaeth Board, 8 November 1875.
72 Cross Commission, 2nd Report, p. 289.
73 NEWAR, Blaenau Llangernyw British, 17 July 1885.
74 *CCE, Report 1878–9*, p. 672.
75 PbA, Solva, 23 January 1873.
76 MRO, Bethel Board, 19 June, 7 July, 16 September, 31 October 1881.
77 PA, Gwenddwr National, 9 October 1865.
78 *Report of the CCE, 1888–89*, p. 347.
79 PA, Staylittle Board, 4 January 1888, 25 January 1889, 29 April 1890.
80 *Report of the CCE, 1886–87*, p. 357.
81 CA, Llanwenog National, 23 June 1880.
82 CRO, Llanrug National, 1 November 1878.
83 Schools Inquiry Commission, *General Reports by Assistant Commissioners. Vol VIII: Midland Countries and Northumberland* (London, 1868), pp. 7–8.
84 E. M. Sneyd-Kynnersley, *HMI: Some Passages in the Life of One of H.M. Inspectors of Schools* (London, 1913), p. 48.
85 For example, PA, Trecastell British, 17 March 1882.
86 AA, Llangristiolus, 28 October 1881.
87 PbA, Solva British, 13 August, 25 November 1875.
88 PA, Trecastell British, 8 December 1882.
89 CmA, Cwmcothi, 24 November 1882.
90 NEWAH, Rhuddlan Boys National, 17 January 1868.
91 *Report of the CCE, 1863–64*, p. 215.
92 *Report of the CCE, 1868–69*, pp. 164–5.
93 For examples see the recollections of difference approaches in J. Lloyd Williams, *Atgofion Tri Chwarter Canrif, cyf. II* (London, 1942), p. 130; *Atgofion Tri Chwarter Canrif, cyf. IV* (London, 1945), pp. 239–40.
94 Geraint Wyn Jones, *Dyddiadur Ysgol: Ysgol y Manod 1867–1967* (Blaenau Ffestiniog, 1997), p. 38.
95 Logbook entry, 11 February 1881, in Kate Davies and T. Llew Jones, *Canrif o Addysg Gynradd: Ysgol Tregroes, 1878–1978* (Llandysul, 1978).
96 *Reports of Assistant Commissioners appointed to inquire into State of Popular Education in England*, vol. II (1861) [hereafter Newcastle Report], p. 557; *Report of the CCE, 1865–66*, p. 67.
97 For example, CA, Swyddffynnon 1884 scheme. Arithmetic might even be a bit simpler in English because Welsh numbers included formats such two and fifteen for seventeen.

98 For example, CRO, Abergwyngregyn National, 18 January 1874, 9 August 1875.
99 Cross Commission, 2nd Report, p. 285; PA, Uwchygarreg National, 2 February 1883; CwyA, Rowen, 34th week, 1873.
100 CRO, Caernarfon British, 1 February 1866.
101 Roger Hawkins, *How Second Languages Are Learned* (Cambridge, 2019), ch. 10.
102 R. T. Jenkins, *Edrych yn Ôl* (London, 1968), p. 61.
103 *Report of the CCE, 1865–66*, p. 56.
104 J. Walker, *The Handy Book of Object Lessons from a Teacher's Note Book*, 3rd edn (London, 1873).
105 Anne Digby and Peter Searby, *Children, School and Society in Nineteenth-Century England* (London, 1981), pp. 160–3.
106 D. R. Fearon, *School Inspection* (London, 1887), p. 16.
107 PbA, Mynachlog-ddu, 9 July 1897, 31 March 1896.
108 CA, Llanrhystid, 28 February 1896.
109 Myra Evans, *Atgofion Ceinewydd* (Aberystwyth, 1961), p. 79.
110 *Report of the CCE, 1886–87*, pp. 360–1. Using object lessons to teach basic English vocabulary was strongly advocated in Jones, *A few Plain Hints and Suggestions on Teaching English*, pp. 7–8. For an example of it in practice see PA, Rhiwhiriaeth Board, 16 August 1878.
111 *Report of the CCE, 1884–85*, p. 349.
112 CA, Swyddffynnon scheme for 1884.
113 For example, CA, Llandysul National 1866 HMI report.
114 *Report of the CCE, 1870–71*, p. 275.
115 PbA, Solva British, 18 November 1875.
116 MRO, Bethel Board, 19 November 1880.
117 Jones, *A few Plain Hints and Suggestions on Teaching English*, pp. 12–13.
118 CA, Llanon British, 21 October 1871.
119 *Report of the CCE, 1875–6*, pp. 391–2.
120 *Reports of the CCE, 1882–3* (p. 424) and *1868–69* (p. 164).
121 For examples of complaints about physical conditions see NEWAR, Brymbo and Broughton British, 8 January 1863; CmA, Cwmbach British, 11 November 1868.
122 For example, PA, Sarn National, 11 December 1865, 12 April 1866.
123 MRO, Bethel Board, 3 December 1880.
124 *Report of the CCE, 1888–89*, p. 345.
125 PA, Sarn National, 27 May 1868.
126 Newcastle Report, vol. II, p. 553.
127 CA, Trewen British, 6 June 1890.
128 NEWAR, Bryncroes Board, 15 September 1882, 26 January 1883, 2 November 1883, 11 July 1884.
129 CRO, Garth Board 1897 HMI report.
130 *Report of the CCE, 1875–6*, pp. 392–3.
131 PA, Staylittle Board, 25 March 1874; Williams, *Atgofion Tri Chwarter Canrif*, cyf. IV, p. 176.

132 MRO, Bethel, 13 August 1880.
133 Lynda Mugglestone, 'Talking Proper': The Rise of Accent as Social Symbol (Oxford, 2003), p. 1.
134 Cross Commission, 3rd Report, p. 29.
135 Frank Smith, *A History of English Elementary Education, 1760–1902* (London, 1931), p. 274.
136 *Report of the CCE, 1888–89*, p. 367.
137 D. J. Davies, 'On the necessity of teaching English through the medium of Welsh in Elementary Schools in Welsh spoken Districts', *Y Cymmrodor*, 5 (1882), 1–13.
138 On the society see J. Elwyn Hughes, *Arloeswr Dwyieithedd: Dan Isaac Davies, 1839–1887* (Cardiff, 1984) and B. L. Davies, 'The right to a bilingual education in nineteenth-century Wales', *Transactions of the Honourable Society of Cymmrodorion* (1988), 133–51. For the society's aims see the Society for Utilizing the Welsh Language, *Memorial Presented by the Council to the Royal Commission on Elementary Education* (Llandilo, 1886).
139 Cross Commission, 3rd Report, p. 1.
140 David T. Roberts, 'The genesis of the Cross Commission', *Journal of Educational Administration and History*, 17, 2 (1985), 30–8.
141 For a school putting flowers in a classroom on the advice of an inspector see NEWAR, Dyserth National, 7 May 1881.
142 *Report of the CCE, 1884–85*, p. 342.
143 W. Gareth Evans, 'The Welsh Intermediate and Technical Education Act, 1889: a centenary appreciation', *History of Education*, 19, 3 (1990), 195–210; David Allsobrook, '"A benevolent prophet of old": reflections on the Welsh Intermediate Act of 1889', *Welsh Journal of Education*, 1 (1989), 1–10.
144 In 1888 just sixteen schools were teaching Welsh as subject. *Report of the CCE, 1888–89*, p. 369.
145 Education Department, *Code of Regulations* (London, 1889).
146 Education Department, *Code of Regulations* (London, 1893); Society for Utilizing the Welsh Language, *Welsh as a Specific Subject for Elementary Schools, Stage 1* (Cardiff, 1891).
147 *Report of the CCE, 1892–3*, p. 440.
148 Davies, 'The right to a bilingual education', 150.
149 Society for Utilizing the Welsh Language, *Scheme of Instruction for Use in Elementary Schools in Wales* (Caernarfon, 1893), p. 4.
150 Editorial, *South Wales Daily Post*, 24 March 1893, 2.
151 'Wales and Welsh', *South Wales Daily Post*, 20 February 1893, 2.
152 Quoted in H. G. Williams, 'Elementary Education in Caernarvonshire, 1839–1902' (unpublished PhD thesis, University of Wales, Bangor, 1981), 435.
153 'Scheme 10 for Small Country School in Welsh Speaking District with Average Attendance of From 20 to 60 Older Children', in *Report of the Board of Education, 1900–01*, p. 238.
154 AA, Aberffraw, 18 September 1894.
155 *Report of the CCE, 1896–7*, p. 172.

156 Evidence of Owen M. Edwards in Intermediate Education (Ireland) Commission, *Final Report of the Commissioners* (1899), section A, p. 61.
157 Honourable Society of Cymmrodorion, *Report of the Committee Appointed to Inquire into the Advisability of the Introduction of the Welsh Language into the Course of Elementary Education in Wales*, quote from appendix, p. 3.
158 'Bilingualism in Welsh schools', *Pontypridd District Herald*, 1 April 1893, 5.
159 W. R. Jones, *Bilingualism in Welsh Education* (Cardiff, 1966), pp. 67–8.
160 Evans, *Atgofion Ceinewydd*, p. 99.
161 *Report of the CCE, 1896–97*, p. 172.
162 J. Ifor Davies, *The Caernarvon County School: A History* (Gwynedd Archives, 1989), pp. 134–5.
163 Robert Smith, *Schools, Politics and Society: Elementary Education in Wales, 1870–1902* (Cardiff, 1999), pp. 196–7.
164 'Welsh in board schools', *Evening Express*, 1 March 1902, 3.
165 'Welsh in board schools', *South Wales Daily News*, 13 July 1893, 4.
166 *Report of the CCE, 1896–97*, p. 182.
167 For example, Thomas Owen, 'The Teaching of Welsh in Schools', *Young Wales*, 1, 7 (1895), 167–8.
168 William Evans, 'Defnyddioldeb yr ysgol sabbathol', *Y Diwygiwr*, March 1895, 81–4.
169 Michael Gareth Llewelyn, *Sand in the Glass* (London, 1943), p. 120.
170 *Welsh in Education and Life: Being the Report of the Departmental Committee Appointed by the President of the Board of Education to inquire into the Position of the Welsh Language and to Advise as to its Promotion in the Educational System of Wales* (London, 1927), p. 68.
171 Isambard Owen, *The Welsh Language Society: Scheme and Rules of the Society* (Bangor, 1901).
172 'Merioneth Education Committee', *Cambrian News*, 24 June 1904, 7.
173 Board of Education (Welsh Department), *Code of Regulations for Public Elementary Schools in Wales* (London, 1907).
174 Owen M. Edwards, *A Short History of Wales* (Chicago, 1907), p. 126.
175 Report on the teaching of English in the elementary schools of Caernarvonshire (1912). Reproduced in Gwilym J. Evans, *The Entrance Scholarship Examination in Caernarvonshire, 1897–1961* (Caernarfon, 1966), pp. 121–2.
176 'Welsh for Wales: protest from a rural district', *Western Mail*, 1 November 1919, 10.
177 John Hughes, *Education in a Changing Wales* (Llandysul, 1932), p. 19.
178 Mrs Stephens, St Fagans oral history, interview 3032–1.
179 Miss Jones, Llanilar, St Fagans oral history, interview 7313.
180 NLW, Cyfweliad â William Christmas Williams gan Medwen Roberts.
181 RBA, Wilfred E. Timbrell, 'Memories of Tumble from 1894'.
182 Talk, Welsh Not, https://en.wikipedia.org/wiki/Talk:Welsh_Not/Archive_1 (accessed 25 March 2024).
183 *Western Mail*, 1 January 1901, 3.
184 RR, 'Yr iaith Gymraeg a'n hysgolion dyddiol', *Yr Haul*, September 1890, 274–5.

185 Honourable Society of Cymmrodorion, *Report of the Committee appointed into the Advisability of the Introduction of the Welsh Language into the Course of Elementary Education in Wales*, pp. 5, 7.
186 Williams, 'Elementary Education in Caernarvonshire', 413, 437.
187 Quoted in 'Memorandum by the Commissioners of National education to the Chief Secretary', *The Gaelic Journal*, 2, 15 (1884), 94.
188 PA, Trecastell British, 25 October 1872; CRO, Llanystumdwy National, 14 January 1872.
189 Smith, *Schools, Politics and Society*, p. 238. For an extended discussion of the variety of teachers see Anon., *A Schoolmaster's Difficulties, Abroad and at Home* (London, 1853).
190 W. Llewelyn Williams, 'Yr iaith Gymraeg', *Y Llenor*, 6 (April 1896), 77–94, 87.
191 'Elementary teachers' conference at Carnarvon', *North Wales Express*, 2 October 1885, 7. For an example of a teacher privately worrying about money see Bangor University Archives, Diary of David Griffith, 31 December 1869.

6
ENEMIES OF THE WELSH LANGUAGE? HER MAJESTY'S INSPECTORS AND THE BRITISH STATE

The role of the state in the Welsh Not is perhaps its most emotive question. In the popular imagination, the Welsh Not was implemented by a government attempting to stamp out the Welsh language. In reality, it was never state policy. Indeed, the British state had relatively few policies in terms of what should happen in classrooms. Nor did the state have consistent views in terms of what it wanted to happen because it had no single mind, being made up of multiple actors, of different levels of power and responsibility. There was no education minister but, from the creation of the Committee of Privy Council on Education in 1839, there was something that can be called a department of education. Yet its chairman and senior administrators were relatively limited in their powers. They ran no schools and employed no teachers and, instead, handed state funds to school boards and managers to spend.

The rudimentary control over education was emblematic of the wider nineteenth-century state. Although it grew significantly, the British state remained a somewhat chaotic patchwork with local government far more important than Westminster in the provision of services. Even at the end of the century, most welfare provision was charitable rather than the work of local or national government. Both local and national government were also highly moralistic and deeply worried about costs.[1] This was an era of laissez-faire politics and the idea of a state department that interfered in classroom practices would have won little support. After all, the state did not even insist that children had to go to the school until 1880 or make education free until 1891.

There is no evidence that the leadership of the education department had any appreciation of the Welsh language. They probably shared the views of the Blue Books and Newcastle Commission that Welsh was a hinderance to both the Welsh people and the administration of the country. But, more often, they seem to have given the language little thought. Neither the 1862 Revised Code nor the 1870 Education Act made any reference to Welsh, and English was simply assumed to be the default language of instruction. Wales was peripheral to thinking in Westminster and its need for distinct policies usually went unnoticed by lawmakers.

But it should not be assumed that the state was instinctively hostile to Wales. Queen Victoria was not much interested in education but in 1849 she told the marquess of Lansdowne, her minister responsible for education, that 'Welsh should be taught in Wales as well as English'. Lansdowne promised that Welsh would be combined with English in schools and that this would influence the choice of inspectors.[2] It was through Her Majesty's Inspectors (HMIs) that the state was able to wield some influence on schools. Both before and after the Revised Code it was they who visited schools and decided on grant levels; it was they who advised teachers on what to do and who passed on the education department's thinking. They were thus the bridge between schools and the education department, interpreting and implementing the state's regulations. The state may have been an abstract concept but, in the inspectorate, it had a real and human face.

Since they worked in Wales, inspectors were far more aware of the issue of language than their employer, but historians have not been kind about them. Robert Smith criticises the inspectorate for not taking enough account of either the impact of Welsh on learning or of the value of Welsh in itself.[3] W. Gareth Evans argues that, with exceptions, inspectors were very hostile to the language, and that they exerted 'rigorous controls' over Welsh; he maintains that Wales was treated as an internal colony and that it was state policy to remove cultural differences such as the existence of different vernaculars.[4] But, like the state itself, the inspectors had no single mind and their annual reports to the department show they often varied significantly in opinion. As this chapter will show, some made it clear that Welsh should be employed; one made it very clear that it should not; most offered no substantive comments on the issue. Inspectors varied in personality too. Some saw themselves as supporting teachers, whereas others were aloof and even condescending. Regardless of their approaches and views, their influence over schools was limited by the fact they tended to only visit each once a year. During that visit they might not see a school in its normal state of affairs, as teachers attempted to show themselves and their pupils in their best light. This meant there were occasional unannounced informal visits but these were rare.[5] Nor were inspectors always listened to and what they told schools to do was not necessarily the same as what schools actually did. No nineteenth-century teacher anywhere in the UK was an employee of the state and they had considerable freedom to teach how they saw fit, including when it came to the language of instruction.

Promoting the use of Welsh: Longueville Jones and the Welsh Paper

School inspection began in 1840 in response to growing state expenditure on education. It was not intended to control schools or to interfere in their running but instead to advise and assist to ensure government money was not wasted.[6] Indeed, under its head, James Kay-Shuttleworth, the education department was paternalist, with a vision of teachers as guiding children to 'affectionate industry and disciplined liveliness'. But after Kay-Shuttleworth's retirement in 1849, the department became more bureaucratic and centralised.[7] It grew in size but still had no grand vision of what should be happening in the classrooms it helped pay for and inspectors retained considerable freedom to work as they saw best. Every school in receipt of government money was subject to inspection, although in the early years this was not an annual ritual. In theory, inspectors had no powers to order schools to do anything but they did award state grants and, after the introduction of the 1862 Revised Code, their examinations of pupils helped decide the levels of those grants. This gave them significant influence but it also threatened to turn their job into a bureaucratic exercise, and one inspector complained that he and his peers were victims of 'a vicious administrative system'.[8]

To appease the religious bodies whose schools were being looked at, the Anglican clergy inspected National schools, while British schools were looked at by laymen, although they might work vigorously in promoting the British Society's work and cause.[9] Recruitment to the inspectorate often occurred in rather haphazard ways, with appointees sometimes having little or no direct experience in education but the right social background or contacts.[10] These Oxbridge and upper-middle-class men might have little prior experience with schools but their reports do suggest they cared about education and wanted its expansion and improved standards. Their approaches to achieving this varied significantly, however. Some were considered kind, patient and tactful men who tried to put pupils at ease.[11] Others were picky, prejudiced and complained of things as trivial as dust on ledges.[12] Their social background did diversify as the size of the inspectorate grew significantly with the expansion of the number of schools to visit after the 1870 Act. This brought men from more different backgrounds into the inspectorate, including some who had worked as teachers.[13] By 1894, there were twenty-four inspectors in Wales, examining 1,437 schools and more than a quarter of million pupils.[14]

Under pressure from campaigners in Wales and aware of the furore that followed the Blue Books, the education department decided in 1848 that it would endeavour to appoint additional inspectors who were 'natives of the Principality, acquainted with the Welsh language'.[15] This led to the appointment of Harry Longueville Jones (1806–70) as inspector for National schools in Wales, a position he held from 1849 until 1864. Born in London but from a wealthy Wrexham family, he was an Anglican priest who learned Welsh, was deeply interested in Welsh history and settled on Anglesey in 1846. The decision to employ Jones was a deliberate recognition of Welsh difference but within a year the leadership of the education department changed with the appointment of Ralph Lingen, one of the three Blue Books commissioners and not someone sympathetic to Wales.[16]

Jones repeatedly highlighted Wales's distinct needs in his annual reports, particularly in the early years when anger over the Blue Books was still fresh. Most notably, he made it clear that Welsh should be employed as a medium of instruction. In 1849, for example, he celebrated the techniques used at the Bevan school at Llangrannog, where the master taught children to translate to and from English.[17] In 1850, he stated that the question of two languages had been solved through experience:

> the greater part of the instruction given in Welsh schools is conveyed in English, at the express desire of the parents, yet it is found that the more the two tongues are taught concurrently, – and so taught as to elucidate and explain each other, – the greater is the progress made in the knowledge of each other.[18]

He argued that young minds were well suited to learning languages and that once the work of Welsh scholars in forming 'good vocabularies and grammars' had matured,

> the knowledge of English will penetrate rapidly to every fireside among our mountains; not to displace the ancient language of the country, but to illustrate and to aid it. The Cymric nation, as a body, is anxious to acquire the Anglo-Saxon tongue, at the same time that it carefully maintains the use of its own. It is aware of the immense importance of a knowledge of English to all who desire to rise in life, or to fight a good battle with a struggling world.[19]

Such comments were partly what his employer wanted to hear but they were also rooted in Jones's own belief that Welsh was valuable in its own right.[20]

Jones called for bilingual books, support for Welsh music, provision to serve Wales's maritime needs, the teaching of Welsh history and extra grants for Welsh schools in light of their challenges. He was thus a believer that some policies should be different in Wales where there were distinct needs. His report for 1855–6 summed up:

> Regulations that will apply on the shores of the Bristol Channel will not hold good, in all cases, amidst the moors of Montgomeryshire; and it does not follow that, because a London plan may be good for Swansea, therefore it should be equally suitable to a village at the foot of Snowdon.[21]

The education department, however, wanted administrative uniformity and Jones came to be seen as something of a troublemaker. In 1862, he had to amend his report to remove sections encouraging managers and teachers to report regulations they felt were unclear. The department refused to publish his 1863–4 report, which led to questions in the Commons and an inquiry since inspectors were meant to be free to articulate their judgements and comments on policy. Jones suffered a stroke while giving evidence to the inquiry and retired soon afterwards.[22]

Historian H. G. Williams called Jones a 'champion of cultural diversity resisting the administrative state's attempts to impose cultural homogeneity', and an 'opponent of English domestic imperialism'. He argues that Williams's retirement was an 'unmitigated disaster' for Wales since it removed from office the only man who had sought to promote a 'distinctive educational system for Wales within a British framework'.[23] But this overplays Jones's influence and the amount to which anything changed after he left the inspectorate. Jones certainly argued for Welsh interests, but he had not changed policy, partly because when it came to language in the classroom, there was no language policy to change and partly because of hostility to the use of Welsh within Wales itself.

Moreover, Jones was not quite the champion of Wales Williams portrays him as. Even with his Welsh sympathies, Jones never escaped the prejudices of his upper-middle-class Anglican background. His report on Newtown National school in 1863, for example, recommended that special attention be paid to raising the moral tone of younger children because 'home influences' in the locality were 'not very favourable'.[24] He worried about children's religious knowledge and this was one reason for his desire to see children taught in a language they understood.[25] His interest in Wales had something of a whiff of wanting to protect and nurture an exotic and somewhat backwards culture. He argued there was a need for more encouragement and intervention in Wales because the people were:

> not naturally prone to help themselves; they require words and deeds of encouragement, and above all that the stiff formalities of Anglo-Norman laws and regulations should not be applied with too rigorous uniformity to Celtic minds, a course that will never overcome the inertness and passive resistance of the Welsh people.[26]

Elsewhere, he claimed that stiff official forms should be simplified to help 'a peculiar district and a peculiar people'.[27] His vision of a bilingual Wales certainly existed within a British context and he stressed to the education department that protecting Wales would not undermine the United Kingdom. In 1849, he expressed that a bilingual Wales would be for the common good, harmonising and binding together 'the different races, of which our mighty empire is composed'. He went on:

> I feel confident that the mass of people will not join in any mischievous agitation for making the distinction of language an engine of political hostility between the Cymro, and the Saxon, nor for getting up on a small scale a repeal of the union and a reversal of the Norman conquest. The more intimately the two nations are blended together, the more rapidly they tend to imitate the good example of each other.[28]

Jones may thus have been an advocate of the use of Welsh and the recognition of Welsh needs, but he was condescending in doing so and his vision of Wales existed firmly within a British imperial context.

Jones's initial appointment had come at a time when the education department was making an effort to recognise Welsh needs to deflect some of the criticisms brought about by the Blue Books. Lobbying from Sir Thomas Phillips, a clergyman and the principal of the new training college at Carmarthen, led to a 'Welsh paper' being set from 1850. It consisted of grammar questions and translation tasks, and could be taken as part of a trainee teacher's qualification tasks. The examination did not attract many takers and in 1857 it was removed from counting towards a teacher's certificate. But the exam remained on offer and those who were marked as 'good' or 'excellent' received an extra £5 salary from the state when they worked in schools where an inspector felt that a knowledge of Welsh was 'needful'.[29]

In 1859, the inspection report on Anglican training colleges was highly critical of the Welsh examination. It noted that no candidates in Carmarthen had taken the exam that year and only eleven at other colleges had. None had done well enough to earn the £5 grant for proficiency in Welsh. The inspector went on:

> From inquiries made in Wales, of schoolmasters, local managers, and others, I have been led to think that the Welsh paper set at the Christmas examination is a mistake. Welsh parents object to their children being taught Welsh; they want them to learn English. In some cases they have been known to withdraw their children from schools where Welsh was taught. To teach Welsh on paper, and grammatically, to students, is therefore unnecessary. Nobody wants it. Nobody will have it, if they can help it. It is a hindrance and not a help in the progress of national and general education.

He urged the abandonment of the exam and recommended instead that the £5 annual bonus be paid to any certified teacher who spoke colloquial Welsh, something he called 'a real advantage and one much valued for the sake both of children and their parents'.[30] With the introduction of the Revised Code, the Welsh examination – and thus additional financial support for the teachers who passed it – came to an end. It was 1893 before teachers could again take an examination in Welsh towards their certification.

That inspector was probably right that the low numbers taking the exam, despite the financial inducement, owed much to how Welsh was not valued. It is probable too that some saw teaching as a route out of Wales and thus did not feel the need for a qualification that only paid in schools where Welsh was needed. But the low numbers were also a reflection of the exam itself, which required the translation of complex materials. Many students had not learned to write Welsh formally and their knowledge of the language was colloquial. The state was trying promote the cause of Welsh-speaking teachers but doing this in such a formal way was pointless if the language was not taught in elementary schools.

Other voices and the Reverend Shadrach Pryce

Jones was not alone in the inspectorate advocating a case for Welsh before the 1880s.[31] The annual reports of other inspectors also make assertions that Welsh should be used in classrooms. Joseph Fletcher (1813–52) was an English lawyer and an inspector of British schools from 1844 to 1852. His 1846 report noted the practical effects of excluding Welsh:

> So strong, indeed, is this desire for English, that it is a fundamental rule of the day-schools, that English only shall be spoken in them; a rule to which it must be very difficult indeed to get a practical obedience, and scarcely less cruel to attempt it; for it deprives the little things of all explanation of their hard technical tasks, however glibly they may be enabled to run off the words before them.[32]

In 1849, Fletcher maintained the teachers in the remotest parts of Wales deserved special attention and support. Although he regarded Welsh as the 'great stumbling block of the whole race', he argued that English being a foreign tongue seldom heard should be taken into account when judging children and teachers. He thus thought 'a proper use might be made of their own language, now absurdly discarded'. In particular, pupil teachers should have English-Welsh dictionaries and 'make full and active use of the vernacular dialect' to 'vivify' the English texts being read by the children. He concluded that by 'proper use of Welsh' in schools, parents could be made to realise that:

> the acquisition of the language of their desire would be more rapid and sound than upon the old rote system, to which they have so willingly had their children chained, even to making it the greatest of school offences, and that most severely punished to speak their native tongue.[33]

Perhaps sensing this message might not go down well with his employers, his 1851 report said that people would be 'no worse Britons for being good Welshmen'.[34]

Other inspectors made similar points. An 1850s education memorandum on the training college in Carmarthen called the existence of Welsh 'an embarrassment' but said knowledge of it was a necessity for those teaching the poor in Wales.[35] Revd D. Thomas's 1866–7 report on Anglican schools in north Wales stated:

> I do expect that the third standard should be taught to understand pretty fairly what they read, and have the hard words explained to them. This should always be done, as far as possible, by simpler equivalents in English. Should it however be found that Welsh children cannot be made to comprehend the English equivalents, every teacher who understands both languages should take pains to explain in Welsh, his great object being to make every lesson intelligible if he wants his scholars to become good readers, and to acquire the English language.[36]

The Revd Robert Temple, who worked in Montgomeryshire, wrote in his 1877 report:

> I strongly advise teachers in Welsh schools to make full use Welsh in teaching English, instead of tabooing their mother tongue as English is tabooed in the French hours in a 'Young Ladies' Academy'. I am sure that Welshmen will learn English much sooner through Welsh than without it.[37]

Four years later, he complained of an 'absence of care to make the children thoroughly understand what they read'.[38]

Other inspectors, however, had more circumspect attitudes. In 1845–6, Revd John Allen, an English clergyman, complained of Llanfynydd that the teacher spoke to children in Welsh but also recorded: 'An intelligent teacher' would 'take advantage of the two languages to exercise the understandings of the children, by making them translate at every step, and so assuring himself of their apprehension of the meaning of their lessons'.[39] In 1850, an inspector in the north-western district, the Revd W. J. Kennedy, wrote that assuming it was 'desirable' for English to replace Welsh as the language of Wales, it would be better to teach English and not Welsh. But he also noted his diffidence on the issue because 'our greatest living scholar', Bishop Thirwall, believed Welsh should be taught first and then English.[40] Revd H. W. Bellairs, who inspected schools in Monmouth and England, thought Welsh was causing Wales religious, moral, political, and commercial loss by reducing intercourse with the more advanced, richer and developed parts of the UK but he still maintained it was wrong to employ teachers who did not speak the mother tongue of their pupils.[41]

Some inspectors were more prejudiced towards Wales. In 1870, Revd H. Smith, an inspector for Church of England schools in Chester, Flint and Denbigh, considered the difference between schools in his district. He thought that while Welsh schools were equal to English schools in elementary examinations, 'they are certainly inferior in discipline and in general intelligence'. He conceded this might be because Welsh children struggled to understand his English pronunciation but maintained he had 'often noticed a dullness and heaviness in the Welsh children which I do not so often find in a Cheshire school'.[42] The fact that this might be because school was conducted in a foreign language did not seem to have occurred to him.

The most infamous anti-Welsh statement from an inspector came from Matthew Arnold. He became an inspector of British and other Nonconformist schools in 1851 and remained so until 1886. In his first year, he visited schools across much of Wales. He noted that Welsh children seemed quicker in apprehension than English ones but that they were hampered by having to acquire 'the medium of information, as well as the information itself'. Moreover, he claimed:

> There can, I think, be no question but that the acquirement of the English language should be more and more insisted upon by your Lordships in your relations with these schools, as the one main object for which your aid is granted. Whatever encouragement individuals may think it desirable to give to the preservation of the Welsh language on grounds of philological or antiquarian interest, it must always be the desire of a Government to render its dominions, as far as possible, homogeneous, and to break down barriers to the freest intercourse between the different parts of them. Sooner or later, the difference of language between Wales and England will probably be effaced, as has happened with the difference of language between Cornwall and the rest of England; as is now happening with the difference of language between Brittany and the rest of France; and they are not the true friends of the Welsh people, who, from a romantic interest in their manners and traditions, would impede an event which is socially and politically so desirable for them.[43]

These words later gained a certain infamy when they were quoted by Saunders Lewis in his iconic 1962 'Fate of the Language' radio broadcast. Politicians may well have agreed with Arnold but the passage should not be taken as evidence that the inspectorate or the education department thought schools should destroy the Welsh language or that it had no practical place in the classroom. They were written at the beginning of Arnold's career, when he was still finding his feet. As one biographer said of Arnold, 'He began as a naïve H.M.I. and became, in time a mediocre one.'[44] Moreover, in 1886 he told the Cross Commission that even at the start of his career he had understood that having the two languages in the classroom was an advantage. Arnold remained unsympathetic to the future of Welsh as a living language, but he had no further opportunity within the education department to call for Wales to be rendered homogenous with England because in 1853 the country was removed from his area of responsibility.[45]

The most hostile of the inspectors was a Welsh speaker himself. Shadrach Pryce (1833–1914) was a Cambridge-educated clergyman who had taught at the grammar school in Dolgellau and was an inspector from 1867 to 1894, working across different parts of mid Wales.[46] His annual reports show he had little love for his mother tongue, while the census reveals that he and his Welsh-speaking wife did not bring up their six daughters to speak it.[47] He felt education would make Welsh a 'dead language' in a few generations and that this would help Wales educationally, intellectually and commercially.[48] He claimed children spoke colloquial Welsh and that the language lacked the vocabulary to deal with what schools taught. He thus maintained that children were unable to explain in Welsh what they read in English.[49] But he also argued that language did not present 'any real difficulty' at school because the Welsh as a people were quick to pick up languages and being examined in English 'quickens their intellect'. He maintained that the work of the lower standards was so mechanical that it did not matter whether a child spoke much English and by the third standard children would know enough English to understand the teacher and 'the general scope' of reading lessons. He thus concluded a good and efficient teacher who spoke simple English to the children as soon as they started school, and used Welsh 'as sparingly as possible', would see the language 'difficulty' disappear in the higher standards. He even claimed that Welsh children had 'a special aptitude for learning a new language' and that if an English child was taught French or German in the time it took a Welsh child to learn English, they would be seen as 'quite a young prodigy'.[50]

With the use of Welsh increasing in schools, he dwelled on the topic at length in his 1882–3 report. He again outlined how Welsh was unsuitable for schools because of a lack of textbooks and technical terms in the language, as well as children's own simple vocabulary in their mother tongue. Instead, he 'unhesitatingly' felt, on the basis of years of experience and his numerous enquiries with teachers, that the best way to teach English was:

> to exclude Welsh altogether, so far as this is practicable, from the school during school hours. I have invariably found higher intelligence in the upper standards, and a more thorough knowledge of the subject matter of the reading book where this plan prevailed ... If a child is to become familiar with a new language, he should be sent among those who speak it, and where he himself is obliged, in order to make his wants known, to speak it as best he can.[51]

He maintained that an indolent teacher might make free use of Welsh to save himself 'much trouble', but:

> [a] prudent teacher, knowing that excellence in the upper classes largely depends upon a careful training in the infants' school or class, grapples with the difficulty at once, and endeavours to make the children forget Welsh and adopt English during school hours. His object is to instil a habit into the children of speaking English on all points connected with school work.[52]

It was in these attitudes that the root of the Welsh Not's persistence existed. Pryce surely informally advised teachers he was inspecting to exclude English, and whether he suggested it or not, the Welsh Not was one method of achieving that. But we should also note his 'so far as this is practicable' and his evidence that Welsh was not excluded in all schools he saw. Even he accepted the importance of making lessons pleasant and interesting and thus he acknowledged that, with younger children, 'a few Welsh words might occasionally be introduced by way of explanation.

1. 'Y *Welsh Note*'. *Trysorfa y Plant* (October 1879).

The phrase – Welsh Note – might be unfamiliar to all the children of Wales. We have not seen nor heard so much as its name for many years. But forty and fifty years ago, the children of the day schools of Wales knew well what the Welsh Note was. It drew more reproaches and tears than can be described in words to many men who are still alive and well.

2. Welsh Not found at Capel Pen-rhiw, Drefach Felindre, Carmarthenshire (Courtesy of Amgueddfa Cymru).

3. Welsh Not found at Garth school, Bangor (Courtesy of Storiel).

4. A depiction of a school in the 1820s from Charles Dickens, *The Old Curiosity Shop* (1840–1). Note the Dunce's Cap on the shelf.

5. British Infants School, Newport, built 1856 (Courtesy of Amgueddfa Cymru).

6. A rural post-1870 school in New Radnor (Courtesy of National Library of Wales).

THE
REGULATIONS
OF THE
ABERGWILLY
NATIONAL SCHOOL.

1. Children are not admitted till the Age of Six.

2. Each Child to pay One Penny per Week to the Master or Matron, every Monday Morning in advance.

3. Children must come to School clean and neat in their Persons, or they will be sent back.

4. Children must have their Hair cut short, and well combed, to come to School.

5. Morning School to commence at Eight in the Summer, and Nine in the Winter, and end at Twelve o'Clock at Noon. Afternoon School to begin at Two, and end at Five in the Summer, and Four in the Winter.

☞ Parents are earnestly requested to be very strict in enforcing Regularity of Attendance; as all Children who make a Practice of coming late, or staying away from School without Leave, will not be allowed to continue at the School.

W. Evans & Co., Printers, Carmarthen.

7. Regulations of the Abergwili National school. Probably from the first half of the century (Courtesy of Carmarthenshire Archives).

8. Pupils of Y Wern school, Llanbryn-mair, Montgomeryshire, 1890s
   (Courtesy of National Library of Wales).

9. Extract from the 1875 logbook of Aberffraw Board school noting the introduction of a form of Welsh Not (Courtesy of Anglesey Archives).

1877

August 22. Some of the parents complained of their children being allowed to speak Welsh. I cautioned the children, and made use of a (Welsh stick).

" 24. Attendance fair this day. Introduced a new song this afternoon called (Addewideon Mawr a gwerthfawr.)

" 27. Mr. Rich.d Parry attendance Officer for the Llanrwst School Board District visited. No. present 22 Boys and 23 Girls total 45. Singing (Knocking Knocking; who is there?)

" 30. Holiday. Annual Agricultural Show held at Llanrwst.

Sept. 3rd. Few extra lessons given this day at 1.30. to the second standard in Arithmetic. Attendance not so good as in the previous week owing to several of the first class children being obliged to stay at home to work in the corn.

" 5. Admitted Robert Davies Groesffordd. The Rev.d T. Jones Rector of the Parish called here this morning.

10. Extract from the 1877 logbook of Llanddoged school. Note how children were being subject to a Welsh Not and taught a song in Welsh (Courtesy of Conwy Archives).

No hard and fast rule should be laid down.' Thus, given how Pryce emphasised the importance of getting young children to understand, surely even he would have felt that the Welsh Not was unsuitable for children beginning on their journey towards understanding English. But, after the infants' stage, he felt 'English is emphatically the school language' and that 'Welsh has no place' except to 'explain the meaning of some difficult word in the lower standards'.[53]

Yet Pryce himself was not as strict on Welsh as he made out and he too made use of the language. He supported its use in object lessons for young children and in testing the understanding of older children when they read poetry and the like.[54] In 1868 he recorded his examinations were entirely in English but that before he began he often addressed 'a few kind words to the children in Welsh, to win their confidence', while he sometimes asked children in the second and third standards to give words from their reading in Welsh to see if they understood. He also used Welsh in examinations when children got something wrong but their teacher claimed they would know if asked in their own language.[55] When older children had to write down a dictated passage or compose their own version of it, he allowed teachers to first give the children a translation of it. With composition he felt this ensured children put the story into their own words rather than repeating the words they could remember.[56] As the campaign for Welsh to be recognised as part of the curriculum gathered pace at the end of the 1880s, he made his opposition very clear but even then he accepted that in examinations children should be allowed to translate a passage from Welsh rather than write their own composition.[57]

One historian has called Pryce an enemy of the Welsh language.[58] His views are certainly out of kilter with present-day views on Welsh and education, but he illustrates the complexity of what was happening in the inspectorate. He spoke against the use of Welsh but still supported its use in moderation and some contexts. Nor does he seem to have been one to impose his views on teachers or to behave in a hostile way at inspections. A 'very large' number of teachers from across Carmarthenshire attended a presentation to mark his retirement. On his death, it was said that his 'geniality and sympathetic disposition were greatly admired' by teachers.[59] What mattered with inspectors was not just what they said, but what they did.

The inspectors at work

What inspectors wrote in their reports to the education department mattered little to the teachers who were not reading them. What mattered to them was what happened on inspection day. The visit of an inspector was a momentous occasion for any school. It was prepared for with a thorough cleaning of the school and its equipment.[60] Children were told to dress as smartly as possible and were often very nervous. School hours might be extended in the weeks before, as children practised and crammed. They might also have to suffer greater use of the cane from anxious teachers, thus adding to the general sense of 'terror' around the day.[61] The inspection might be something of a spectacle too, with local people coming into the school to watch, much to the annoyance of some inspectors.[62] For teachers, the whole thing was very stressful because it decided not just their professional standing, but, in the era of the Revised Code, sometimes their wages too. Contracts where teachers were given a share of the grant were common because this enabled committees to pay smaller basic wages and it was felt to act as an incentive for more effective teaching. A man from Rhymney summed up:

> No one who was present can forget the examination day; it was like a funeral and the Judgement Day rolled into one. The hectic preparation at home, the girls in their spotless pinafores, the boys doubly brushed and scrubbed, the arrival of that terrifying ogre, Her Majesty's Inspector, with his strange English name.[63]

Certainly, some inspectors did behave in aloof, pompous ways and there were national, class and gender dynamics to their relations with the poor teacher and children they were examining.[64] Inspectors saw their examinations as ensuring the quality of education, something important because they thought teachers could be subject to 'delusions' about what they were doing and unaware of their failings.⁶⁵ Inspectors thus did not always bite their tongues or treat teachers they did not rate with respect. A young female assistant teacher remembered being called lazy by an inspector and made to promise to work harder.⁶⁶ The master at Bala British school complained he had been told to mind his own business when making suggestions on inspection day.⁶⁷ Inspector Sneyd-Kynnersley recalled that he told teachers the results on the day only if he was a 'good fellow and trustworthy' but not if he was likely to complain that the marking and exercises were too hard.⁶⁸ At Llangedwyn National school, the managers complained formally in 1865 that the inspector 'being an Englishman could not understand the children who happened to have a strong Welsh accent'. They maintained that two pupils had not made a single mistake in their reading but were still not passed.⁶⁹ Children too might struggle to understand the inspector's formal English. Even simple instructions could flummox children. One teacher remembered a girl putting her head on the desk when the inspector told the children to put their pen (also Welsh for head) down.⁷⁰ Sneyd-Kynnersley, who worked in north Wales in 1871, recalled that if he insisted on 'giving out the Dictation, my deplorable English accent will be fatal; and if I laugh at the children's efforts to talk English, they will close up like tulips in a shower'.⁷¹ He understood this was not their fault but another teacher recalled an English inspector who assumed pupils were stupid when they were unable to understand him.⁷²

Before the Revised Code, inspectors had much freedom and many were more understanding of the challenges schools faced than some historians and teachers gave them credit for. An inspector working outside Wales recorded that 'he was free to do what he thought best for those under his charge, free to take account of and adapt his teaching to varying degrees and kind of ability'.⁷³ The Newcastle Commission noted that inspectors were 'practically almost uncontrolled by the central office'.⁷⁴ The Revised Code changed this by making conducting examinations an inspector's primary role: some thus complained that they were therefore not allowed to explore what children knew and thought.⁷⁵ In contrast, other inspectors did things their own way. Sneyd-

Kynnersley noted the education department wanted every fourth infant to be strictly examined but he did not do this: 'A little experience taught me that infants should be left in the hands of their own teachers, and that the inspectors should look on.' Only an enthusiastic inspector would, he claimed, carry on enquiries 'to any length'.[76]

It was this freedom that laid the basis for Welsh to have some place in both the examinations and advice of HMIs. Rather than being agents of an alien British state, the inspectors muted the effect of its policies and, regardless of their views of the place of Welsh, they made clear in their annual reports to the education department the difficulties Welsh schools faced. In their reports, they also seemed to have glossed over how little was being learned and understood, probably for fear of discouraging managers and teachers. Most notably, inspectors exercised some judgement in deciding what constituted a grant-earning pass under the Revised Code. Across England and Wales, most inspectors, if not all, were generally generous when it came to deciding results. Hurt argued that after the Revised Code, 'Bad teaching and harsh discipline could have been penalised. They seldom, if ever, were.'[77] One reason for this leniency was that inspectors knew perfectly well that cutting the grant of a poor school 'only aggravates the evil'; maybe leaving it unable to buy new books, employ a pupil teacher or a better master.[78]

Teachers and managers in Wales often felt disadvantaged by the fact that Welsh-speaking children were subject to the same examinations as children in England but they did not see how inspectors took into account the linguistic challenges their schools faced.[79] In 1870, William Williams, then inspecting British schools across Wales, reported: 'it would be unreasonable to expect children to read with due emphasis and expression what they only imperfectly understand'.[80] Sometimes inspectors' lack of Welsh led them to err on the side of generosity because they could not actually test the children's understanding by asking questions in their own language as some other inspectors did. In 1867, D. R. Fearon, an Englishman who examined British schools, adopted a Welsh Standard and an English Standard. Noting how there were localities where 'very little English is understood, and where parents and children never speak it except when they are compelled to do so', he stated it would be 'very harsh' to apply the same standards used in examining English schools. In Welsh schools he did not require that the children read 'with perfect correctness or with intelligence' and was content to pass them 'if they can decipher the text mechanically, and read intelligibly, though with a foreign accent'. He gave shorter dictations and allowed the teacher to read it to the children. In arithmetic, he read the sums more slowly and more distinctly and gave the pupils more time than he allowed in schools in English-speaking areas. He noted with children unable to translate even simple words, reading could only be mechanical and all that was required was to be able to pronounce words seen in print.[81]

His method generated some complaints that it meant it was easier for British rather than Anglican schools to get a grant.[82] This was perhaps true since Revd B. J. Binns, then inspector for Church of England schools in south Wales, was rather less sympathetic. In his 1863 report, he had responded to concerns around holding Welsh and English children to the same standard, that a pass was 'easily reached' if children were sent to school young enough and taught properly. He did, however, concede that in the north, where English was less spoken, matters might be different.[83] In response to concerns that different standards were being applied, a common method was agreed among inspectors, although it did not, formally at least, make Fearon's distinctions, except in dictation.[84] Indeed, one of the Anglican inspectors Fearon was supposed to have come to an arrangement with was Pryce, who refused teachers and managers' request that he use some Welsh to test children's religious knowledge.[85] But Pryce also said that in examining reading in Welsh-speaking districts he gave children 'the benefit of the doubt'.[86]

The reports on individual schools also show that inspectors were generally understanding and flexible. Schools where the logbooks were a litany of complaints about linguistic problems could still receive good inspection reports.[87] Some annual reports made it explicit that the inspector had taken into account the school's linguistic situation. The 1868 report for Croes-goch, for example, noted: 'The reading in most of the standards is rather weak, but this is due in some degree, to the fact that the reading books used in the various classes are too difficult for a rural school'.[88] The annual report on Hope Board school in 1878 said the grammar was passable, 'making some allowance for the special difficulties of Welsh-speaking children'.[89] The 1879 report for Dylife National school noted that the lower part of the school was 'so bad' that it was only a consideration of the difficulties faced by 'a purely English master ... in a purely Welsh district that prevents me from advising a reduction of the grant'.[90] The Revd Robert Temple awarded a merit grant to Pennant National school in 1889 seemingly because of the challenge he recognised of the school being very small, 'exceedingly Welsh' and under one teacher rather than because of its exam results.[91] Indeed, inspectors often seemed softer than their teachers. In 1874 the new master of Llandysul National school complained: 'Most of the children spell words readily, but are totally unacquainted with their meaning.' Yet the previous year's inspection report had been very positive and contained no such complaint.[92]

Such leniency was the product of inspectors' experience. Some teachers thus claimed that when a new inspector came into Wales from England pass rates dropped substantially.[93] Flexibility was officially sanctioned in 1875 when inspectors were formally allowed to use Welsh to test the understanding of children.[94] This was supposed to increase the emphasis on teaching children the meaning of what they read, something which could only be done by employing their mother tongue. Some inspectors were already doing that but others now adopted the technique. At Meifod National school, the inspection report for 1876 noted that the teacher had been hitherto 'used to think too much of routine and too little of general knowledge and intelligence, but I have no doubt that the bracing effects of the Code of 1875 will cure this'.[95] In 1883, inspectors everywhere were told to 'make reasonable allowance' for 'special circumstances', such as a 'shifting, scattered, very poor or ignorant population'.[96] In response, John Bancroft, an inspector in Pembrokeshire, said he had always made allowance for the special circumstances of Welsh-speaking districts and always would do so.[97]

Encouraged, some inspectors pushed for further changes to recognise the difficulties faced by Welsh-speaking schools. In 1888, the inspector for the Merthyr district argued that, given children were learning a language not colloquially familiar to them, one reading book in Welsh should also be used. In Pembrokeshire, Bancroft started using a composition task with Standard V where he read a story in Welsh and English and asked children to write their own version of it. Composition was particularly difficult for children in Welsh-speaking areas and, at the end of the 1880s, the chief inspector in Wales called for it to be dropped from examinations and replaced by translations from Welsh into English.[98] This was implemented in 1890 when inspectors were officially allowed to replace composition with a translation into English of 'an easy piece' of Welsh writing from the blackboard or a story read to them twice.[99] The fact that this was not required by the education department again illustrates how much discretion individual inspectors had.

Not all inspectors were convinced about the value of using Welsh to test children. Pryce called the 1875 ruling 'worthless and impracticable', and stuck to his guns that the most efficient and popular schools were those where no Welsh was used.[100] The Cross Commission heard complaints that inspectors were not using Welsh in their examinations.[101] Even William Williams, the chief inspector for Wales, seemed more concerned with the fluency and expression in reading than whether children understood the meaning. He said he never examined in Welsh but sometimes asked children to translate words to see if they understood what they read.[102] Some inspectors did not like using Welsh because they felt the children's ability in that language was insufficient. In Glamorganshire, an inspector called the regulation allowing Welsh in inspections 'almost a dead letter', since most scholars' Welsh 'is limited to what suffices for everyday purposes, and they are wholly unable to translate a short passage from their reading book, either orally or in writing, with approach to correctness'.[103] This was probably overstating things or perhaps even a degree of snobbery about what constituted correct Welsh. There were claims that inspectors' Welsh was too formal and removed from the colloquial Welsh of children. Children's apparent problems in answering questions in Welsh when being examined may just have been a question of practice because they were not used to talking about lessons in their mother tongue. There were also suggestions that children might even be reluctant to use Welsh having 'been accustomed to doubt the value of his native language'.[104]

The discretion allowed and different approaches of inspectors meant schools were not all subject to the same pressures when it came to using and managing Welsh in the classroom. What teachers were told or advised came down to who they were inspected by, and that was not the same person each year. It seems very unlikely that any inspector advised that children should be physically punished for speaking Welsh. Although they might report that general discipline was not strict enough, most inspectors pushed against the excessive use of physical punishment.[105] In 1848, for example, one inspector composed a letter to be given to teachers newly appointed to a workhouse school. In it he reminded them of the rule that only boys should be given corporal punishment and not until two hours after the offence. He concluded, 'I beg of you not to resort to this mode of punishment except in extreme cases where every milder means shall have proved fruitless. Kindness and firmness are by the far the most effective powers.'[106]

No inspector made any comment on the Welsh Not itself in their reports, but that does not mean that Pryce and others did not encourage its use, even if only indirectly. The 1868 report for Llanwenog National school, for example, stated:

> I would advise the managers to recommend the master to discontinue talking Welsh to the children except when there is an absolute necessity for doing so and even then to use it most sparingly; experience has proved that this ultimately is the best plan both with regard to discipline and efficiency.[107]

In 1878, the report for Ystumtuen said that: 'The mistress ought not to speak Welsh to the scholars as she does but should train them to understand and speak English.'[108] At Capel Evan, where there was a rule of no Welsh during school hours, the report for 1872 noted: 'The teacher should endeavour to get the Scholars to speak English more than they do now.'[109] Such examples made no reference to the Welsh Not but it could have come up in the inspector's informal discussions with the teacher, or the teacher might have turned to it of their own volition in response to the written report.

In contrast, far more schools received the opposite advice. At Penyrheolgerrig Infant school, the 1881 inspection report stated: 'The children being almost entirely Welsh need more care than usual to make them thoroughly comprehend what they learn.'[110] Brithdir was criticised in 1887 because children did not know the meaning of the words they read. In 1896, its inspection report declared: 'Efforts should be made to secure better expression in the Reading, to increase the intelligence of the children, and widen their knowledge of English, by explaining and translating the books read.'[111] In 1875, Staylittle Board school was criticised for making no effort to develop the intelligence of older scholars, which meant employing Welsh to test and enhance their understanding. However, no deduction in the grant was made on account of there being no pupil teacher to help and in 'consideration of the purely Welsh character of the children'. The year before, the school had been told that pupils should know twelve secular songs and it did not matter if they were in Welsh or English. After struggling with English songs because the children did not understand the words, the master taught 'Ar Hyd y Nos' instead.[112] The advice had come from the Revd Robert Temple who was a particular advocate for the use of Welsh. He told Rhiwhiriaeth Board school that pupils should 'be made to give Welsh equivalents of English words and vice versa as the best way of teaching them English'.[113] A teacher who used the Welsh Not at Llanfihangel was criticised by inspection reports for lacking energy in his work and for his pupils being backwards.[114] In contrast, where Welsh was used, inspectors might offer praise in the formal reports, something which mattered when managers who might hold different views to teachers, were reading. The 1876 report on Llanerfyl, for example, attributed the pupils' good knowledge to the use of Welsh in the school.[115] In 1895, the report for Pennant National school, which employed an English-monoglot teacher, recorded: 'The children are totally Welsh speaking and it is highly desirable that the teacher should have some knowledge of Welsh.' No grant was recommended because the inspector was 'unable to report that the staff is efficient'. Two days after receiving the report, the teacher sent in his resignation. The next teacher employed did speak Welsh and his first report noted a marked improvement in results and methods of teaching.[116] Sometimes the advice was more forceful. A man born in 1881 remembered an inspector coming to his school, asking a question in Welsh and no one replying. When the inspector asked the children in English why they did not answer, one child said they were afraid of the master. The inspector then told them, and the teacher, they would be allowed to speak Welsh from the following day.[117]

Such advice was partly a product of how the inspectorate was changing. It expanded significantly after 1870 and some of the new assistant inspectors were former teachers and were very sympathetic to Welsh and the travails of their formal peers.[118] In recommending the use of Welsh some inspectors were also drawing upon their own memories of being at schools where it was excluded.[119] The ability to speak Welsh seems to have been part of the reason why some individuals were recruited; by the late 1880s it was asserted that the majority of inspectors could speak Welsh, although the education department thought this was not 'a necessity'.[120] In the wake of the 1886–7 Cross Commission, one campaigner maintained that while there were still some of inspectors of the old mould, 'the present generation has seen rather a remarkable change of front, or at any rate, the beginning of such a change, which it is much to be hoped will be a considerable factor in introducing a healthier state of things both socially and intellectually into the principality'.[121]

But encouraging the use of Welsh as a means of explanation was not the same as encouraging its free use. Bancroft asked children to translate sentences into Welsh in his inspections and argued that the use of Welsh in teaching English was very desirable and no intelligent teacher would not do this.[122] But he also felt that children should be speaking English. In his 1880 report on Elerch, he instructed: 'It is highly desirable that more intelligence should be thrown into the teaching and the use of English should be encouraged.'[123] The Revd E. T. Watts, who inspected in the north, told Irish educationalists that using Welsh for explanations was sensible but he feared that it was too often 'indulged in', with the result that children's acquisition of English was being held back. He argued children learned the language fastest in schools where Welsh was 'sparingly' used or where teachers did not speak the language.[124] The chief inspector in Wales, who accepted Welsh had some use in education, noted how composition was the least satisfactory topic in Welsh schools because 'children have been in the habit of speaking Welsh, and can command but a very limited vocabulary in English'. He noted that some teachers encouraged children to speak English and had them practise oral translation which produced very praiseworthy results.[125] Even at the end of the 1890s, by when Welsh was formally allowed as a topic in itself, some inspection reports were still recommending Welsh only be used 'when really necessary'.[126]

Whether they encouraged or discouraged the use of Welsh, inspectors were sure that Welsh schools were not losing out under their inspections. In 1885, Bancroft compared schools in the English- and Welsh-speaking areas of Pembrokeshire and found similar results for the merit grant, with Welsh schools actually having a higher proportion of students graded as good rather than fair. He concluded the Welsh schools 'have no cause for complaint'.[127] This was also broadly true at a national level. In 1887–8, for example, the overall pass rates in Wales were lower than the average for England and Wales but by less than a percentage point in reading and writing and less than three in arithmetic.[128] However, in defending their comparative treatment of Welsh-speaking and English-speaking schools, inspectors did unwittingly reveal how much pass rates varied between different HMIs rather than different languages. The Revd H. Smith examined Church schools in Chester, Flint and Denbigh and in 1870 reflected that there was little difference in examination results, with 91.4 per cent passes in English schools and 91.3 per cent in Welsh schools. This, he argued, showed they had not suffered from 'the supposed disadvantage of having an English instead of a Welsh-speaking inspector'. But other HMIs had both different pass rates and patterns. The Revd E. T. Watts inspected Church schools in north Wales in the same year and compared them to Wiltshire. Arithmetic was significantly worse in Wiltshire but reading was worse in every Welsh county by a few percentage points. Overall, the pass rate ranged from 84.2 per cent in Denbigh to 76.9 in Meirionnydd. In Wiltshire, it was 75.4 per cent.[129] The diversity of individual opinions was also evident when HMI reports are compared with those from the diocesan inspectors who visited National schools. In 1887, for example, Ruabon Boys National school's HMI report stated that 'the work of this school is by no means what it should be', whereas that year's diocesan report concluded, 'This is a very good school.'[130]

Even allowing for the different patterns, the fact that everywhere the majority of pupils entering examinations were passing is also a reminder of the shortcomings of the Revised Code. However much an inspector adapted things, they were still ultimately tests of preparation. If a child had learned to read or write a passage with relative fluency, it did not matter much to the outcome whether they understood it or not.[131] An inspector might work out that children did not understand much but that did not mean they would withhold the grant for something regurgitated from memory and practise. Indeed, inspectors learned not to expect too much. In 1881 the HMI report for Llanfihangel National school said children should: 'understand to some extent when they read'.[132] The 'to some extent' showed they too lacked in ambition.

The influence of inspectors

Some inspectors recorded that teachers appreciated their counsel and the opportunity to discuss issues.[133] Pryce said he had had no 'unpleasant friction' in his dealings with teachers and 'my suggestions have generally been acted upon, and even any necessary fault finding was, I believe, received in no unkindly spirit'.[134] Some teachers also reported that they were indebted to the inspectors' suggestions over methods and the general conduct of schools.[135] After a very poor examination, the master of Blaenau Llangernyw British school said he did not blame the inspector who had been 'very kind indeed'.[136] After being visited by an English diocesan inspector, a teacher in Capel Curig recorded that the inspector had been sympathetic and understanding of the difficulties faced by the rural school teacher. He found the visit and positive report uplifting.[137] That was written in private and seemed a genuine sentiment. Others perhaps only took on board advice in the hope of receiving a sympathetic inspection the following year. After Staylittle Board school was criticised for not developing or testing the intelligence of scholars, the master made it very clear in his logbook in subsequent months that he was working with pupils on their understanding. He also recorded that the children 'seemed pleased with the method' and that their English was rapidly improving.[138] That was probably true, but it is still difficult not to think that by recording it the teacher was making it clear to his inspector that he had listened.

Other teachers had very different experiences. They could feel looked down upon or patronised. Some distrusted inspectors because they were churchmen contemptuous of Nonconformists.[139] Others felt ill at ease with inspectors because they were both English and from a higher class. This might result in the use of condescending language that offended, even when it was not intended to. Despite speaking Welsh himself, the Revd E. T. Watts, for example, wrote in his 1871 report on Corris British school: 'All the children however read with more than ordinary expression and intelligence considering the Welshey character of the district.'[140] Census entries show that Watts did pass the language on to his own children and thus he was not someone who wanted to see Welsh disappear. Yet others did apparently want that, or at least were thought to by some teachers. In 1885, a Glamorganshire teacher claimed that inspectors were not allowing children to answer their questions in Welsh, even though the regulations permitted this. He concluded: 'The great majority of the inspectors are rank Englishmen, whose hobby it is to stamp out the Welsh language altogether.'[141] There were stories of inspectors making misleading statements. William Williams was said to have told the master at Rhydlewis, an Englishman who had learned Welsh, that he was 'breaking the law' by teaching them Welsh songs.[142] Perhaps it was no surprise then that in 1893, O. M. Edwards listed prejudiced inspectors as one of the problems facing the place of Welsh in schools.[143]

The behaviour and demeanour of some inspectors led some teachers to not understand the freedom and discretion they had to use

Welsh if they wished to. Some teachers seem to have prohibited Welsh because they thought that was what inspectors wanted them to do. One later excused his use of the Welsh Not at Garndolbenmaen Board school in the 1870s by pointing to how he had experienced it as a pupil and what he described as the hostility of inspectors and the education department towards Welsh. He wrongly remembered that it was a rule of the department that no Welsh should be used in school. There was perhaps a degree of trying to shift the blame here, but his confusion was not surprising given he was told off for teaching a Welsh song by the inspector Revd E. T. Watts who said 'How can you expect them to learn English when you actually teach them Welsh? You must never do such a thing again.'[144] Another inspector recalled being told by a teacher that he read a chapter of the Bible every morning in English because Welsh was 'discouraged' by the education department. When asked if the children understood it, the teacher replied, 'Well, no, indeed; but it is just while they are coming in, and it doesn't matter.'[145] Most inspectors, especially as the century progressed, did accept teachers utilising Welsh but it does seem that some were not emphatic enough in making that clear, with their patronising and superior demeanours leading some schools to adopt precisely the opposite practice.

But teachers did not just accept what inspectors said or did. For some teachers, the Revised Code meant the inspectors were there to be beaten rather than worked with. They might appeal to inspectors to interpret the code leniently but also strove to ensure the children would not fail. Everything was practised and practised so the examination became a test of memory rather than ability. Teachers might also mislead or cheat inspectors. When they knew an inspector would allow them to choose the subject of a composition, they would get children to learn what they would write beforehand.[146] Another trick was to bend the reading book from which the inspector would choose a random passage so that it fell open on a section that the teacher had prepared with the class.[147] Registers might be altered to show higher attendances or add fictious children in order to raise the potential grant. Children who had left school or were from elsewhere might be substituted for those less able to pass the exam. Stories of such practices were 'generally believed' by inspectors but they were difficult to uncover when children had so few surnames, particularly if the inspector was unable to speak Welsh and thus could not make enquiries.[148]

Teachers also made sure inspectors knew the challenges they faced by filling their logbooks with accounts of poor attendance and linguistic difficulties. Pryce, in his determination that language was not a problem, felt references to it were an excuse for hopeless, careless or indolent teaching, but other inspectors were probably more understanding.[149] Inspectors were not just enforcers of regulations, they did listen to teachers and communicated what they learned to the education department.[150] Indeed, the inspectorate became an important force in making schools and the education department more hospitable to the Welsh language. It was the feedback of inspectors, inspired by what they saw and heard from teachers, that saw the gradual modifications of the Revised Code. Their use of Welsh in inspections, formally sanctioned from 1875, encouraged teachers to do the same. From 1890, inspectors were allowed to replace composition examinations with translation exercises. This, in turn, encouraged schools to teach children to translate into both Welsh and English. The new generation of inspectors who came in after 1870 were an important part of the push for Welsh to be recognised as a subject rather than just as a means of explaining. A particularly important voice was Dan Isaac Davies (1839–87), who knew the value of Welsh from his own experience of being a teacher and inspecting schools in the south. He wanted a bilingual Wales and actively campaigned for the place of Welsh in schools, publishing a series of letters on the subject in *Baner ac Amserau Cymru*, which were then released as a book.[151] For Davies, making Welsh a subject was not just about money or practicalities: he valued the language for its national and literary worth and wanted literary Welsh taught so that children were not just speaking the patois of the street.[152] His voice helped persuade the education department to start recognising Welsh as a distinct subject. There were still sceptical voices within the inspectorate, but they were now up against central pressure. In 1893, the code was changed to instruct inspectors to draw teachers' attention to the advantages of using Welsh and make use of it themselves in testing children.[153] By 1908, one newspaper was noting that inspectors in the north did not speak a word of English to the children and that schoolmasters blushed to hear them greet the children in Welsh. What a change since the days of the Welsh Note, it reflected.[154] By then Welsh had still not firmly established itself within the curricula of schools but that was down to local decisions, not the guidance of inspectors.

Conclusion

Like the grants made to teachers who passed an exam in the 1850s or the sanctioning of inspectors' use of Welsh in examinations, the changes of the 1890s were not the product of some big shift of mindset in the education department, but rather listening to the campaigning in Wales and the comments of the inspectors. It was not that the department was hostile to Welsh but more that it did not think about the issue unless it was forced to. The 1870 Act made no special provision for Wales because there was no pressure on government to do so and the education department seemed incapable of thinking about Welsh needs without repeated prompting. Despite the fact that from 1874 its annual report bore the subtitle 'England and Wales', England was always its default mindset and for who its codes and regulations were written. This could result in some silly situations. In 1884, for example, a teacher at Bryngwran Board school complained how hard it was to teach children, who were 'totally ignorant of the meaning of the commonest English words', why some were verbs and others nouns. Indeed, he wondered what the point of this was, but noted that the 'powers that be' required him to do at Standard II and he was 'duty bound to obey them to the best of our ability'.[155]

The inspectors working in Wales were a bulwark against such situations but their repeated assertions of the need to take into account Welsh conditions were slow to hit home. In 1878, Revd B. J. Binns, an inspector in Glamorgan, felt the omission of Wales from the code's description of geography for Standard III was 'perhaps an accidental omission', but argued that, 'A knowledge of their own country is certainly desirable in Welsh children, and ought by no means to be taken for granted.'[156] But it still took the department another fifteen years, and the forcible calls for Welsh needs to be addressed in the Cross Commission, for it to formally allow Welsh geography to be taught. Even after making concessions in the 1890s, the department was still not fully attuned to Welsh linguistic needs. It failed to commission the bilingual books that might have helped both the teaching of Welsh and other subjects. In 1897, it appointed Albert G. Legard as chief inspector for Wales only to face a backlash because he did not speak Welsh. The government defended this by pointing to how little use had been made by schools of their new right to teach Welsh. Nonetheless, Legard made clear that he 'fully approved' of the use of Welsh for the more efficient teaching of English.[157]

It is unsurprising that some contemporaries felt the state was deeply hostile to the language considering the state's slow and hesitant action on the position of Welsh in schools. One former teacher later wrote that the board schools were erected by the education department to worship the English language.[158] In 1888, one campaigner argued that the education department had long regarded Welsh as a 'vexatious obstacle to the unification of the country', had ignored it as much as possible, and ridden roughshod over the idea that Wales required different treatment to England.[159] Some thought the state was working towards the extinction of Welsh. This was perhaps not surprising given how Welsh was often seen by state administrators as a backwards relic from the past. The memories of what had been written in the Blue Books and elsewhere lingered long. Angry at the failure of a proposal to allow Welsh children to be examined at an older age than those in England, in 1862, the editor of *Carnarvon and Denbigh Herald* claimed:

> it is the sound policy and the firm determination of the English governments, be they Radical, Whig or Tory, to extirpate the tongue of Wales; and that as a means to that end, they will visit the sons of Cambria with every possible lingual evil, giving them not only English law, English judges, English bishops and English

schools, but forcing them to learn English and teach it to their children by making the same age for examination hold with respect to the child of English parents resident in Wales and the poor monoglot youngsters of Wales itself, who know and have from infancy known no other language than that of their native hills.[160]

Such broad interpretations misrepresented how much power the state actually had and its reluctance to interfere in any sphere of life beyond the defence of the realm. In 1862, education was neither compulsory or free, and the state only funded it via third parties which it had limited control over. Public administration was in English but did not mean that there was an actual policy or determination to kill Welsh. Schools were in English but that had been the case before government intervention because they were run by and for Welsh people and that was what people wanted. Of course, the state wanted the people of Wales to learn English too but, as Osterhammel notes, 'Popular education could not be simply forced down people's throats. It could be successful only if they associated their own desires and interests with it.'[161]

As modern nation states developed across Europe, there was a sense that linguistic uniformity was desirable and useful, and education could help bring this about. Hobsbawm argues that this was 'entirely democratic ... How could citizens understand, let alone take part in, the government of their country if it was conducted in an incomprehensible language?' But achieving this was not easy. As Hobsbawm again put it, 'in the absence of a willingness to change languages, national linguistic homogeneity in multi-ethnic and multi-lingual areas can be achieved only by mass compulsion, expulsion, or genocide'.[162] Such extreme action was not in the character of the British state, at least at home. Moreover, the state knew this was not needed. Once the turmoil of the 1830s and 1840s had passed, Welsh was seen as an 'inconvenience' rather than a threat.[163] The sense that Welsh was a language of the past meant its death was regarded as inevitable. If people could not be compelled, there was no need to go through such an unpleasant and difficult exercise when all the evidence from Wales said people wanted to learn English. The British state, in its desire for linguistic uniformity, was content to facilitate the teaching of English, in order to eradicate Welsh monolingualism, and then sit back and wait for Welsh to die.

The state also had wider reasons for funding education, both in Wales and the rest of the UK. An educated people able to read the Bible was thought to be more accepting of the social order and more moral in its behaviour. The state sought to combat problems such as destitution, drunkenness, disease and violence by raising the morals and prospects of the working class and infusing them with bourgeois values such as hard work, discipline and thrift.[164] As Richard Johnson put it, 'Supervised by its trusty teacher, surrounded by its playground wall, the school was to raise a new race of working people – respectful, cheerful, hard-working, loyal, pacific and religious.'[165] But achieving any of this with a limited budget, a laissez-faire attitude and all schools under local control was a different matter. In these circumstances, all the state could do was use its funding and inspections to try to dictate and direct. But this depended on inspectors being willing to implement its rules, and training colleges, schools and teachers being willing to follow them. All had their own minds and ideas.

The inspectors were the most important part of this chain since it was through them that schools learned of what they were supposed to do and were assessed on how well they did it and thus how well funded they would be. The inspectorate was far from perfect. Some were not from Wales and did not understand the communities they were visiting. Some of those that were from Wales had little sympathy for their native linguistic culture and encouraged teachers to banish the language from schools. Many were snobs. Too many were more concerned with religious rather than educational needs. Their words could seem unsympathetic too, although describing a lack of English as 'ignorance' or 'backwards, or calling Welsh 'the great stumbling block', were not meant quite as harshly as they now sound.[166] But even inspectors with these prejudices played an important role in persuading teachers to employ the language. They were a key reason why the language gradually found a place at schools and why both the practice and spirit of the Welsh Not were banished. This was, however, slow work and not helped by the inspectors not speaking in a single voice on the issue. It also faced the problem of how deeply ingrained prejudices towards the use of Welsh were in communities and among many teachers. There was also the very practical issue that an annual visit was never going to be an effective means of enforcing change in the rest of the year. This lack of unanimity in Wales over the need for Welsh to be used in schools might explain why, despite the recommendations of the Blue Books, Newcastle Commission, Cross Commission and others, the education department did not explicitly state that Welsh should be used in schools until 1900.

Wales was on the geographical and mental periphery of the United Kingdom. Most of the time, it was out of Westminster's sight and mind. Education policies were typical of this. They were not intentionally anti-Welsh in any explicit way. Their impact on Wales had simply not been thought about by anyone in a position of authority within the British state. There were voices telling them of the need to treat Wales differently but they were not loud or unanimous enough. It was thus easy for them to take the second place to the desire for administrative uniformity. But, regardless of intention, the impact on Wales – its people, its culture, and its language – was nonetheless detrimental. The British state may not have taken actions intended to hurt Welsh but nor did it do anything to protect or nurture it either. Unlike, for example, the Austria-Hungary Empire from 1867, which gave children a right to education in their mother tongue and used schools to develop a vision of the state as a 'family of nations', the British state had a blinkered understanding of its national identity.[167] Its Britishness was not the United Kingdom's multinational reality but a narrow and often conceited Englishness. It failed to place any value on nurturing bilingualism because it assumed the English language and culture were superior and more important. But this view was shared in Wales too, not because people were brainwashed by the state but because the economic realities of an English-centric union had created that situation.

Notes

1. Oliver MacDonagh, 'The nineteenth-century revolution in government: a reappraisal', *Historical Journal*, 1 (1958), 52–67; David Eastwood, *Government and Community in the English Provinces, 1700–1870* (London, 1997); Philip Harling, 'The centrality of locality: the local state, local democracy, and local consciousness in late-Victorian and Edwardian Britain', *Journal of Victorian Culture*, 9, 2 (2004), 216–34.
2. This viewpoint was influenced by her views on Scottish Highlanders: she thought a Gaelic education would keep them in 'their simplicity of character'. The fact that the government did not seek to ensure either Welsh or Gaelic were taught showed the limits of Royal power. Arthur Christopher Benson and Viscount Esther (eds), *The Letters of Queen Victoria*, vol. II (London, 1908), p. 255.
3. Robert Smith, *Schools, Politics and Society: Elementary Education in Wales, 1870–1902* (Cardiff, 1999), p. 275. For a more sympathetic overview see Russell Grigg, 'Origins and development of the inspectorate in Wales, 1839–1907', in Ann Keane (ed.), *Watchdogs or Visionaries? Perspectives on the History of the Education Inspectorate in Wales* (Cardiff, 2022), pp. 21–45.
4. W. Gareth Evans, 'The British state and Welsh-language education, 1850–1914', in Geraint H. Jenkins (ed.), *The Welsh Language and its Social Domains* (Cardiff, 2000), pp. 459–82, 466; W. Gareth Evans, 'The "bilingual difficulty": HMI and the Welsh language in the Victorian age', *Welsh History Review*, 16, 4 (1993), 494–513.
5. Bryncroes Board school (CRO) opened in 1882 and by 1900 had received just six visits without notice.
6. *Minutes of the CCE, 1840–41*, p. 1; Russell Grigg, '"Wading through children's tears": the emotional experiences of elementary school inspections, 1839–1911', *History of Education*, 49, 5 (2020), 597–616, 600.
7. Anne Digby and Peter Searby, *Children, School and Society in Nineteenth-Century England* (London, 1981), pp. 7–8.
8. Edmond Holmes, *In Quest of an Ideal: An Autobiography* (London, 1920), p. 62.
9. This is particularly true in the case of Joseph Bowstead who helped recruit teachers and encouraged the formation of British schools in communities. His 1854 report to the education department was published as a pamphlet by the British Society under the title *British Schools Best Adapted to the Educational Wants of Wales* (1855). Idwal Jones, 'The voluntary system at work: a history of the British School Society', *Transactions of the Honourable Society of Cymmrodorion*, (1931–2), 72–164, 120, 125.
10. Holmes, *In Quest of an Ideal*, p. 17.
11. R. M. Theobald, *Memorials of John Daniel Morell, M. A., LL. D. Her Majesty's Inspector of Schools* (London, 1891); CA, Newgate British, 27 September 1864.
12. Michael Gareth Llewelyn, *Sand in the Glass* (London, 1943), p. 7.
13. J. E. Dunford, 'Biographical details of Her Majesty's Inspectors appointed before 1870', *History of Education Society Bulletin*, 28 (1981), 8–23.
14. *Report of the CCE, 1894–95*, p. 115.

15 *Minutes of the CCE, 1847–48*, p. xxvii.
16 H. G. Williams, 'Longueville Jones and Welsh education: the neglected case of a Victorian H.M.I.', *Welsh History Review*, 15, 1 (1990), 416–42.
17 *Minutes of the CCE, 1848–49–50*, vol. II, p. 210.
18 *Minutes of the CCE, 1850–51*, vol. II, p. 511.
19 *Minutes of the CCE, 1850–51*, p. 511.
20 Williams, 'Longueville Jones', 427.
21 *Minutes of the CCE, 1855–56*, p. 449.
22 H. G. Williams, 'Jones, Harry Longueville (1806–1870), inspector of schools and antiquary', *Oxford Dictionary of National Biography;* H. G. Williams, 'Nation state versus national Identity: state and inspectorate in Mid-Victorian Wales', *History of Education Quarterly*, 40, 2 (2000), 145–68, 164–6; H. G. Williams, 'Longueville Jones, Ralph Lingen and inspectors' reports: a tragedy of Welsh education', *History of Education*, 25, 1 (1996), 19–36.
23 Williams, 'State and inspectorate', 146, 167.
24 PA, Newtown National, 1863 report.
25 *Minutes of the CCE, 1854–55*, p. 602.
26 *Minutes of the 1856–57*, pp. 505–6.
27 *Report of the CCE, 1858–59*, p. 140.
28 *Minutes of the CCE, 1848–49–50*, vol II (London 1850), pp. 206–7.
29 Evans, 'The "bilingual difficulty"'.
30 *Report of the CCE, 1859–60*, p. 297.
31 Evans, 'The "bilingual difficulty"', 325.
32 *Minutes of the CCE, 1846*, p. 305.
33 *Minutes of the CCE, 1848–49–50*, vol. II, pp. 293–6.
34 *Minutes of the CCE, 1851–52*, p. 502.
35 *Minutes of the CCE, 1852–53*, p. 387.
36 *Report of the CCE, 1866–67*, pp. 217–18.
37 *Report of the CCE, 1877–78*, p. 566.
38 *Report of the CCE, 1881–82*, p. 455.
39 *Minutes of the CCE, 1845*, pp. 77, 73.
40 *Minutes of the CCE, 1848–49–50*, vol II, p. 186.
41 *Minutes of CCE, 1854–55*, p. 408.
42 *Report of the CCE, 1870–71*, p. 189.
43 *Minutes of the CCE, 1852–53*, vol. I, pp. 674, 675.
44 Park Honan, *Matthew Arnold: A Life* (London, 1981), p. 258.
45 *First Report of the Royal Commission appointed to Inquire into the Working of the Elementary Education Acts, England and Wales*, vol. 1 (London, 1886), p. 219 [hereafter Cross Commission]; Nicholas Murray, *A Life of Matthew Arnold* (London, 1996), pp. 120, 132. For Arnold's views on Welsh see his *On the Study of Celtic Literature* (London, 1867).
46 For more on Pryce see W. Gareth Evans, '"Gelyn yr iaith Gymraeg": Y Parchedig Shadrach Pryce A.E.M., a meddylfryd yr Arolygiaeth yn Oes Fictoria', *Y Traethodydd*, 149 (1994), 73–81.

47 Census entry for Pryce family, Bryneithyn, Llandilofawr, Carmarthenshire, 1891.
48 *Report of the CCE, 1868–69*, pp. 165–6.
49 *Report of the CCE, 1878–79*, p. 674.
50 *Reports of the CCE, 1868–69*, pp. 164–5; *1878–79*, p. 674.
51 *Report of the CCE, 1882–83*, pp. 420–1, 422.
52 *Report of the CCE, 1882–83*, p. 421.
53 *Report of the CCE, 1882–83*, pp. 421–2.
54 *Report of the CCE, 1888–89*, p. 366.
55 *Report of the CCE, 1868–69*, p. 165.
56 *Reports of the CCE, 1882–83*, pp. 422–3; *1888–89*, pp. 345–6.
57 *Report of the CCE, 1886–87*, p. 364.
58 Evans, 'Gelyn yr iaith Gymraeg'.
59 'Presentation to the Rev. Shadrach Pryce', *Aberystwith Observer*, 21 February 1895, 3; 'Death of the Rev Shadrach Pryce', *Carmarthen Weekly Report*, 25 September 1914, 1.
60 Abel J. Jones, *I was Privileged* (Cardiff, 1943), p. 74. For a description of an 1890s inspection see Thomas Richard, *Atgofion Cardi* (Aberystwyth, 1960), ch. 4.
61 Edmund Stonelake, *The Autobiography of Edmund Stonelake* (Bridgend, 1981), p. 48.
62 *Minutes of the CCE, 1870–71*, p. 150; John Hurt, *Education in Evolution: Church, State, Society and Popular Education, 1800–1870* (London, 1971), p. 130.
63 Thomas Jones, *Rhymney Memories* (1938; Llandysul, 1970), p. 49. Also see Llewelyn, *Sand in the Glass*, pp. 9–10; E. M. Sneyd-Kynnersley, *HMI: Some Passages in the Life of One of H.M. Inspectors of Schools* (London, 1913), p. 42.
64 Pamela Horn, *Education in Rural England, 1800–1914* (Dublin, 1978), p. 128; Anon., *A Schoolmaster's Difficulties, Abroad and at Home* (London, 1853), pp. 108–9.
65 D. R. Fearon, *School Inspection* (London, 1887), pp. 2–3.
66 Elizabeth Williams, *Brethyn Cartref* (Llandysul, 1951), pp. 52–3.
67 MRO, Bala British, 1866 inspection report.
68 Sneyd-Kynnersley, *HMI*, pp. 43–4.
69 NEWAR, Llangedwyn National, 19 August 1865.
70 Williams, *Brethyn Cartref*, p. 86.
71 Sneyd-Kynnersley, *HMI*, p. 46.
72 J. Lloyd Williams, *Atgofion Tri Chwarter Canrif, cyf. II* (London, 1942), p. 42.
73 John Kerr, *Memories Grave and Gay: Forty Years of School Inspection* (Edinburgh, 1902), p. 48.
74 *Report of the Commissioners Appointed to Inquire into the State of Popular Education in England*, vol. I (1861), p. 230.
75 Holmes, *In Quest of an Ideal*, p. 64.
76 Sneyd-Kynnersley, *HMI*, pp. 43–4.
77 Hurt, *Education in Evolution*, pp. 62–5, 216.

78 *Report of the CCE, 1870–71*, p. 150.
79 For example, J. Lloyd Williams, *Atgofion Tri Chwarter Canrif, cyf. IV* (London, 1945), p. 164.
80 *Report of the CCE, 1870–71*, p. 275.
81 *Report of the CCE, 1867–68*, pp. 321–2.
82 *Report of the CCE, 1867–68*, p. 325.
83 *Report of the CCE, 1863–64*, p. 48.
84 *Report of the CCE, 1867–68*, p. 325.
85 *Report of the CCE, 1868–69*, p. 165.
86 *Report of the CCE, 1888–89*, p. 345. He argued his results were better than in the rest of Wales or in England but denied that this was due to leniency: *Report of the CCE, 1882–83*, p. 420.
87 See CRO, National, Abergwyngregyn, Bangor in the 1870s and early 1880s.
88 PbA, Croes-goch, 4 December 1868.
89 NEWAH, Hope Board (Llanfynydd), 1878 HMI report.
90 M. J. Evans, 'Elementary education in Montgomeryshire 1850–1900', *The Montgomeryshire Collections*, 63, 1 (1973), 1–46, 8.
91 PA, National school Pennant, Llanbryn-mair, 1889 HMI report.
92 CA, Llandysul National, 21 January 1874.
93 Cross Commission, 2nd Report, p. 289.
94 Education Department, *1875. New Code of Regulations* (London, 1875), p. 7.
95 PA, Meifod National, 1876 HMI report.
96 *Report of the CCE, 1882–83*, p. 157.
97 Address by John Bancroft quoted in PbA, Amblestone Board, 29 October 1883.
98 *Report of the CCE, 1888–89*, pp. 346–7, 355.
99 *Minute of 10th March 1890 establishing a New Code of Regulations* (London, 1890).
100 *Report of the CCE, 1878–79*, p. 674.
101 Cross Commission, 3rd Report, p. 25; 2nd Report, p. 281.
102 *Report of the CCE, 1884–85*, p. 352; 'Memorandum by the Commissioners of National education to the Chief Secretary', *The Gaelic Journal*, 2, 15 (1884), 94.
103 *Report of the CCE, 1877–78*, p. 412.
104 Cross Commission, 3rd Report, pp. 4, 24, 29.
105 Hurt, *Elementary Schooling*, p. 164. For an example of criticism of poor discipline see PA, Llanllwchaearn National, 1862 HMI report.
106 *Minutes of the CCE, 1847–48–49: Schools of Parochial Unions* (London, 1849), p. 300.
107 CA, Llanwenog National, 1868 HMI report.
108 Quoted in Griffith G. Davies, 'Addysg elfennol yn Sir Aberteifi, 1870–1902', *Ceredigion*, 4, 4 (1963), 367.
109 CmA, Capel Evan British, 29 November 1872.
110 GA, Penyrheolgerrig Infants, 30 April 1881.
111 MRO, Brithdir, HMI 1887 and 1896 reports.
112 PA, Staylittle Board, 1874 and 1875 HMI reports, and entries for 28 September and 23 November 1874.

113 PA, Rhiwhiriaeth Board, 1875 HMI report.
114 CA, Llanfihangel National, HMI reports for 1876 and 1877.
115 Evans, 'Elementary education in Montgomeryshire', 13.
116 PA, Pennant National, HMI reports for 1895 and 1896.
117 St Fagans oral history collection, Mr Jones, Y Tymbl.
118 For the life of one such inspector see T. H. Parry-Williams, *John Rhŷs, 1840–1915* (Cardiff, 1954).
119 *Report of the CCE, 1896–97*, p. 172.
120 Cross Commission, 1st Report, pp. 70, 79; 3rd Report, p. 9; *Cambrian News*, 7 June 1889, 9.
121 John E. Southall (ed.), *Bilingual Teaching in Welsh Elementary Schools or Minutes of Evidence of Welsh Witnesses before the Royal Commission on Education in 1886–87* (Newport, 1888), p. i. Pryce, inevitably, was one such hostile voice. With Welsh in the code on the horizon, he wrote that he earnestly trusted 'that this will be made subservient to the more effectual teaching of English, and not with the vain endeavour of extending and prolonging the use of the Welsh language', *Report of the CCE, 1888–89*, p. 366.
122 *Report of the CCE, 1888–89*, p. 366.
123 CA, Elerch school logbook, 26 April 1880.
124 'Memorandum by the Commissioners of National education to the Chief Secretary', *The Gaelic Journal*, 2, 15 (1884), 94.
125 *Report of the CCE, 1884–85*, p. 353.
126 Geraint Wyn Jones, *Dyddiadur Ysgol: Ysgol y Manod 1867–1967* (Blaenau Ffestiniog, 1997), p. 39.
127 *Report of the CCE, 1884–85*, p. 344.
128 *Report of the CCE, 1888–89*, p. 353.
129 *Report of the CCE, 1870–71*, pp. 188–9, 228. Smith speculated that the reason might be a Welsh boy had 'a new language to learn, but he has nothing to unlearn'. In contrast, a boy in Cheshire had to 'unlearn almost the whole alphabet, certainly every vowel'. He concluded that he was inclined to think that most schoolmasters would prefer to teach English to a foreigner than 'to undergo the labour of undoing the *Cheshirisms* learnt from the mother's knee'.
130 NEWAR, Ruabon Boys National school, HMI report 1887. Diocesan inspectors predominantly examined religious knowledge and they often used Welsh in doing so. See Deiniol Wyn, 'Rhai adgofion am bersonau a pethau', *Yr Haul*, 6, 67 (1890), 208–9.
131 Cross Commission, 2nd Report, p. 289.
132 CA, Llanfihangel National annual report 1881.
133 *Report of the CCE, 1872–73*, p. 22.
134 *Report of the CCE, 1882–83*, p. 427.
135 Newcastle Commission, vol. II, p. 521.
136 NEWAR, Blaenau Llangernyw British, 10 June 1885.
137 Bangor University Archives, Diary of David Griffith, 5 April 1873.
138 PA, Staylittle Board, 22 November, 13 December 1875, 2 February, 12 June 1876. The master at Rowen similarly made clear that he was devoting time to

translation and 'word explaining' in response to an inspection report that called for 'greater efforts' to 'cultivate the intelligence of the children': CwyA, Rowen, 3 May 1873.
139 Williams, *Atgofion Tri Chwarter Canrif, cyf. IV*, p. 174.
140 MRO, Corris British school, 1871 HMI report.
141 Honourable Society of Cymmrodorion, *Report of the Committee Appointed to Inquire into the Advisability of the Introduction of the Welsh Language into the Course of Elementary Education in Wales: The Introduction of Welsh as a Specific Subject. Appendix* (Aberdare, 1885), p. 16.
142 Abel J. Jones, *From an Inspector's Bag* (Cardiff, 1944), pp. 106–7.
143 O. M. Edwards, 'Cymraeg yn yr ysgolion dyddiol', *Cymru*, 15 September 1893, 133–4.
144 Williams, *Atgofion Tri Chwarter Canrif, cyf. IV*, pp. 118, 109, 110–1.
145 Sneyd-Kynnersley, *HMI*, p. 11.
146 *Report of the CCE, 1875–76*, p. 393; *Report of the CCE, 1888–89*, p. 348.
147 Williams, *Brethyn Cartref*, pp. 54–5.
148 Sneyd-Kynnersley, *HMI*, p. 11; Dewi Môn, 'Ysgol genedlaethol o'r hen ffasiwn', *Y Geninen*, October 1902, 258–63; *Report of the CCE, 1882–83*, p. 397.
149 *Report of the CCE, 1868–69*, p. 165.
150 Christopher Bischof, *Teaching Britain: Elementary Teachers and the State of the Everyday, 1846–1906* (Oxford, 2019), p. 160.
151 J. Elwyn Hughes, *Arloeswr Dwyieithedd: Dan Isaac Davies, 1839–1887* (Cardiff, 1984); Dan Isaac Davies, *Yr Iaith Gymraeg 1785, 1885, 1985! Neu, Tair Miliwn o Gymry Dwy-Ieithawg mewn Can Mlynedd* (Dinbych, 1886).
152 Revd Principal Edwards, chairman of the Society for Utilizing the Welsh Language, *Cambrian News*, 7 June 1889, 9.
153 *Report of the CCE, 1893–94*, p. 424.
154 *Y Goleuad*, 22 July 1908, 4.
155 AA, Bryngwran Board, 12 November 1884.
156 *Report of the CCE, 1877–78*, p. 414.
157 'Welsh schools', *Evening Express*, 12 January 1897, p. 2; 'The chief inspectorship of schools in Wales', *Young Wales*, 3, 26 (1897), 44.
158 Williams, *Atgofion Tri Chwarter Canrif, cyf. IV*, p. 111.
159 Southall, *Bilingual Teaching in Welsh Elementary Schools*, p. i.
160 'Injustice to Wales', *Carnarvon and Denbigh Herald*, 10 May 1862, 4.
161 Jürgen Osterhammel, *The Transformation of the World: A Global History of the Nineteenth Century* (Princeton, 2014), p. 790.
162 Eric Hobsbawm, 'Language, culture and national identity', *Social Research*, 63, 4 (1996), 1065–80, 1069, 1071.
163 Merfyn Jones, 'Notes from the margin: class and society in nineteenth century Gwynedd', in David Smith (ed.), *A People and a Proletariat: Essays in the History of Wales, 1780–1980* (London, 1980), pp. 199–214, 208.
164 Stephen Humphries, *Hooligans or Rebels? An Oral History of Working-class Childhood and Youth, 1889–1939* (Oxford, 1981), p. 31; Sascha Auerbach,

"'Some punishment should be devised": parents, children and the state in Victorian London', *The Historian*, 71, 4 (2009), 757–79.

165 Richard Johnson, 'Educational policy and social control in early Victorian England', *Past & Present*, 49, 1, (1970), 96–119, 119.
166 HMI Joseph Fletcher claimed that Welsh was 'the great stumbling block of the whole race', *Minutes of the CCE, 1848–49–50*, vol. II, pp. 293–4.
167 Scott O. Moore, *Teaching the Empire: Education and State Loyalty in Late Habsburg Austria* (West Lafayette, 2020), pp. 40, 49.

7
VICTIMS AND REBELS: CHILDREN AND THE WELSH NOT

The tendency in modern thinking about the Welsh Not has been to portray children as victims. Indeed, one recent novel had its protagonist so traumatised by school that he developed a condition where he was unable to talk at all.[1] In contrast, Beriah Gwynfe Evans, a former teacher and then secretary of the Society for Utilizing the Welsh Language, gave the 1887 Cross Commission a more nuanced picture of the impact on children of Welsh not being used:

> In the first place, it lessens the child's confidence in himself, it makes him nervous, afraid to give expression to his thoughts, and doubtful of his own powers. In the second place, it instils into his mind a hatred of one of the two languages. Either he must hate the language of his home, which he is led to regard as a thing to be ashamed of, or, if he has any spirit in him or the least spark of patriotism, it fills his youthful mind with a deep-seated hatred of the foreign language, in favour of which his legitimate mother tongue is placed in the position of a bastard. In the third place, again, it affects the light in which he regards school. He associates school with English, and home with Welsh; these counteract each other where they should assist.[2]

Such arguments moved beyond just thinking of children as victims of an unfair system and highlight the plurality of responses. Individuals can have very different reactions to the same experiences. What traumatises some, others shrug off. What some accept, others reject.

As this chapter will show, the Welsh Not and other ways of excluding Welsh was a traumatic and insidious experience for many but victimhood is only half the story. As Evans noted above, children were not without agency. They may have been subject to adult thinking and action, but they chose how to respond. They could perpetuate, manipulate or resist the actions of adults. Their agency was constrained by the conditions imposed upon them by adults, but they could still survive and adapt on their own terms.

Remembering school and the Welsh Not

Drawing upon recent evidence from around the globe, a range of disciplines suggest that the psychological impact of being punished at school for speaking one's mother tongue would have been great. An indigenous Alaskan who had had his mouth washed for this recounted, 'Whenever I speak Tlingit, I can still taste the soap.' Citing this, David Crystal argues that the result of such experiences was 'a growing sense of inferiority or shame about one's language for fear of evoking further condemnation, and a natural desire to avoid having one's children exposed to the same experience'.[3] Modern educational psychology sees deriding or rejecting a child's language or accent as causing them to feel belittled or rejected.[4] Drawing parallels with the Welsh Not, educationalists have claimed that 'the violence is still very real' when contemporary teachers reprimand children from minority-linguistic backgrounds for speaking their mother tongue and advise their parents to speak the majority language at home. They argue that children internalise the shame and 'lose the power to control their own lives in situations where they interact with members of the dominant group'.[5] Meanwhile, psychologists and others argue that making children feel ashamed can damage their self-esteem and mental health.[6]

Historians have made similar arguments of the past. The language historian Andrew Dalby argued that the children being punished for speaking their mother tongue 'tended to devalue it in the children's own minds, meanwhile instilling a feeling in communities beyond the school that indigenous languages were something to be ashamed of'.[7] However, proving such ideas in the Welsh historical context is not simple because no child recorded what they felt at being punished for holding the Welsh Not. There are sources on what adults thought and remembered but none written by children themselves.

Education was certainly an emotional experience as much as an intellectual one.[8] It was a place where children learned about authority and rules, where they found frustration and fun, where they met and socialised with their peers. The experience of being punished, and being denied access to knowledge because school was conducted in a foreign language, surely brought some emotional response. Yet whether adults could accurately recall those emotions when they recorded their memories years later is a different matter. Historians must be cautious of assuming what people remember feeling is the same as what was felt at the time being recalled.[9] Julie-Marie Strange has argued that some working-class autobiographers probably censored themselves 'to omit difficult experiences', while for others their past trauma was 'pivotal to telling their story'.[10] Both cases seem to be true of retrospective accounts of the Welsh Not. There is also the question of whether the memories recorded are representative. This is always an issue for historians but especially when dealing with education as those who wrote down their memories were people who had received a good enough education to become fairly literate or important enough for someone to publish them. The emotional reactions of those completely failed by education are almost entirely lost to the historian.

Many of the published reminiscences of the Welsh Not are full of anger and resentment. A 1904 editorial in *Celt Llundain*, for example, said that most people would not soon forget the cruelty of the Welsh Note and being forbidden to speak Welsh.[11] The memory of physical pain was central to such sentiments. In 1915, Henri Bourassa, the Quebec political leader, recounted how David Lloyd George had told him that he could still feel his fingers burn with the strokes of the rod he had received at school when he spoke his mother's tongue.[12]

An account of the Welsh Not in the 1830s noted the injustice of the teacher enjoying giving out the punishment and finished with a reflection on how God would judge such cruelty.[13] Others focused on the unfairness and the public nature of the punishment. A generalised retrospective from 1879 noted while the occasional boy would accept the punishment with indifference, others would be terrified because the rest of the children would mock and make faces at them. It concluded that the Welsh Not brought more tears and shame than could be put into words.[14] One man recalled in 1889 a Caernarfonshire teacher who gave someone the Welsh Not for coughing because the child could not speak English and thus must have coughed in Welsh.[15] It was common in accounts to stress how Welsh was the language of their mother, a common term for a first language but one that also emphasises the innocence and helplessness of children in the matter of which language they spoke. For example, an 1894 retrospective account stated that the Welsh Not raised 'terror in the poor children in case they uttered a word of the old language they had learned on their mother's knees'.[16] In 1922, the *Western Mail* published a Welsh-language poem, in which the author stated he well remembered receiving the Welsh Not long ago for speaking the language of his mother, and the everlasting plague English was to his soul.[17]

A particularly strong sense of injustice came from the fact that children being punished for speaking Welsh often could not speak any other language. Writing in old age, David Davies (b.1849) recorded that he had 'a faint recollection' of school lessons, but his memory of the Welsh Not was 'as vivid' as if it were 'yesterday'. He went on: 'I well remember how, even at that age, I felt hardship of being punished for speaking my mother-tongue, when my command of English was pitiably limited.'[18] Poet Watcyn Wyn (b.1844) briefly attended a school in Cwmaman of which he wrote the only things he could really remember were the rod and the Welsh Note. The school was run by a former soldier who did not care much if the culprit being punished cried out in English but if the child called out for his mother in Welsh he was hit on the back too. Wyn concluded the monolingual Welshman could do nothing in such circumstances but act as if he was dumb.[19] The Revd Aaron

Davies recalled in 1889 that he was of one the 'sufferers of the Welsh note system'. He had been raised in Welsh: 'How, then, could he manage to speak anything else than Welsh though he was to be punished for speaking it?'[20]

Memories are framed and affected by the cultural contexts in which the remembering takes place. From the later nineteenth century, childhood was increasingly celebrated as a time of innocence to be indulged. This was evident not just in laws and regulations against child employment and cruelty, but also in literature, popular culture and new traditions such as Father Christmas. Memories of the Welsh Not were shaped and influenced too. Given how physical punishments were common in many schools for all kinds of demeanours, it is likely that cruelty and unfairness were more central to how the Welsh Not was remembered, rather than how it was thought about by children experiencing it and the wider exclusion of Welsh. This is not to argue that the Welsh Not was not cruel or unfair but rather that it was primarily with adulthood that some sufferers of it came to see it that way. For children, it was not so much that the Welsh Not was brutal but more that many things in schools were and that normalised cruelty to the extent that injustice became matter of fact.

The context of national revival in Wales also framed memories of the Welsh Not. The first stirrings of this were after the Blue Books but it took off in the late nineteenth century. Then Welsh culture was much celebrated and there were the beginnings of serious discussions about home rule. This does seem to have led some people to look back at their experiences through a lens of national identity that they probably had not considered as children. One writer, attempting to persuade people of the need for Welsh-language education, complained in 1848 that 'No Welsh to be spoken here' was the first thing pupils heard at National schools and that no worse could be done to Welsh children if they were slaves of the most barbarous nation on the face of the earth.[21] The poet Gwilym Wyn (b.1852), in recounting his memory of the Welsh Not being introduced at his school, called it a 'Coercion Act with a vengeance' to bend Wales's children into speaking English.[22] In 1907, the Revd D. L. Thomas told an education conference that he spoke from experience when he said that one of the first objects of a schoolmaster thirty years earlier had been to 'make little Welsh children speak English and English only during the time they were in school'. He concluded that it was 'a great moral injustice' that children should be made to feel that English 'was in any sense superior to the language of their hearth and home'.[23] Such accounts were partially driven by concerns for the future of the Welsh language, which by the Edwardian period seemed to be in retreat in industrial districts. A poem about the Welsh Not in 1909 called school a prison for every Welshman, where they learned nothing but a foreign language. It finished with an appeal to people to embrace the Welsh language and culture.[24]

By the twentieth century, the story of the Welsh Not had become infamous enough that some people who had not experienced it felt they needed to make that clear when writing an account of their life.[25] Yet, even without a Welsh Not, a school's emphasis on the English language could still leave bitter memories of an alienating experience. One man recalled how a teacher had pronounced his name in an anglicised fashion rather than in the Welsh way he and his family used.[26] Another remembered the injustice of not knowing what he was being caned for when the teacher chastised him in English he did not understand.[27] Such accounts are particularly characteristic of people who went to school later in the century and went onto become Welsh-language writers. Poet and scholar T. Gwynn Jones (b.1871) remembered that the first time he was punished at school was for speaking Welsh. Unable to understand the English book he was given, he had asked what it meant. Jones claimed he then asked how he was supposed to learn if no one told him the meaning of words, to which the master laughed. Jones wrote he would find how badly he had been taught English funny were it not for the fact that the failings still affected him.[28] Poet T. E. Nicholas (b.1879) attended the Board school at Hermon and said that he had no joy looking back because he was taught in a language he did not understand, was hit by the pupil teachers, and left hating education and without having learned anything. He called the whole experience unfair and degrading.[29]

Professor of Welsh W. J. Gruffydd (b.1881) called the school he attended in Bethel until he was thirteen the most oppressive period of his life and largely a waste of time. Much of the teaching was left to pupil teachers, 'none of whom spoke the language through which they purported to teach us'. He remembered his classmates loathed school, became bitter and played truant or wept and wailed every morning. Their teachers considered them stupid and incapable of learning. It was only thanks to help from his mother that he had learned to read.[30] Clergyman and recorder of Welsh traditions, D. Parry-Jones (b.1891) was educated near Newcastle Emlyn. He remembered that the English of his teachers conveyed nothing but fear to him and that he may as well as have been 'put down in China'. Welsh was allowed in the playground but he recalled in the classroom:

> I felt utterly cowed before the strangeness of this alien atmosphere. Imagine the cruelty of a system that drove a child to this pitch of nervousness for his first lesson. We were taught everything through the medium of a foreign tongue of which we knew nothing but the negative and the affirmative. Progress was necessarily laborious, slow and baffling. The dreadful result was that we were taught neither our own tongue nor the English tongue. Of our own, it was assumed it did not exist, of English, that it was well known and familiar.

He contrasted this with Sunday school where he was taught in Welsh and made 'extraordinary progress'.[31]

It is notable that three of the above four writers were at the very least cultural nationalists and had a strong political sense of Wales. However, that does not mean that their politics had entirely clouded and shaped their memories of alienation. Rather it might be that these experiences contributed to their politicised sense of Welshness. National identity is not a thing or a category, but a feeling and experience. Like class, it is not just there but is made and remade by those who feel and experience it.[32] The Welsh Not was one of those emotive experiences. It could be that people's anger and resentment at what they experienced at school helped make them into nationalists of various types.[33] Certainly, their Welshness was defined by their sense that the Welsh language was not accorded equal status with English, and that was something they first learned at school. Thus, perhaps, it was not so much that writers politicised the question of language in schools, but rather that their experience of this helped politicise the writers. At least one person recognised this. William George, who attended a school where Welsh-speaking was punished, later wrote that the:

> contempt in which the Welsh language was held by the authorities in my early days, fostered in me a determination to devote my main efforts in later years to having the language properly taught in the schools of Wales and recognised by the authorities as an official language.[34]

These published memories, like all accounts of the Welsh Not, were articulated by people who went onto lead educated lives. They saw how school was a missed opportunity and how their learning had come from ministers or others in the community rather than the one person whose job it was to teach them.[35] Indeed, they were part of a wider characteristic of British social mobility where people who had left the working class through their own hard work became resentful at how their elementary education had not equipped them for life.[36] Others who had not been so successful in life perhaps saw education in a different light. Some may have been bitter about their failure to avoid a life of manual work and blamed their education.

But others may have been less angry because they had no sense of missed opportunity and were content in occupations or lives that did not require much education. Certainly, not everyone who wrote accounts of their time at school seemed angry about the Welsh Not. In 1894, one retrospective account said it was so common no one saw anything out of place in it.[37] This might also explain why many memories of school make no mention of it at all (although some of these must be because the writer did not experience it). Seeing the

Welsh Not in a matter-of-fact way was most common in oral accounts. In 1952, one researcher recounted:

> A friend of mine, who knows Anglesey well, asked several old people who were taught under this regime what was their reaction to it. Strangely enough the majority of them did not condemn it, saying 'we already knew Welsh, so it was useful to be taught English as an additional language'.[38]

Similarly, an oral history conducted in 1972 with someone hit for speaking Welsh said that neither the children or their parents saw anything strange or wrong about it.[39] Even if the English they were taught was very limited, some people seemed very accepting of the failings of their schooling. One minister recalled being taught to pronounce English incorrectly by a bad-tempered violent teacher but said a little learning was better than none.[40] Another man recalled in an oral history interview, without any hint of anger, beatings at his Llanuwchllyn school for speaking Welsh, noting a person would not go far in life without English.[41]

Boredom was another powerful memory of school thanks to, as one person put it, rote learning, incomprehensible books and everything in a language they did not speak.[42] Contemporaries agreed with this too. An account from 1892 said the exclusion of Welsh had turned schools into 'scenes of mechanical, irrational drudgery'.[43] Understanding did not always make things better, however. Some pupils were left idle while their teacher concentrated on another standard. Shortages of books and the need to pass the exam meant they read the same book over and over again. Lessons often concentrated on remembering facts rather than thinking about their significance, which could kill a child's potential interest in the subject.[44] Wil John Edwards (b.1888) thus remembered his class 'repeating after the teacher in unsurpassed monotony a series of sentences in sing-song fashion. There were no persons: the individual was lost in the crowd.' For him, leaving school aged twelve for the friendly atmosphere of the coalmine was thus an 'exciting adventure'.[45] Nor was school even comfortable boredom, given the overcrowding, lack of furniture and temperatures that were often too hot or too cold. It was such experiences that helped mute anger about the restrictions on speaking Welsh. They were just another example of an experience that was unpleasant and dispiriting.

With the passage of time, some even came to find humour in their childhood experiences. One 1851 account referred to the Welsh stick and the like as amusing anecdotes.[46] In 1927, a man recalled that the Welsh Not led to his first caning but joked that perhaps it had done some good in storing up energy for his work for the Welsh language society.[47] One man remembered in an oral history interview being nervous and afraid on his first day in school because he was a sensitive child and the teacher was speaking English, but he laughed when he added that years later he had given a lift to that same teacher who checked if he was Welsh before accepting it.[48] Some retellings of the Welsh Not turned it into a humorous anecdote because there was a degree of tragic ridiculousness in its effects. In 1897, one man told of an argument between two boys at Llwyngwril when one tried to pass the Welsh Not onto another for pronouncing his village name correctly rather than in an anglicised fashion.[49] A 1927 letter writer recounted the story of a farm boy who turned up late to school, explaining to the others, 'Our donkey had a small donkey'. He was asked 'when?', but confused this for 'wen', the Welsh word for white and replied 'Nage, un ddu' (No, a black one). For this, he was presented with the Welsh Not.[50] Audiences could find such stories funny too. Speaking to a school prize-giving in 1888, a minister recalled the Welsh Not being used during his education in the 1840s. The newspaper report noted that the audience had laughed after hearing that the boy who had the Welsh Not in his hand at lunch break was 'whipped'.[51] None of this means the adults were dismissing the childhood experiences of themselves and others. As historians have argued, 'laughter is often a weapon of the weak', a way of ameliorating suffering, expressing complaint, and resisting and subverting authority. When the subject of the humour is something not funny on the surface, a joke can critique power relations.[52] Laughing at the Welsh Not was thus a way of laughing at the stupidity of the education system, those who implemented it, and of sympathising with those who suffered it.

Seeing the whipping of children as something funny was also underpinned by how corporal punishment was an accepted part of the education system, even if its use was gradually becoming curtailed. This was not just true of adults but children too, as long as it was utilised in ways that were felt to be fair and clear. Corporal punishment was, Middleton argued, 'simply a hazard of school life, a painful correction to be borne with stoicism and which ultimately had little effect on behaviour'.[53] In giving his memories of the Welsh Not in the 1860s, William Williams recalled that children preferred the cane for speaking Welsh to being kept in after school because the latter would mean a long walk home on their own.[54] Teachers sometimes stressed the support of children for what they did. In 1864, for example, the master of Llyswen National recorded that he had to punish a child for disobedience but 'had the sympathy of the school'.[55] Children could think like this because violence was common in other walks of life. Most fathers and mothers employed physical punishment, or at least the threat of it, to discipline their children. Some witnessed their fathers hitting their mothers. Rural children knew about the short brutal lives of animals. Boys often fought amongst themselves.[56] All this probably meant that corporal punishment in the classroom was just an extension of violence outside the school. In her study of fatherhood, Julie-Marie Strange has noted how few working-class autobiographies discuss corporal punishment, suggesting 'children may have deemed a degree of physical reprimand sufficiently normative to render it unimportant in relating its life stories'. Those memoirs that did report it still expressed love and understanding towards their fathers.[57]

This does not mean that children liked corporal punishment. A bad-tempered teacher who used the cane freely could cause fear and uncertainty, making it difficult to concentrate on lessons.[58] Abel Jones recalled that he found schoolwork easy but that 'the severity of the discipline kept me in an uneasy frame of mind'.[59] This was captured in an 1841 poem where the 'dread birch' was hung above the teacher's head. It was worn to a stump through repeated use and 'Each dunce in school with trembling horror views [it], Shudders, and looks and longs to be at home'.[60] When it arrived, a swish of the cane could cause tears and pain.[61] But these things were accepted, as long as the punishments were deemed fair.

As the memories already discussed show, certainly some adults looking back on being punished for speaking Welsh did not accept what had happened to them. For those unable to speak much English, it is probable that the resentment articulated in later life was felt in childhood too because it would have been seen as unfair. But there are reasons to think that childhood feelings may have been more complex. Certainly, some could remember teachers who had used the Welsh Not with respect and admiration, thus suggesting there was no universal resentment of it.[62] Much of how schools worked must have seemed arbitrary and unfair to children and for some the Welsh Not may have been another example of that. A 1904 poem asked readers whether they remembered the old schools with drunk teachers, beatings and the Welsh Not and everything but learning.[63] It may be that because the Welsh Not had rules to it, it appeared less unjust than the flashes of temper for other offences that could come from teachers. The shame of being punished must also have been muted by the fact that the Welsh Not was passed around, thus creating an emotional community of sorts. If many people suffered it, the humiliation was shared, and children were tied together by the experience. One man, born in 1844 who encountered the Welsh Not, described his school near Pwllheli as a place where pupils learned but also suffered together.[64] The public shame and disgrace the Welsh Not produced was not a unique experience. There were memories of children early in the century being washed in front of others, which, no matter what the intentions of the teacher, must have been humiliating.[65] Robert Roberts recalled how coming into contact with the better dressed children of richer farmers created a resentment in him: 'My poverty galled me and made me gloomy and morose, I fancied slights when none were meant, and became, in short, a disagreeable boy.'[66] In 1900, one Welsh inspector looked back on the harshest days of the Revised Code and said children were driven by: 'The fear of not passing, of being left behind by more fortunate comrades. The child of the present day has no conception of the terrible disgrace attached to the expression "failed to pass".[67]

In these circumstances, it could also be that many children did not much reflect on the injustice of language. There were teachers who went to some efforts to explain to children why they felt speaking Welsh at school should not be done. Moreover, English was the language of authority – of government, law and often the gentry. Children might not have much contact with those worlds, but the idea that English was what to be expected from those in positions of authority was a fact of life rather than something for a young mind to think about. Historians argue that emotions are framed and constructed by social contexts. The anger felt at wearing the Welsh Not would thus depend not just on whether it was felt to be fair but whether it was expected too. In a world where unfairness and inequality were all around, the Welsh Not could be just another example. Nonetheless, the school made abstract points of inequality something real in their lives. School was not just somewhere where children learned some English, it was a place where they learned that English was the language of the harsh and alien world of authority and power. It was a place where a wider abstract political fact became a lived reality. They may not have understood that at the time, and many never came to think that way, but for some adults, looking back at the Welsh Not symbolised Welsh culture's inferior status within the United Kingdom. And they were not wrong.

But that does not mean all victims were angry about it, either at the time or later. Just as modern linguists and educationalists suggest, some children who were punished for speaking Welsh may not have felt it was unfair because they had come to believe the teacher's message that speaking the language was wrong, at least in school. A number of nineteenth-century writers did argue that the Welsh Not turned children against the Welsh language.[68] In 1885, one Carmarthenshire master claimed that teaching Welsh as a distinct subject would combat how some children felt Welsh was something to be ashamed of and 'forgotten, and cast aside as soon as possible'.[69] Such feelings explain why some accounts of the Welsh Not pointed not to children's anger at the practice but their 'derision' at their peers holding the Welsh Not.[70]

Yet that was very clearly not a universal case because not all children were able to speak English and thus could not have felt contempt towards those who, like them, only spoke Welsh. All Welsh-speaking children, whether they could speak English or not, also heard Welsh at home, a place where most felt loved and safe, which would have counteracted against ideas that it was a shameful language. Thus, as Rose argued, children interacted with schooling according to their own circumstances.[71] They did not simply accept what they were told. This is very evident in how, as the next section shows, children subverted the Welsh Not. While some may have internalised the idea that Welsh was shameful, many others clearly did not and, in the places where the Welsh Not was applied most vigorously by excluding all Welsh from a school, children could not have rejected their mother tongue because they did not learn enough English to use it instead.

Fighting back: children's agency

Dalby has argued of the punishments and humiliations handed out for speaking Welsh: 'Only the most stubborn and self-sufficient of pupils were likely to put up determined resistance to repeated moral and physical abuse of that kind.'[72] In fact, many children were both more determined and resilient than this perspective suggests. Children had a strong sense of independence and did not simply sit back and accept how they were treated in school or beyond. Thompson has written of the streets and playgrounds of the Edwardian period:

> a remarkably independent children's culture flourished, with its own secret pacts and passwords, ancient rhymes and adaptations from Edwardian music halls, old seasons and new fashions. This children's culture was in its own way as savage, competitive and hierarchical as that of adults.[73]

Humphries's oral history of childhood from 1889 to 1939 paints a picture of a powerful culture of resistance to teachers' efforts to control and manipulate children. He sees this as more than just the anti-authoritarianism of a rough working class but as a form of 'violent class conflict over the form of education that working-class children should receive'.[74]

It is perhaps misleading to see children's resistance at school in class terms since most teachers were working-class figures, like their pupils. But the existence of an assertive culture of resistance in Welsh schools is undoubted. The most common act of resistance was to play truancy and not turn up at all. Harsh punishments could be one cause of that and, in 1876, the master at Llangunnock attributed a fall in attendance to his recent implementation of stricter discipline.[75] Children could be assertive at school too. In 1889, an Aberystwyth clergyman described a school of fifty years earlier where the drunk teacher would sleep on the floor and the boys would place benches over him so he could not get up when he awoke.[76] Some teachers recalled being shouted at or having things thrown at them.[77] One recorded being threatened with a thrashing unless he left a pupil to do what he wanted.[78] In 1872, a boy walked out of Llechryd school after being caned and returned with a horsewhip to threaten the pupil teacher who had punished him.[79] A pupil teacher in Llanrwst from 1867 to 1872 recalled that some older children would kick the headmaster when he tried to punish them.[80] Other pupils refused to hold out their hands to be caned or ran out of school when punishment beckoned.[81]

In the first half of the century, there was a tradition in some communities of locking a teacher out of school when the children decided it was time for a holiday. This could result in physical struggles and one account claimed, probably dubiously, that children carried guns to emphasise their point. Such cases were often the result of long-standing tensions but they were not complete rejections of school. Instead, they were assertions that a master's powers were not infinite, with everyone knowing that the normal hierarchy of power would resume after the holidays.[82] Such traditions did persist in some places and became rather ritualistic, with both sides treating it as something of a game with a foregone conclusion.[83] Yet some teachers did resist. In 1870, encouraged by stories from old people in the village, children at Croes-goch tried to shut the master out of school to finish for the summer. He refused and had to stay in at lunchtime to ensure the children could not lock him out. When the children refused to come back in after lunch, he locked them out and told them to return the next day for their books. This caused some to cry and the teacher relented and broke the school up for the summer after all.[84]

Such acts of resistance always ran the risk of a teacher unwilling to capitulate turning to violence to enforce their authority. News might also get home, resulting in a beating there instead. Children might thus turn to more covert ways of getting back at unpopular teachers. In 1872, the master of Llanon British school had his rods removed from his desk three nights in a row by children who entered the school at night. Two weeks later, he came into school and found things torn down from the wall and the registers hidden. Within a few weeks, he had left the school.[85] One woman born in the 1850s remembered that children would put a goat or sheep in the garden of an unpopular teacher as they tried to punish them for every 'horrific beating'.[86] There are examples too of children going on strike in protest at homework, holiday dates or hours. In 1889, there was a national school strike, which spread as pupils heard about it from newspapers. In Cardiff and Swansea, stones were thrown at school windows and two boys were charged with assaulting teachers. In Holyhead, too, the strike saw teachers 'subjected to rough treatment by their pupils, who armed themselves with sticks and cabbage stalks'.[87]

These are extreme examples and more common acts of resistance were disputing or taunting teachers. Edward Hughes (b.1856) remembered he often argued with the teacher and was sent home regularly for being unmanageable. His mother was more assertive with him and took him back to school to apologise and promise to obey in future.[88] New teachers faced particular problems with noise and discipline, as pupils tested their mettle.[89] Some never managed to exert their authority. Samuel Nutall (b.1833) remembered that at the National school in Mold, the children would shout 'Perry Winkle', the teacher's nickname, when his back was turned, and then look innocent when he turned to see who had done it. This could continue all morning and, with the children also fighting each other, Nutall described the school as 'pandemonium'.[90] At Ruthin British school, the master was praised in the Blue Books for instilling in pupils a 'a desire for knowledge' but the commissioner was less impressed at their manners:

> When any movement was required, his pupils rushed pell-mell to their places, thwarting and tripping each other; then mounted the desks and sat upon them with their caps on, swinging their legs; some peeling sticks, others caning those near them with the master's cane, the rest struggling together, talking, or playing tricks with anything that happened to be at hand. The answer sent by one boy, when summoned by the master to his place, was, that he could not come.[91]

Another extreme example comes from the Blue Books' report of the Church school at Llanfynydd (Flint):

> The master had no idea of governing his school, and did not attempt to suppress the tumult, uproar, and disorder which prevailed during my visit, but allowed the scholars to continue laughing, playing, and jumping upon each other's backs, boys and girls promiscuously, with such contempt for all authority, that I was under serious apprehension lest a general fight should ensue before my examination could be concluded.[92]

Such descriptions owed something to middle-class disgust and apprehension at working-class behaviour. But even members of that class could be somewhat afraid of the children. Robert Roberts said of his first teaching post at a school in Amlwch:

> When the school door was opened in the morning, in rushed a crowd of boys such as I never saw except in a gutter: half of them had no shoes or stockings, most of them had evidently not been washed for some days past, and all were unruly as wild colts.[93]

Logbooks also hint at a rebellious and disruptive culture later in the century, with records of children making noises when a teacher's back was turned or laughing during prayers. In 1874, the master of Llangollen National school ruefully recorded: 'The children are very unruly and it is with difficulty that anything like order is maintained.'[94] Discipline was not helped by the reliance on monitors and pupil teachers. Some struggled to maintain control over their charges; some were the cause of the disturbances themselves.[95] Indeed, they might be younger than those they were teaching and it is important to remember that, throughout the century, schools could also contain teenage and adult pupils who were looking to make up what they had missed in their younger years.[96] This must have added to the potential for classrooms to be places of rebellion and resistance. It was this potential for disorder that explained why some teachers used the cane so freely. For them, it was not a pedagogical tool or even about correcting individual failings, but about keeping general order and discipline.

Most acts of resistance or ill-discipline were fairly mundane. With teachers having to deal with large numbers of children, there were plentiful opportunities to talk amongst themselves, work slowly or not at all, or get up and wander around.[97] Boredom could be averted by furtive games such as playing noughts and crosses on slates. Teachers' authority could be undermined in subtle ways too. Calling them a nickname behind their back was a risk-free way of demeaning them. The pain of corporal punishment could be blunted, at least in playground folklore, by spitting on the palm or putting a hair across it.[98] Teachers from England trying to learn some Welsh could be taught the wrong words.[99] In all these small things, children were not rebelling against education itself. Instead, they were regaining some pride and dignity in an oppressive system that too often denied them just that. They were making fair a system that teachers had made unfair.

As chapter 4 explored, children regularly resisted orders not to speak Welsh too. In 1863, the master of Cemais British school recorded: 'Endeavoured to get the children to make a practice of talking English on the play-ground. Noted that unless continually watched they spoke Welsh.'[100] Of course, this owed much to children's poor or non-existent

English, but it does seem children made little effort to comply unless they had to. This suggests that rather than internalising the message that Welsh was inferior, they rebelled against it. One Cardiganshire teacher tried banning Welsh in the playground for the third standard and above. After two weeks of this, he recorded: 'Can't get them to speak English in the playground because those who can play with those who cannot.'[101] It might be such rebellion was not just about language but the general tenor of a school: speaking one's own language was an easy way to assert some independence against the strict climate of school. Certainly, getting away with rule breaking, avoiding punishment or tricking the teacher could be a source of pride for children.[102] Thus one 1612 observer of attempts to make children speak Latin rather than English noted that children 'will speake English, and one will winke at another, if they be out of the Master's hearing'.[103] Similar behaviour could be found around the Welsh Not. An 1824 account recalled how pupils in the playground might agree not to pass the Welsh Not on so they could play in their own language.[104] There are memories of people vigorously rebelling against being punished for speaking Welsh, which suggests a deep resentment of the Welsh Not. William Williams, who went to school in Blaenau Ffestiniog in the 1860s, remembered a few brave children would throw the Welsh Not over the hedge rather than betray their language, as he later put it.[105] One writer recounted an anecdote told by his father of how a teacher had informed pupils he would not use the Welsh Not on any day they heard him speak Welsh. One pupil later overheard the teacher curse in Welsh. Thus, when that pupil and others were lined up to receive their punishment for speaking Welsh, he kicked the teacher hard in the shin. The teacher roared in Welsh and the boy shouted at him that they could no longer be punished.[106]

Such acts required some courage, not least because they might also lead to a beating at home if the teacher spoke to the parents. A less dangerous way of exerting agency was to take pride in the punishment. As one teacher who became a professor of education pointed out, there was 'a certain glory in bearing stripes without flinching', making the victim a hero amongst his peers.[107] Another Welsh teacher noted corporal punishment created a 'spirit of indifference' in a child rather than urging 'him to improve himself'.[108] Owen M. Edwards was not alone in recounting proudly how he was punished more frequently than others for speaking Welsh.[109] Such feelings were probably rooted in a masculine self-esteem where toughness mattered. Boys might not yet have the tough bodies so central to working-class adult masculinity but by resisting or withstanding physical punishment they could still show they were men.[110]

This is indicative of how the Welsh Not could be gendered. Education itself was patriarchal, with schools perpetuating the gender structures of society, something clear in the Revised Code's requirement that girls be taught sewing.[111] Girls were instructed in basic literacy and arithmetic but the expectations of them were generally lower among both parents and the state. Unless they were going into service, English was seen as a less useful skill for women since they were going to spend their lives as housewives. This, in itself, probably discouraged their punishment for speaking Welsh. As a result of such attitudes, far fewer girls than boys were sent to school in the first half of the century, when the Welsh Not was at its height. Again, this probably meant that the experience of being punished for speaking Welsh was more a male experience. However, the latter part of the century did see feminist stirrings across society and rejections of the idea that girls were intellectually inferior and thus less in need of educating.[112] In 1869, for example, the girls section of Gresford National school was told in its inspection report that great pains should be taken to 'awaken their intelligence', by questioning pupils on the meaning of what they read.[113] But this did not change how girls were subject to different disciplinary expectations and, for most of the century, there was a reluctance to physically punish them.[114] Some teachers, free with the strap for boys, might not hit girls at all.[115] A pupil, who remembered the Welsh Not as a 'most barbarous practice', noted that girls were exempt from it at his mid-century school at Pontgarreg.[116] None of the first-hand accounts of the Welsh Not were written by women. This must be partly because the patriarchal nature of society gave women fewer opportunities to publish their life stories, but it does further suggest that the Welsh Not's use against girls was less common. Nonetheless, there are occasional male memories of girls being punished. In 1902, one vicar claimed that the Welsh Not had been used for both sexes but girls were tapped not flogged and as a result did not care if they got the token or not.[117] Logbooks also show that girls could be physically punished for speaking Welsh.[118] Ideas of chivalry further complicated things and boys would sometimes take the punishment for girls. As one account put it: 'Mother, being a lively child, was in frequent possession of the Welsh Not, but was never allowed to pay the penalty; a chivalrous boy cousin always asked for it in Welsh and took the punishment himself.'[119] Again, here we see a child humanising a system that was anything but by subverting it in his own little way.

The impact of the Welsh Not could be muted by turning it into a game where children provoked and tricked each other into speaking Welsh. One 1851 description elaborated on this:

> The unfortunate wight who held the Welsh stick was at liberty to pass it off on another, and this he did not at all scruple to do, treating it as men do bad money, making due haste to get rid of it. Sometimes the unsuspecting victim was drawn into a conversation which more than taxed his stock of English, when a *Welsh* word would drop out, and the *stick* was thrust upon him to the no small joy of the successful tempter; or if the tempted was too much on his guard to be inveigled into conversation, he was pinched so unmercifully in some tender part of his person, that the suddenness of the attack would betray him into venting his ire in the vernacular, and the obnoxious stick was in an instant on his book or in his pocket.[120]

Watcyn Wyn (b.1844) remembered in class the larger boys tended to get the Welsh Not because they spoke the loudest and most daringly but it did not bother them much because they knew they could get rid of it in the playground to children who were smaller or less wily than themselves. He described the playground as a 'Welsh Not fair', as boys tried to pass it off on others.[121] This drew upon a competitive playground culture where name calling, fighting and bullying were common.[122] But such games were also coping mechanisms. They helped bring a degree of fun to something otherwise harsh; more importantly, they were also an exertion of agency that gave children some power over what was happening. For those at the receiving end, however, this was not true. Indeed, the trickery and force involved maybe made the pain worse because the cause of the punishment was unfair. One memory from Pembrokeshire was that small boys who were tricked into receiving the Welsh Not at playtime would swear or shout for their mother in Welsh.[123]

Teachers could also exploit children's sense of competition and spite and encourage such games. One man remembered that the Welsh Not was given to a boy at the start of the day who was then free to speak Welsh to try and get others to do so. This, he recalled, caused many hot battles between the boys.[124] A variation on this was to give the Welsh Not to a pupil as the children walked home for lunch. He would be allowed to speak Welsh to try to get the others to.[125] In an account of the Welsh Not in the Gwaun Valley, the teacher asked for volunteers to take it at the start of the day and 'a dozen hands' would go up. The 'detective' was called the 'Corryn' (spider) by the children and was commended after the punishment of each child who had held the Welsh Not. That this was no light-hearted game is evident in how the writer recalled that his body still bore the marks of this 'ancient infliction'.[126]

There were thus distinct limits to the idea of children's agency.[127] They could not always avoid punishment. They did not subvert or deny the wider hegemonic notion of the importance of both education and the English language. Children's resistance was not going against such central tenets in Welsh culture but instead negotiating how they functioned. Children may have altered how teachers operated but they could not, and did not try to, challenge the principles of education. Yet this, in itself, might be seen as a form of agency. Children who went along with and tried to make the most of what education purported to offer were just as much making a choice as those who openly or silently rebelled.[128]

The failures and indignities of education

How children negotiated and felt about such experiences should not detract from what happened to them. The exclusion of Welsh made school a thoroughly miserable experience for many. Even play and companionship could lose its appeal if it was forced to be in a foreign language that a child struggled to speak.[129] One stark example of the inhumanity of the situation was the case of a girl who felt she needed to ask for permission to speak Welsh before explaining to her teacher that a fellow pupil had swallowed a coin and needed help.[130] The complete or partial exclusion of Welsh also meant education failed many children in its primary function, to teach them English. Of course, this was not just down to teachers' pedagogical shortcomings. Learning a language is easiest when the new one being learned resembles the one already spoken, but this was not the case with Welsh and English.[131] Too many children went to school too infrequently and for too short a period. In rural areas, they rarely heard English outside school and thus had little opportunity to practise and develop their linguistic skills. Nonetheless these challenges were exacerbated by the prohibitions on Welsh and, as this book has argued, they failed in the very thing they were meant to aid: the spread of the English language.

As those prohibitions faded away and Welsh found a growing place in classrooms in the 1880s and 1890s, the efficiency of English teaching improved. This is clear in the language results of the 1901 census, the first to be broken down by broad age categories, and which clearly showed the effects of better education in how English-speaking was higher among those who had completed school. Across all Wales, the proportion of Welsh monoglots was lower amongst those aged fifteen to twenty-four than it was among children aged three to fourteen. Even allowing for some people developing their English after school, the statistics, particularly in rural counties, showed that schools were now teaching a majority of children English. Nonetheless in rural counties in the west, anything from a quarter to four in ten teenagers and young adults were recorded as unable to speak English.

Table 7.1. Language ability by age, 1901 census[132]

	Language spoken	Age 3–14 %	Age 15–24 %
Denbigh	Welsh	20.7	12.4
	Both	36.7	47.7
Flint	Welsh	7.9	4.0
	Both	32.5	43.2
Cardigan	Welsh	59.1	33.9
	Both	35.5	56.6
Carmarthen	Welsh	41.0	25.0
	Both	48.4	65.3
Pembroke	Welsh	13.9	7.7
	Both	15.9	23.3
Anglesey	Welsh	57.0	39.4
	Both	34.9	52.5
Caernarfon	Welsh	55.8	37.2
	Both	35.4	52.7
Meirionnydd	Welsh	60.6	36.1
	Both	34.4	58.4
Brecon	Welsh	10.2	6.2
	Both	23.5	34.4
Montgomery	Welsh	17.4	11.7
	Both	21.9	32.8
Radnor	Welsh	0.1	0.3
	Both	1.6	3.9
Glamorgan	Welsh	6.2	4.5
	Both	29.9	38.1
Monmouth	Welsh	0.5	0.5
	Both	5.3	9.4
Wales	**Welsh**	**15.9**	**10.5**
	Both	**27.3**	**37.4**

The official census report, however, did not focus on the failures and instead produced more detailed data for Meirionnydd to demonstrate the positive impacts of education.[133] This data showed how monolingual Welsh numbers fell with each year of school.

Table 7.2. Percentage of children in Meirionnydd recorded as monolingual Welsh by age, 1901 census

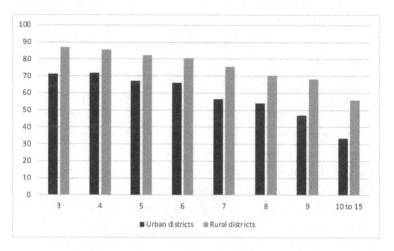

But these statistics again showed how education was not teaching every child English, especially in rural areas. More than half of 10- to 15-year-olds being unable to speak English in rural Meirionnydd was a damning indictment of a schooling system whose central purpose was to teach them that language.

The census was (and is) a crude measure of linguistic ability, which failed to embrace how fluency was a spectrum rather than something that people either had or did not have. Contemporary comment was better at noting the limitations of what children were able to do in English. An 1867 enquiry into agriculture noted that children left school 'too young to have acquired sufficient English even for colloquial purposes'.[134] In 1895, the headmaster of Aberystwyth Grammar School wrote that the result of the Welsh Not ('so prevalent some years ago') and the exclusion of Welsh from schools was that comparatively few former pupils were able 'to take pleasure in reading an English book or newspaper, or to hold an ordinary conversation in that language, and fewer still able to express themselves in writing'.[135] In 1900, John Rhŷs, who had been a teacher in Anglesey and then an inspector in north-east Wales in the 1870s, concluded that in rural areas children left school before they had mastered enough English to have a free conversation in the language and at most they retained enough to 'be able to answer simple questions addressed to them in very plain terms'.[136] In 1895, a new teacher at Cil-y-cwm did not think his older children could even do that and recorded that they were unable to answer 'questions of the most elementary kind'.[137] In her rural Cardiganshire school, Cassie Davies (b.1898) learned to read and write English well enough to win a scholarship to the secondary school but she recalled she had not been taught to speak the language and was thus very much afraid when she started her new school.[138] Whether children in such positions were recorded as bilingual or Welsh monoglots on the census came down to their parents' judgement.

In both rural and industrial areas, much of the English that children spoke was not what the English middle classes would have called correct. Of course, this was also true of much of England where regional dialects remained powerful throughout the century. But in Wales differences in spoken English were more significant because the syntax and sentence structure employed might take a Welsh form rather than follow conventional English. Children might confuse tenses or reproduce Welsh idioms in English, even though they made little sense in that language.[139] This was most common in industrial areas where the two languages intermingled. In contrast, spoken English in rural areas, even amongst teachers, could be very formal because it had been learned from books that employed traditional and arcane language and not developed in informal everyday settings.[140] The result was claims that Welsh people felt their English was poor when they met English working-class people in a way they would not had they encountered the English upper classes.[141]

The failures of schools to make many children fluent in English would have mattered less had children been literate in their own language. But, as one report put it of children aged six and seven: 'the language he reads he cannot understand, and the language he understands he cannot read'.[142] Whether children got beyond this in Welsh depended on whether they attended Sunday school and the character of education that local ministers or congregations could offer there. Many Sunday schools taught children to read Welsh but not to write it.[143] The result could be, as one former teacher pointed out, that those who moved away might find themselves forced to write to their mother in a language they had never spoken to her in.[144] Indeed, one Cardiganshire teacher claimed in 1885 that Welsh was 'falling fast into disuse' as a written language and that it was 'ridiculous' that the present generation could express themselves better in writing in English than their mother tongue.[145] But not everyone went to Sunday school and thus there were those who could not read or write either language.[146] A lack of literacy in Welsh cut people off from their own culture. Despite snide English remarks about Welsh literature, there was a wealth of newspapers, books and periodicals in that language. In 1886, the chief inspector concluded that in Welsh-speaking areas, 'the bulk of the scholars' left school 'without acquiring sufficient knowledge of English to understand or take pleasure in reading an English book, whilst their mere colloquial knowledge of Welsh is insufficient to enable them fully to appreciate a Welsh book'.[147] This may have had long-term consequences for people's decision around language transmission too. If people were not comfortable writing and reading Welsh then they may not have wanted to raise children in a language they were not literate in, even if it was their mother tongue.

The indignities and failures of education extended beyond language. Whilst the best teachers were praising, the worst ones were criticising and even humiliating. That may have faded with the growing professionalisation of teachers, but few schools gave individual children much credit or encouragement unless their performances really stood out. The chief inspector for Wales argued attendance would be better if teachers made children feel they were making continual progress.[148] Moreover, the whole nature of too many lessons was crude and rudimentary, focused on facts and recitals rather than curiosity and inquiry. Some children learned to pass the annual examination very well, perhaps thanks to a good memory, but floundered when asked to do something that had not been prepared beforehand.[149] The utility of rote learning passages, poetry, and geographical and historical facts was very limited, particularly if children were not encouraged to use this knowledge to think for themselves or cultivate a wider taste for reading. Failures in education thus denied working-class children not only the chances for better jobs but access to thinking about the world in different ways and windows into places beyond their horizons. Their mental wings were clipped.

Other children were failed by the structural inequalities of society. Countless children had to leave school at a young age because their families needed them to start work. Before this, weeks of school could be missed because children had to help with harvests, stone picking and the like. Some farmers' children worked from 5.30 a.m. before school, helping their father milk, and then worked on the farm again after school, denying them not only opportunities to play but probably the sleep they required to concentrate at school.[150] Some missed school because they had no shoes or their clothes were unsuitable.[151] In some places, children were made to leave school because their parents were in arrears with the fees, although schools could often be lenient on this issue.[152] Some were never sent in the first place. As late as 1884, only 75 per cent of school-aged children in Anglesey and 83 per cent in Caernarfonshire were on school registers.[153]

For too many children, the whole experience of school was something to be endured until they could begin working. This was especially true in industrial districts where work was inherently linked to manhood, and wage earning brought privileges at home such as a better share of food.[154] Walter Haydn Davies (b.1903) remembered school as a chore and singing 'Down the pit we want to go, Away from School with all its woe, Working hard as a collier's butty, Make us all so very happy!'[155] Edmund Stonelake (b.1873), who grew up in Aberdare, remembered that the boys all looked forward to 'the day of our emancipation' and 'freedom from the boredom and imprisonment provided by the four walls of a cell, called school'.[156] Such sentiments probably owed something to naivety about what the world of work was like and some retained their anger towards school even after leaving or came to lament that education had not rescued them from manual toil.[157] In 1878, a boy at work returned to Solva British school one dinnertime and 'wilfully tore the Regulations to pieces'.[158] He seems to have been just one of thousands of Welsh children who found school to be an alienating and futile experience.

The power of education

But education was not a universally negative experience. Children adapted to difficult circumstances and found happiness where they could.[159] School was a chance to be with friends and might be an escape from overcrowded and cold homes. There could be days out and prizes and special teas from the local gentry or school managers.[160] Michael Gareth Llewelyn was alienated by the Englishness of his education but still recalled there was a sense of 'learning together' and 'helping each other'. He thought that children being left to work on their own developed their self-reliance and made learning into 'a happy adventure in which all could join and assist'.[161] Some schools clearly developed a sense of community and loyalty, something clear in the ways pupils from National and British schools sometimes fought or vandalised each other's premises.[162]

Where children did learn English, something which became more common with the greater use of Welsh, school gave them a skill that brought prestige and was of practical use in later life in commerce and dealings with authority. The son of a teacher remembered a successful horse and cattle dealer coming to the house and saying 'Govnas, often I thanked you for teaching me my 'Rithmetic and how to speak the English.'[163] Children, too, were surely aware of the practical advantages of English, having heard that message at home and from teachers, and witnessing how wealthy people in their own communities spoke it. Teacher J. Lloyd Williams wrote in his autobiography that his pupils had been eager to learn English.[164] Nor did they always have to learn very much to derive some benefit. Historian David Howell argued that rural children found even a little English useful for begging from tourists.[165]

The growing use of Welsh was not the only improvement in classrooms. As the century progressed, there was a growing emphasis on better ways of teaching and ensuring the children were interested. Where teachers successfully negotiated language issues, and were willing to go beyond the requirements of equipping children to pass the annual examination, education could be an enlightening, even transformative experience. Teachers recorded the interest of pupils when things were explained to them rather than just left in a foreign language.[166] At Aberaman, the master noted how pupils were taken with stories from the Bible and that his use of them on Friday afternoons increased attendance, although it was not clear what language these stories were told in.[167] After the opening of a school at Llidiart-y-waun in 1872, the master wrote that the children were well behaved and all seemed 'most anxious to learn'.[168] At Bryncethin National school, attendance was patchy and the teacher struggled with the children's lack of English, but he blamed parents and said the children were 'very fond of school'.[169] Even the annual examinations were a chance to show off what had been learned and to receive recognition. The Revd B. K. Binns, inspector for Church of England schools in south Wales, wrote in 1863 that: 'The examinations evidently excite a high degree of interest among the scholars, and serve to impress them with a greater sense of the importance of their work. They are anxious to acquit themselves to the best of their ability.'[170] At Trefriw, the master recorded that the children were anxious to know how they had done in their examination and 'much delighted' when informed they had passed 'excellently'.[171]

R. T. Jenkins (b.1881), who knew some English before going to school, remembered it as a happy time with no language problems, even saying they deserved the frequent canings they received for talking.[172] E. D. Rowlands looked back fondly upon his time at the National school in Llanuwchllyn in the 1880s, the village where Owen M. Edwards had gone to school and received the Welsh Not. He noted that the teachers were very pleasant, the cane was not used and the children were allowed to speak Welsh and had things explained to them in that language.[173] In such conditions, and even where the cane was used, children could gain productive educations. At Capel Isaac British school in the 1880s, older children were reading books such as *The Vicar of Wakefield* and *Swiss Family Robinson*. The inspector recorded: 'They had evidently been taught not only to read but to enjoy it.'[174] By the end of the century, larger industrial towns had built higher-grade elementary schools for older children where important practical and technical skills were taught to the benefit of both the children and their industrial communities.[175] Secondary education in Wales expanded with the 1889 Welsh Intermediate Education Act and many local authorities provided scholarships to ensure talented children could attend them for free. Through those schools a few working-class children made their way into university and the professions. Slowly, formal education was becoming a route to genuine learning and social mobility.

But even for those children who did not take that route, learning did not have to stop with the end of school. Across all Wales, there was a strong culture of adult education through night schools, Sunday schools, miners' institutions, trade unions and community libraries. Secular adult education was most common in industrial areas where the population was large enough to support classes. At Aberaman, for example, funded by a local works, there was a large night school at the local boys' school. When it opened it found a significant demand amongst teenagers employed in local industry. In 1868, it had nineteen members under the age of twelve, 131 between the ages of twelve and twenty-one, and eleven members older than twenty-one.[176] However, adult education only reached a minority, not least because elementary school had turned many off learning or had denied them the basic skills to even get going with educating themselves. Attending a night school also meant missing out on free or rest time. Thus, in 1864, attendance fell off at Dafen Tin Plate Works' night school, with the 'lads' saying they were too tired for school after work.[177] Education, whether for children or adults, was always something very individual. Some struggled through and made the most of what they could. Others hated every element of it. As every teacher knows, even the best pedagogies will not inspire everyone.

Conclusion

Childhood is a time of 'emotional formation' when children learn what is expected of them, how they should behave and what they should feel. But it is also an 'emotional frontier', and children are subject to competing expectations which they have to negotiate and navigate.[178] In Victorian Wales, the messages of school and community did collide. School told children English was the language that mattered, but home and chapel told them, sometimes explicitly but certainly implicitly, the opposite. This meant it cannot be assumed that children just absorbed and accepted the messages of education. Certainly, some adults recalled their time at school with anger and frustration because of the linguistic insults and challenges they experienced. Others maybe internalised a sense that Welsh language and Welsh culture were inferior, and this could have shaped their attitudes as adults and to their own children. Yet some children were remarkably tolerant of what happened, sometimes because the exclusion of Welsh was just another example of a repressive or pointless education and sometimes because they felt they were still learning something. Whatever they felt, children were not just victims of a system. They exerted agency and could find dignity and even fun in resisting and subverting what was asked of them. Even deciding to comply with adults' demands can be seen as a form of childhood agency. But none of this changes the bare fact that there were children beaten and punished for speaking their mother tongue. Even if they were not angry about it, this was, surely, an injustice.

Notes

1. Myrddin ap Dafydd, *Under the Welsh Not* (Llanrwst, 2019).
2. *Third Report of the Royal Commission appointed to inquire into the Working of Elementary Education Acts, England and Wales* (London, 1887) [hereafter Cross Commission], p. 3.
3. Nora Marks Dauenhauer and Richard Dauenhauer, 'Technical, emotional, and ideological issues in reversing language shift; examples from southeast Alaska', in Lenore A. Grenoble and Lindsay J. Whaley (eds), *Endangered Languages: Language Loss and Community Response* (Cambridge, 1998), pp. 57–98, 65; David Crystal, *Language Death* (Cambridge, 2000), p. 85.

4   See for example, P. Trudgill, *Accent, Dialect and the School* (London, 1975), pp. 58, 67.
5   Jim Cummins and Tove Skutnabb-Kangas, 'Introduction', in Tove Skutnabb-Kangas and Jim Cummins (eds), *Minority Education: From Shame to Struggle* (Clevedon, 1988), pp. 1–6, 5.
6   Ann Monroe, 'Shame solutions: how shame impacts school-aged children and what teachers can do to help', *The Education Forum*, 73, 1 (2009), 58–66.
7   Andrew Dalby, *Language in Danger* (London, 2002), p. 165.
8   Claudia Soares, 'Emotions, senses, experience and the history of education', *History of Education*, 52, 2–3 (2023), 516–38.
9   Rebecca Clifford, *Survivors: Children's Lives After the Holocaust* (New Haven, 2020), p. 7.
10 Julie-Marie Strange, *Fatherhood and the British Working Class, 1865–1914* (Cambridge, 2015), p. 149.
11 'Ysgol Sirol Tregaron', *Celt Llundain*, 19 January 1901, 5.
12 Henri Bourassa, *La Langue Francaise au Canada* (Montreal, 1915), p. 37.
13 J. B. Jones, 'Welshnot', *Yr Arweinydd*, August 1880, 208–10.
14 'Y Welsh Note', *Trysorfa y Plant*, October 1879, 271–2.
15 'Society for utilizing the Welsh language', *Aberystwyth Observer & Merionethshire News*, 8 June 1889, 5.
16 Andronicus, 'Yr ysgol: pennod III: dim Cymraeg', *Cymru'r Plant*, November 1894, 313–17.
17 David Davies, 'Atgofion mebyd', *Western Mail*, 27 November 1922, 6.
18 David Davies, *Reminiscences of My Country and My People* (Cardiff, 1925), pp. 28–9.
19 Watcyn Wyn, 'Haner cant o flynyddau', *Y Diwygiwr*, September 1894, 261–7.
20 *Cambrian News*, 7 June 1889, 10. Nonetheless, when he told this story in a public meeting the audience laughed when he said he recalled getting seven slaps for speaking Welsh seven times 'and the schoolmaster did not mince matters'.
21 'At y werin weithyddawl Gymreig', *Seren Gomer*, February 1848, 42–3.
22 Quoted in Hywel Gwyn Evans, *Pum Ysgol* (Llandysul, 2003), p. 5.
23 'Teaching of Welsh', *Brecon County Times*, 25 January 1907, 6.
24 'Adgofion am y "Welsh Note" yn yr Ysgol Ddyddiol', *Pembroke County Guardian and Cardigan Reporter*, 8 October 1909, 2.
25 For example, Hugh Evans, *Cwm Eithin* (Liverpool, 1933), p. 193.
26 R. E. Jones in 'Y Welsh Not yn Llangernyw', *Llafar Gwlad*, 64 (1999), 17.
27 William Williams, 'Cymru fu', *Cymru*, 15 June 1892, 34.
28 T. Gwynn Jones, *Gwedi Brad a Gofid* (Caernarfon, 1898), p. 56.
29 In a 1942 letter quoted in Hefin Wyn, *Ar Drywydd Niclas Y Glais: Comiwnydd Rhonc a Christion Gloyw* (Talybont, 2017), p. 34.
30 W. J. Gruffydd, *The Years of the Locust*, trans. D. Myrddin Lloyd (Llandysul, 1976), pp. 87–90.
31 D. Parry-Jones, *Welsh Country Upbringing* (London, 1948), pp. 19–20, 148.
32 E. P. Thompson, *The Making of the English Working Class* (London, 1963), preface.

33 W. C. Elvet Thomas recalled that his father, who was born in 1878, was very bitter at how English his education had been and became determined that his own sons should know Welsh history: W. C. Elvet Thomas, *Tyfu'n Gymro* (Llandysul, 1972), p. 34.
34 William George, *My Brother and I* (London, 1958), p. 55.
35 David Thomas, *Silyn: Robert Silyn Roberts, 1871–1930* (Liverpool, 1956), pp. 5–7.
36 Emma Griffin, *Bread Winner: An Intimate History of the Victorian Economy* (New Haven, 2020), pp. 272–3.
37 'John Jones, Junior: Sef anturiaethau Cymro ieuangc mewn bywyd cyhoeddus', *Baner ac Amserau Cymru*, 12 December 1894, 12.
38 A. Bailey Williams, 'Education in Montgomeryshire in the late nineteenth century', *Montgomeryshire Collections Relating to Montgomeryshire and its Borders*, 52 (1952), 83–106, 93.
39 South Wales Miners' Library, Josiah Jones interview (1972).
40 E. Davies, *Cofiant Y Diweddar Barch. Morris Roberts* (Utica, 1879), pp. 22–3.
41 St Fagans oral history collection, Mr Jones, Rhosygwalia, Y Bala (b.1892).
42 Glaslyn, 'Adgofion bore oes', *Cymru*, 15 October 1904, 149–54.
43 John E. Southall, *Wales and her Language* (London, 1892), p. 78.
44 *Minutes of the CCE, 1870–71*, pp. 153, 156; J. Lloyd Williams, *Atgofion Tri Chwarter Canrif, cyf. II* (London, 1942), p. 71.
45 Wil John Edwards, *From the Valley I Came* (London, 1956), p. 16.
46 'Addysg yn Nghymru', *Y Dysgedydd Crefyddol*, June 1851, 166–9.
47 'Schoolmasters I have known', *Welsh Outlook*, 14, 5 (May 1927), 124.
48 St Fagans oral history collection, 8720–1.
49 'Wales day by day', *Western Mail*, 29 January 1895, 4. For similar memories of being made to pronounce and spell a village name's incorrectly see 'Y Welsh Not yn Llangeryw', *Llafar Gwlad*, 64 (1999), 17.
50 'The Welsh Note', *Western Mail*, 7 October 1927, 13.
51 'Wrexham British Schools', *Wrexham Advertiser*, 17 March 1888, 6.
52 Strange, *Fatherhood and the British Working Class*, pp. 146–7; Andy Medhurst, *A National Joke: Popular Comedy and English Cultural Identities* (London, 2007); Peter Bailey, *Popular Culture and Performance in the Victorian City* (Cambridge, 1998).
53 Jacob Middleton, 'The experience of corporal punishment in schools, 1890–1940', *History of Education*, 37, 2 (2008), 253–75, 270.
54 NLW, 'Yr Hen Ysgol, 1864–7', William Williams papers.
55 PA, Llyswen National school, 4 May 1864.
56 Ellen Ross, *Love and Toil: Motherhood in Outcast London, 1870–1918* (Oxford, 1993), pp. 149–51; Griffin, *Bread Winner*, pp. 243–4; Jane Humphries, 'Childhood and violence in working-class England, 1800–1870', in Laurence Brockliss and Heather Montgomery (eds), *Childhood and Violence in the Western Tradition* (Oxford, 2010), pp. 135–40. For memories of fighting see J. Lloyd Williams, *Atgofion Tri Chwarter Canrif, cyf. I* (London, 1941), pp. 63–4.

For memories of accepting being hit see Edwards, *From the Valley I Came*, pp. 13, 26, 27–8.
57 Strange, *Fatherhood and the British Working Class*, pp. 181, 184.
58 See the memories of such a teacher in Maesteg in Philip Boswood Ballard, *Things I Cannot Forget* (London, 1937), p. 24.
59 Abel J. Jones, *I was Privileged* (Cardiff, 1943), p. 7.
60 'The school room', *The Cambrian*, 9 January 1841, 3.
61 Maude Morgan Thomas, *When I was a Girl in Wales* (New York, 1936), p. 45.
62 Isfryn, 'Pan oeddym ny yn blant yn yr ysgol', *Perl y Plant*, April 1900, 125–6.
63 Granellian, 'Ysgolion Cymru fu', *Tywysydd y Plant*, 34, 4 (1904), 115.
64 Henry Jones Williams, 'Hunangofiant enwogion', *Y Geninen*, 28, 2 (1910), 124–9.
65 Sir Henry Jones, *Old Memories* (London, 1922), pp. 108–9.
66 Robert Roberts, *A Wandering Scholar: The Life and Opinions of Robert Roberts* (Cardiff, 1991), p. 110.
67 Edward Robert, HMI, 'Address delivered to teachers at Llangefni', 23 August 1900; leaflet contained in CRO, Bryncroes Board school logbook.
68 'Adeiladu addoldai', *Cronicl y Cymdeithasau Crefyddol*, December 1875, 323–6.
69 Honourable Society of Cymmrodorion, *Report of the Committee appointed into the Advisability of the Introduction of the Welsh Language into the Course of Elementary Education in Wales: The Introduction of Welsh as a Specific Subject: Appendix to Report* (Aberdare, 1885), p. 14.
70 Darius Dare, 'Captain R. Davies', *South Wales Star*, 25 November 1892. This account stated: 'The holder of the "Welsh mark" was an object of derision to the whole of the scholars, and in this way Welsh boys were taught early in life to be ashamed of their noble old language, and to look upon one who spoke it as belonging to a lower caste.'
71 Jonathan Rose, 'Willingly to school: the working-class response to elementary education in Britain, 1875–1918', *Journal of British Studies*, 32, 2 (1993), 114–38.
72 Dalby, *Language in Danger*, p. 88.
73 Paul Thompson, *The Edwardians: The Remaking of British Society*, 2nd edn (London, 1992), p. 39.
74 Humphries, *Hooligans or Rebels?*, pp. 29, 87–8. For more on children's resistance see Laura M. Mair, 'They "come for a lark": London Ragged School Union teaching advice in practice, 1844–70', *Studies in Church History*, 55 (2019), 324–46.
75 CmA, Llangunnock Vaughan's charity, 22 December 1876.
76 *Cambrian News*, 7 June 1889, 10.
77 See *The Carmarthen*, v, 3 February 1901, 50–1, cited in Grigg, *Trinity College*, p. 124.
78 NEWAR, Dyserth National school, 26 February 1880.
79 CA, Llechryd school, 2–7 December 1872.
80 Williams, *Atgofion Tri Chwarter Canrif*, cyf. II, p. 56. For more memories of pupil violence see James Williams, *Give Me Yesterday* (Llandysul, 1971), p. 21.

81 For example, CA, Llanon British school, 15 October 1869.
82 Evan Jones, *John Jones yn yr Ysgol: Ffug-hanesyn, yn Rhoddi Darluniad o Ysgolion Gwledig Cymru, oddeutu'r Flwyddyn 1840*, 2nd edn (Lampeter, 1904), p. 34; Gareth W. Williams, 'The disenchantment of the world: innovation, crisis and change in Cardiganshire, c.1880–1910', *Ceredigion*, 9, 4 (1983), 303–21, 307–8; D. Parry-Jones, *Welsh Children's Games and Pastimes* (Denbigh, 1964), p. 163.
83 Davies, *Reminiscences of My Country*, p. 29.
84 PbA, Croes-goch, 10 August 1870.
85 CA, Llanon British, 10 and 24 February 1872.
86 Gwyneth Vaughan, 'Bryn Ardudwy a'i bobl: ein hysgolfeistri', *Yr Haul*, 6, 65 (May 1904), 225–30.
87 'The school boys' strike: extension to Swansea', *Western Mail*, 11 October 1889, 3; 'Strike of Cardiff school children', *Western Mail*, 9 October 1889, 4; 'The school boys' strike at Swansea', *Western Mail*, 21 October 1889, 3; 'The schoolboy strike', *South Wales Echo*, 15 October 1889, 3. See Humphries, *Hooligans or Rebels?*, ch. 4, for a discussion of the strikes.
88 NEWAH, Autobiography of Edward Hughes.
89 MRO, Bala British, 4 and 5 January 1869.
90 NEWAH, Autobiography of Samuel Nutall.
91 *Reports of the Commissioners of Inquiry into the State of Education in Wales. Part III: North Wales* (London, 1847), p. 25.
92 *Reports of the Commissioners of Inquiry into the State of Education in Wales. Part III*, pp. 24–5.
93 Roberts, *A Wandering Scholar*, p. 311.
94 MRO, Llangollen National, 7 January 1869, 1 May 1874.
95 For example, NEWAR, Ruabon Boys National, 13 September 1892 and 13 October 1893.
96 In 1867, a man in his forties registered as a pupil: NEWAH, Bodelwyddan National, 8 January 1867.
97 CA, Llanon British, 5 April 1872; Llanwenog National, 3 June 1869; Ferwig, 28 March 1868; PA, Newtown National, 27 April 1864.
98 Parry-Jones, *Welsh Children's Games and Pastimes*, pp. 162, 150; William George, *My Brother and I* (London, 1958), p. 40.
99 See the memory in Kate Davies and T. Llew Jones, *Canrif o Addysg Gynradd: Ysgol Tregroes, 1878–1978* (Llandysul, 1978), p. 5.
100 PA, Cemais British, 24 March 1863.
101 CA, Newgate British, 27 May, 12 June 1867.
102 David James, 'Myfyr Emlyn: y tudalen cyntaf yn hanes ei fywyd', *Y Geninen*, March 1897, 46–50.
103 John Brinsley, *Ludus Literarius or the Grammar Schoole*, ed. E. T. Campagnac (1612; London, 1917), p. 219.
104 Carnhuanawc, 'Ysgolion Cymreig', *Seren Gomer*, April 1824, 114–15.
105 NLW, 'Yr Hen Ysgol, 1864–7', William Williams papers. Similarly, a 1920s appeal for folk tales produced an account, dated to the 1840s, of a boy who claimed he had heard no one speaking Welsh and had thus not passed the Welsh

Not on. He was caned for lying: NLW, David Thomas, Aberystwyth papers, Elerch B30.
106 Michael Gareth Llewelyn, *Sand in the Glass* (London, 1943), pp. 8–9.
107 James Pillans, *Contributions to the Cause of Education* (London, 1856), p. 339.
108 NEWAR, Dyserth National, 25 February 1880.
109 For example, 'Hanes hynod, ond gwir', *Tarian y Gweithiwr*, 30 August 1888, 3.
110 On embodied working-class masculinity see Stephanie Ward, 'Miners' bodies and masculine identity in Britain, c.1900–1950', *Cultural & Social History*, 18, 3 (2021), 443–6.
111 Carol Dyhouse, *Girls Growing Up in Late Victorian and Edwardian England* (London, 1981); A. Turnbull, 'Learning her womanly work: the elementary school curriculum, 1870–1914', in Felicity Hunt (ed.), *Lessons for Life: The Schooling of Girls and Women 1850–1950* (Oxford, 1987), pp. 83–100.
112 W. Gareth Evans, *Education and Female Emancipation: The Welsh Experience, 1847–1914* (Cardiff, 1990), p. 255.
113 NEWAR, Gresford National, April 1869.
114 Jacob Middleton, 'Thomas Hopley and mid-Victorian attitude to corporal punishment', *History of Education*, 34, 6 (2005), 599–615, 606; Middleton, 'Experience of corporal punishment', 272. A punishment book for Llandderfel Board school was kept between 1900 and 1906 and it showed that seventy-six incidents of corporal punishment being inflicted but only two were to girls and none were to a child under eight: MRO, Llandderfel Board school punishment book.
115 Davies and Jones, *Canrif o Addysg Gynradd*, p. 6.
116 St Fagans archives, Note by John Griffiths (1925).
117 A. N. Cooper, 'Wales in November Sunshine', *Yorkshire Post and Leeds Intelligencer*, 25 November 1902 6.
118 At Llanwenog, the master recorded that he had punished three girls for 'talking Welsh in school contrary to the rules': CA, Llanwenog National, 16 December 1880. Also see PbA, Dinas, 3 May 1870.
119 Mrs Hugh Lewis, 'School days fifty years ago', *Welsh Outlook*, 18, 5 (1931), 123–5.
120 James Rhys Jones (Kilsby), 'A Lecture on the educational state of Wales' (1851), *Mid Wales Herald*, supplement no. 1 (1860).
121 Watcyn Wyn, *Adgofion Watcyn Wyn* (Merthyr, 1907), p. 16; Wactyn Wyn, 'Trem yn ol', *Y Geninen*, 22, 3, (1904), 181–5, 182. Also see E. Pan Jones, *Oes Gofion neu Fraslun o Hanes fy Mywyd* (Bala, 1911), p. 11.
122 Jacob Middleton, 'The cock of the school: a cultural history of playground violence in Britain, 1880–1940', *Journal of British Studies*, 52, 4 (2013), 887–907.
123 J. Brynach Davies, 'Ysgolion', *Pembroke County Guardian and Cardigan Reporter*, 7 July 1904, 5.
124 W. Jones, 'Talybont a'r gymydogaeth haner can' mlynedd yn ol', *Y Negesydd*, 3 January 1896, 1.
125 'Y bobloedd', *Tarian y Gweithiwr*, 31 August 1899, 3.

126 W. Meredith Morris, *The Renaissance of Welsh Literature* (Maesteg, 1908), pp. 261–2.
127 For a critical view of the idea of children's agency see David F. Lancy, 'Unmasking Children's Agency', *AnthropoChildren*, 1, 2 (2012), 1–20.
128 Mona Gleason, 'Avoiding the agency trap: caveats for historians of children, youth, and education', *History of Education*, 45, 4 (2016), 446–59, 457; Susan Miller, 'Assent as agency in the early years of the children of the American Revolution', *Journal of the History of Childhood and Youth*, 9, 1 (2016), 48–65.
129 Cross Commission, 3rd Report, p. 3; NLW, 'Yr Hen Ysgol, 1864–7', William Williams papers.
130 J. Lloyd Williams, *Atgofion Tri Chwarter Canrif, cyf. IV* (London, 1945), p. 118.
131 Nicholas Ostler, *Empires of the Word: A Language History of the World* (London, 2005), p. 556.
132 Dot Jones, *Statistical Evidence Relating to the Welsh Language, 1801–1911* (Cardiff, 1998).
133 *Census of England and Wales, 1901: General Report* (London, 1904), section X: Languages in Wales and Monmouthshire.
134 *Commission on the Employment of Children, Young Persons, and Women in Agriculture (1867), Third Report of the Commissioners* (London, 1870), p. 56.
135 Thomas Owen, 'The teaching of Welsh in schools', *Young Wales*, 1, 8 (1895), 189.
136 Sir John Rhys and David Brynmor Jones, *The Welsh People; Chapters on their Origin, History, Laws, Language, Literature, and Characteristics* (New York, 1900), p. 529.
137 CmA, Cil-y-cwm school, 2 October 1895.
138 Atgofion cyffredinol Cassie Davies, British Library sounds collection.
139 Williams, *Atgofion Tri Chwarter Canrif, cyf. IV*, pp. 177–8; *Report of the CCE, 1886–87*, p. 356. For Welsh-language influences on spoken English in Wales see Robert Penhallurick, 'English in Wales', in David Britain (ed.), *Language in the British Isles* (Cambridge, 2007), pp. 152–70.
140 Rhys and Jones, *The Welsh People*, p. 528; Williams, *Atgofion Tri Chwarter Canrif, cyf. IV*, p. 239.
141 For reflections on this see Lewis Edwards, *Yr Athrawes o Ddifrif* (Caernarfon, 1859), pp. xiv–xv.
142 Quoted in Alfred T. Davies (ed.), *OM (Sir Owen M. Edwards): A Memoir* (Cardiff, 1946), p. 86.
143 For memories of learning to read at chapel see NEWAH, Autobiography of Edward Hughes (b.1856). For memories of struggling to write in Welsh see Thomas Jones, *Rhymney Memories* (1938; Llandysul, 1970), p. 52.
144 J. Lloyd Williams, *Atgofion Tri Chwarter Canrif, cyf. III* (Dinbych, 1944), p. 118.
145 Honourable Society of Cymmrodorion, *Report of the Committee Appointed to Inquire into the Advisability of the Introduction of the Welsh language. Appendix*, p. 10.
146 Cross Commission, 2nd Report, p. 287.
147 *Report of the CCE, 1886–87*, pp. 364–5.
148 *Report of the CCE, 1888–89*, p. 343.

149 *Report of the CCE, 1878–79*, p. 655.
150 See the evidence of a farmer in *First Report of the Royal Commission on Land on Wales and Monmouthshire* (London, 1894), pp. 97–8.
151 For children missing school because of a lack of shoes see GA, Georgetown Girls, 11, 14 and 21 September 1863. For missing school because clothes were 'so bad' see Richard Burton archives, St David's RC, 11 November 1873.
152 For example, NEWAH, Rhyd-y-mwyn, 12 July 1873; Nercwys National, 3 August 1883.
153 *Report of the CCE, 1884–85*, p. 337.
154 Griffin, *Bread Winner*, ch. 7.
155 Walter Haydn Davies, *The Right Place, the Right Time: Memories of Boyhood Days in a Welsh Mining Community* (Swansea, 1975), p. 90.
156 Edmund Stonelake, *The Autobiography of Edmund Stonelake* (Bridgend, 1981), p. 49.
157 See the frustrations in Roberts, *A Wandering Scholar*, p. 115.
158 PbA, Solva British, 5 April 1878.
159 Jamie L. Bronstein, *The Happiness of the British Working Class* (Stanford, 2023), p. 40.
160 For example, Bangor University Archives: Diary of David Griffith, 16 September 1868, 31 December 1869.
161 Llewelyn, *Sand in the Glass*, p. 19.
162 For memories of this Williams, *Atgofion Tri Chwarter Canrif, cyf. I*, ch. 6; Laura M. Mair, '"Give my love": community and companionship among former ragged school scholars', *Family & Community History*, 21, 3 (2018), 166–79.
163 Llewelyn, *Sand in the Glass*, p. 16.
164 Williams, *Atgofion Tri Chwarter Canrif, cyf. IV*, pp. 116–17.
165 David W. Howell, *The Rural Poor in Eighteenth-century Wales* (Cardiff, 2000), pp. 108–9.
166 For example, PA, Trecastell British, 14 January 1863 and Crickhowell British, 19 February 1868.
167 GA, Aberaman Boys, 13 September and 13 December 1867.
168 PA, Llidiart-y-waun, 6 December 1872.
169 GA, Bryncethin National, 4 November 1870, 2 February 1871, 7 April 1871.
170 *Report of the CCE, 1863–64*, p. 48.
171 CwyA, Trefriw, 8 June 1869.
172 R. T. Jenkins, *Edrych yn Ôl* (London, 1968), pp. 61, 64.
173 E. D. Rowlands, *Atgofion am Llanuwchllyn* (Nant Peris, 1975), p. 78.
174 *Report of the CCE, 1882–83*, p. 424.
175 Smith, *Schools, Politics and Society*, p. 145.
176 GA, Aberaman Boys, 1868.
177 CmA, Dafen Tin Plate Works National, 12 February 1864.
178 Stephanie Olsen, 'The history of childhood and the emotional turn', *History Compass*, 15 (2017), 1–10, 6.

8
PARENTAL AND COMMUNITY ATTITUDES TOWARDS EDUCATION AND THE WELSH LANGUAGE

Life was not easy for most people living in rural Wales. Both farmers and their labourers lived on diets dominated by potatoes and bread. Meat was rarely eaten and even cheese was a luxury. Hunger was common, especially for the labourers. Homes were cold, damp and overcrowded. Working hours were long: dawn to dusk in winter and sometimes twelve hours a day in the summer. Whether at work or not, life was a constant struggle against the weather, with the comforts of family and religion the only respite for most. To escape, tens of thousands of people moved to the mining and iron districts, where pay – and thus food – was better but working hours were still long and arduous and the housing just as unhealthy and uncomfortable. These industrial communities were growing too fast; there were no sewars, running water was scarce and sanitation was a constant problem. Inevitably, there was disease and ill health. Roads were filthy with cinders, coal, mud, dust and household waste. The air was polluted by the constant thick plumes of industrial smoke. The rivers fared little better, as they were used to dispose all manner of human, animal and industrial waste. As in the countryside, there was little recreation beyond what people could make themselves, although alcohol supplemented prayers in giving people hope and escape. Of course, there were ebbs and flows in the state of the Welsh economy, and wages did gradually rise as the century progressed, but life was never easy for those who made their living with their hands.

These basic facts framed and shaped popular attitudes to schools. Education was regarded as a means for children to escape such a life because it taught them to speak English. The belief that the English language was a route out of poverty was so strong that it meant very few working-class people thought Welsh should have a place in schools. Yet, at the same time, going to school prevented children from working to earn a little money that might alleviate some of the poverty that their families were enduring.

Parental attitudes had a very direct influence on how schools operated. British and National schools competed with each other for pupils and did not want to do anything that might turn parents away. Even the post-1870 Board schools were still dependent on attendance and enrolment for their grants and thus had to ensure they did not alienate local opinion. The influence of parents was muted by the attendance by-laws that were introduced in some areas after the 1870 Act, but this was a slow and gradual process. Not until 1880 was attendance compulsory everywhere and, even then, children could still work from the age of ten if they had reached certain education standards. Moreover, enforcing attendance was never easy, even with the force of the law, and thus parental attitudes continued to have a significant influence. Such arguments emphasise the agency of the working class. Despite the poverty they endured, people were not passive victims. Just as their children did, parents argued and resisted. Whatever the state and teachers wanted education to be, communities helped fashion it to their own needs and interests. Or at least they tried to.

Parental attitudes to education

Since parents were not forced to send their children to school for most of the century, many chose not to. The Blue Books, for example, argued that in north Wales just 22 per cent of children under fifteen were at school.[1] Some observers claimed this was because parents did not value education. The High Constable of Merthyr blamed children leaving school to work in mines or ironworks on the 'greed' of parents.[2] Others thought that parents did not appreciate education because they were not educated themselves. Teachers were often not very sympathetic either. Logbooks are full of their complaints about the apathy of parents. In 1871, for example, the master of Solva British school complained the instruction was 'greatly crippled by the extremely irregular attendance of children who are only sent to school when their parents can find nothing else for them to do'.[3]

Such perspectives failed to appreciate how much of an issue the cost of education was. Until 1891, most elementary schools charged fees, unless they enjoyed a significant charitable bequest. Fees were typically one or two pennies a week, although they could be higher. Llyswen National school charged the children of farmers as much as 4d a week, although the children of their labourers only had to pay 2d.[4] The sums involved might not sound much but they were unaffordable for many families, especially if they had a large number of children. In 1871, one departmental official said about one-fifth of children in Caernarfon were unable to pay fees because of the poverty and thriftlessness of their parents.[5]

Logbooks are thus full of complaints about arrears. Some schools were active in chasing these. In 1885, the Trefor Welsh Granite Quarry Company sent an angry circular to parents: 'The neglect of parents is simply disgraceful! and we are not going to educate your children for nothing. Besides which it is grossly unfair to those decent honest people who do pay.' This prompted the parents of twelve children to withdraw them from the company school.[6] Moreover, some schools expected parents to supply books, slates and pencils, which added to the cost. The expectation, real or imagined, that children dress smartly for schools also discouraged some poor parents from sending their children.[7] It was little wonder that Penrhyndeudraeth British school complained it was losing pupils to a rival school where fees were cheaper, books free and there was a clothing club to help parents.[8] Local authorities did pay the fees of some impoverished children, while some schools or teachers decided not to charge parents unable to pay, although this was easier at larger schools that had bigger incomes.[9] But such charity was never on sufficient scale to overcome the issue that many children missed out on an education because the costs involved were beyond their parents' means. Indeed, even after fees were abolished, finances could still keep children at home. In 1892, for example, an attendance officer told the master at Ruabon Boys National school there was little he could do because a miners' strike meant parents did not have enough food to give their children to attend and they were needed to help pick coal from waste tips.[10]

Going to school also meant losing out on opportunities to work and supplement the family income. On farms, young children were employed to scare birds away, pick stones from fields, and help herd sheep and cattle. Older ones looked after livestock and helped sow and harvest crops and hay. Indeed, many farms depended on child labour if tasks were going to be completed in the short windows that the weather allowed. In industrial districts, ironworks and mines created even more employment opportunities for children. After 1842, legislation outlawed the employment underground of those under the age of ten, but this was not always enforced and it did nothing to prevent older children working. Such restrictions were not always popular with parents in need of the extra wages. Working-class finances were so precarious that every penny could matter.[11] A labourer's wife in the Bridgend district told a commission on child employment that she could not afford to lose the small wages of her four children: 'I know it is a good thing to have learning, but still the sixpences are a great help.' The same inquiry also heard the words of a Cardiganshire labourer who spoke a little English, earned 1s. 6d a day and had six children, none of whom could read or write:

> There is no school in the parish where I live, and if there was I could not afford to send my children to it. I never get meat, except now and then a bit of bacon. I live upon potatoes, bread and cheese, and a little butter. The labour of children becomes valuable after 10; a boy of that age can earn 1*l*. 10*s*. a year, besides getting his meals at

the farm house ... Education is a good thing, but bread for a poor man is better.[12]

Thus, in both rural and industrial areas, education was a financial cost to parents, both in terms of its direct expenses and the lost opportunity for wages. The irony was that education could be a route to alleviate or escape such poverty. Many parents knew this, and an appreciation of education was part of the wider culture of self-help, moral discipline and respectability that Nonconformity in particular pushed. Some made significant sacrifices to send their children to school. A Flintshire lead miner told an investigator at the end of the 1840s that his children were a great comfort to him after a day at work and he ensured they all went to school, even though it cost two or three pence per week each. This was not easy: 'We have strived very hard to keep them in school, eating dry bread many times to be able to do this for them.'[13] Some made sacrifices for very practical reasons. Lacking in concentration, stamina and strength, young children were very limited in what kind of paid work they could actually do. Sending them to school meant they did not have to be looked after by their parents, neighbours or older siblings.[14] An 1843 report on Cardiff Infant School, which noted the kindness there towards children, claimed that parents had expressed gratitude for how the school had made their children less sullen and better behaved at home.[15] Parents were also reacting to the inducements laid down by local elites. There were local charitable clubs which would help parents clothe their children if they attended school regularly.[16] Industrialists valued schooling as developing self-control, discipline, cleanliness and the like. Some employers would not take on children unless they had attended school for some time.[17] Joseph Marryat, owner of an ironworks at Ystradgynlais, would not employ children unless they had learned English. This encouraged attendance at the school attached to his works.[18]

Some observers tried to make clear that the Welsh labouring classes did value education. The bishop of St David's was reported as saying it was very rare that the poor were unaware of the benefits of education, even if, and sometimes because, they had received none themselves.[19]

Inspector Shadrach Pryce argued there was 'a genuine love of learning' among the Welsh people.[20] Binns, another inspector, said in 1863:

> Education is becoming more generally appreciated, and wherever the means of obtaining it are duly supplied the labouring population promptly avail themselves of them. Considerable sacrifices are willingly made to obtain good schooling, and school fees above the usual rate are in many cases cheerfully paid.[21]

Such interpretations went too far and education was not universally popular amongst either parents or employers. In slate-quarrying areas, there was a belief that boys became better workmen if they started work early. This encouraged their withdrawal from school at just nine or ten.[22] In coal and iron districts, employment opportunities were plentiful which reduced the practical need for and advantages of literacy.[23] Not all rural parents thought it useful either. In 1869, the master of Llangeitho British school recorded that a father had come to school complaining that, amongst other things, his son was being taught reading and arithmetic, subjects which 'he considered to be useless'.[24] Such antipathy could be from experience. Parents might remember the failings of their own education or see that their children had not learned much and were still unable to speak English.[25] This was especially true of dame schools, which, according to one of the Blue Books commissioners, caused parents to be indifferent about education: 'Money, they say, has been wasted – time wasted – and but little learnt.'[26] Some farmers, meanwhile, feared that educated children would not want to work anymore. David Davies MP, who was also chairman of a schoolboard, reported that one farmer told him of a 13-year-old he had taken on: 'the first thing he does is to take up a newspaper, and if I tell him to get on with his work, he snubs me telling me he knows more than I do'.[27] Some children of farmers actually received less education than those of their labourers. The latter would not be employed regularly until they entered service, usually between the ages of nine and thirteen, but farmers' young children might be made to look after stock or scare birds from a very early age because there was no need for parents to pay them.[28]

In 1885, the Bwlchysarnau logbook recorded that a father took his girl out of school on her first day because she did not like it. He said he would not send her to school 'against her will'.[29] This points to how not educating children could be out of love, but it also hints at the widespread belief that school was not as important for girls. The Blue Books calculated there were almost 20 per cent fewer girls than boys in north Wales schools.[30] In 1851, the census found that 57 per cent of pupils enrolled at Welsh schools in receipt of public funding were male.[31] A winning entry at the 1861 National Eisteddfod in Conwy claimed some mothers equated the education of girls with the promotion of vanity and laziness. Such attitudes were not just the product of ingrained prejudices but also rooted in the knowledge that there were few opportunities for educated women.[32] Attitudes were slowly becoming more progressive, but change was slow. In 1886, for example, the British school at Menai Bridge had eighty-two boys but just fifty-seven girls.[33]

There was thus a widespread but far from universal desire for education, even if many parents were unable to afford to send their children to school. One reason for the varied perspectives was how different individual schools were. The vicar of Llanbadarnfawr noted that: 'Parents are very quick in appreciating a good school, and will make sacrifices to give their children the advantage of it', but that they would not send them to 'a bad one'. Similarly, an 1867 report on children's employment reported a parent would not make children walk three or four miles to school every day 'if he doubts the capacity of the master or the value of the instruction imparted'.[34] Others did make their children walk that distance to a school they respected, even though there was a nearer inferior one.[35]

Some parents clearly took an interest in what they were getting for their fees. They might thus quiz their children on how much English had been learned.[36] At Dyserth, the master received complaints in 1880 from parents that children were being neglected and no notice taken of their homework.[37] At Llwydcoed, a father wrote to the teacher asking that his son be given more attention because he was not making much progress. The father threatened to remove the child 'if he don't learn little beter [sic]'.³⁸ W. J. Gruffydd (b.1881) recalled how parents in Bethel all wanted to see their children do better than other people's. They were determined their children get on in the world and be better than quarrymen. He was forced to go to school when ill so he could get a medal for attendance.³⁹ However, it was not easy for poorly educated parents to assess how their children were progressing. In 1846, one writer complained that some children were removed from school because they were being taught to pronounce English differently to the incorrect ways their parents had learned at school.⁴⁰

Parents were thus not passive consumers of their children's education. Matthew Arnold, then inspecting schools in Wales, wrote in his 1852 report that parents paying 6d a week in fees are apt to 'criticize nicely, though not always judiciously … They desire this and that for their child, and they object to this and that, and, being often not very reasonable persons, they greatly embarrass a teacher.'⁴¹ These were better-off parents but it was also true of many poorer ones too. In the first week of a new school at Aberaman, the master recorded that he found 'parents in this neighbourhood are not deficient in the art of scolding'.⁴² A teacher in Anglesey said that notices of non-attendance sent to parents caused offence leading them to complain, keep their children away even more, or change the school they were registered at.⁴³ A teacher who worked in Brynaman in the 1870s recalled that some mothers came into the school and, in strong language and in front of the children, told the master what they thought of him, sometimes manhandling him in the process.⁴⁴ Robert Roberts recalled of his teaching career: 'I found a considerable amount of unreasonableness among the parents, unreasonable expectations of rapid progress, silly complaints about trifling matters of discipline and other little disagreements of that sort: but that annoyance wore away as the parents acquired confidence in me.'⁴⁵

The agency parents were willing to exert and the rivalry between British and National schools meant that teachers and managers could not afford to alienate parents. Some National schools did not teach the catechism for fear of upsetting Nonconformist parents, with clergymen saying 'If we did not do this our schools would be nearly empty.'[46] Others tried but gave up in the face of parental opposition.[47] In 1869, an inspection of Llanon National school criticised how moderate the religious instruction was but recorded that this was due to the opposition of parents.[48] At Corris, a local quarry-owner had wanted to establish a National school but, because parents were opposed, he founded and funded a non-denominational school with a Methodist master instead. National and Church schools that did insist on the catechism being taught might experience low attendances. In Edeyrn, after the rector insisted that children attended church on a Sunday, so many children were withdrawn that the school had to close.[49] When the catechism was not taught and there was no requirement to attend a local church, parents seemed quite happy to send their children to a National school. Even if Anglican ideas were taught, some Nonconformist parents did still send their children there if it had a very good reputation for the secular education it provided.[50] Religious differences mattered intensely to some but far less so to others.

There is also evidence that parents exerted pressure on schools over other parts of the curriculum. The 1861 Newcastle Commission reported that there could be parental hostility to the teaching of grammar and geography, something which schools had to handle carefully. It noted that this did not just come from working-class parents but also from small tradesmen, underagents at works and farmers who wanted education to concentrate on accounts and good handwriting, probably because they felt most deficient in these in their own lives.[51] In 1875, a teacher at Solva recorded that he had abandoned grammar and geography because the parents would not have it.[52] At Caio Board school, parents complained about the 'uselessness' of learning poetry, although the teacher stuck with it because he felt it cultivated children's memory and familiarity with English.[53] The son of a teacher in industrial Carmarthenshire remembered that when his mother introduced sewing, an irate parent had complained, 'I do send her to school to be learned to do readin', writin', and 'rithmetic. I can teach her how to sew myself.'[54]

Parental agency and attitudes to punishment

Thus, it seems likely that had parents objected to schools being in English, there would have been complaints. Similarly, had parents objected to their children being punished for speaking Welsh they would have complained. Just as parents could influence what was taught, they also had an influence on discipline in schools. As Middleton has argued, attitudes to corporal punishment were 'complicated and often contradictory'.[55] The popular image of Victorian tyrannical fathers is a myth. Instead, parental love was powerful, with families offering people material and emotional security.[56] Yet physical punishment was widely accepted as a way of disciplining one's own children. According to one teacher, some people even believed that physical punishment was necessary for boys to become men.[57] Such attitudes extended to schooling. Parents seem to have generally accepted that teachers had the right to physically discipline their children, at least when it came to conduct at school.[58] The poet Isfoel (b.1881) remembered that his teacher at Pontgarreg used the cane almost every day but also had an array of other punishments, including making children stand on a chair on one foot, pulling their hair or ears, and making them put their head between their knees and having to stay still. Yet, he said, there was no point in the pupils complaining to their parents because they thought the punishments were deserved and that it did the children good.[59] Indeed, parents might have stronger views on the matter than teachers. In 1865, one Caernarfon mother brought in her son to school and asked the teacher to beat him in front of the other boys.[60] In 1873, a mistress recorded that two boys had been withdrawn from her school in Swansea because she was 'too gentle' and did not 'beat & chastise them as a strong master would do'.[61]

However, there was a widespread belief among parents that, as at home, punishment should be proportionate, justified and a last resort.[62] Parents might have different views from teachers of what was legitimate, and the punishment of children was a common cause of conflict. Parents turning up at school to complain that their children had been punished were fairly common complaints in logbooks.[63] At Bwlchysarnau, the master recorded that he would get a scolding from mothers after punishing their children.[64] When Robert Roberts began teaching in Caernarfon, he found the boys were 'thoroughly savage in their manners and behaved so rudely', but if he 'attempted to chastise any of these promising pupils, we were sure to have a crowd about us on our way home; enraged women volleying Billingsgate, and their precious offspring volleying stones after us'.[65] In 1873, a mother turned up at Dyserth National school complaining that her son had been punished, and acting 'like one mad brandishing a sickle and using most profane language'.[66] At Swyddffynnon in 1883, a new girl was given one stripe of the cane and shut in a classroom for disobedience. Her father later came to school and 'abused' the teacher 'in the most shameful manner, threatening to knock me down'.[67] The perceived legitimacy of punishments was also affected by the nature of the offence. At Dafen Tin Plate Works National school, a mother turned up at school after a boy had been punished for teasing a pupil teacher the night before. She was indignant that he was 'taking any notice of what happens out of school' and removed her son from it.[68] Parents seem to have been particularly prone to complain when the punishment came from monitors or pupil teachers.[69] A pupil teacher in Rhondda in the early 1890s later recalled: 'Sometimes irate parents followed me along the streets from the school. Once, I had to run for my life from a wild woman brandishing an axe, with which she was threatening to kill me.'[70] Some parents went further and actual violence against teachers was not unknown. In 1897, for example, a Pentyrch coal dealer found himself in court after hitting a teacher who had ordered his son out of school for being late and having a dirty face.[71]

Some teachers clearly felt that parents interfered too much and without due cause. In 1883, a boy was expelled from Glasfryn Board school after his parents insulted the master. The child had received 'one slight cut' on his palm for talking and playing in class but had been given three warnings first. The teacher complained that some parents insisted they were the only ones who should control the children, depriving him of any authority. He maintained that even when the 'slightest' punishment was inflicted some parents would insult him and thus encourage the children 'to disobedience and render the proper discipline of the school almost a matter of impossibility'.[72] To avoid such cases, some schools had explicit regulations. In the 1840s, the rules of the Abersychan Iron Company school stated that parents were not to interfere with the teacher after punishment was inflicted. If parents considered 'unnecessary severity has been used', they should complain to the school committee who would investigate and take any necessary action. Any parents who interfered contrary to the rule would see their child expelled.[73]

Parents could simply remove their child from a school they did not like. Before attendance by-laws denied them the right to, some parents did withdraw their children from schools where teachers were felt to be too strict on attendance, or too harsh or frequent in their use of physical punishments.[74] Even later in the century, parents argued with and abused attendance officers and lied about the age of their children when they felt their children were unfairly being made to go to school.[75] In 1887, the logbook at Llanllyfni British school recorded complaints about the infants' mistress beating her young charges 'in such a manner that their parents fail to send them to school'.[76] At one Swansea school, the mistress even alleged that parents who had removed a child had been motivated by the 'universal opinion of ignorant parents' that a man would be better at teaching and managing children.[77] Removing children could be easier in Wales because it was not uncommon for there to be British and National schools in the same town. Parents seemed quite willing to take advantage of this and teachers, eager to increase their income, were willing to take in their children as pupils. Indeed, managers of nearby schools sometimes had to come to agreements not to take children from each other except at set points in the year.[78] But even in rural areas where there was not a close rival school, parents might still remove their children. The logbook at Nevern, for example, recorded pupils being removed after being physically punished for crimes such as truancy and not putting a capital letter after a full stop.[79]

Such occurrences, or the threat of them, clearly influenced how schools operated. Teachers had to be mindful of the potential for conflict with parents because attendance levels were key to their pay, both through school fees and government grants. In rural areas, they also generally lived in the same communities as parents and much of their social life must have been affected by how their professional work was perceived locally. Parents' attitudes to teachers were, in the words of one historian of the profession, 'a mixture of admiration and resentment. The teacher was admired because he had risen from the working class and resented because of his "airs".'[80] Those who went against local wishes thus risked both social alienation and reduced incomes. Some inspectors and investigators felt this could create a reluctance to use physical punishment too readily. One of the Blue Books commissioners concluded:

> Beating, to a certain extent, is the prevailing kind of punishment; but I am not of the opinion that it is by any means severely practised, or that cruelty is at all a common feature of Welsh schools. The children are generally self-willed and indulged by their parents, and a master disposed to severity is restrained by his interest.[81]

Matthew Arnold noted in 1852 that children in schools where the teacher's salary depended on fees were often not well disciplined, 'owing to the master's fear of offending parents by a strictness which may appear to them excessive'.[82] Again, there were suggestions that this was a particular problem in areas with National and British schools close to each other.[83] Managers could also use parental influence to explain away discipline issues. After a critical inspection of Llanllwchaearn National school in 1865, the vicar responded that 'the Parents are very averse to having the children corrected & some time ago the father of a child actually struck the late master in the school for detaining his child'.[84]

Yet parental influence over punishment regimes in schools should not be exaggerated. Some teachers refused to bend to local opinion. In Tywyn in 1873, the master recorded that he had to 'inflict' corporal punishment upon two senior girls who were laughing and pinching each other. He felt such behaviour was 'very improper' and thus punished them 'in spite of all the school opposition existing in this little town'. He said he was determined to have good discipline and would not be sorry if the girls left because of it.[85] Parents might not even know that their children were being hit. Evidence from England suggests that some children did not like making a fuss or telling their parents about things at school for fear of what might happen.[86] But, even if they did, in a deeply hierarchical world, challenging teachers required courage and conviction. People embarrassed of their clothes and their poverty were not always willing to confront those with more money and different manners. Throughout the nineteenth century, most of the Welsh working class was not particularly radical. Unions and the Labour Party made slow progress and riots and rebellions against authority only happened at times of extreme economic hardship. Indeed, Ieuan Gwynedd Jones argued that the workers were conditioned to accept the status quo as God's will.[87] Some parents could thus be accepting of what happened at school. After all, many had little schooling themselves and might be unsure of how schools could or should work. Moreover, although historians emphasise the love within nineteenth-century families, that does not mean that there were not uninterested or even cruel parents. Emma Griffin has recently pointed to how a 'substantial minority' of working-class autobiographies include stories of neglect and ill treatment. She situates this within the context of a struggle against poverty which would have strained nerves and relationships.[88] Even if the parents did want to complain, if the teacher did not speak Welsh, then challenging them would have been near impossible. One historian concluded that working-class parents:

> hesitated to grapple with figures of authority who they seem to have held in a curious mixture of respect and contempt. Very occasionally an irate father would threaten a teacher who had over-punished his child, but more often a pupil punished at school would receive a supporting beating at home.[89]

That reasoning probably underplays parents' willingness to interfere in disciplinary matters but it was perhaps the repetition of punishments that sparked parents into action. One woman born in 1852 remembered her very violent teacher being tolerated by the parents for some time. However, he was eventually beaten up by people in the community so badly that he was in bed for a month. But what finally led parents to remove their children from his school was not his violence but their belief that the children were not learning enough English.[90]

Parents and the Welsh Not

Some parents may have felt unwilling or unable to complain but a sizable proportion were far more assertive. The active interest many took in ensuring their children's education, their willingness to remove children from unsatisfactory schools and their financial power over teachers all implies that the Welsh Not could not have been used without general parental support.

Certainly, there is no evidence of any parental opposition to English dominating schools. Longueville Jones, inspector for Anglican schools across Wales, wrote in 1859 that people of all classes were 'really anxious' to learn English and expressed this wish without 'reserve' or 'compulsion'.[91] All commentators agreed that the reasons for this were economic. A report in *The Times* on the conditions that had caused the Rebecca Riots claimed that every Welsh farmer wanted his son to know English because 'he knows that in every branch of industry, it is the language of promotion'.[92] As one character put it in an 1885 novel, 'Well if a man doesn't know a bit of English in these days he's bound to be left behind.'[93] Indeed, there were Welshmen aplenty who told their compatriots of the economic importance of learning English. Perhaps the most famous example came in 1865 when David Davies, a self-made industrialist, told the National Eisteddfod that he had no sympathy with those who reviled Welsh but that he had 'seen enough of the world to know English was the medium to make money'. He thus advised:

every one of his countrymen to master it perfectly. If they were content with brown bread, let them, of course, remain where they were; but if they wished to enjoy the luxuries of life, with white bread to boot, the way to do so would be by the acquisition of English. He knew what it was to eat both.[94]

Parents probably did not need telling this because they could see the advantages of English all around them. In 1869, a schoolmaster at Llanrhaeadr told an inquiry that parents were anxious to have their children taught English 'without which they find that they cannot get good places'.[95]

Former teacher and language campaigner Beriah Gwynfe Evans argued that even the most patriotic person could see that English had more status and it was natural for people to want their children to speak the language. To them, he argued, English seemed a golden key that would open doors, whereas Welsh was an iron bolt keeping them in a prison. They looked around and saw in their communities that Welsh was the language of the quarry worker, the farmer, the bell ringer, the railway worker, whereas English was the language of the overseer, the steward, the vicar and the stationmaster. Welsh was the language of labour, fatigue and hardship; English was the language of those who were easy in their labour, and great in their wages. It was thus, he maintained, no wonder that people wanted to learn English and thought Welsh had to be kept out of schools.[96] Parents did not necessarily expect their children to attain such middle-class lifestyles. Their ambitions were often rather modest. As one man remembered, 'we were sent to school principally to learn English so that we could earn our bread and cheese – and more of it – in some lighter capacity than our parents on the farms, who knew only the hard, unremitting, unrewarding toil of the fields'.[97]

However, the desire for English ran far deeper than just economic ambitions. Not being able to speak English was a particular hinderance in dealing with the law. Although Welsh was used in courtrooms, English was the official language of the law and, in giving evidence or being tried, the monoglot Welshman could be at the mercy of the skills of an interpreter when a jury or judge did not speak Welsh.[98] One of the

Blue Books commissioners thought there were matters of dignity at play too, with Welsh people finding it painful and damaging to their self-esteem not to be able to articulate themselves properly when English was needed. He argued this was exacerbated by how a 'certain power of elocution' in Welsh was universal amongst the working class so that being without it was 'a sort of stigma'.[99] This was not an unreasonable interpretation. One teacher told an 1860s enquiry that Welsh farmers' experience of trying to make themselves understood to Englishmen at markets or fairs was 'a bitter lesson on the value of education, which they are not slow to appreciate' and thus they sought to place their sons 'in a better position'.[100] In 1847, one Welsh-language writer argued that monoglot Welshmen were treated like barbarians from the mountains and always lost out to English, Scottish or Irishmen for jobs of responsibility.[101] A canal worker in Llangollen with broken English told travel-writer George Borrow that he had 'a great dislike for the English' who 'were in the habit of making fun of him and ridiculing his language'. Another man Borrow met told him that he was used to seeing Englishmen 'swaggering about Llangollen, and looking down upon us poor Welsh'.[102] Even if such prejudice was not intended, it could still be felt. Thomas Marchant (b.1845), who had worked across Wales, told the Cross Commission that the Welsh were shy and embarrassed when they met English people and felt that simply being Welsh was a disadvantage to them.[103]

Being able to speak English would overcome such humiliations and add to people's status. Many people in both rural and industrial communities were preoccupied with questions of status. In a world where so many were denied so much, people clung to anything that offered some dignity or raised them above others. Communities that seemed homogenous from the outside could be anything but. Quarrymen in Gwynedd thus often looked down upon the local agricultural workers, calling them sheep or pigs.[104] Those who drank too much or were bad husbands were gossiped about and sneered at. When people saw the educated children of their neighbours getting good jobs, it encouraged them to educate their own children.[105] In a world where not everyone spoke English, being able to do so was a status symbol in itself and something to distinguish oneself or one's children from the neighbours. Schools themselves fed this by sometimes holding public exhibitions, where children showed off their reading, spelling and the like to parents and local dignitaries. The names of prize winners might appear in the local paper, which must have further increased the pride of parents and the connections between education and local status.[106] Perhaps then it should be no surprise that education could also create jealousy and a belief that it lifted people beyond their station or was a sign of too much pride.[107]

It was this desire for English that shaped the language policies of schools. The Revd R. Bowen Jones of Narberth told the Rebecca Riots inquiry that a school in his parish had failed because it taught in Welsh, whereas if 'the schoolmaster has to teach them English, and to talk English in the school, there is no room in the school-room to admit all that come'.[108] One minister told the Blue Books that parents had complained when he taught children to read the Bible in Welsh, saying their children could 'learn Welsh at home'.[109] In 1850, inspector Longueville Jones stated the 'greater part' of instruction was in English 'at the express desire of the parents'.[110] The son of one teacher in industrial Carmarthenshire remembered a parent saying, in Welsh, 'Learn you my boy to speak English for him to get on in the world. To get the better of them English cattle dealers in Trosafon, I do want him.' He also described his father's account of a teacher saying 'I am here to learn you English. That is for what your father and mother do pay me your school pence.'[111]

Such attitudes also seem to have underpinned the exclusion of Welsh from schools. One Blue Books commissioner complained of 'the prejudice of Welsh parents against the employment of their own language, even as a medium of explanation'.[112] When the Honourable Society of Cymmrodorion surveyed teachers in 1885 about the introduction of Welsh as a subject, parental hostility was frequently cited as a reason why this should not be done. Some teachers reported complaints from parents when Welsh was used, even occasionally. The society's report concluded some parents were 'strongly impressed with the idea that the exclusion of Welsh from schools' was the surest way of teaching English.[113] In 1888, inspector Shadrach Pryce said any use of Welsh except in connection with improving English would not be 'favourably received. An experience of 21 years as a school inspector tells me that the less Welsh is spoken in the day school the more popular the school is with the parents.'[114] It was such attitudes that led some parents to believe that teachers who were unable to speak Welsh were a good thing. A farmer told a Blue Books commissioner he would pay double for a teacher who knew no Welsh.[115]

In wanting Welsh to be kept out of schools, parents were following the line advocated by many teachers – that this helped children to develop their English skills.[116] But this does not mean that parents openly supported their children being punished for speaking Welsh. Yet, in some cases, the prohibition of Welsh, and thus its punishment, does seem to have come directly from the parents. An 1867 commission on children's employment heard that in Llanboidy National school: 'The parents are most anxious that their children should learn English, and have requested that the school children should be made to speak English during play hours.'[117] At Llanddoged, a new teacher recorded in 1877: 'Some of the parents complained of their children being allowed to speak Welsh, I cautioned the children, and made use of a (Welsh Stick).'[118] This was probably not common but, in their explicit or implicit support for Welsh being excluded from school, parents would have known what rule breaking could lead to. Indeed, many of them would have themselves experienced being punished and humiliated for speaking Welsh at school, and they seem to have been willing for the same thing to happen to their children. A man born in 1881 remembered telling his parents about being hit for speaking Welsh and expecting some sympathy, only to be told that he knew the rules so should have expected it.[119]

This does not mean that there was universal acceptance of no-Welsh rules and punishments. At Pentraeth in 1876 the teacher recorded:

> Yesterday I endeavoured to get the school to speak English when out playing. I succeeded very well, but today I find a decreased attendance in consequence of the pressure put upon them. There

are but few parents who cooperate with me in an attempt of this kind.[120]

Given how unusual this case was, it may be that the issue was more how he had enforced his new rule rather than the rule itself. In a similar vein, an 1880s fictionalised account of schools forty years earlier depicts parents threatening a teacher because of the punishment that followed the Welsh Not and how it scared the children. In this case, the teacher decided not to use it at playtime anymore for fear for he might be strangled by mothers. However, this was fiction, although the author maintained his general account was rooted in fact.[121] These are isolated examples and, significantly, there do not seem to be cases in logbooks of fathers or mothers turning up at school to complain that their children had been punished for speaking Welsh.

Some observers felt the dominant tolerance of school language policies showed antipathy towards the future of Welsh itself. Inspector Dan Isaac Davies felt parents were in ignorance when it came to education and language: 'they fancy that a man cannot have two mother tongues; that if you wish to learn English you must give up Welsh'.[122] But, whatever Davies thought, parents, by looking around them, would have understood that it was possible to be fluent in two languages. An investigator on the commission on the employment of children in 1867 reported:

> I heard hopes frequently expressed by farmers that as a living language Welsh would soon become extinct. They feel its inconveniences daily. It interferes with their business transactions with their English neighbours, and it keeps the country, as they say, a century behind England in civilization.

Yet this investigator himself did not speak Welsh and noted how this meant he had to rely on professional peoples and the farmers and labourers who could speak English.[123] Had he spoken to those unable to speak English he would have found quite different attitudes. Some, however, did not believe when they were told or heard a desire for

Welsh to live on. Dr Thomas Nicholas told the National Association for the Promotion of Social Science in 1868 that by promoting English education the people of Wales 'were giving up the idea of continuing the Welsh tongue although it would not be possible to make them confess this'.[124] The Blue Books commissioner who investigated north Wales said he was frequently told that parents 'would not endure any encroachment upon their language'. This, he felt, showed that many people were ignorant of what the poor thought; but the commissioner was confusing a desire for English with a desire for English monolingualism..[125]

One of the other commissioners was more attuned to what people thought. He reported that 'on all hands' he found a desire for English. 'Yet, if interest pleads for English, affection leans to Welsh. The one is regarded as a new friend to be acquired for profit's sake; the other as an old one to be cherished for himself, and especially not to be deserted in his decline.' He noted that every part of community life was in Welsh, 'partly, it may be, from necessity, but, in some degree also, from choice'.[126] Many commentators agreed and argued that the Welsh were, as the minister at Lady Llanover's Church at Abercarn put it, 'very much attached to their own language'.[127] Edward Crompton Lloyd Hall, a barrister in Cardiganshire, told the Rebecca Riots inquiry that he felt people would support more systematic attempts to teach English if it was done with judgement, 'and if nothing was said about getting rid of the Welsh language'.[128] Inspector Longueville Jones argued that the people's universal desire for English was 'without yielding in one iota of respect and affection for the mother-tongue of our beloved country'.[129] In 1879, the sociolinguist E. G. Ravenstein was told by a correspondent in Glamorgan that, 'There is an abiding love of Welsh which clings to the people with great tenacity.'[130]

Historian Ieuan Gwynedd Jones argued that the Welsh working class clung on to their language because it was *their* language. It was a way of 'expressing social difference', marking them off from 'the English aristocracy and the anglicising middle-classes' and symbolising their Welshness, connecting them with a national past. More than this, it gave them dignity and a class consciousness at a time when everything else reduced them to dehumanised and brutalised slaves.[131] However, there is a degree of wishful thinking in this. Welsh was, first and foremost, a means of communication rather than a political symbol. Given the crushing poverty so many endured, finding a better way of life must have been the priority for most. Inspector Joseph Fletcher argued that 'the mass of the population' were 'exceedingly desirous that their children' learn English but 'with no *express* intention' of abandoning Welsh, while 'comparatively careless whether it be retained in after generations or not'.[132] Such attitudes were particularly strong in areas where English was rapidly gaining ground, such as border communities and eastern industrial districts. Here there were claims that parents were speaking English to their children, even if they did not speak the language well themselves.[133] In other areas, however, it thus seems likely that the strong support for education centring on English as a means of economic liberation co-existed with a pride in the Welsh language. Certainly, most bilingual parents passed on Welsh to their children in communities where it was the dominant language. This was partly natural, but it was also because to not do so would have harmed their children more than not speaking English did. Welsh was essential to life in such communities. What we see here is how language was about function rather than something all pervasive. Beyond the countryside, the reality of life of Wales was increasingly bilingual rather than monolingual. Not speaking one or the other was a disadvantage. As a consequence, English parents in Welsh-speaking areas saw some utility in the teaching of the local language in order to ensure their children were not disadvantaged.[134]

School boards and managers

Thus the Welsh Not was used with the tacit consent of parents but not because they wished to kill the Welsh language. If any school did have linguistic practices that parents disapproved of, they would have faced at least some forceful complaints. Yet that did not happen, and few teachers would have risked it anyway, given the financial and reputational damage parental opposition would lead to. The Welsh Not's goal (to teach

English) and its method (controlled punishment) was entirely in line with what parents wanted from school and how they accepted schools should operate. But parents were not the only influence on teachers. Those not running their own private schools were employees, usually of a local works or a local committee, or, after 1870, a school board. Such bodies tended to be dominated by the local elite who saw such work as part of their paternal responsibilities towards communities. But, in both rural and industrial communities, there was not always a significant cultural divide between the middle and working classes, and many of the people on school boards and committees shared the same linguistic attitudes as parents. Indeed, many were parents themselves.

How much school managers and committees shaped the daily running of schools varied. Robert Roberts recalled that when he taught at Amlwch National school in the 1850s, 'not one of the better classes' ever visited the school or took the 'slightest interest in it'.[135] Inspector Shadrach Pryce argued that, in poor schools, managers did not supervise teachers closely enough, sometimes only visiting on inspection days.[136] But logbooks also show some managers and board members visited regularly and took a close interest in schools' running. Indeed, some were intrusive and felt they knew better than the teachers, leading to disputes between teachers and their employers.[137] It is clear that, in a few cases, it was managers and committees that were responsible for the exclusion of Welsh from schools. In 1849, the inspection report for Llangoedmor noted that the population was 'altogether Welsh; but the education is carried on totally in English, by order of the Committee, and no Welsh is allowed to be spoken by either teachers or pupils'.[138] The bishop of St David's also argued that it was the managers of schools who prevented 'all use of the language in school hours'.[139] Later in the century, a few school boards and committees were against Welsh being used, at least in the 1870s.[140] At the new Crai Board school, the logbook recorded in 1872: 'Cautioned children about talking Welsh both in School and playground having had special order to that effect from the School Board.'[141] Two years later, the board at Llangeinwen recorded its 'wish to press upon the teachers the importance of keeping strictly to the use of the English Language in the schools'.[142] In 1876, a new teacher at

Trefriw recorded: 'Being unable to speak Welsh I find it very difficult work, but have resolved to make the children speak English, as I find that this is the wish of the managers when they speak to me.'[143] Teachers who did bring Welsh into the classroom could find themselves at odds with their boards and not stay long; the Cross Commission reported it had heard of a case of a teacher being dismissed for using Welsh in his teaching.[144]

Cases of managers and boards intervening on language were unusual and do not mean there was a community hostility to Welsh or an attempt to stop the children speaking it in their wider lives. As Bassett points out, it was often the same people – local community leaders – who promoted both Sunday schools, where Welsh dominated, and day schools, where it was English that ruled the roost.[145] Their attitudes reflected the wider idea of separate spheres where English was the language of business and officialdom, and Welsh was for home, hearth and the sacred. Thus school managers who ordered no Welsh in their institutions, like the teachers who implemented the Welsh Not and the parents who supported it, would generally speak the language at home. The chair and clerk of the Crai Board that ordered no Welsh to be spoken in school was Owen Price, whose census entries show him to be a wealthy bilingual farmer. In 1901, he had eight children living with him, all of whom he had raised to be bilingual.[146]

His initial order was perhaps the naivety of a new board finding its feet and it later made Welsh an option on the curriculum. The fact that some committees were instructing teachers to exclude Welsh from their schools shows how little they understood the mechanics of education. Indeed, some apparently gave the practicalities of language no or little thought. The Blue Books commissioner for north Wales argued that a majority of promoters of schools were 'unconscious' of the fact that children they heard reading and reciting English did not understand the language.[147] That observation may have been the result of locals' unwillingness to discuss the issue with outsiders or admit that Welsh was required to overcome the problem. It could be that the general English disdain for Welsh created a defensiveness amongst committees on the matter. In 1849, the committee of a school in Brecon was quoted as saying that they did not want 'to promote an exclusive spirit of nationalism', but that it must not be forgotten that if Welsh was not occasionally fallen back 'for illustrations or incitements' it would not have much influence on people's character.[148]

Educational providers may not have been hostile to Welsh having some place in schools but nor were they often proactively supportive of the language being used. When the grant to Welsh-speaking teachers was brought to an end with the creation of the Revised Code, there were no complaints or voices of dissent from educationalists in Wales. Not until the 1880s was the whole absence of Welsh in schools a matter of public controversy. Before that, those people sponsoring, running and commenting on schools were far more concerned with religious than linguistic matters.[149] The way religion dominated community and public discussions of education is evident in how Anglicans and Nonconformists often failed to co-operate to overcome local shortcomings in the provision of schools. In some rural communities, neither religious grouping could afford to build and maintain a school on their own, so nothing was done. Elsewhere, both British and National schools were built in small communities where the number of children only required one school.[150] Financed by a local quarry owner, there was a subsidised clothing club attached to the National school at Bethesda to discourage parents from sending their children to the local British school.[151] Efforts to co-operate could break down. In Aberdyfi, for example, there were angry public accusations that Anglicans had misled local Nonconformists, had gone back on promises to work together and instead set up their own school.[152]

Such rivalries dominated the public discussions of education in Wales, marginalising and pushing aside practical questions over the effects of the exclusion of Welsh. This owed much to how the British and National societies agreed that the teaching of English was their primary educational goal in Wales. The British Society's main supporters in Wales showed no interest at all in fostering the Welsh language, probably because they knew that chapels did that already. Citing the possibility of a prisoner in court being unable to understand proceedings and local officials unacquainted with the language of their instructions, the society's 1848 report stated: 'the importance of establishing English Schools in Wales can scarcely be over-rated'.[153] Nonconformists continued to worry about Anglican influence and Welsh debates around the 1870 Education Act and the subsequent election of school boards were dominated by religious issues. Nor were the tensions just between church and chapel: there were cases where teachers alleged they had lost their job for belonging to the wrong Nonconformist denomination.[154]

Anglicans themselves saw National schools as a way of bringing the Nonconformist majority back into the Church of England, and many realised the Welsh language was needed if children were to be taught both English and the Scriptures properly. The National Society and prominent leaders such as Connop Thirwall, bishop of St David's from 1840 to 1875, supported the employment of Welsh-speaking teachers and produced a number of books to teach people Welsh reading and religious knowledge. James Henry Cotton, dean of Bangor cathedral, meanwhile, argued in 1831:

> In affording instruction to the rising generation in the English language, it is obvious that it is not intended thus to supersede their native tongue, nor in teaching them in another language to teach them to despise or to neglect their own. On the contrary the [local diocesan] committee are persuaded that the best preparatory step towards the study and acquisition of their own language is an early acquaintance with the English tongue.[155]

Yet, despite influential supporters of the place of Welsh in National schools, the National Society itself never made any definitive statement or policy in favour of using Welsh and local practices ultimately came down to teachers and managers.

Regardless of their religious affiliations, most school boards and committees did not see their role as dictating to teachers how schools should operate pedagogically. The minute books of school boards are dominated by financial and administrative issues and suggest there was little discussion of educational matters. School committees and boards could exert influence through who they chose to employ and in

National, British and Board schools there was a growing recognition of the importance of Welsh-speaking teachers as the century progressed. In 1866, the Revd Dr T. Pryce, a minister in Aberdare and a manager of the British school, told a select committee that while they did not make it a requirement that masters spoke Welsh, it was an advantage, not just in explaining things to children but also in dealing with parents who had 'somewhat more confidence' in someone who spoke their own language.[156] By 1887, one inspector noted 'as a matter of fact' that Welsh teachers were preferred to English ones.[157] In that same year, the Llanfihangel-y-Creuddyn Lower school board formally resolved that in future it would not appoint Englishmen as headmasters.[158]

One way to recruit a Welsh speaker was to advertise in the Welsh-language press. In January 1876, for example, there were twelve advertisements in *Baner ac Amserau Cymru* for teaching vacancies. Although only two stated 'Welsh indispensable', the advertisements must have been placed there with the aim of securing a Welsh-speaking teacher.[159] Explicit requirements for Welsh become more common as the century progressed. In one 1891 issue of the Welsh-language paper *Y Llan*, there were four advertisements for teaching jobs in the north-west. Whereas in Corris and Machynlleth churchmen and good disciplinarians were sought, a vacancy in Betws-y-coed wanted a single woman with a knowledge of Welsh, while Trefnant National school said it preferred a married Welshman.[160] But the shortage of teachers within Wales meant most advertisements were published in the UK-wide *The Schoolmaster* and not in the local press. In the 1880s and 1890s, some advertisements in that paper did state Welsh was 'indispensable', 'necessary' or 'desirable', but the majority did not. In January 1892, *The Schoolmaster* contained advertisements for vacancies in seventy-eight locations in Wales, with just eleven stating any preference for Welsh speakers and all coming from rural communities.

Even if a school deliberately recruited a Welsh-speaking teacher, this did not mean that he or she would use the language, and ultimately the influence of those who managed and financed schools on classrooms practices was always limited. Instead, the support of some boards for Welsh was evident in how they used the language themselves. Some rural boards always held their meetings in Welsh, sometimes because they had Welsh-monoglot members, but also because it helped marginalise the influence of English-monoglot Conservatives and Anglicans.[161] In 1899, the Llansantffraid board voted to keep its minutes in Welsh.[162] Seeking Welsh-speaking teachers may have been a matter of practicality but this gesture was clearly a celebration of the Welsh language in its own right.

The old prejudices, however, were only slowly dying away. In 1896, the Ruthin school board discussed whether Welsh should be a desirable or essential qualification for a teaching post. Practical concerns were clear, as well as a concern for the experience of children. One board member recalled a 'splendid' elementary teacher 'who, being unable to understand Welsh, was made all manner of fun of by the boys'. The board chairman wanted to ensure that a teacher would not 'in any way inconvenience the children in his care' by not being able to speak their language, but the headmaster felt this was not essential since he spoke Welsh himself. It was decided to advertise with Welsh as desirable rather than essential.[163]

When boards did decide to not employ Welsh-speaking teachers at the end of the century they could face parental opposition. In 1888, there were prolonged objections that the Swansea school board had appointed a teacher who did not speak Welsh as master of Cwm school. One complaint called the board 'lovers of the Welsh knot'.[164] It is significant that this was in a large urban area. In such places Welsh was clearly in retreat late in the century because of the effects of migration from England. This seems to have generated some public support for Welsh to be more formally recognised. In response to the new regulations of the 1890s that allowed the language to be taught as a subject, some boards in anglicised areas consulted parents on the matter and found much support for the teaching of Welsh. In Cardiff, for example, 15,000 ballots were distributed to parents: 8,124 voted in favour of teaching of Welsh and 1,770 against.[165]

In contrast, in rural areas the many remaining National schools seem to have done little to introduce Welsh lessons, while attempts to promote the language by boards ran into local opposition. Some inspectors argued that it was a lack of support from parents that was stopping teachers and managers introducing Welsh as a subject. The chief inspector put parental attitudes down to a misunderstanding that Welsh would replace English.[166] As a consequence, one inspector argued in 1891 that parental demand should not decide language policy in schools because they did not understand how teaching Welsh was not to the detriment of learning English.[167]

A few people outside education were outwardly alarmed by the developments. The *Western Mail* ran an editorial in 1885 arguing against Welsh being taught in schools, maintaining that the language was of no use to helping the working class 'compete in the battle of life' and was 'in fact a positive disadvantage'.[168] In 1892, one letter writer, who signed himself Cymro, claimed that it was now almost impossible to get children to answer simple questions in English:

> Six or seven years ago, the children of the same districts would answer questions in English with the greatest ease. I remember once passing through a small village in the heart of Cardiganshire, and hearing the children using English in their play in the village street. Now in the same place it is almost impossible to obtain a simple Yes or No. I find upon inquiry, that this decay of English speaking among our school children dates from the commencement of the 'Welsh in school' craze some seven or eight years back.

He bemoaned the loss of the days when 'The master, as a rule, spoke English only to his pupils, and English only was allowed in the school and play-ground.' But even this man was not entirely hostile to Welsh. He wanted children to 'talk in English, sing, play, think and compose in English while they are in school', but he also accepted they would get 'plenty of Welsh at home and in the Sunday School'.[169] Indeed, it was because Welsh felt safe and secure in such communities that perhaps people did not worry about the long-terms effects of excluding the language from schools. We can see this as a mistake now, but that is to look at the past through twenty-first-century eyes rather than those of the nineteenth century, more concerned with the welfare of their children than the nation and its culture.

Conclusion

Amidst such debates, an 1894 newspaper story, probably intended to influence unconvinced readers, described a mother complaining that her son's back was black and blue after being repeatedly hit for speaking Welsh. She showed it to the local vicar and complained that it was wrong her child had been punished for using Welsh in the playground. She accepted his right to punish the use of Welsh in the school but still asked the vicar where Wales was going if this was what happened for speaking their own language. The vicar was persuaded, the teacher was replaced and Welsh translations began to be used in the school.[170] Whether this account was true or not, it was not in line with dominant views through the century. The managers and patrons of schools slowly came to support the place of Welsh in education. Parents were not coerced to send their children to school until 1880 and they did so because they thought it was important for them to learn English. This did not mean they wanted Welsh to die away but many did seem to have thought this required the exclusion of Welsh from classrooms. This should not be surprising given that many teachers thought the same too, but attitudes in the teaching profession evolved quicker than in wider communities and the financial and practical influence of parents on schools meant their views shaped language policies and practices in education until the end of the century. Seeing all this, some commentators, angry at what was happening to the Welsh language and culture, blamed parents and worried that society was becoming too individualistic.[171]

In 1851, the famous minister J. R. Jones argued that the use of the Welsh Not was evidence of how deep the popular desire to acquire English ran.[172] Such perspectives were rooted in how parents not only voluntarily sent their children to schools where it was used but paid to do so too. However, parental comment on the Welsh Not was minimal.

Although parents complained more to teachers about the punishment of their children than anything else, there was no real criticism of the Welsh Not but nor was there open support for it. Part of the problem here is the nature of the historical record, where the views of working-class parents were not recorded unless they intruded on schools. Contemporaries aplenty recorded how parents wanted English to dominate the schools and feared the use of Welsh might hinder their children in learning the new language. That probably translated into tacit rather than open support of the Welsh Not. Parents wanted children to learn English and, if schools thought the Welsh Not was the way to achieve this, then they went along with that.

Many parents would have experienced the Welsh Not themselves. This should have made them aware of how it hindered rather than helped the learning of English. They might too have remembered the pain, humiliation and boredom it could induce. Perhaps their lack of vocal opposition suggests that its harm was muted by the fact that school itself was not a pleasant experience. Perhaps some had forgotten what they experienced. Their thinking may have been clouded by the depths of the poverty they endured. Perhaps they were so desperate for their children to avoid the same fate that they were willing to let them go through the pain of the Welsh Not with the hope of something better for them afterwards. This interpretation is appealing to those who do not like the decisions that parents took. It frees them from blame for what happened and passes the responsibility onto economic systems. But it also reduces the working class of Wales to unthinking victims rather than individuals fighting to fashion their own lives and identities and to make their own histories. Of course, their options and actions were curtailed by the cultural and economic conditions they lived in, but the working class were not unthinking pawns and they negotiated their own routes to survive and escape. For them, learning English was not a matter of oppression but of liberation. There was no reason this had to lead to the decline of Welsh. Education could have made Wales into a bilingual nation. But, as the next chapter explores, the fact that this did not occur was not down to what happened in schools, but in communities.

Notes

1. *Reports of the Commissioners of Inquiry into the State of Education in Wales. Part III: North Wales* (London, 1847), p. 35 [hereafter Blue Books].
2. Evidence of Thomas Stephens, *Reports of Assistant Commissioners appointed to inquire into State of Popular Education in England*, vol. II (1861), pp. 588–9 [hereafter Newcastle Commission].
3. PA, Solva British, 8 November 1872.
4. PA, Llyswen National school. Subsequent children from the same family were half price.
5. H. G. Williams, 'A study of the Kynnersley educational returns for Caernarfonshire', *Welsh History Review*, 13, 3 (1987), 300–27, 304.
6. CRO, Trefor Welsh Granite Quarry Company, 6 November 1885.
7. Newcastle Commission, vol. II, p. 579.
8. MRO, Penrhyndeudraeth British, 20 November 1863, 24 March 1864.
9. Newcastle Commission, vol. II, p. 525. *Commission on the Employment of Children, Young Persons, and Women in Agriculture (1867), Third Report of the Commissioners* (London, 1870), p. 130 [hereafter Employment of Children Commission].
10. NEWAR, Ruabon Boys National, 15 September 1892.
11. Emma Griffin, *Bread Winner: An Intimate History of the Victorian Economy* (New Haven, 2020), p. 199. On child labour see Jane Humphries, *Childhood and Child Labour in the British Industrial Revolution* (Cambridge, 2010)
12. Employment of Children Commission, pp. 9, 130.
13. Reproduced in Jules Ginswick (ed.), *Labour and the Poor in England and Wales, 1849–51: Vol. III The Mining and Manufacturing Districts of South Wales and North Wales* (London, 1983), p. 230.
14. Emma Griffin, *Liberty's Dawn: A People's History of the Industrial Revolution* (New Haven, 2013), p. 63.
15. 'Cardiff infant school', *The Glamorgan, Monmouth & Brecon Gazette, Cardiff Advertiser* and *Merthyr Guardian*, 2 December 1843, 3.
16. *Minutes of the CCE, 1855–56*, p. 440.
17. W. B. Stephens, *Education, Literacy and Society, 1830–70: The Geography of Diversity in Provincial England* (Manchester, 1987), p. 30.
18. Newcastle Commission, vol. II, p. 600.
19. Quoted in *Hansard Debates*, vol. 84, col. 852, 10 March 1846.
20. *Report of the CCE, 1874–75*, p. 343.
21. *Report of the CCE, 1863–64*, p. 49.
22. Newcastle Commission, vol. II, p. 478.
23. On factors holding back the working-class desire for literacy see David F. Mitch, *The Rise of Popular Literacy in Victorian England: The Influence of Private Choice and Public Literacy* (Philadelphia, 1992).
24. CA, Llangeitho British, 25 March 1869.
25. For example, 'Addysg yn Nghymru', *Y Cronicl*, March 1846, 40–2, 40.
26. Blue Books, Part II, p. 266.
27. *Hansard*, 4 July 1878, col. 785.

28 David W. Howell, *Land and People in Nineteenth-century Wales* (London, 1977), pp. 94–5; Employment of Children Commission, pp. 56, 165.
29 H. L. V. Fletcher, *Portrait of the Wye Valley* (London, 1968), p. 54.
30 Blue Books, Part III, p. 36.
31 *Census of Great Britain, 1851, Education: England and Wales, Report and Tables* (London, 1854), p. 6. Figures exclude Monmouthshire.
32 W. Gareth Evans, *Education and Female Emancipation: The Welsh Experience, 1847–1914* (Cardiff, 1990), p. 17.
33 Cross Commission, 2nd Report, p. 280.
34 Employment of Children Commission, pp. 129, 56.
35 *Report of the CCE, 1870–71*, p. 158.
36 J. Lloyd Williams, *Atgofion Tri Chwarter Canrif, cyf. IV* (London, 1945), pp. 116–17.
37 NEWAR, Dyserth National, 12 February 1880.
38 GA, Llwydcoed mixed, 6 September 1879. The letter was entered in the logbook, presumably to show its poor spelling and grammar. The teacher replied that the boy was rather troublesome and a poor attender who he would be happy to lose.
39 W. J. Gruffydd, *The Years of the Locust*, trans. D. Myrddin Lloyd (Gomer, 1976), pp. 87–90.
40 'Addysg yn Nghymru', *Y Cronicl*, February 1846, 24–6, 24.
41 *Minutes of the CCE, 1852–53*, vol. 1, p. 671.
42 GA, Aberaman Boys, 22 June 1866.
43 Cross Commission, pp. 281–2.
44 Henry Jones, *Old Memories: Autobiography* (London, 1922), p. 110.
45 Robert Roberts, *A Wandering Scholar: The Life and Opinions of Robert Roberts* (Cardiff, 1991), p. 284.
46 Newcastle Commission, vol. II, p. 553.
47 Tim Williams, 'Language, Identity and Education in a Liberal State: The Anglicisation of Pontypridd, 1818–1920' (unpublished PhD thesis, University of Wales, Cardiff, 1989), 456–7.
48 CA, Llanon National school, 1 September 1869.
49 Newcastle Commission, vol. II, p. 574, 517; H. G. Williams, 'A study of the Kynnersley educational returns for Caernarfonshire', *Welsh History Review*, 13, 3 (1987), 300–27, 322.
50 Evidence of Jno. Thomas in Newcastle Commission, vol. II, p. 582; *Minutes of the CCE, 1857–58*, p. 496. For a passionate defence of National schools, their respect for parents' wishes and the willingness of Nonconformists to embrace such institutions see Connop Thirwall, *A Letter to J. Bowstead [commenting on his Letters] … concerning Education in South Wales*, 2nd edn (1861).
51 Newcastle Commission, vol. II, p. 548.
52 PbA, Solva British, 25 November 1875.
53 CmA, Caio Board, 9 September 1869.
54 Michael Gareth Llewelyn, *Sand in the Glass* (London, 1943), p. 7.
55 Jacob Middleton, 'Thomas Hopley and mid-Victorian attitude to corporal punishment', *History of Education*, 34, 6 (2005), 599–615, 600.

56 Carol Beardmore, Cara Dobbing and Steven King (eds), *Family Life in Britain 1650–1910* (Basingstoke, 2019); Emma Griffin, 'The emotions of motherhood: love, culture, and poverty in Victorian Britain', *American Historical Review*, 123, 1 (2018), 60–85.
57 Williams, *Atgofion Tri Chwarter Canrif, cyf. IV*, p. 114.
58 Jacob Middleton, 'The Experience of Corporal Punishment in Schools, 1890–1940', *History of Education*, 37, 2 (2008), 253–75, 263. In 1880, for example, the master of Swyddffynnon recorded that there had been a 'row' from the parents after he punished three boys for misconduct on a Sunday. The teacher recorded 'my authority does not extend further than the time during which they are in school': CA, Swyddffynnon, 23 April 1880.
59 Isfoel, *Hen Ŷd y Wlad: Atgofion Isfoel* (Llandysul, 1966), pp. 32–3.
60 CRO, Caernarfon British, 15 September 1865. For a similar case see GA, Llwydcoed mixed, 3 May 1878.
61 Richard Burton Archives, St David's RC school, 15 July 1873.
62 Julie-Marie Strange, *Fatherhood and the British Working Class, 1865–1914* (Cambridge, 2015), pp. 180–1; Paul Thompson, *The Edwardians: The Remaking of British Society*, 2nd edn (London, 1992), pp. 45–6.
63 For example, CRO, Bethel Board school, 14 October 1881.
64 H. L. V. Fletcher, *Portrait of the Wye Valley* (London, 1968), p. 54. For examples of parents forcefully objecting to the unfair physical punishment of their children by teacher see Strange, *Fatherhood and the British Working Class*, pp. 188–9.
65 Roberts, *Wandering Scholar*, p. 257.
66 NEWAH, Dyserth National, 28 February 1873.
67 CA, Swyddffynnon, 4 September 1883.
68 CmA, Dafen Tin Plate Works National, 31 July 1866.
69 NEWAR, Ruabon Boys National, 9 November 1893.
70 Abel J. Jones, *I was Privileged* (Cardiff, 1943), p. 13.
71 'Assault upon a Pentyrch School Master', *Glamorgan Free Press*, 6 November 1897, 3. Similarly, 'Threatening a schoolmaster', *Evening Express*, 8 December 1900, 4.
72 CmA, Glasfryn Board, 7 February 1883.
73 Blue Books, Part II, p. 284.
74 J. S. Hurt, *Elementary Schooling and the Working Classes, 1860–1918* (London, 1979), p. 161. For a memory of being removed in response to being hit on the head by a teacher see 'Hen Scwlmistir', *Cymru*, 37 (1909), 121.
75 Sascha Auerbach, '"The law has no feeling for poor folks like us!": everyday responses to legal compulsion in England's working-class communities, 1871–1904', *Journal of Social History*, 45, 3 (2012), 686–708.
76 CRO, Llanllyfni British, 17 June 1887.
77 Richard Burton Archives, St David's Roman Catholic school, 26 May 1873.
78 Employment of Children Commission, p. 88; Cross Commission, 2nd Report, pp. 280, 282.
79 PbA, Nevern, June 1878 entries and 6 June 1894.

80 Asher Tropp, *The School Teachers: The Growth of the Teaching Profession in England and Wales from 1800 to the Present Day* (London, 1977), p. 34.
81 Blue Books, Part II, p. 28.
82 *Minutes of the CCE, 1852–53*, vol. 1, p. 672.
83 *Report of the CCE, 1875–6*, p. 391.
84 PA, Llanllwchaearn National, 5 December 1865.
85 MRO, Tywyn Board, 10–14 March 1873. As it turned out, only one girl left the school.
86 Middleton, 'Experience of corporal punishment', 261.
87 Ieuan Gwynedd Jones, 'Language and community in Nineteenth Century Wales', in David Smith (ed.), *A People and a Proletariat: Essays in the History of Wales, 1780–1980* (London, 1980), pp. 47–71, 66–7.
88 Griffin, 'The emotions of motherhood', 85.
89 John Burnett (ed.), *Destiny Obscure: Autobiographies of Childhood, Education and Family from the 1820s to the 1920s* (London, 1982), p. 152.
90 Gwyneth Vaughan, 'Bryn Ardudwy a'i bobl: ein hysgolfeistri', *Yr Haul*, 6, 65 (May 1904), 225–30.
91 *Report of the CCE, 1859–60*, p. 154.
92 'State of south Wales', *The Times*, 16 December 1843, 5.
93 Daniel Owen, *Rhys Lewis*, ed. Trans. Robert Lomas (2018), loc. 5874.
94 'The Eisteddfod', *Aberystwith Observer*, 20 September 1865, 4.
95 Employment of Children Commission, p. 95.
96 Beriah Gwynfe Evans, 'Addysg plant Cymru ddoe a heddyw', *Tywysydd y Plant*, April 1910, 108–11.
97 D. Parry-Jones, *Welsh Children's Games and Pastimes* (Denbigh, 1964), pp. 15–16.
98 On the use of Welsh in courts see J. Gwynfor Jones, 'The Welsh language in local government: Justices of the Peace and the Courts of Quarter Sessions, c.1536–1800', in Geraint H. Jenkins (ed.), *The Welsh Language Before the Industrial Revolution* (Cardiff, 1997), pp. 181–206.
99 Blue Books, Part I, pp. 6–7.
100 Evidence of Evan Davies, *Schools Inquiry Commission, Vol. V: Minutes of Evidence taken before the Commissioners Part II* (1868), p. 347.
101 'At athrawon yr Ysgolion Brutanaidd', *Y Cronicl*, October 1847, 309–11, 310.
102 George Borrow, *Wild Wales: Its People, Language and Scenery* (1862; London, 1977), pp. 50, 54, 57.
103 Cross Commission, 3rd Report, p. 26.
104 Merfyn Jones, 'Notes from the margin: class and society in nineteenth century Gwynedd', in David Smith (ed.), *A People and a Proletariat: Essays in the History of Wales, 1780–1980* (London, 1980), pp. 199–214, 207.
105 Newcastle Commission, vol. II, p. 477.
106 For example, 'Examination at the Dr Coke Memorial Schools', *Brecon County Times*, 8 July 1876, 5.
107 For a contemporary description of this see Daniel Owen, *Fireside Tales*, ed. trans. Adam Pearce (1895; Talybont, 2011), p. 40.

108 *Report of the Commissioners of Inquiry for Turnpike Roads, South Wales* (London, 1844), p. 102.
109 Blue Books, vol. 1, p. 32.
110 *Minutes of the CCE, 1850–51*, vol. II, p. 511.
111 Llewelyn, *Sand in the Glass*, pp. 7–8.
112 Blue Books, part III, p. 22.
113 Honourable Society of Cymmrodorion, *Report of the Committee Appointed to Inquire into the Advisability of the Introduction of the Welsh Language into the Course of Elementary Education in Wales: The Introduction of Welsh as a Specific Subject* (Aberdare, 1885), p. 6 and appendix pp. 5–6, 8–9.
114 *Report of the CCE, 1888–89*, p. 366.
115 Blue Books, Part I, p. 32.
116 Newcastle Commission, Vol. 2. p. 569; Cross Commission, 3rd Report, p. 26.
117 Employment of Children Commission, p. 46.
118 CwyA, Llanddoged, 22 August 1877.
119 St Fagans oral history collection, Mr Jones, Y Tymbl.
120 AA, Pentraeth British, 22 September 1876.
121 *John Jones yn yr Ysgol: Ffug-hanesyn, yn Rhoddi Darluniad o Ysgolion Gwledig Cymru, oddeutu'r Flwyddyn 1840*, 2nd edn (Lampeter, 1904), pp. 61–2.
122 Cross Commission, 3rd Report, p. 8.
123 Employment of Children Commission, pp. 56–7.
124 Birmingham Meeting, 1868, *Transactions of the National Association for the Promotion of Social Science* (London, 1869), p. 453.
125 Blue Books, Part III, p. 34.
126 Blue Books, Part I, p. 6.
127 *Report from the Select Committee on Education* (1866), p. 290.
128 *Report of the Commissioners of Inquiry for Turnpike Roads, South Wales* (London, 1844), p. 240.
129 *Minutes of the CCE, 1848–49–50*, vol. II, p. 207.
130 E. G. Ravenstein, 'On the Celtic languages in the British Isles: a statistical survey', *Journal of the Royal Statistical Society*, 42 (1879), 621–2.
131 Jones, 'Language and community', pp. 67–8.
132 *Minutes of the CCE, 1846*, pp. 111–12.
133 Blue Books, Part III, p. 338; Employment of Children Commission, p. 59.
134 'Carnarvon School Board', *Carnarvon and Denbigh Herald*, 8 March 1889, 3.
135 Roberts, *A Wandering Scholar*, pp. 311–12.
136 *Minutes of the CCE, 1870–71*, p. 150.
137 Anon., *A Schoolmaster's Difficulties, Abroad and at Home* (London, 1853), ch. 4. For an example of this in practice see CmA, Glasfryn Board, 29 June 1883.
138 *Minutes of the CCE, 1848–49–50*, vol. II (London, 1850), p. 241.
139 Quoted in Sir Thomas Phillips, *Wales: The Language, Social Condition, Moral Character and the Religious Opinions of the People, considered in Relation to Education* (London, 1849), p. 27.
140 This happened at Dwyran. See David Pretty, *Two Centuries of Anglesey Schools, 1700–1902* (Llangefni, 1977), p. 211.

141 Quoted in Glenville Powell, 'Hanes plwyf Crai: VI Addysg yng Nghrai', *Brycheiniog*, 10 (1964), 39–68, 49.
142 AA, Llangeinwen school board, minute book, 2 December 1874.
143 CwyA, Trefriw, 24–8 January 1876.
144 Cross Commission, 2nd Report, pp. 288–9. Also see the case of Dan Jenkins at Cilcennan in 1877–8: Alan Leech, *Dan Jenkins: A Biography* (Talybont, 2011), ch. 3.
145 T. M. Bassett, 'The Welsh circulating schools', in Jac L. Williams and Gwilym Rees Hughes (eds), *The History of Education in Wales* (Swansea, 1978), pp. 70–82, 79.
146 See 1901 census entry for Owen Price, NantyRharn, Crai.
147 Blue Books, Part III, p. 34.
148 Henry Griffths, 'Addysgiaeth', *Y Traethodydd*, October 1849, 416–46.
149 This can be seen in 'At athrawon yr Ysgolion Brutanaidd'. This article does note the importance of using Welsh if children are going to understand but it is dominated by a discussion of religious matters relating to schools.
150 Evidence of David Williams, magistrate, in Newcastle Commission, vol. II, p. 580; *Minutes of the CCE, 1854–55*, pp. 639–40.
151 Roberts, *Wandering Scholar*, pp. 288–9. At Llanllechid, a similar clothing club patronised by the same Pennant family also required parents to attend the parish church. See its rules in CRO, Llanllechid National.
152 See the case made in a bilingual leaflet produced to raise money for a British school: MRO, 'Elementary education at Aberdovey', August 1894.
153 Brunel University archives, *43rd Report of the British and Foreign School Society 1848*, p. 31.
154 See the account in J. Elwyn Hughes and André Lomozik, *Canmlwyddiant Ysgol y Cefnfaes Bethesda ynghyd â Hanes Canolfan Gymdeithasol y Cefnfaes* (Bethesda, 2007), pp. 5–6. For wider religious tensions around the 1870 Act and its implementation see Robert Smith, *Schools, Politics and Society: Elementary Education in Wales, 1870–1902* (Cardiff, 1999).
155 Quoted in H. G. Williams, 'Learning suitable to the situation of the poorest classes: the National Society and Wales 1811–1839', *Welsh History Review*, 19, 3 (1999), 425–52, 449. On Thirwall see J. Vyrnwy Morgan, *Welsh Political and Educational Leaders in the Victorian Era* (London, 1908), pp. 105–6.
156 Report from the Select Committee on Education [Pakington Committee] (1866), p. 169.
157 *Report of the CCE, 1886–87*, p. 365.
158 CA, Llanfihangel-y-Creuddyn Lower school board minute book, 24 December 1887.
159 'School boards, teachers etc', *Baner ac Amserau Cymru*, 5 January 1876, 1.
160 'Hysbysiadau blaendaliadol rhad', *Y Llan*, 21 August 1891, 5.
161 Smith, *Schools, Politics, and Society*, p. 121.
162 PA, Llansantffraid school board minute book, 3 March 1899.
163 'The Ruthin School Board and Welsh', *Denbighshire Free Press*, 19 September 1896, 6.

164 'A Welsh-speaking master for Cwm', *South Wales Daily News*, 8 May 1888, 3.
165 'Welsh for Cardiff schools', *South Wales Daily News*, 23 July 1897, 4; 'Welsh in board schools', *South Wales Daily News*, 28 September 1892, 3; 'Bilingualism in Welsh schools', *Pontypridd District Herald*, 1 April 1893, 5; Smith, *Schools, Politics and Society*, p. 196.
166 *Report of the CCE, 1888–89*, p. 366.
167 *Report of the CCE, 1890–91*, p. 409.
168 *Western Mail*, 12 June 1885.
169 'Welsh in schools', *Cambrian News*, 4 November 1892, 2.
170 'John Jones, Junior: sef anturiaethau Cymro ieuangc mewn bywyd cyhoeddus', *Baner ac Amserau Cymru*, 12 December 1894, 12.
171 For example, D. F. Davis, 'Gwaseiddiwch y Cymry', *Seren Cymru*, 12 October 1888, 3; Morgan Williams and R. Prys Morris, 'Yr Iaith Gymraeg yn yr ysgolion Cymreig', *Y Genedl Gymreig*, 6 April 1887, 7.
172 James Rhys Jones, 'A Lecture on the educational state of Wales' (1851), *Mid Wales Herald*, supplement no. 1 (1860).

9
EDUCATION AND THE ANGLICISATION OF WALES

In 1868, the Welsh-speaking schools inspector Shadrach Pryce wrote that education would mean the language would be dead in a few generations:

> the young lad from school, though continuing to speak Welsh at home, has acquired a taste for reading English books, the English newspaper is sought after and read by him for the sake of getting the latest intelligence about the state of the markets, etc., his accounts and correspondence are carried on in English; this result of school education, together with other auxiliary causes, such as railways, and the introduction of English capitalists and labourers into the country, will slowly drive away Welsh even from its last retreat, the hearth and altar.[1]

Twenty-three years later, following requests from within Wales, the government counted the number of Welsh speakers for the first time. What the 1891 census, and the one that followed it a decade later, showed was that education had far from transformed Wales into either a bilingual or English-speaking society.

Table 9.1. Number and proportion of Welsh and English speakers, 1891 and 1901 censuses

	1891 (age 2+)		1901 (age 3 +)	
Welsh only	508,036	30.4%	280,905	15.1%
Welsh and English	402,253	24.0%	648,919	34.9%
English only	759,416	45.4%	928,222	49.9%
Total Welsh speakers	910,289	54.4%	929,824	50.0%
Total English speakers	1,161,669	69.4%	1,577,141	84.8%

Officials seemed surprised and unbelieving that English was not more widely known in Wales. In the official report on the 1891 census, a section headed 'Untrustworthiness of the returns' complained that 'many' bilinguals had returned themselves as Welsh monoglots.[2] Although it offered no reasoning, the 1901 census report claimed the numbers for Welsh-speaking 'may, and probably do, err on the side of overstatement'.[3]

The official scepticism was not entirely out of place. In 1891, there had been a public campaign for people with limited English to return themselves as Welsh monoglots.[4] But the far bigger problem was how the census relied on the notion that people either could or could not speak a language, when language skills are a spectrum that range from complete fluency to no knowledge at all. In 1891, some people were uncertain about what level of competency in Welsh or English was required to record themselves as a speaker of that language, while others apparently interpreted the question as being about their mother or most commonly used tongue rather than their language ability.[5] This might explain examples such as the Glanaman mother returned as a Welsh monoglot, while her two youngest children were returned as English monoglots.[6]

Many, indeed probably most, people recorded as Welsh monoglots would have known some English. This might be just a few common words, but it could also be that they understood far more than they could speak due to their schooling and encounters with the language in adult life. Linguists call such people 'passive bilinguals', people able to understand a language without speaking it. These realities could, despite the census results, lead visitors to Wales to conclude 'it is only in the wildest regions that natives are occasionally to be found who do not understand any English'.[7] But the reverse could also be true. In rural areas and some industrial districts, many English monoglots must have picked up a little Welsh because it was all around them. They may not have recorded this from a lack of confidence in Welsh or because they did not want to be associated with what they perceived as a lower-status language. Similarly, the status associated with speaking English may have meant some people returned themselves as bilingual even though they had quite limited skills in that language.

The census failed to capture the nuances of this spectrum of language ability or education's effect. Schools had given many people limited English but made far fewer fluent. Nor did the census reveal anything about how many people were what linguists call 'balanced bilinguals' (those with equal skills in both languages), or 'dominant bilinguals' (those with a preference and more ease with one language).[8] The census did, however, complicate the idea that Welsh was in retreat. That was true when percentages were considered but, with the population growing, there were more Welsh speakers in 1901 than 1891. What is most significant about the figures is the growth of bilingualism. By 1901, there were nearly a quarter of a million more bilingual people than a decade before. In the longer term, the tragedy for Wales, and the Welsh people, was neither the spread of English nor the retreat of Welsh monolingualism but the fact that the bilingualism that was so prevalent at the end of the nineteenth century did not persist.

Thinking about bilingualism shifts linguistic change from being something traumatic – an erosion of Wales's indigenous culture and distinctiveness – to something empowering, where people gain rather than lose a language. Yet such societies do not always stay bilingual when one language has a strong advantage over the other and thus bilingualism can be a stage towards homogenisation.[9] This is what happened in many Welsh industrial communities but this perspective relies on a knowledge of what happened next. Like any emphasis on the longer-term change, it misses the dynamics of the particular moment. As this chapter will argue, it is misleading to say English had all the power in the nineteenth century. Across all Wales, Welsh had very considerable cultural capital because of its role in religion. In many communities, the sheer numbers of Welsh speakers meant English monoglots faced considerable daily problems: they were outsiders. Thinking closely about what underpinned bilingualism also helps makes clearer what the determining factors behind linguistic change were. Too often the emphasis has been on what caused the spread of English rather than what lay behind the abandonment of Welsh. Education had a role in both, but religion emerges as a key factor too. Its strength had ensured that Welsh was not a second-class language, and thus, when secularisation grew, the rug began to be pulled from underneath the language's feet. In rural communities, Welsh survived this because it remained the dominant language and thus not to speak it was a practical problem; in industrial areas, where migration was introducing more and more English, the weakening of religion would prove fatal for Welsh.

Language and communities

The slow decline of Welsh monolingualism was not just down to the failures of education. Linguistic skills are not fixed and can improve or deteriorate according to how frequently they are used. In many rural areas, especially in the north and west, English was rarely heard outside the classroom. In such communities, people might quickly lose what they had learned at school. At Croes-goch, the master, who did use Welsh to explain things, remarked: 'It is almost incredible how soon Welsh children under 12 age will forget the little English they learn at school when they do not have a word of English at their homes.'[10] The master of Menai Bridge British school told the Cross Commission that children in rural areas forgot most of the English they learned just a year after leaving school.[11] This could happen in industrial communities too if there were few English or Irish migrants. Thus, as the manager of Dowlais works put it in around 1860, 'younger persons often forget much of what they were imperfectly taught'.[12] In contrast, English children who moved to areas where they were very much in a minority could pick up Welsh quickly without being taught it at school. This was simply because it was all around them. One man recalled how quickly English migrants in his Welsh-speaking industrial community learned Welsh: 'they had to learn it or be outside the society of the other children altogether'.[13] This all reflects recent research that shows the benefits of learning a new language as a child rather than as an adult are muted when exposure to it is limited.[14]

The importance of community contexts in shaping linguistic abilities is evident in the parish of Llanbryn-mair (Montgomeryshire). Iorwerth Peate (b.1901) remembered of his childhood that English was only heard within the walls of the school.[15] The 1891 census recorded just 8.2 per cent of people in the community as bilingual. Without reinforcement outside the classroom, schools struggled to teach English in such places: of children aged two to fifteen in Llanbryn-mair, 325 were recorded as Welsh monolinguals, fifteen as bilinguals and seven as English monolinguals. In contrast, just ten miles away was the town of Machynlleth, with a railway and market, both of which meant far more English was used and heard in the community. In 1891, 63.9 per cent of its population was bilingual, 9.8 per cent English monolingual and 26.3 per cent Welsh monolingual. Of children aged two to fifteen, 25.9 per cent were Welsh monoglots, still a substantial proportion but far less than in the nearby countryside.[16] In rural towns like Machynlleth, Welsh monoglots made up the majority of people over sixty but bilingualism was coming to characterise community life. Education had laid a basis for this by teaching people some English, but it was wider social changes that were more important because they allowed children and adults to develop their linguistic skills and gave them reasons to do so. Railways were key here. They brought English visitors and workers into the countryside, and created jobs where the language was useful and often, in the eyes of English railway companies at least, essential.[17] In seaside towns, entertainments and even some religious services were held in English to cater for the needs of visitors.[18] Such dynamics meant some middle-class figures were speaking Welsh less and less, even if they lived in rural towns. Some even became uncomfortable in their first language. In 1858, William George, a teacher at Pwllheli British school, wrote:

> I wished to say a few words to you in Welsh – but I am sorry that I cannot do so, although Welsh is my mother tongue – and I knew very little English until I was nine years of age – but I have used English almost ever since. The English language has done with me what the English people have done with our country – taken possession of the richest and largest part of it. No sooner do I use two or three Welsh words than their bolder English brethren thrust forward and the poor timid Taffies shrink back to hide themselves and I cannot, in spite of the utmost effort, find them again in time.[19]

This was probably an extreme example, but it is indicative of the complexity of linguistic change.

Even in rural communities where English was rarely spoken, the language did have a growing presence through consumer goods, post boxes, advertising and newspapers. Nor was this always something coming from outside. The language's status meant some monoglot Welshmen had business signs and even gravestones in English.[20] Thus the seeds were being sown of English becoming a more familiar language. Inspector Shadrach Pryce argued:

> a fair proportion of the children, unless of a very tender age, are not totally ignorant of English, even in country districts, when they first enter school. They have learnt a few English expressions at the market town, or at the railway station, or from an English family settled in the neighbourhood, and in numberless other ways the language of the great outside world has been brought under their notice.[21]

This was also happening through Welsh people's own journeys. Sailors and soldiers travelled the world. Farmers headed to English towns to sell milk, cattle, sheep and ponies. All brought back not just stories but English words and phrases they had picked up. Working outside Wales was possible because it did not require fluency in English. Even trade and exchange could happen with relatively limited vocabularies. Drovers claimed that 200 words of English was sufficient to do business when trade was good but if things were poor, and more bargaining was needed, then better English was required.[22] None of this was enough to overcome education's inadequacies, but as schools got better at teaching English, their lessons were slowly reinforced and made effective by everything from shop signs to boxes of tea.

Historians of language have argued that migration 'is the basic seed of language spread' and far more influential than conquest, because personal interaction is key to developing language ability.[23] This remained rare in rural areas, but industrial districts were magnets for young adults seeking better wages and more exciting lives than that offered by the countryside. At first, this migration happened within Wales. It thus buttressed the Welsh language by growing communities already rooted in Welsh culture with more Welsh speakers. In the middle of the century in the central and eastern valleys, or later to the west where migration from England was always small, those who came from England tended to learn some Welsh. As Brinley Thomas argued, 'The unrighteous Mammon in opening up the coalfields at such a pace unwittingly gave the Welsh language a new lease of life.'[24]

However, from the 1870s, English migrants into the Glamorgan valleys outnumbered those from Wales and, between 1901 and 1911, the Welsh only made up one-third of incomers.[25] This gave adults opportunities to keep up and develop the English they had learned at school. As the numbers of English migrants, and the English skills of Welsh people grew, discussions in public settings such as workplaces, pubs and community meetings began to switch from Welsh to English. This affected not just the linguistic dynamics of day-to-day life, but also, perhaps, people's attachment to Welsh since it lost some currency as a marker of local identity. Perhaps most significantly, children were using English more and more outside the home. Playing with the children of English migrants reinforced and developed their own English skills. Just as today, it is often through play and informal settings that children learn a new language most effectively. This is because they learn implicitly (that is unconsciously and without reflection) but that does require substantial time with the new language and opportunities to exchange and communicate in it. Unlike in some schools under the Revised Code, playing gave them that: it involved real communication, exchanges of ideas and sustained efforts to ensure comprehension. However, schools can reinforce the learning gained through play and help children understand the rules and grammar of a language.[26] Thus, in industrial communities, schools and migration reinforced each other in making people fluent in English.

Some individuals made their own personal determined efforts to become fluent in English. Relatives could help but others had to make do themselves.[27] Percy Watkins, born in Montgomeryshire in 1871, remembered that his father improved his English by reading a dictionary before breakfast every day.[28] Daniel Parry-Jones, born in Carmarthenshire in 1891, recalled that he was never taught to speak English at school: 'that I had to do on my own as best as I could'. By fourteen, he was taking a Welsh-English dictionary everywhere and using it to help him read English books; he kept a notebook where he wrote new words and their Welsh equivalent. Nonetheless, working from written sources, he still struggled with knowing how to pronounce words.[29] Those without a dictionary struggled even more but could still develop their English reading by looking at the context of words that they did not understand and working things out for themselves.[30] In industrial areas, there were a variety of institutions that offered people access to books, newspapers, lectures, evening classes and debating societies.[31] This rich educational environment did more than just develop people's political and intellectual interests; it was also part of the way that the English language developed and took root in communities and individuals' lives.

The 1861 Newcastle Commission was correct in that education's role in linguistic change was:

> that of an adjunct, and a most powerful one, to the physical ones ... But we mistake, and over-estimate its influence, if, as is often done, we look at the school as the sole or even the principal agency

in the change of a population from the use of one language to that of another.[32]

What education did was lay the foundations for the spread of English; it was migration that built on this and created actual linguistic change. Education was the facilitator, but migration was the executor. Yet the spread of English was still a slow process. In 1891, 29.6 per cent of the Pontypridd registration district and 32.1 per cent of the Merthyr district were recorded as Welsh monoglots. In rural areas, with little or no migration, English remained very much a minority language. Welsh monolinguals made up well over half the population in Cardiganshire (56.5 per cent), Caernarfonshire (65.8 per cent), Meirionnydd (74.5 per cent) and Anglesey (71.4 per cent) at the 1891 census. In some registration districts, such as Pwllheli, Bala and Anglesey in the north and Tregaron and Newcastle Emlyn in the south, Welsh monoglots made up more than 80 per cent of the population. Quite simply, there were many rural communities at the end of the century where it was rare to hear English outside a school. In such places, education had largely failed in its goal of teaching and spreading the English language.

The decline of Welsh

Sociolinguists notes there is a common sequence in all situations where language replacement occurs. The first stage is significant pressure on people to speak the dominant language. This might be cultural, economic, political and can come from above in the form of laws or from below in terms of fashions or material conditions. It is followed by a second stage of bilingualism, where people have competency in both their mother tongue and the learned dominant language. In the third stage, people, especially younger ones, begin to use their mother tongue less and less. They might even feel shame about using it, especially outside the home. They might not pass it on to their children thus changing the language of the family.[33] Through this process comprehensive language change within a community, and even a family, can happen in little more than a generation. In Wales, this meant monolingual Welsh grandparents could have bilingual children and monolingual English grandchildren. Language replacement is not inevitable in bilingual communities. The ability to speak English did not have to mean the decline of Welsh, although that was often what contemporaries assumed would happen. What decides if bilingual communities move from the second stage to the third stage is how the less dominant language is seen.

Nineteenth-century comment suggests that some communities were already moving into the third stage of language abandonment. The 1861 Newcastle Commission claimed that in towns where people spoke Welsh and English: 'the vernacular Welsh of the parents is exchanged for English in the next generation, while the Welsh is gradually abandoned, and in the third generation is not found'. It suggested that the death of Welsh was inevitable because people did not need two languages.[34] In border counties, both early and late in the century, there were similar claims of Welsh-speaking parents talking English to their children.[35] An 1883 report noted:

> The extent to which English has superseded Welsh in the last twenty years is a subject of general remark among school managers. In the Gwenddwr National schools, Breconshire, the children at present speak only English, and have actually lost their knowledge of Welsh, though the parents of these very children continue to speak Welsh among themselves.[36]

It is difficult to be conclusive about how widespread this was. Dan Isaac Davies recorded in 1885 that when he visited Abermorlais Board school there were 510 children there over the age of eight. Ninety-six children had Welsh-speaking parents and could understand Welsh but not speak it. Another 100 could not understand or speak it, although their parents spoke the language.[37] That same year, a Montgomeryshire teacher reported around half of the children at his school spoke English at home but had Welsh-speaking parents.[38] In contrast, Philip Jones's study of the census for mining communities in Glamorgan led him to conclude that the dominant pattern was for children to learn the language of their parents. In his investigation, just 8 per cent of the Welsh-speaking couples in a sample had not passed the language onto their children.[39] This was far more common in the twentieth century. Research for a 1927 education inquiry found that around a quarter of pupils at secondary school had one or two Welsh-speaking parents but did not speak the language at home. This was least common in rural counties but in Merthyr half of secondary schoolchildren had at least one parent who spoke Welsh but the language was not used habitually at home.

Table 9.2. Home language of secondary schoolchildren, 1927[40]

	% speaking Welsh habitually at home	% not speaking Welsh habitually at home but with 2 Welsh-speaking parents	% not speaking Welsh habitually at home but with 1 Welsh-speaking parent
Meirionnydd	80.0	3.3	6.3
Cardigan	79.0	2.5	12.2
Anglesey	75.3	2.1	17.0
Caernarfon	74.0	3.0	6.3
Carmarthen	58.5	15.0	13.7
Denbigh	32.7	11.7	14.6
Montgomery	25.9	1.2	14.6
Glamorgan	23.2	18.9	18.1
Brecon	22.3	8.0	18.4
Flint	17.2	24.2	15.5
Swansea CB	15.4	15.1	20.0
Pembroke	13.0	4.7	10.5
Merthyr Tydfil CB	12.4	30.1	20.2
Cardiff CB	3.2	5.3	8.0
Monmouth	2.4	5.2	10.6
Newport CB	0.6	2.1	5.7
Radnor	0.4	1.8	6.1
Total	28.0	12.3	14.1

These regional figures disguised how widespread parents not passing on Welsh could be within specific communities. In Dunvant, for example, only ten out of 257 children at the school spoke Welsh but 100 of them had Welsh-speaking parents.[41]

Such cases were particularly common where one parent spoke Welsh but the other did not. Speaking English to the child may have been the natural outcome of speaking English to one's partner rather than a conscious decision not to teach them Welsh. Studies of languages across the world have shown men were more susceptible to external linguistic influences because women's lives were more focused on the home.[42] This also made women crucial to linguistic decisions and influences on children. The effects of linguistically mixed marriages and the influence of women was clear in a study of Dowlais in the 1891 census. In 94.2 per cent of households with two Welsh-speaking parents, all the children spoke Welsh. In contrast, all children were Welsh speakers in just 7.7 per cent of households where the father was bilingual and the mother an English monoglot. The figure was 30.2 per cent in households where the mother was bilingual and the father an English monoglot.[43]

There are few historical sources that reveal why people chose not to pass the language onto their children but choices are not made in a cultural vacuum. Regardless of whether people could speak one or both languages, it would have been obvious to all that Welsh and English were not equals. English was clearly the language of power, business and law. The fact that so much of the local gentry only spoke English reinforced the idea that it was a language of status.[44] So, too, did the vast British Empire and the migratory allure of the USA. This explains people's desire to gain that language, but not to lose their own. However, notions of status are also relational and the power of English in turn implied the inferiority of Welsh, even when this was not actually put into words.[45] Abel Jones, an inspector in Glamorgan early in the twentieth century, argued, 'Children heard so little about the language and history of their native land in school that there was a tendency to despise their own country, and to over-estimate the greatness of other countries.'[46] Thus the exclusion of Welsh from so many official, educational and business spheres gave the impression that it was not a language of modern worth.

Indeed, even when speaking Welsh, people tended to use the English words for school and master rather than 'ysgol' or 'athro'.

At times, the supposed inferiority of Welsh was explicitly articulated. The criticisms of the Blue Books, all made under the official stamp of government, left what Geraint H. Jenkins called a 'psychological scar ... so deep that the Welsh intelligentsia lived in fear of further indictments at the hands of the English establishment'.[47] And there were further indictments. Newspapers, tourists and postcards sometimes joked about the strangeness of Welsh and Welsh place-names.[48] In 1866, an editorial in *The Times* called Welsh 'the curse of Wales', excluding people from civilisation, prosperity, literature and progress. 'Their antiquated and semi-barbarous language', it concluded, 'shrouds them in darkness'.[49] Of course, few people in Wales read *The Times* or government reports but some of the middle class did, and the Blue Books and other comments were widely reported in Welsh papers. Thus, when in 1863 *The Spectator* called Welsh 'uncouth gibberish', the comment was reported in a number of Welsh newspapers and periodicals.[50] Yet people did not believe everything they read. The Blue Books and *The Spectator*'s comments both drew angry retorts: *Seren Cymru*, for example, called the latter wicked untruths.[51]

Some in Wales, however, clearly shared such views, sometimes for religious reasons and sometimes out of a sense of paternalism. In 1818, the rector of Aberporth told an inquiry on the education of the poor that because so many people could not speak English, they were 'prey to illiterate bigoted fanatics, who undertake to teach them in night schools, which is a source of much immorality, of dissent from the Church of England, and of bastardy, by which they become worse men and more disloyal subjects'.[52] A 1842 commission on the employment of children was told by a Welsh-speaking Cyfarthfa overman that teaching the language in schools and using it in chapels 'stultifies the children, and prevents their progress in education'.[53] In 1858, Enoch Gibbon Salisbury, a Welsh-speaking barrister and MP for Chester, declared at the opening of the Vale of Clwyd railway that while he was a proud Welshman he was not ashamed to say 'and I say it boldly – that I shall be delighted to see the Welsh people anglicised'.[54] Major

R. O. Jones of Bala told the Aberdare Committee in 1881 that in the interest of 'the humbler classes ... the sooner the Welsh language becomes a dead language the better'.[55] How widely such comments were disseminated is difficult to know but they surely reflected what was being said in communities and, like the similar comments from outside Wales, all this attributed negative connotations to the Welsh language. These were not necessarily automatically accepted or absorbed, but they framed the decision taken by some parents not to pass on the language in communities where people could see it had retreated in their own lifetime. They also contributed to the idea that English was the language of the future, while Welsh of the past and thus dying out, an idea articulated in newspaper articles.[56] This notion was far less judgemental and often articulated with sorrow or regret, with calls that nothing should be done to speed up the process.[57] But the idea that Welsh was dying was deeply injurious to the language nonetheless since it probably discouraged speakers from keeping the language up and passing it on.

However much anti-Welsh attitudes might be dressed up in paternalist tones, they were also rooted in snobbery. If English was the language of power, then by implication Welsh was the language of the working class. This reinforced external ideas that Welsh was uncivilised. As James Vernon has argued, 'The poor were increasingly conceived less as a separate class than as a race apart and were frequently equated to "primitive" and "savage" peoples across the empire.'[58] Such attitudes explain why a teacher reported that in towns those with some schooling adopted English to show their civility but would feel shame if an Englishman they met detected a Welsh accent.[59] Similarly, an 1868 schools inquiry was told that it was becoming unfashionable for middle-class girls to know Welsh.[60] In 1888, the principal of Bangor Normal College criticised the bilingual middle class for seeing Welsh 'as a language which would do for servants but not for themselves'.[61] The association of Welsh with the working class was felt outside the middle class too. This was clear in a story where a man walking on a mountain knocked at a farmhouse and asked in Welsh for a glass of milk. As the old woman who answered the door went off to fetch it, he heard her say: 'You said a gentleman was coming to the door but the man is a Welshman!'[62] It was thus perhaps unsurprising that throughout the century there were claims that the Welsh lacked self-confidence in themselves and their nationality.[63] Inspector Dan Isaac Davies, an advocate for the language who worked across industrial Wales, went further and said many in Wales felt a shame about speaking Welsh.[64]

Late in the century some attitudes towards Welsh did start to change and the language began to become associated with an imperial modernity.[65] There was a new interest in Welsh history and a growing understanding of the United Kingdom's inherent diversity as a characteristic strength rather than a threat. By 1894, a new periodical founded by Owen M. Edwards entitled *Wales* declared proudly there had been 'an outburst of national feeling' in recent years.[66] It was this movement that produced the 1880s campaign for Welsh in schools, but it had been slowly growing since the Blue Books encouraged a backlash that celebrated and defended Wales. As early as 1861, the rector of Merthyr told the Newcastle Commission that the feeling from half a century earlier that it was ungenteel to speak Welsh no longer existed to any great extent.[67] Yet the national revival never displaced the old ideas of Welsh inferiority that worked at an abstract level, hovering in the background, occasionally coming into focus, but often unseen and unnoticed, influencing people's mindsets in small and subtle ways when they were not countered by contradictory ideologies and influences.

These messages were most powerful in industrial communities. There, migration was bringing English into communities, making it much easier to believe that Welsh was backwards and dying. This made it easier to take the decision not to pass Welsh on to the children. Indeed, in such communities it might be children themselves who were leading linguistic change in families. Inspector W. Edwards, who lived in Merthyr, claimed that education being in English meant children struggled to express themselves in Welsh. The result, he said, was that they found it difficult to speak to their mothers, forcing her 'to use such broken English as she may possess'. He stated that everyone in

Wales could recall families where, through the influence of schools, the children had been 'weaned from the Welsh-speaking habit' and were thus unable 'to converse with their elders', making them 'foreigners in their own home circles'.[68] This seems an exaggeration and a language was unlikely to be forgotten if it was used every day with friends and family. More credibly, Jack Jones (b.1884) recalled of his youth in Merthyr:

> At first I only knew Welsh from my parents and grandparents, but as I went on playing with Scott, Hartley, Ward and McGill children, I became more fluent than in my native language. Dad was annoyed when I started replying in English to what he had said in Welsh, but our mam said in Welsh: 'Oh, let him alone. What odds anyway?'[69]

That happened because of migration into Merthyr from England, and it was migration that made so much linguistic change a gradual rather than sudden process. As English was spoken more and more in such communities, some families probably came to think Welsh had no future or real use anymore. Indeed, Welsh speakers may themselves have gradually spoken more English at home as their use of the language outside it increased.[70] This might explain why the census reveals families where the older children were bilingual but the younger ones English monoglots. Individuals reacted differently to this. As the above example from Jack Jones shows, there could be different ideas within families too. There are even suggestions that migration from within Wales could undermine the language. Oral histories hint at parents' view of the value of Welsh being undermined by the differences in dialects between locals and Welsh migrants who had moved into industrial areas.[71]

Imperfect language skills and environments where two languages might be heard and valued led people to switch between languages, even within sentences, according to what was being talked about and their knowledge of vocabulary. This is what linguists call code switching and it was strongest in areas where communities that were frontiers between areas dominated by Welsh and those dominated by English. In the novel *Rhys Lewis* (1885), people in Buckley (Flintshire) were said to speak Welsh and English mixed up.[72] Pembrokeshire was a particularly complex county, with English predominating in its south and Welsh in its north. A visitor to Fishguard – near the county's linguistic border – at the start of the nineteenth century noted that some people spoke a mixture of Welsh and English that was 'unintelligible to either ear'.[73] In 1902, a poem appeared in a newspaper that switched between languages in single lines and said people in the county spoke neither English nor Welsh, but 'Half and half ar ol eu mixio' (Half and half after they have mixed).[74]

Some code switching was emotional and unconscious. The 1936 autobiography of a woman from Pontypool remembered of her childhood:

> The older folks would usually begin a conversation in English, which was all right for the preliminaries, but as the subject became more interesting, they would abandon the English and lapse into their beloved Welsh, which has a fiery, excitable sound, well suited to dramatic discussions.[75]

But code switching could also be very conscious. Sometimes one language was felt to be more effective or suitable for a particular subject. One Montgomeryshire boy told travel writer George Borrow that his horses would not respond to Welsh oaths and curses and English needed to be used.[76] Another man recalled that in his childhood some farmers with very little English still spoke that language to their dogs and gave them English names.[77] English seems to have been preferred when it came to anything formal, especially written. This might be because people did not know how to write Welsh if they had not been to Sunday school but it was also rooted in numeracy being taught in English. Thus one school inspector noted that in Carmarthenshire a dealer and farmer would bargain in Welsh but that the bill and receipt would be issued in English.[78]

In such situations, where the intermingling of languages, even within conversations, was common, the process of linguistic change was organic and gradual. Doyle has suggested that in Ireland there was not even a conscious point of abandoning one since the two had become intertwined, and that this helps explain why there was little contemporary trauma from the process.[79] The reaction of Jack Jones's father suggests it would be wrong to say there was no trauma. Similarly, in the 1880s novel *Rhys Lewis*, a mother complains that her sons now spoke so much in English that she did not know what was happening in her own house.[80] Such examples further point to how, for many, which language was spoken at home was often a conscious and sometimes emotional decision. The complexities of parents' thinking are illustrated by one Rhondda family. Abel Jones was born in 1878, to a couple who spoke little English. When Jones was five, his father decided to offer a prize to whichever of his children spoke the least Welsh at home for a month. But the parents became alarmed at how much English was being spoken by the children so they followed it with another prize for the child who spoke the least English for a month.[81]

Some parents seem to have made decisions to raise the children in English despite their own limitations in that language. The vicar of Cwmdauddwr (Radnorshire) claimed that in the Cefn valley in his parish, 'there are many cases of parents hardly knowing anything but Welsh, and their children all knowing hardly anything but English'. He put this down to people thinking English was of 'more use' to the children.[82] Similarly, a writer claimed in 1888 that there were parents in Glamorgan teaching English to their children when they only understood a few words of the language themselves.[83] Perhaps such families were influenced by the limitations of their own education. They knew from experience that schools could not be relied on to make children fluent in English and that it was using the language outside the classroom that really developed people's fluency. Thus speaking English rather than Welsh to a child was probably sometimes an effort to compensate for poor education and ensure their children were fluent. But such cases were surely exaggerated or at least very unusual because to speak to one's children in a language that one was far from fluent in must have felt unnatural and uncomfortable.[84] People may have tried to but achieving this was quite a different matter.

The resilience of Welsh

There were influences and ideologies that worked against the power of English. The most powerful was everyday life in communities. This mattered far more than the negative tropes around Welsh and was key to why the language did not decline at anything like the rate that commentators suggested. Dalby has argued that language death occurs when bilingual people feel their traditional language has no use and thus decide not to pass it on.[85] Any language widely spoken in a community clearly has practical use and contemporary research shows the influence of the linguistic dynamics of a community on parents' decision-making in language transmission.[86] Whether people in nineteenth-century Wales felt Welsh had no use depended on where they lived and what they did for a living. Table 9.2 showed how rare it was in rural counties for Welsh-speaking couples not to speak the language to their children. In such communities to not pass on Welsh would have been seriously disadvantageous to a child. Every simple, local transaction with a neighbour, tradesman or shop would have been a challenging experience. Moreover, sociolinguists argue that to stop speaking a language is also to risk being ostracised or resented.[87] Those without Welsh in rural villages could find it an isolating experience with few to talk to and they did sometimes feel ostracised by their neighbours.[88]

Across Wales, there were other powerful reasons for people not to give up Welsh. Despite the image of English as the language of business, the ability to speak Welsh had economic value too. It was essential for shopworkers and tradesmen in not just Welsh-monoglot communities but many bilingual ones too. This is evident in job advertisements in newspapers. Some were in English but placed in Welsh-language newspapers, presumably out of a desire for a Welsh speaker. Others, for positions in retail, agriculture and trades, sometimes explicitly asked for

Welsh speakers, even in industrial areas.[89] One 1860s enquiry noted in Swansea Welsh had much declined but 'shopkeepers and others, however, still learn it in order to be able to communicate with country persons'.[90] Some industrial companies realised that having Welsh speakers in key management positions helped industrial relations.[91]

Welsh was not just protected by its practical uses. Languages without political capital can still have significant cultural capital as an expression of identity that ties together families and communities. In such cases, it is a language's inward-looking and local character – the very thing that outsiders criticised – that matters.[92] Welsh was something that shut outsiders out and that gave it some status as a marker of identity and some utility as a tool to laugh at strangers and others.[93] Local gentry or clergy who had tried to learn Welsh, something some did to deal with tenants and exert local leadership, might find themselves mocked by native speakers for their poor grasp of the language.[94] It was thus little wonder that local squires could feel disadvantaged or frustrated by not understanding the people they met and having to use interpreters.[95] Such dynamics might also explain the anger George Borrow said he encountered when people learned he, an Englishman, could understand their Welsh.[96]

Moreover, Welsh had deep emotional resonances for many of its speakers. Family and community were integral to most people's lives and Welsh was integral to both. It was the language people loved and lived in, and it was widely used in the spheres that gave people security and hope. It was the language of hearth, eisteddfodau, chapels, taverns and other places that help people resist the brutal, dehumanising existences that poverty could otherwise inflict.[97] One writer called Welsh the language of prayer, love, affection, sadness, rejoicing, wailing and song.[98] Moore-Colyer has described Welsh as representing 'an expression of cultural continuity', conferring 'a sense of belonging and security' and a 'bulwark against an uncertain and dangerous world outside'. He sees it as thus providing people with a 'sort of psychic cohesion and social cement'.[99] Indeed, researchers have shown in other multilingual contexts sentimental factors have an influence on which language people chose to use, with emotive letters being written in the mother tongue.[100] All this would have mitigated against negative ideas around the language derived from school. As Ravenstein put it in 1879, 'a language to which the people who speak it cling with affection dies a slow death, and Welsh may survive for centuries to come, if not, for ever'.[101]

There were also ideological forces protecting the language. Welsh communities faced contradictory pressures through the nineteenth century. The idea that Welsh was a language of the past rather than modernity may have turned some away from the language but for others this made it more important. English may have been seen as a language of modernity but that also meant it was associated with greed, money and thus questionable morals.[102] Particularly amongst Nonconformist ministers and thinkers, there was a sense that the Welsh language protected communities from some of the immoral influences of the outside world and thus holding on to it mattered. This created a schizophrenic attitude which Ieuan Gwynedd Jones summed up as: 'Learn English, my boy, to get on; but learn English and risk being damned, and what is more, risk bringing about the dissolution of the society we have created.'[103]

It was religion that was the strongest buttress against the abandonment of Welsh.[104] Ostler, a historian of language, has argued that 'ultimately the association of a language with profound religious truths gains the most loyal adherents'.[105] Religion was not a discrete sphere of life but integral to how people lived and thought. Through the chapels Welsh became associated with good moral conduct but, more importantly, it was a language in which the word of God, the key to everlasting salvation, could be heard and understood. In 1937, W. J. Gruffydd argued that religion had given Welsh in the previous century the highest dignity any language could have and its exclusion from classrooms accentuated its connection with the spiritual. Thus, he argued, at school Welsh was the servant but in the higher world of religion it sat on the throne.[106] Ieuan Gwynedd Jones concluded that the alliance of religion and language was 'so powerful' that it was 'able to contain the challenge of English culture' up to 1914.[107] Religion also explains a key difference between Welsh and Irish. In Ireland, the Catholic church did not promote the language, but the Protestant church did – not out of love for the language but to try and find a way into Irish communities. Yet what this did was associate Irish with what many perceived as an alien church, to the detriment of the language's reputation.[108]

By the end of the century, a form of secularisation was creeping into Welsh society. This was not so much a growth of atheism or agnosticism but a more casual attitude to religion. Nonetheless, this still undermined its emotional pull and thus the status religion could bestow on Welsh. Chapels increasingly found themselves at odds with some of the new aspects of popular culture, such as sport. This hurt their support amongst younger people, which in turn had a detrimental effect on those people's attitudes towards the language that chapels operated in.[109] In industrial areas, some chapels were also turning their backs on the Welsh language to try to win the support, and save the souls, of migrants from England. Before 1860, 85 per cent of Baptist chapels in the Glamorgan valleys operated in Welsh. By the 1880s, this had fallen to 57 per cent.[110] All this undermined the Welsh language. A bilingual people only stays so if it values both languages. The two languages do not have to be equal in status but both have to have a use. Once Welsh declined as a language of religion then people's reasons to retain it were severely undermined.

Sociolinguist Robert Page argued that linguistic choices were 'acts of identity', conscious attempts to identify with one group or another.[111] There is nothing to suggest that not speaking Welsh to one's children was a conscious rejection of being Welsh. It could be that such people were rejecting not Wales itself but the poverty they associated with their personal or family past. This is made more likely by how Welshness itself was being remade into an identity less rooted in language and more anchored in personal and community sentiments. The rise of a popular patriotism in sport and music were the most obvious examples of this.[112] Migration was key here but so too were changes in religion. Nonconformity retained its position as symbol of Welsh difference and identity but it gradually stopped reinforcing the idea that the Welsh language was part of this, as some chapels in industrial communities switched to English. Welsh thus got caught in a vicious circle where its declining status began to undermine the idea that Welsh nationality was rooted in language. This then may have made it mentally and emotionally easier for more people to leave the language behind since to reject it was not to reject Wales itself.[113]

The influence of education on language choices

In the popular imagination, the Welsh Not is a key reason why some Welsh speakers did not pass on the language to their children. There are family stories of a grandparent being punished for speaking Welsh and then never uttering a word of the language again.[114] Contemporary or first-hand evidence of that happening does not exist but some contemporaries did raise the possibility that the Welsh Not turned people against the language and Wales itself. The academic Isambard Owen asked the Cross Commission:

> Is it calculated to conduce to the formation of habits of self-confidence and self-respect in the children of Wales, that the first lesson impressed upon them when they enter school should be this, that their own native language is a thing to be straightway [sic] forgotten and despised; that the language learned at their mother's knee, the language in which the associations of their homes are bound up, the language in which the truths of religion have been imparted to them, the language which is to them the badge of their country and nationality, is a thing to feel ashamed of, and to get rid of as soon as possible? Children are impressionable, and little given to drawing fine distinctions. Is there then no danger that the lesson should be transferred in the child's mind from the language itself to its associations, and become in effect a lesson of contempt and distrust for his parentage, his home, his religion, his nationality, and himself?[115]

His evidence was part of a campaign to influence the commission to recommend the formal recognition of Welsh in schools, but it is notable that he raised the possibility that education was undermining Welshness rather than saying it actually was. Similarly, Beriah Gwynfe Evans recalled that the Welsh Not, which he himself had used, created a stigma around Welsh but he also stopped short of saying this led children to abandon the language, perhaps because he saw that it stopped children understanding the English they were learning.[116]

It is impossible to say definitively that the Welsh Not made a direct contribution to the decline of Welsh. It was at its height in the first half of the century, when 70 to 80 per cent of children were not attending day schools.[117] Thus only a minority of Welsh people probably ever experienced it. As this book has shown, where children were at schools where Welsh was completely excluded they did not learn much. Welsh could not be beaten out of children if they spoke no other language. In cases where children were prevented from speaking Welsh but teachers employed the language, things might have been different. Moreover, as Welsh found a greater place in the classroom, and thus the teaching of English became more effective, then the general climate of schools could have contributed to future decisions to shun Welsh by adding to the general sense that it was English that mattered. The growing place of Welsh in the classroom did not change this since the primary reason for its employment was to improve the teaching of English. Moreover, those who were successful at school and went onto secondary education would have encountered the same message again. The 1889 Welsh Intermediate Education Act created a system of secondary schools. These were important routes to social mobility for those able to access them, but they were also places where Welsh was marginalised and children might be punished for speaking it. Secondary school could thus further alienate children from their native language and culture.[118] But, without evidence that education made people devalue Welsh, these are hypothetical suppositions.

Humphries argues that working-class children did not 'automatically absorb the values encouraged by schools'. The behaviours, values learned in family, street and neighbourhood instead exerted more influence on children, especially since their time at school was relatively short with most children earlier in the century leaving at around ten, and later on at twelve.[119] The way some people had their sense of Welshness intensified rather than undermined by school showed that. So, too, did the general agency children could show at school (see chapter 7). However, some teachers did feel they were changing children's habits when it came to language. Some references to the Welsh Not and similar rules did claim to be having an effect. At Dwyran in 1878, for example, a week after recording his desire to 'overcome' Welsh-speaking, the master recorded that a 'great deal' of it had disappeared. Yet he also noted that older children were unable to undertake simple translations from English into Welsh, which suggests what he, and other teachers who noted the success of their anti-Welsh rules, might have done was create more silence rather than more English being spoken.[120] More significantly, the master of Swyddffynnon, who had occasionally punished boys for speaking Welsh, recorded in 1883: 'The practice of speaking English in the Playground and on the road to and from school has very much increased among the children, especially the boys. Several people in the neighbourhood have commented upon it favourably.'[121] He may have been exaggerating to impress his school board or the inspectors, but this is a rare piece of evidence from a teacher that claims education did bring about linguistic change outside school. Occasionally, people external to education also claimed that children outside industrial districts were leaving Welsh behind. In 1903, for example, there was a complaint in the press that secondary schools were anglicising children by discouraging pupils from speaking Welsh. It claimed the young were speaking English in the streets of Caernarfon, something that never happened a decade before.[122] Nonetheless, at the 1901 census, 35.5 per cent of children aged three to fourteen in Caernarfon municipal borough were still recorded as being Welsh monoglots.

Thus the influence of education on language choices cannot be discounted but it has to be set against the considerable weight of evidence that pointed in the opposite direction. As chapter 5 showed, one of the reasons that teachers punished children for speaking Welsh was because they could not get pupils to stop doing so. Much would have depended on how the teacher approached his or her task. Using the cane did not make teachers' interventions any more influential since children had a strong sense of what was fair and resisted authority in all sorts of ways when they felt rules were unfair. One writer on corporal punishment claimed:

> I do not find a spark of gratitude for any flogging I ever received. The remembrance is of hatred to the punishment, of vexation with the inflicter of it, be he father or schoolmaster. I do not feel that the love of truth, of honesty, or other virtue, was implanted in me by flogging; or that any vice was ever eradicated.[123]

Persuasion was much more effective in changing habits. A good teacher was inspirational and did have some hold over pupils and even local communities, especially if what they asked of children was reinforced in other spheres, such as church or chapel or fitted with community norms. The influence persuasion could achieve was evident at Llidiart-y-waun in Montgomeryshire. The master there complained how sheep washing and shearing was a general holiday in his community, with children invited to watch. It could keep them away from school for several days and two years after raising this, he recorded that he had, by persuasion, 'almost stamped out the custom' in the interests of the 'welfare of the school'.[124] That argument would have had some influence with parents given the value many placed on education. As chapter 4 showed, some teachers also tried to reason with and persuade children not to speak Welsh at school. There is no evidence that they tried to extend this outside the classroom, on the playground or journey to school but that does not mean it did not happen. More common probably were more subtle messages about the value of Welsh. Cassie Davies (b.1898) remembered her teacher would only speak Welsh to the children on Sundays and was constantly telling them that the language would be of no use to them outside their own small corner of Cardiganshire.[125] Given the general value placed on social mobility and English in general in rural communities, any such message from a teacher would have had some influence. But it would also have run contrary to the fact that children heard Welsh in the loving sanctuary of their homes and in the sacred space of the chapel.

What is more likely is that educational experiences affected how people behaved as adults rather than as children. Rather than stopping speaking Welsh themselves, it is more likely that negative experiences might have encouraged them not to pass the language on in contexts where the language was already diminishing in communities and thus losing its practical use. Yet evidence of people stating that they did not speak Welsh to their children because of their school experiences seems to be non-existent. It could be that people's internalised sense of shame meant they kept it hidden or did not discuss it, making it difficult for the historian to later understand what was felt.[126] One hint that this could happen is J. Lloyd Williams (b.1854), who worked as a teacher in Caernarfonshire in the 1870s and 1880s, where he used the Welsh Not. He later confessed to thinking that Welsh was inferior and speaking English at home; he wrote that it was not until he moved to London that he realised the value of his own language and he did go on to raise his children in Welsh.[127]

Further weight to the possibility that educational experiences may have turned people against Welsh in the longer term comes from considering other countries. Anticolonial writers have argued that when colonial regimes tried to persuade people of the inferiority and inadequacy of their languages for modern life, their very identity and self-confidence were undermined.[128] Education was part of that process. In the 1950s, the British colonial regime in Kenya assumed control of schools and made English their formal language. The punishment for speaking the indigenous language was a fine, the cane or being made to wear a metal plate that said 'I am stupid' or 'I am a donkey'. This was implemented through children passing a button to whoever was heard speaking their mother tongue. Ngũgĩ wa Thiong'o wrote, from personal experience, that this was humiliating. He maintained that it broke children's connections between learning and home, alienating them from their domestic environment.[129] Post-independence, fluency in English has remained the goal of Kenyan education but at the 2019 census just 8 per cent of Kenyans in urban areas and 3 per cent in rural areas spoke English as their primary language.[130] If the British regime was trying to kill African languages, it clearly failed. Indeed, excluding a language from education could have the opposite effect to what was intended. Jernsletten has argued that the exclusion of the Sami language from Norwegian schools meant the institutions became isolated from Sami society. Thus, while schools were meant to make the Sami people Norwegian, they resulted in an estrangement between Sami and Norwegian society and thus the preservation of the Sami language and culture.[131]

The evidence of other nations shows that wider contextual factors are more influential on the future of languages than harsh educational practices. In the USA, from the late nineteenth century, native American children were often forcibly sent to boarding schools where they were educated in English and punished for speaking their own languages. Rule 41 of the 1881 Reservation Boarding Schools stated that: 'Pupils must be compelled to speak with each other in English, and should be properly rebuked or punished for persistent violation of this rule. Every effort should be made to encourage them to abandon their tribal language.'[132] Andrew Woolford called the process genocide, although he also stresses the ways indigenous peoples resisted vigorously what was being done to them.[133] John Reyhner has shown there was an awareness in the nineteenth century that education was not obliterating Indian culture or language. Just as in Wales, there were contemporary calls for children to be taught English through their own language because they were learning how to read without understanding the meaning of what they read. Moreover, after school many returned to their reservations and tribal lifestyles, blending into the population rather than transforming it. By the 1950s, native American education continued to focus on developing English but regulations no longer allowed stopping children use their own language because it was accepted that this was necessary for the development of thinking skills and that children learned English faster if use was made use of their native tongue.[134] By then, Indian culture had been deeply wounded by decades of racism, violence, forced removals, religious persuasion, cultural contempt and economic forces. For those who wanted to eradicate the native peoples of North America, there was simply less need to try to do this through beating them for speaking their own languages.

Nineteenth-century France was also marked by linguistic diversity but French was spreading because of internal migration, military service and education. In schools, there were a variety of practices when it came to the language of instruction and, as in Wales, complaints that children were learning to speak French like parrots and unable to understand what they read if their mother tongue was not employed.[135] In Brittany, Breton was widely, but far from universally, used in schools for much of the century, but after 1870 attitudes hardened. In the 1870s, the French government banned bilingual and Breton textbooks and instructed that only French could be taught in schools. In that decade, the *vuoc'h koad* or *simbol*, an instrument similar to the Welsh Not, became popular, although it was never officially sanctioned by the government. Without the use of Breton in classrooms, French could not flourish and there were still more than 1.4 million Breton speakers at the end of the century, not least because the language continued to have a role in popular religion.[136]

Most other languages in France were more vulnerable because they were much closer to French in structure and vocabulary and thus much easier to learn. In Provence, there was a tool similar to the Welsh Not called the sign. One inspector in the 1890s said of it:

> Since I introduced the sign into my school nearly two years ago, I have noticed a very real progress in the way in which my pupils speak and read French ... Little by little patois is disappearing from the school, from the playground, the street, the family itself. Everyone gains by this, and no one has protested against my method, which I have therefore every reason to think is a good one.[137]

But linguistic change in Provence was driven more by economic integration, as its ports boomed due to their proximity to the French empire in north Africa. Everywhere in France, language change was pushed along by people's desire to learn French because it 'stood for mobility, advancement, economic and social promotion, and escape from the restrictive bonds of home'. But the effect of this was most significant in those areas where there were economic and political opportunities to take advantage of. As Weber concludes, 'the success or failure of the schools simply reflected their linguistic environment, either predisposed to French or alien to it'.[138]

At the start of the nineteenth century, Irish was already significantly weaker than Welsh and its subsequent decline was far starker. Historians estimate that in 1800 only around 45 per cent of the population spoke Irish. Fifty years later, at the time of the first language census, the figure had fallen to 23 per cent.[139] Mass migration and the potato famine were key to this but some historians see education as having an important role too. Notably, Neville has argued that Irish speakers internalised an association between their language and stupidity.[140] Some contemporaries also claimed that education was sparking a process of linguistic change: one inspector claimed that the children of Irish monoglots were becoming bilingual, and, in nine out of ten cases, their children in turn were monoglot English.[141]

But, as in Wales, the direct evidence for education itself being the key cause of people not raising their children in Irish is weak, not least because Irish did have a place in many schools early in the century when it suffered the most damage. In the rural 'hedge schools', attended by the sons of Catholic farmers, the emphasis was on teaching English but teachers also used Irish as a medium of instruction. Protestant schools also often employed Irish as a means of reaching the rural Catholic working classes and, between 1816 and 1831, there was also some state financial support for Irish-medium non-sectarian religious teaching.[142] In 1831, a new system of state-funded National schools was introduced. It did not promote the use or teaching of Irish and there were examples of children being physically punished for its use.[143] As in Wales, there was little pressure from parents for anything different and instead a strong desire for children to be taught English. Early in the century there were similar tools to the Welsh Not being used. However, de Fréine argues that the tally sticks, wooden gags and the humiliation used to encourage children away from Irish were not the causes of language change but rather themselves the result of people's own prior decision to give up Irish, a 'social self-generated movement of collective behaviour'.[144] The status of the language was actually stable between the 1851 census (when 23.3 per cent of the population were recorded as Irish speakers) and 1881 (23.9 per cent), suggesting that any immediate harm caused by the spread of education was not dramatic. Moreover, while the education system may have been heavily anglicised, it did not stop Irish nationalism growing through the century, a further stark example of the limitations of what schools could do for the state.

As in Wales, excluding children's mother tongue made little educational sense and there were calls, in and outside the education system, for Irish to be used as a medium of instruction, with blame placed on teachers for not following what common sense suggested was imperative. Some of these calls drew directly upon the similar arguments being made by inspectors in Wales.[145] In 1879, the education board made Irish an 'extra' subject, which meant that teaching it could earn schools money. In 1883, it formally allowed Irish to be used as a medium of instruction, although this was not widely taken up. Partly influenced again by developments in Wales, this provision was reinforced in 1900.[146] Yet these two decades of an increasing place for Irish in schools did little to help the language and instead helped spread English by making its teaching more effective. By 1901, there were just 20,953 Irish monoglots, a mere 0.47 per cent of the population, while another 13.9 per cent were bilingual.[147]

Ultimately, the emphasis in the historiography of Irish is on linguistic change as a voluntary rather than forced process.[148] This does not mean that the influence of education is discounted but rather that it is part of a complex mix of different influences. It facilitated rather than caused change. Notably, Mary Daly has shown that the influence of education was most significant in parts of Ireland where there was the greatest migratory labour.[149] In other words, the educational message that Irish did not matter hit home because people could see its decline where they lived. Thus, as Woolf concludes, 'Irish declined because English became the language of economic advancement and political dominance rather than the language of invasion and oppression as it once had been.'[150]

In Scotland, Gaelic was predominantly a rural language early in the century. It had suffered from being associated with poverty, Jacobinism and Catholicism, and had then been undermined by the demographic upheaval of the Highland Clearances. There was a widespread sense that education, 'preferably in English', was the answer to all the area's perceived problems. As in Ireland and Wales, English was seen as a route to social mobility. At first there was a belief that the best way to teach it was through excluding the mother tongue. Gaelic had been nominally prohibited as a medium of instruction in the schools run by the SSPCK, the region's most important provider of education, although the society and its teachers also appreciated the language's utility for teaching English and religious knowledge. There was more open support for using and teaching the language from 1826, although English remained the ultimate goal of such schools.[151] The growing state support for schools did not change this and the pattern reflected Wales, with schools devoted to teaching English and the better teachers employing Gaelic out of necessity, and the worst ones punishing the use of the language. Nonetheless some teachers put on Gaelic lessons outside normal school hours as 'a labour of love', with financial support from parents and local dignitaries for books.[152] The 1872 Education Act (Scotland) made no provision for Gaelic but its teaching was formally allowed from 1878 and it was recognised as a grant-earning subject in 1885. Yet, like Irish and Welsh, it continued to have a peripheral place in schools, used for pragmatic reasons but with little official or popular enthusiasm. There have been academic claims that education alienated and coerced children away from Gaelic and that the use of the hanging stick, an equivalent of the Welsh Not, continued well into the twentieth century, although without providing evidence for this latter assertion.[153] A language question was first asked in the Scottish census in 1881, by when just 6.76 per cent of the population were returned as Gaelic speakers, although in some communities the figure was over 70 per cent.[154] Twenty years later, there were just 28,106 monolingual Gaelic speakers recorded.[155]

Withers has concluded that the 'decline of Gaelic owed much to education' but this seems to rest on the assumptions that children were learning sufficient English and then, when they became parents, declined to pass the language on because of their schooling.[156] Again, education could only teach English effectively if it utilised Gaelic, which undermines the idea that children were coerced away from their mother tongue. This does not mean that education did not make some feel there was no point passing on the language and it certainly did little to encourage people to value and transmit their language. But education was far more important in facilitating the growth of English rather than the decline of Gaelic. The answer to the latter lay in wider social and economic forces that meant English was required for better paid jobs. Education was not the cause of Gaelic's marginal place in Scottish society but a reflection of it.

In both Ireland and Scotland, disentangling the precise influence of education from wider social and economic forces is near impossible. Instead, some better insight into the effect of schooling comes from England. There, migrants' languages, with little reinforcement in the wider community, quickly faded in subsequent generations and oral histories suggest negative comments at school may have been part of the cause. Anna Davin cited the testimony of a woman who grew up as a Yiddish speaker in 1920s London, stopped speaking the language to her parents, but then came to regret that in later life, saying 'if you're made to feel that your language is second-rate it does something to your self-image, which it probably takes you the better part of your lifetime to recover from'.[157]

In England, education also pushed against regional forms of English. Education manuals, training colleges and inspection reports often stressed the importance of accent and 'correct' speech and advocated that teachers should correct their children's ways of speaking. An 1852 manual for use in village schools noted that a classically educated man could not 'ignore his education as to address a congregation in the jargon and patois of the village ... We may and ought to raise them to our standard; we cannot, without profaneness in sacred things, descend to theirs.'[158] Speaking what was regarded as correct English probably became more of an issue after the Revised Code, when children were being judged on how they read aloud and this was sometimes concentrated on to the cost of ensuring that the pupil understood what they were reading.[159] But the ethos lasted much longer. The 1920s Newbolt report on teaching declared: 'It is emphatically the business of the elementary school to teach all its pupils who either speak a definite dialect or whose speech is disfigured by vulgarisms, to speak standard English and to speak it clearly.'[160]

The effect of all this was that English working-class children could feel alienated by the environment they were learning in. One Leicestershire man remembered that his teachers threatened children with a 'trouser-dusting' if they used local dialect after being warned. This, he said, worked and he never saw any canings in his two years at the school.[161] But this is to overstate the impact of such actions. In 1860, one inspector working in Kent, Surrey and Sussex complained that some teachers' chief occupation seemed to be 'lying in wait for provincialisms', which made children get worked up about the 'constant fault finding'. Apart from the effect on the children, the inspector felt there was little point since the 'home influences' made 'the vernacular dialect too strong, to be materially shaken'.[162] Even if children did change their speech inside school, they did not necessarily stick to that. The English heard at school was counteracted by the language heard at home and on the streets. Indeed, the Newbolt report denied that it aspired to suppress dialect and instead hoped, 'as often happens', that children would become 'bilingual', speaking both standard English and their regional version of it.[163] One interwar teacher remembered this happening, with children talking 'broad Tyneside' outside school but the 'King's English' inside it.[164] Despite what schools were trying to do, accents and dialects remained a central feature of the English language in the nineteenth century. Indeed, some people felt that they picked up a local accent at school rather than lost one.[165] As Patrick Joyce put it, 'it is striking how little formal schooling eroded dialect'. This, he argued, was down to how dialect was celebrated as a symbol of local identity. Thus while it might be denigrated by outsiders and self-help books, 'It was their own perceptions of their own language that finally mattered, rather than others' ideas of the people's English.'¹⁶⁶ Much the same could be argued of Wales and Welsh.

The evidence from other nations suggests a general sense that education did play a role in linguistic change but this only occurred when education was effective at actually teaching a new language and was supported by wider social, economic and cultural forces. Education could teach people a new language but that did not necessarily mean they would then abandon their mother tongue. People only took that decision when the old language already seemed to be no longer of value to them. The same was true of Wales. Where teachers refused to use Welsh too, then children's English skills were rudimentary at best. An adult unable to speak English very well could not have just given up speaking Welsh. However, as education improved and more English was heard in the communities then the rejection of Welsh from classrooms, even though now usually done in more humane ways, perhaps became more significant. But, most importantly, there were factors that showed Welsh still had a use and this offset the cultural pressures on people to turn their back on the language. The reason that so few did was that Welsh still had considerable significant cultural prestige and practical use. In a 1972 interview, a miner born in 1890 was asked what effect his education all being in English had on language in his community. None, he replied (in Welsh): everyone in the village spoke Welsh and no English people had moved in.¹⁶⁷ Thus the fact that he had been hit for speaking Welsh had no impact on linguistic choices because it made no sense to give up a language that everyone in a community spoke. The Welsh Not was most common in those areas where Welsh was and remained strongest. This suggests that it had no direct influence on the language's decline. Moreover, the Welsh Not probably also protected the position of Welsh in communities by undermining the teaching of English. As the Blue Books suggested, had Welsh been more used in schools, then the language would have declined faster.

Britishness beyond English

The influence of education on the anglicisation of Wales was not just a linguistic matter. The education department thought schools should be building a sense of national cohesion, but its sense of the nation was Englishness cloaked as Britishness. Heathorn has argued that schools sought to instil a sense of national and imperial belonging and patriotism, turning pupils into good citizens. He shows how reading books emphasised English virtues, such as manliness and good government, and argues patriotism 'became hegemonic from the sheer interconnectedness of the many symbols and narratives of identity … The various emblematic recitals of Englishness all seemed to reinforce each other, and because of their ubiquitous "ordinariness" seemed to be simple "common sense".'[168]

Geography and history were particularly important here and inspectors were told to encourage the subjects' use to foster patriotic feeling amongst children.[169] In Wales, neither subject ever became more than peripheral in most schools, but geography was taught far more widely than history. It was often not much more than learning the names of capitals, capes and rivers but it was supposed to open pupils' eyes to what was beyond their immediate area and to help them understand their position as citizens of an empire that connected far-flung places and their own homes.[170] History taught similar messages. Although it sometimes descended into a litany of dates, history books celebrated English valour and heroes within an imperial context through stories that were supposed to inspire children.[171] Both geography and history might, on the surface, have alienated Welsh children since they tended to use the name England rather than Britain. Yet children and teachers did not necessarily see it that way since 'Britain' and 'British' were words often associated with the empire, while 'England' might signify the island and government of Britain. Indeed, as Bischof argues, by exploring different places, geography could encourage a sense of the diversity of Britishness and an empire based on different races, languages and religions.[172] In this sense, it might have helped children be comfortable with being both Welsh and British. Furthermore, since geography clearly taught ideas of racial superiority, it could also have offset any sense of individual inferiority among Welsh children that came from having their language marginalised.[173] Nor was Wales entirely invisible in geography or history: schools were encouraged to teach about their local areas, which some teachers extended to giving lessons specifically about Wales.[174]

Songs were another way of encouraging national pride amongst children. 'God Save the Queen' was widely taught but it was far from the only patriotic example. Amongst the songs taught in Caernarfonshire in the 1880s and 1890s were 'Let English boys their duty do', 'Britain by waves caressed', 'Oh I'm a British boy sir', 'Hurrah for England', 'Victoria! Victoria! Victoria!' and 'Rule Britannia'.[175] Some schools did teach Welsh songs and, indeed, were sometimes encouraged to do so by inspectors. The 1879 report for Talybont noted that the Welsh song performed at the inspection was 'a very sweet one' and 'well sung'.[176] The inspector for Denbigh and Flintshire wrote in his 1882–3 report that songs like 'Rule Britannia', 'Men of Harlech' and 'Hen Wlad fy Nhadau' 'send a delicious thrill through the system; and, apart from this passing delight, they impart a twofold instruction – a love for music, and simple (though all prevailing) domestic and patriotic truths'.[177] Most teachers, however, do not seem to have embraced the opportunity for Welsh songs, perhaps because they saw singing as an opportunity to reinforce language skills.

The British patriotism encouraged in schools would have had some influence because it was not at odds with wider community understandings of nationality. Few were in doubt that Wales was a British nation and the Welsh-language press was supportive of the empire.[178] This was clear in an 1857 Welsh-language book for children that declared proudly that Britain's wealth, arts and trade were without comparison, while its inhabitants' knowledge, and its law and constitution were a wonder to all the nations of the earth.[179] Such Welsh Britishness drew upon a vague sense that the Welsh were the original Britons and had inhabited the island before the English.[180] But it was also rooted in a belief that being part of the empire was a marker of Wales's modernity. Nonetheless, there were increasing concerns that Wales's distinct identity was not being fostered in schools. One 1889 writer bemoaned children knowing about other countries but not the history, geography and literature of Wales.[181] Efforts to proclaim and defend Welsh national identity had been kickstarted by the Blue Books but peaked in the last quarter of the century. The promoting of Welsh songs and the limited teaching of Welsh history and geography were an outcome of this. So, too, was the place that Welsh found on the formal curriculum of some schools in the 1890s. By late in that decade, some schools in both the rural west and urban south were giving St David's Day as a holiday, while a handful of schools celebrated it with special concerts.[182] But it is important not to exaggerate the influence of such feelings or attempts to foster them. Even the campaigners for Welsh did not envision the language as having anything but a marginal place in popular education. The demands for Welsh history and geography were not conceived of as challenges to the importance of Britishness, but rather its instinctive Englishness. Ultimately, education did very little to foster any sense of Welshness among children.

Historians of empire have cautioned against assuming the surfeit of imperial images in popular culture were just absorbed or accepted.[183] Whatever schools were trying to do, children might have other ideas. For some, songs were probably just a welcome break from the tedium of the 3Rs. In history and geography, many children probably paid little attention, bored by the litany of facts. Others though maybe thought about what they read. Maps that showed England and Wales as the same country could have encouraged children to see their nation as just a corner of England, but a few were maybe annoyed at or critical of this.[184] Much probably depended on what, if anything, their teacher said to them. Even if they had the time to discuss the lessons, teachers might not actually share in the intense Britishness patriotism intended by textbooks and songs. Linda Colley has argued, in remote rural communities 'intense localism' was the norm and people lived in little worlds 'cut off for most of the time by custom, poverty, ignorance and apathy'.[185] Everywhere in the UK, except during exceptional events such as a war, national identity tended to be in the background and rarely thought about much. It was secondary in what mattered to people to home, family and community.[186] This is not to say that there was not an awareness of empire and Britishness but that it did not matter very much for most of the time. Daniel Parry-Jones recalled of his rural childhood at the start of the twentieth century that they never thought much about England, although school reminded them that English was 'the language of the boss-nation. Vaguely we knew that something had happened in the past to bring about such a state of things, which we now calmly accepted and went our own way of business.'[187]

One key reason for such apathy was that lessons were not always intelligible. For children to absorb or reject the intended messages, they had to be able to understand the songs and history and geography readers they studied and the lessons they heard. As chapter 5 showed, pupils' poor English and the unwillingness of some teachers to explain lessons meant this was far from always the case. It may thus be that in rural communities, the Britishness of lessons fell on deaf ears more often than not, while in industrial Wales, where English was much more widespread, more Britishness was absorbed. This could even partly explain why it was more common in such places for Welsh speakers not to pass the language on to their children.

Conclusion: the Welsh Not, the state, colonialism and language shifts

The British state saw education as a 'good thing'. It would help tame and civilise the working classes, making them easier to govern and more respectable. In Wales, the need for this was felt to be particularly acute because the majority did not speak English, something which was seen as both a practical and moral barrier to their incorporation into the mainstream of society. Teaching people English did not have to involve stopping them speaking Welsh but even in the nineteenth century there were those who believed that the goal of the state and schoolmasters was to destroy the Welsh language and identity. In 1884, the principal of Bangor Normal College claimed that the 'taboo' on Welsh in schools was part 'of the old policy to stamp the Welsh out of existence'.[188] In

1893, a leading Welsh newspaper argued that: 'In every way, direct and indirect, attempts have been made to crush out of existence the Welsh language.' It went on:

> Our schoolmasters have vied with the politicians of England in their endeavour to stamp out Welsh. No Welsh was allowed to be used in our schools, and the 'Welsh mark' was held to be a disgrace to its recipients. In these and countless other ways, every effort has been made to degrade Welsh from its position as one of the languages of the world to a street slang, a mere *patois* of chance or trick, unworthy of the respect of other languages.[189]

An 1894 review of educational history for children said that if schoolmasters had their own way, Welsh would have disappeared from the land and places of worship and the Welsh Bible would now only be found in libraries and museums.[190] The Welsh Not was viewed as part of this, an instrument to teach children to hate their own language and nation, as T. Gwynn Jones put it.[191]

As this book has argued, there was little love for Welsh in the British state, but it had neither the means nor inclination to bring about the language's demise. Instead, its position was based on spreading the English language, with the assumption that this would probably see the eventual end of Welsh, simply because it was not a language suited to modern life. This reflected its policies in the empire, where education was seen as a way of turning people into good colonial subjects, people who accepted rather than challenged the political order.[192] Yet colonial powers rarely had the resources or patience to carry such ideas out on any grand scale, not least because teaching anyone a new language was not easy unless the existing language was employed. Since using local languages in schools seemed a retrogressive step to some, there could be vigorous debates among both colonised and colonisers about which language education should take place in.[193] The success of colonial education owed more to people seeking English rather than having it forced upon them. Osterhammel argues that the spread of English in India and Ceylon was not 'as a result of ruthless Anglicization policies on the part of the colonial rulers, but as a combination of cultural prestige and mundane career advantages' which made it "advisable to master the language".[194] The founder of the Welsh Patagonian colony, Michael D. Jones saw this and argued that it was the Welsh that let the English language into homes, chapels and trade, and it was up to them whether the language lived or died.[195]

Such perspectives move beyond seeing imperialism as a one-way process where colonial subjects were just victims, there to be manipulated and moulded. It accepts they could respond to, resist and take advantage of colonial projects. Even the harshest educational system could not simply mould pupils into the kind of citizens desired if they did not want to be so moulded. Across the empire, indigenous languages remained strong and popular in places where incoming migrants were in a minority. For most colonial subjects, gaining a new language did not mean abandoning an old one. The exception was in the heart of the British Empire – the United Kingdom itself. Irish, Gaelic and Welsh were all denigrated, but the state had no power to stop those languages being spoken at home, play or prayer. The primary cause of those languages declining was not acts to stop them being used but people's own choices not to pass on the language to their children. People took those decisions on a scale that did not happen in most of the empire because migration, communication and trade brought English into those communities on a scale that gave it a significant foothold. The only other parts of the empire where that happened were the white dominions where indigenous languages were swamped by the number of settlers.

Education helped enable this linguistic shift because it was one of the ways people learned English. But it was often ineffective. Many children only attended school for short periods and irregularly. Even at the end of the century, there were many children not going at all. When schools refused to employ the local language, then they were very ineffective at teaching English. When this happened, education held back the spread of English rather than enabled it. It was only as Welsh, like Irish and Gaelic, were used more in schools that education became a vehicle for the spread of English. But, again, the spread of English did not have to require the abandonment of people's mother tongues. In Wales at least, that only happened when people felt the language had no use anymore. That only occurred in communities where migration from England was large enough to change the local linguistic dynamics and where religion lost its potency as a bastion of the language. Thus, as Mary Daly has argued, 'any discussion of changes in literacy or linguistic patterns must be couched in micro rather than macro terms. For while the broad changes in Irish culture, economy and society are undoubtedly of importance, specific local circumstances played a key role.'[196] It is this that explains the very significant differences in linguistic situations between the mining districts and rural Wales. Both were subject to the same educational practices but in the countryside Welsh remained entrenched as the community language, whereas many industrial areas were in the middle of a process of change, where, gradually, Welsh was becoming a language of old people and English of the young.

In this light, education was a facilitator or enabler of linguistic change rather than its cause. It was key to the collapse in Welsh monolingualism from 30.4 per cent of the population in 1891 to 8.7 per cent in 1911. But this enabling role does not mean that education played no role in encouraging individuals not to pass the language onto their children. The popular image of people being shamed into turning their back on their native language is surely not completely wrong. Sociolinguists argue that people do internalise external prejudices towards their way of speaking.[197] Some Irish writers have certainly seen the process of linguistic change as a colonial process where Irish people internalised its dynamics to such an extent that they helped bring it about by their own thinking and actions.[198] In Wales, chronology is important here. The key period for people not passing the language on was in the twentieth century, long after the height of the Welsh Not. The idea that the Welsh Not influenced people not to transmit the language is undermined by the fact that the language remained strongest precisely in those isolated rural communities where its use was most common. Children being punished for speaking Welsh was not the main influence, but that the language of schooling was English, thus associating that language with modernity and social advancement. But, again, most people only acted on this in terms of language transmission once it was clear that Welsh was not needed in communities. As inspector Thomas Darlington noted in 1894, 'the exclusion of Welsh from the day-schools has undoubtedly tended, in many districts *already* bilingual to depress Welsh-speaking in favour of English'.[199] The Englishness of education continued well into the twentieth century – despite efforts from government to challenge that – and the significance of that grew as the number of bilingual communities did.

Even if negative experiences of education alone did not lead many Welsh speakers to abandon the language, they did reveal the national inequalities within the United Kingdom. It was not that Wales was deliberately or actively oppressed but rather that it was out of governments' sight and thus its problems and situation were not understood or acted upon. There were local officials who did understand what was going on, but they were hamstrung by their lack of power and the unwillingness of those above them to act or to treat Wales differently. There was no centralised Welsh polity, no Welsh public funds, not even a Welsh capital to act as a focal point and stimulant for national discussions and campaigning. There was almost no attempt to foster the Welsh language for its own sake.

Welsh's marginal place in education was not the cause of the language's unequal political status with English but symptomatic of it. As in wider politics, there were concessions made to Wales and greater calls for Welsh needs and difference to be recognised. Official changes that began in 1875 with a regulation allowing the use of Welsh in inspections, gathered pace in the 1890s with the formal place of the language in the curriculum of schools who wanted it, and culminated in 1900 when Welsh was encouraged as the medium of instruction for younger children in Welsh-speaking districts. These were all important but they were far from revolutionary. Welsh education remained a variation on the English system. Welsh schools were run by the same regulations and funding arrangements as English schools. Inspectors may have been organised into a Welsh division and employed the language but they were still following the same broad principles and goals as their peers in England. Even the creation of a Welsh Board of

Education in 1907 did not change this. Above all English remained the basis of the educational system, with Welsh primarily employed either as a distinct subject or as a means towards English fluency. The state did not recognise anyone's right to an education in their mother tongue.

Yet very few were calling for that. The idea of Welsh-medium education does not seem to have been considered by many beyond a few isolated voices.[200] Some historians have seen the late nineteenth century as a missed opportunity to create such a system and to establish the language's place in national institutions more broadly.[201] But this is to view the past too much through modern eyes, which see both the subsequent demise of Welsh and the nation's political problems. In the late nineteenth century, the future of Welsh seemed more secure because of its associations with religion, while Wales itself was enjoying a renaissance within the United Kingdom and global status through its position in the empire. Yet English was the cultural, political and economic hegemony and in the longer-term Welsh stood little chance against this.

The Welsh Not itself was a product of this power imbalance. It was not a primary cause of linguistic change but the result of pedagogical misunderstandings and people's desire for English. The first owed much to how underdeveloped education was, while the latter was rooted in Wales's subordinate position within the United Kingdom. The Welsh Not was not imperialism in a direct sense, not least because the state never sanctioned it, but it was an example of how the Anglo-centricity of the United Kingdom produced cultural forces that had the similar effects to more overt imperialistic practices in the empire. The political, economic and cultural power of English was the direct cause of the decline of Welsh because it underpinned why so many Welsh people wanted to learn the language and why they decided not to pass on their mother tongue. It was those decisions that were the immediate cause of the decline of the language. It was not beaten out of anyone. When the Welsh Not was implemented in a rigid fashion and the language was excluded from schools, children were failed because they did not learn English and thus, ironically, educational practices actually protected Welsh culture and the Welsh nation by holding back the English tide. It was only where the Welsh Not was abandoned, in both spirit and letter, that schools did what they were supposed to and spread the English language. In doing that, education could be emancipatory for individual Welsh people because it gave them access to the wider corridors of economic and political power. But whether they succeeded in teaching English or not, schools reinforced the idea that in the secular world English was a superior language and what was needed to succeed in a modern world. In this, it perpetuated and exacerbated a linguistic power imbalance that would prove disastrous for the Welsh language once secularisation and migration swept the carpet from beneath its feet. Education thus did lay the basis for individual and collective change. The best schools served the Welsh people but failed the Welsh nation. The worst schools failed both.

Notes

1   *Report of the CCE, 1868–69*, p. 166.
2   *Census of England and Wales 1891, vol. IV: General Report* (London, 1893), section IX: Languages in Wales and Monmouthshire.
3   *Census of England and Wales, 1901: General Report* (London, 1904), section X: Languages in Wales and Monmouthshire.
4   David Llewelyn Jones, 'The Welsh language in Montgomeryshire, *c.*1800–1914' in Geraint H. Jenkins (ed.), *Language and Community in the Nineteenth Century* (Cardiff, 1998), pp. 63–99, 86.
5   John E. Southall, *The Welsh Language Census of 1891* (Newport, 1895), p. 13.
6   R. J. Moore-Colyer, 'Landowners, farmers and language in the nineteenth century', in Geraint H. Jenkins (ed.), *The Welsh Language and its Social Domains, 1801–1911* (Cardiff, 2000), pp. 101–30, 102.
7   Wirt Sikes, *Rambles and Studies in Old South Wales* (London, 1881), p. 202.
8   Anita Pavlenko, *The Bilingual Mind and What it Tells us About Language and Thought* (Cambridge, 2014), p. 23.
9   Aidan Doyle, *A History of the Irish Language: From the Norman Invasion to Independence* (Oxford, 2015), p. 135. For a historical investigation of the importance of the bilingual stage in linguistic change in Ireland see Margaret Kelleher, *The Maamtrasna Murders: Language, Life and Death in Nineteenth-century Ireland* (Dublin, 2018).
10 PbA, Croes-goch, 29 February 1872.
11 *Second Report of the Royal Commission appointed to inquire into the Working of Elementary Education Acts, England and Wales* (London, 1887), p. 287 [hereafter Cross Commission].

12 Evidence of G. T. Clark in *Reports of Assistant Commissioners appointed to inquire into State of Popular Education in England*, vol. II (1861), p. 595 [hereafter Newcastle Commission].
13 Michael Gareth Llewelyn, *Sand in the Glass* (London, 1943), p. 48.
14 Jenifer Larson-Hall, 'Weighing the benefits of studying a foreign language at a younger starting age in a minimal input situation', *Second Language Research*, 24, 1 (2008), 35–63.
15 Iorwerth C. Peate, *Rhwng Dau Fyd: Darn o Hunangofiant* (Dinbych, 1976), p. 9.
16 Jones, 'Welsh language in Montgomeryshire', pp. 88–91.
17 Dot Jones, 'The coming of the railways and language change in north Wales 1850–1900', in Geraint H. Jenkins (ed.), *The Welsh Language and its Social Domains* (Cardiff, 2000), pp. 131–49.
18 David Llewelyn Jones and Robert Smith, 'Tourism and the Welsh Language in the Nineteenth Century', in Geraint H. Jenkins (ed.), *The Welsh language and its Social Domains* (Cardiff, 2000), pp. 151–75.
19 Quoted in W. R. P. George, *The Making of Lloyd George* (London, 1976), p. 45.
20 Michael D. Jones, 'Difodi y Gymraeg yn barhad o oresgyniad Cymru', *Y Celt*, 27 June 1890, 3; Simon Brooks, *Why Wales Never Was: The Failure of Welsh Nationalism* (Cardiff, 2017), p. 63.
21 *Report of the CCE, 1882–3*, p. 421.
22 C. Skeel, 'The cattle trade between Wales and England from the fifteenth to the nineteenth centuries', *Transactions of the Royal Historical Society*, 9 (1926), 135–58, 152.
23 Nicholas Ostler, *Empires of the Word: A Language History of the World* (London, 2005), pp. 534–5.
24 Brinley Thomas, 'Wales and the Atlantic Economy', *Scottish Journal of Political Economy*, 6, 3 (1959), 169–92, 192. Also see his 'A cauldron of rebirth: population and the Welsh language in the nineteenth century', *Welsh History Review*, 13, 4 (1987), 418–37.
25 Philip N. Jones, 'The Welsh language in the valleys of Glamorgan, c.1800–1914', in Geraint H. Jenkins (ed.), *Language and Community in the Nineteenth Century* (Cardiff, 1998), pp. 147–80, 155.
26 On implicit learning see Marianne Nikolov (ed.), *The Age Factor and Early Language Learning* (Berlin, 2009). On children learning more formally see K. Roehr-Brackin and A. Tellier, 'The role of language-analytic ability in children's instructed second language learning', *Studies in Second Language Acquisition*, 41, 5 (2019), 1111–31. For contemporary comment on how children using English with each other was likely to affect the long-term prospects of Welsh see Newcastle Commission, vol. II, pp. 451–2.
27 Watcyn Wyn, 'Haner cant o flynyddau', *Y Diwygwir*, September 1894, 263.
28 Sir Percy E. Watkins, *A Welshman Remembers* (Cardiff, 1944), p. 3.
29 D. Parry-Jones, *Welsh Country Upbringing* (London, 1948), pp. 109–10. Similarly, see Robert Roberts, *A Wandering Scholar: The Life and Opinions of Robert Roberts* (Cardiff, 1991), p. 113.
30 J. Lloyd Williams, *Atgofion Tri Chwarter Canrif, cyf. I* (London, 1941), p. 87.

31 See the account of Abercarn Scientific Institution in 'Labour and the poor', *Morning Chronicle*, 13 May 1850, 5–6. For another example of a town with such institutions see Brynley F. Roberts, 'Welsh Scholarship at Merthyr Tydfil', *Merthyr Historian*, 10 (1999), 51–62.
32 Newcastle Commission, vol. II, p. 455.
33 David Crystal, *Language Death* (Cambridge, 2000), pp. 78–9.
34 Newcastle Commission, vol. II, p. 453.
35 John E. Southall, *Wales and Her Language* (Newport, 1892), p. 347; *Reports of the Commissioners of Inquiry into the State of Education in Wales. Part III: North Wales* (London, 1847), p. 338; *Commission on the Employment of Children, Young Persons, and Women in Agriculture (1867): Third Report of the Commissioners* (London, 1870), p. 59.
36 *Report of the CCE, 1882–3*, p. 419.
37 Dan Isaac Davies, 'Cymru ddwyieithog', *Y Geninen*, July 1885, 206–12, 209.
38 Honourable Society of Cymmrodorion, *Report of the Committee Appointed to Inquire into the Advisability of the Introduction of the Welsh Language into the Course of Elementary Education in Wales: The Introduction of Welsh as a Specific Subject* (Aberdare, 1885), appendix, p. 9.
39 Jones, 'Welsh language in the valleys of Glamorgan', p. 177.
40 *Welsh in Education and Life: Being the Report of the Departmental Committee Appointed by the President of the Board of Education to inquire into the Position of the Welsh Language and to Advise as to its Promotion in the Educational System of Wales* (London, 1927), p. 224 and appendix.
41 Anon., *Dunvant School Centenary, 1877–1977* (1977), p. 24.
42 Andrew Dalby, *Language in Danger* (London, 2002), p. 77.
43 Mari A. Williams, 'Dowlais', in Gwenfair Parry and Mari A. Williams (eds), *The Welsh Language and the 1891 Census* (Cardiff, 1999), pp. 175–200, 185–6. These figures disguise families where some but not all children could speak Welsh. They thus underestimate Welsh transmission.
44 On the anglicised gentry see David W. Howell, *Patriarchs and Parasites: The Gentry of South-west Wales in the Eighteenth Century* (Cardiff, 1986) and Melvin Humphreys, *The Crisis of Community: Montgomeryshire, 1680–1815* (Cardiff, 1996).
45 For this point in an Irish context see Tony Crowley, 'English in Ireland: a complex case study', in Terttu Nevalainen and Elizabeth Closs Traugott (eds), *The Oxford Handbook of the History of English* (Oxford, 2012), pp. 470–80, 478.
46 Abel J. Jones, *From an Inspector's Bag* (Cardiff, 1944), p. 61. On the global status of English see Jürgen Osterhammel, *The Transformation of the World: A Global History of the Nineteenth Century* (Princeton, 2014), p. 783.
47 Geraint H. Jenkins, 'The historical background to the 1891 census', in Gwenfair Parry and Mari A. Williams (eds), *The Welsh Language and the 1891 Census* (Cardiff, 1991), p. 19.
48 For an example of such 'humour' about Welsh place-names see 'The difficulty', *Illustrated London Life*, 9 July 1843, 13.
49 Editorial, *The Times*, 8 September 1866.

50 For example, *Usk Observer*, 19 September 1863, 5.
51 'The Eisteddfod and the English Press', *Wrexham and Denbighshire Advertiser*, 17 October 1863, 8; 'Barn "Cockney" am yr Eisteddfod – "Y Spectator" etto', *Seren Cymru*, 2 October 1863, 3. For a wider discussion of English attacks on Welsh and the response see Aled Gruffydd Jones, '"One language is quite sufficient for the mass": metropolitan journalism, the British state and the "vernacular" periodical', in David Finkelstein (ed.), *The Edinburgh History of the British and Irish Press* (Edinburgh, 2020), pp. 313–36.
52 *A Digest of Parochial Returns made to the Select Committee Appointed to Inquire into the Education of the Poor: Session 1818* (1819), p. 1205.
53 *Children's Employment Commission, First Report of the Commissioners: Mines* (London, 1842), p. 503.
54 Quoted in Herbert Williams, *Davies the Ocean: Railway King and Coal Tycoon* (Cardiff, 1991), p. 99. Similarly, see, for example, 'Ymfudo: llythr III', *Y Cronicl*, February 1851, 51–5.
55 *Report of the Committee Appointed to Inquire into the Condition of Intermediate and Higher Education in Wales*, vol. II (London, 1881), p. 236.
56 H. J. Lewis, *The Teaching of Welsh* (Federation of Education Committees, Wales and Monmouthshire, 1925), pp. 10–11. For example, 'Mr Samuel on Welsh nationality', *The Welshman*, 1 April 1864, 3.
57 For example, Cross Commission, 3rd Report, p. 18.
58 James Vernon, *Distant Strangers: How Britain Became Modern* (Berkley, 2014), p. 43.
59 J. Lloyd Williams, *Atgofion Tri Chwarter Canrif*, cyf. *III* (Dinbych, 1944), pp. 118–19.
60 Schools Inquiry Commission, *General Reports by Assistant Commissioners. Vol VIII: Midland Countries and Northumberland* (London, 1868), p. 7.
61 'The Society for Utilising the Welsh Language', *North Wales Chronicle*, 14 April 1888, 7.
62 Translated from Williams, *Atgofion Tri Chwarter Canrif*, cyf. *III*, p. 122.
63 For example, Principal Reichel, 'The future of Welsh education', *Transactions of the Liverpool Welsh National Society*, second session (1886–7), 3–22, 6.
64 Dan Isaac Davies, 'Cymru ddwyieithog', *Y Geninen*, July 1885, 206–12, 211.
65 Aled Jones and Bill Jones, 'The Welsh world and the British empire, c.1851–1939: an exploration', *Journal of Imperial and Commonwealth History*, 31, 2 (2003), 57–81, 75.
66 R. D. Roberts, 'A Welsh movement', *Wales*, 1, 1 (1894), 5.
67 Evidence of Revd John Griffiths in Newcastle Commission, vol. II, pp. 620–1.
68 W. Edwards, *The Direct Method of Language Teaching: A Suggestion in the Education of Wales* (Newport, 1900), pp. 6–7.
69 Jack Jones, *Unfinished Journey* (London, 1938), p. 22. For other memories of a family where the children spoke back in English to their Welsh-speaking parents see St Fagans Oral history collection 2685–1. This was noted on the coast of Glamorgan in a survey from 1879: E. G. Ravenstein, 'On the Celtic languages

in the British Isles: a statistical survey', *Journal of the Statistical Society of London*, 42, 3 (1879), 579–643, 615.
70 This is depicted in the novel Daniel Owen, *Hunangofiant Rhys Lewis, Gweinidog Bethel* (Wrexham, 1885).
71 Sian Rhiannon Williams, 'The Welsh language in industrial Monmouthshire, c.1800–1901', in Geraint H. Jenkins (ed.), *Language and Community in the Nineteenth Century* (Cardiff, 1998), pp. 203–29, 229.
72 Owen, *Rhys Lewis*, p. 368.
73 Benjamin H. Malkin, *The Scenery, Antiquities, and Biography of South Wales* (London, 1804), p. 456.
74 Not the hired man, 'The language of "Shir Bembro"', *Pembroke County Guardian and Cardigan Reporter*, 26 April 1902, 9.
75 Maude Morgan Thomas, *When I was a Girl in Wales* (New York, 1936), pp. 20–1.
76 George Borrow, *Wild Wales: Its People, Language and Scenery* (1862; London, 1977), p. 342.
77 Llewelyn, *Sand in the Glass*, p. 59.
78 *Report of the CCE, 1882–83*, p. 419.
79 Doyle, *A History of the Irish Language*, p. 138.
80 Owen, *Rhys Lewis*, p. 161.
81 Jones, *From an Inspector's Bag*, pp. 59–60.
82 *Commission on the Employment of Children, Young Persons, and Women in Agriculture (1867)*, p. 165.
83 D. F. Davis, 'Gwaseiddiwch y Cymry', *Seren Cymru*, 12 October 1888, 3. For a similar point in Monmouthshire see *Commission on the Employment of Children, Young Persons, and Women in Agriculture (1867)*, p. 59.
84 Dalby, *Language in Danger*, p. 90.
85 Dalby, *Language in Danger*, p. 219.
86 Mercedes Durham and Jonathan Morris, 'An overview of sociolinguistics in Wales', in Mercedes Durham and Jonathan Morris (eds), *Sociolinguistics in Wales* (London, 2016), pp. 3–28, 11.
87 John Edwards, *Sociolinguistics: A Very Short Introduction* (Oxford, 2013), p. 37.
88 Borrow, *Wild Wales*, pp. 117, 373.
89 See the examples in *South Wales Daily News*, 12 July 1898.
90 Schools Inquiry Commission, *General Reports by Assistant Commissioners. Vol VIII*, p. 7.
91 Williams, 'Welsh language in industrial Monmouthshire', p. 218.
92 Crystal, *Language Death*, p. 81; Edwards, *Sociolinguistics*, pp. 37–8.
93 Nicholas Wolf, '"Scéal Grinn?" Jokes, puns, and the shaping of bilingualism in nineteenth-century Ireland', *Journal of British Studies*, 48, 1 (2009), 51–75.
94 For example, Tom Macdonald, *The White Lanes of Summer* (London, 1975), p. 149 and Roberts, *Wandering Scholar*, p. 9.
95 For example, Diary of Charles Morgan (Gower), 10 August 1849, online at http://www.southwalesrecordsociety.co.uk/33/1849.htm (accessed 25 March 2024).

96 Borrow, *Wild Wales*.
97 Jones, *Mid-Victorian Wales*, p. 23.
98 Evan Davies, *Hanes Plwyf Llangynllo* (Llandysul, 1905), p. 211.
99 Moore-Colyer, 'Landowners, farmers and language', p. 105.
100 Ivana Horbec and Maja Matasović, 'Voices in a country divided: linguistic choices in early modern Croatia', in Vladislav Rjéoutski and Willem Frijhoff (eds), *Language Choice in Enlightenment Europe. Education, Sociability, and Governance* (Amsterdam, 2018), pp. 111–42, 134.
101 Ravenstein, 'On the Celtic languages', 621–2.
102 Moore-Colyer, 'Landowners, farmer and language', p. 109.
103 Ieuan Gwynedd Jones, 'Language and community in nineteenth century Wales', in David Smith (ed.), *A People and a Proletariat: Essays in the History of Wales, 1780–1980* (London, 1980), pp. 47–71, 66. For a contemporary example of the belief in the need for Welsh, whilst also supporting its decline see 'Raise the Welsh character and condition', *The Welshman*, 1 September 1843, 2. For a defence of Welsh see 'Y drefedigaeth Gymreig, a'r iaith Gymraeg', *Y Cronicl*, May 1851, 149–51.
104 Dalby has argued that in cases of language shift where the bilingual stage lasts a long time religion is involved: Dalby, *Language in Danger*, p. 103. On Nonconformity see M. Wynn Thomas, *In the Shadow of the Pulpit: Literature and Nonconformist Wales* (Cardiff, 2009) and Glanmor Williams, *Religion, Language and Nationality in Wales: Historical Essays* (Cardiff, 1979).
105 Ostler, *Empires of the Word*, pp. 551–2.
106 W. J. Gruffydd, *Owen Morgan Edwards: Cofiant. Cyfrol 1, 1858–1883* (Aberystwyth, 1937), p. 49.
107 Jones, 'Language and community', p. 58.
108 See Doyle, *A History of the Irish Language*, pp. 118–24.
109 Ioan Matthews, 'The Welsh language in the anthracite coalfield, c.1870–1914', in Geraint H. Jenkins (ed.), *Language and Community in the Nineteenth Century* (Cardiff, 1998), pp. 125–46, 139.
110 Jones, 'Welsh language in the valleys of Glamorgan', p. 153.
111 Miriam Meyerhoff, *Introducing Sociolinguistics* (London, 2006), pp. 2, 61.
112 Martin Johnes, *A History of Sport in Wales* (Cardiff, 2005), ch. 2.
113 R. J. W. Evans, 'Language and society in the nineteenth century: some central-European comparisons', in Geraint H. Jenkins (ed.), *Language and Community in the Nineteenth Century* (Cardiff, 1998), pp. 397–424, 423.
114 Myrddin ap Dafydd, 'Cysgod y Welsh Not', *Llafar Gwlad*, 64 (1999), 15.
115 Cross Commission, 3rd Report, p. 13. Also see Society for Utilizing the Welsh Language, *Scheme of Instruction for Use in Elementary Schools in Wales* (Caernarfon, 1893), p. 3.
116 Beriah Gwynfe Evans, 'Addysg Plant Cymru ddoe a heddyw', *Tywysydd y Plant*, April 1910, 110.
117 Neil J. Smelser, *Social Paralysis and Social Change: British Working-Class Education in the Nineteenth Century* (Berkeley, 1991), p. 165.

118 See the account of Welsh at Gowerton Boys Grammar in Gilbert Bennet (ed.), *Something Attempted, Something Done* (Llandybïe, 1973), pp. 110–19; Leslie Wynne Evans, *Studies in Welsh Education: Welsh Educational Structure and Administration, 1880–1925* (Cardiff, 1974), p. 27. Also see the memories in W. C. Elvet Thomas, *Tyfu'n Gymro* (Llandysul, 1972), ch. 7.
119 Stephen Humphries, *Hooligans or Rebels? An Oral History of Working-class Childhood and Youth, 1889–1939* (Oxford, 1981), p. 61. Similarly see Susannah Wright, 'Teachers, family and community in urban elementary school: evidence from English school log books *c*.1880–1918', *History of Education*, 41, 2 (2012), 155–73.
120 Some months later he was noting how 'deeply rooted' Welsh was among the children: AA, Dwyran, 8–19 July, 23–8 September 1878.
121 CA, Swyddffynnon, 13 July 1883.
122 *Carnarvon and Denbigh Herald*, 20 and 27 March 1903, 8.
123 Alfred Jones, *The Philosophy of Corporal Punishment: An Investigation into the Policy and Morality of School Coercion* (Edinburgh, 1859), p. 11.
124 Quoted in M. J. Evans, 'Elementary education in Montgomeryshire 1850–1900', *The Montgomeryshire Collections*, 63, 1 (1973), 1–46, 22.
125 Cassie Davies, *Hwb i'r Galon* (Swansea, 1973), p. 49.
126 Ann Monroe, 'Shame solutions: how shame impacts school-aged children and what teachers can do to help', *The Educational Forum*, 73 (2009), 58–66, 59.
127 Williams, *Atgofion Tri Chwarter Canrif, cyf. I*, p. 85; Williams, *Atgofion Tri Chwarter Canrif, cyf. III*, p. 119.
128 Victor Kiernan, 'Languages and conquerors', in Peter Burke and Roy Porter (eds), *Language, Self and Society: A Social History of Language* (Cambridge, 1991), pp. 191–210, 207.
129 Ngũgĩ wa Thiong'o, *Decolonising the Mind: The Politics of Language in African Literature* (London, 1986), pp. 11, 17.
130 See https://www.statista.com/statistics/1279581/primary-languages-spoken-at-home-in-kenya-by-area/#:~:text=Around%2044%20percent%20of%20the%20urban%20population%20surveyed,for%20three%20percent%20of%20respondents%20in%20rural%20zones (accessed 25 March 2024); Grace W. Bunyi, 'Language classroom practices in Kenya', in Angel Lin and Peter Martin (eds), *Decolonisation, Globalisation: Language-in-Education Policy and Practice* (Clevedon, 2005), pp. 131–52.
131 Nils Jernsletten, 'Sami language communities and the conflict between Sami and Norwegian', in Ernst H. Jahr (ed.), *Language Conflict and Language Planning* (New York, 1993), pp. 115–32, 119.
132 Quoted in Ostler, *Empires of the Word*, p. 489.
133 Andrew Woolford, *This Benevolent Experiment: Indigenous Boarding Schools, Genocide and Redress in Canada and the United States* (Lincoln, 2015).
134 Jon Reyhner, 'American Indian language policy and school success', *Journal of Educational Issues of Language Minority Students*, 12 (1993), 35–59; Jon Reyhner, 'American Indian languages and United States Language policy', in Willem Fase, Koen Jaspaert and Siaak Kroon (eds), *The State of Minority*

Languages: International Perspectives on Survival and Decline (Lisse, 1995), pp. 229–48.
135 Eugen Weber, *Peasants into Frenchmen: The Modernization of Rural France, 1870–1914* (Stanford, 1976), pp. 69, 306, 311–13, 336–7.
136 Rhisiart Hinks, 'The Breton language in the nineteenth century', in Geraint H. Jenkins (ed.), *Language and Community in the Nineteenth Century* (Cardiff, 1998), pp. 369–95.
137 Quoted in Eileen Holt, 'The Provencal Not', *Planet*, 8 (1971), 33–5.
138 Weber, *Peasants into Frenchmen*, ch. 6, quotes from pp. 84, 85.
139 Doyle, *History of the Irish Language*, p. 129.
140 Grace Neville, '"He spoke to Me in English, I answered him in Irish": language shift in archives', in Jean Brihault (ed.), *L'Irlande ses langues: Actes du Colloque 1992 de la Société Francaise d'Étude Irlandaises* (Rennes, 1993); Doyle, *History of the Irish Language*, p. 118.
141 Appendix G, in P. J. Keenan, 'Head Inspectors' Reports on Schools Inspected and Teachers Examined', in *The Twenty-second Report of the Commissioners in National Education in Ireland* (Dublin, 1856), p. 75.
142 Doyle, *History of the Irish Language*, p. 96; Tom O'Donoghue and Teresa O' Doherty, *Irish Speakers and Schooling in the Gaeltacht, 1900 to the Present* (Basingstoke, 2019), pp. 25–8.
143 On teaching methods in such schools see John Logan, 'Book learning: the experience of reading in the national school, 1831–1900', in Bernadette Cunningham and Máire Kennedy (eds), *The Experience of Reading: Irish Historical Perspectives* (Dublin, 1999), pp. 173–95.
144 Seán de Fréine, 'The dominance of the English language in the 19th century', in Diarmaid Ó Muirithe (ed.), *The English Language in Ireland* (Cork, 1977), pp. 71–87, 84.
145 O'Donoghue and O' Doherty, *Irish Speakers and Schooling*, pp. 28–36; Doyle, *History of the Irish Language*, p. 118. For an example of a call drawing on Wales see appendix G, in P. J. Keenan, 'Head Inspectors' Reports on Schools Inspected and Teachers Examined', in *The Twenty-second Report of the Commissioners in National Education in Ireland* (Dublin, 1856), pp. 75–6.
146 O'Donoghue and O' Doherty, *Irish Speakers and Schooling*, p. 48; Máirtín Ó Murchú, 'Language and society in nineteenth-century Ireland', in Geraint H. Jenkins (ed.), *Language and Community in the Nineteenth Century* (Cardiff, 1998), pp. 341–68, 366.
147 *Census of Ireland, 1901. Part II: General Report* (Dublin, 1902), p. 8.
148 See the overview in Niall Ó Ciosáin, 'Gaelic culture and language shift', in Laurence M. Geary and Margaret Kelleher (eds), *Nineteenth-century Ireland: A Guide to Recent Research* (Dublin, 2005), pp. 136–52.
149 See Mary Daly, 'Literacy and language change in the late nineteenth and early twentieth centuries', in M. Daly and D. Dickson (eds), *The Origins of Popular Literacy in Ireland: Language Change and Educational Development 1700–1920* (Dublin, 1990), pp. 153–66.

150 Nicholas M. Woolf, 'History and linguistics: the Irish language as a case study in an interdisciplinary approach to culture', in Nils Langer, Steffan Davies and Wim Vandenbussche (eds), *Language and History, Linguistics and Historiography* (Oxford, 2012), pp. 49–64, 53.
151 Charles W. J. Withers, 'A social history and geography of Gaelic in Scotland, 1806–1901', in Geraint H. Jenkins (ed.), *Language and Community in the Nineteenth Century* (Cardiff, 1998), pp. 316–40, 331–5; Ewan A. Cameron, 'Education in rural Scotland, 1696–1872', in Robert Anderson (ed.), *The Edinburgh History of Education in Scotland* (Edinburgh, 2015), pp. 153–70; Victor Edward Durkacz, *The Decline of the Celtic Languages* (Edinburgh, 1983), chs. 2–3; Elizabeth Ritchie, '"Alive to the advantages of education". In using the new statistical account of research education: a case study of the Isle of Skye', *Northern Scotland*, 7 (2016), 85–92, 85.
152 Christopher Bischof, *Teaching Britain: Elementary Teachers and the State of the Everyday, 1846–1906* (Oxford, 2019), pp. 186–7.
153 Kenneth MacKinnon, 'Education and social control: the case of Gaelic Scotland', *Scottish Educational Studies*, 4 (1972), 125–37, 130–1.
154 Kenneth MacKinnon, 'The Gaelic language-group: demography, language-usage, -transmission, and -shift', *The Edinburgh Companion to the Gaelic Language* (Edinburgh, 2010), pp. 128–45.
155 *Eleventh Decennial Census of the Population of Scotland, 1901*, vol. 1 (Glasgow, 1902), p. xxviii.
156 Withers, 'Gaelic in Scotland, 1806–1901', p. 335.
157 Quoted in Anna Davin, *Growing Up Poor: Home, School and Street in London, 1870–1914* (London, 1996), p. 201.
158 Samuel Best, *Elementary Grammar for the Use of Village Schools* (1852), quoted in Ian Michael, *The Teaching of English from the Sixteenth Century to 1870* (Cambridge, 1987).
159 Mugglestone, *'Talking Proper'*, ch. 7; D. R. Fearon, *School Inspection* (London, 1887), p. 33.
160 *The Teaching of English in England* (London, 1926), p. 65.
161 Jacob Middleton, 'The experience of corporal punishment in schools, 1890–1940', *History of Education*, 37, 2 (2008), 253–75, 266; Sam Shaw, *Guttersnipe* (London, 1946), pp. 23–4.
162 *Report of the CCE, 1860–61*, p. 88.
163 *Teaching of English in England*, p. 67.
164 Philip Gardner, 'The giant at the front: young teachers and corporal punishment in inter-war elementary schools', *History of Education*, 25, 2 (1996), 141–63, 145.
165 F. H. Spencer, *An Inspector's Testament* (London, 1938), p. 66.
166 Patrick Joyce, 'The people's English: language and class in England *c*.1840–1920', in Peter Burke and Roy Porter (eds), *Language, Self and Society: A Social History of Language* (Cambridge, 1991), pp. 154–90, 157, 161.
167 South Wales Miners' Library, Josiah Jones interview (1972).

168 Stephen Heathorn, *For Home, Country, and Race: Constructing Gender, Class, and Englishness in the Elementary School, 1880–1914* (Toronto, 2000), p. 178.
169 *Report of the CCE, 1877–8*, p. 334.
170 Bischof, *Teaching Britain*, pp. 93–4.
171 Peter Yeandle, *Citizenship, Nation and Empire: The Politics of History Teaching in England, 1870–1939* (Manchester, 2015).
172 Bischof, *Teaching Britain*, p. 94.
173 For an example of racism in a popular textbook see *Royal Geographical Readers: First Book (For Standard II)* (London, 1881), p. 33.
174 For example, in 1894 the conquest of Wales was taught as an object lesson at Garth Board school (14 September 1894).
175 H. G. Williams, 'Elementary Education in Caernarvonshire, 1839–1902' (unpublished PhD thesis, University of Wales, Bangor, 1981), 422.
176 CwyA, Talybont HMI report 1879.
177 *Report of the CCE, 1882–3*, p. 398.
178 Paul O'Leary, 'The languages of patriotism in Wales, 1840–1880', in Geraint H. Jenkins (ed.), *The Welsh Language and its Social Domains, 1801–1911* (Cardiff, 2000), pp. 533–60, 546.
179 *Anerch i Ieuenctyd Cymru* (Bethesda, 1857), p. 224.
180 For this sense being articulated outside the public sphere see the account of an 1890 railway journey quoted in Eileen Holt, 'Mistral and the Welsh', *Transactions of the Honourable Society of Cymmrodorion* (1983), 157–63, 160.
181 H. Howell, 'Y cyfarfod adloniadol: Cymraeg yn yr ysgolion ddyddiol', *Cyfaill yr Aelwyd*, January 1889, 20–2.
182 Geraint Wyn Jones, *Dyddiadur Ysgol: Ysgol y Manod 1867–1967* (Blaenau Ffestiniog, 1997), p. 18; GA, Albany Road, 1 March 1898; Russell Grigg, '"You should love your country and should ever strive to be worthy of your fatherland": identity, British values and St David's Day in elementary schools in Wales, c.1885–1920', *Welsh History Review*, 29, 1 (2018), 99–125.
183 Bernard Porter, *The Absent-Minded Imperialists: Empire, Society and Culture in Britain* (Oxford, 2004).
184 On children's agency in reading see Ute Frevert et al., *Learning How to Feel: Children's Literature and the History of Emotional Socialization, c.1870–1970* (Oxford, 2014).
185 Linda Colley, *Britons: Forging the Nation, 1707–1837* (London, 1994), pp. 372–3.
186 Peter Mandler, 'What is "national identity"? Definitions and applications in modern British historiography', *Modern Intellectual History*, 3, 2 (2006), 271–97, 280; Philip Harling, 'The centrality of locality: the local state, local democracy, and local consciousness in late-Victorian and Edwardian Britain', *Journal of Victorian Culture*, 9, 2, (2004), 216–34, 218; T. M. Devine, *Scotland's Empire: The Origins of the Global Diaspora* (London, 2004), p. 352.
187 D. Parry-Jones, *My Own Folk* (Llandysul, 1972), p. 47.

188 Honourable Society of Cymmrodorion, *Preliminary Report upon the Use of the Welsh Language in Elementary Schools in Welsh-Speaking Districts* (London, 1884), p. 15.
189 Editorial, 'Wales and Welsh', *South Wales Daily Post*, 20 February 1893, 2.
190 Andronicus, 'Yr ysgol: pennod III: dim Cymraeg', *Cymru'r Plant*, November 1894, 313–17.
191 T. Gwynn Jones, *Gwedi Brad a Gofid* (Caernarfon, 1898), p. 55.
192 Catherine Hall, 'Making colonial subjects: education in the age of empire', *History of Education*, 37, 6 (2008), 773–87.
193 Lynn Zastoupil and Martin Moir (eds), *The Great Indian Education Debate: Documents Relating to the Orientalist-Anglicist Controversy, 1781–1843* (Richmond, 1999).
194 Osterhammel, *Transformation of the World*, p. 783.
195 Michael D. Jones, 'Difodi y Gymraeg yn barhad o oresgyniad Cymru', *Y Celt*, 27 June 1900, 3.
196 Daly, 'Literacy and language change', p. 165.
197 Edwards, *Sociolinguistics*, p. 36.
198 For example, Gearóid Denvir, 'Decolonizing the mind: language and literature in Ireland', *New Hibernian Review*, 1 (1997), 44–68, 45.
199 Thomas Darlington, 'The English speaking population of Wales', *Wales*, 1 (1894), 11–16, 15; my emphasis.
200 For example, Emyr Llydaw, 'At y werin weithyddawl Gymreig', *Seren Gomer*, February 1848, 42–3; Eiddal Ifor, 'Diwylliant y werin Gymreig', *Seren Gomer*, June 1854, 246.
201 Brooks, *Why Wales Never Was*; cf. Siwan M. Rosser, *Darllen y Dychymyg: Creu Ystyron Newydd i Blant a Phlentyndod yn Llenyddiaeth y Bedwaredd Ganrif ar Bymtheg* (Cardiff, 2020), p. 184.

BIBLIOGRAPHY

Archival material

Amgueddfa Cymru (St Fagans)
Letter, Stuart Maxwell to Iorwerth Peate, 19 June 1953
Note by John Griffiths (1925). St Fagans, 2933

Oral histories
Mr Jones, Rhosygwalia, Y Bala
Mr Jones, Y Tymbl
Mr Thomas, Llangynwyd
Mrs Evans
Mrs Stephens, Abergwili
Miss Jones, Llanilar

Anglesey Archives
School logbooks
Aberffraw Board
Amlwch Board
Bodedern National
Bryngwran Board
Dwyran British
Llanddeusant National
Llanddona British
Llandegfan National
Llangefni British
Llangefni National
Llangeinwen National
Llangristiolus

Llannerch-y-medd British
Malldraeth National
Pentraeth British
Trefdraeth National

Other

Llangeinwen school board minute book

Bangor University Archives

Diary of David Griffith, schoolmaster and curate
Letter from J. Ll. Evans to Ifor Williams, 10 February 1955

British Library Sounds Collection

Atgofion cyffredinol Cassie Davies
Cyfweliad gyda Mr E. D. Jones

Brunel University

43rd Report of the British and Foreign School Society, 1848
Ashley, James, Untitled
The Autobiography of J. D. Jones of Ruthin
Hobley, Frederick, From the Autobiography of Frederick Hobley, a nineteenth-century schoolteacher
Hughes, George Clifton, Shut the Mountain Gate
Lloyd, George, The Autobiography of George Brawd
Raymont, Thomas, Memories of an Octagenarian, 1864–1949

Carmarthenshire Archives

School logbooks

Abergwili National
Alma Board
Ammanford Junior
Bryn British
Bryn Evan Board
Carmarthen Lancastrian
Caio Board
Cil-y-cwm National

Cwmbach British
Cwmcothi Board
Cwmdwr
Dafen Tin Plate Works National
Esgairdawe
Five Roads British
Ffarmers Board
Glasfryn Board
Llanarthne
Llandeilo Tabernacle British
Llangunnock Vaughan's charity
Penygarn Board
Rhydcwmerau

Other

Five Roads Board school, manager's minute book
Saint Clears school board minute book

Ceredigion Archives

School logbooks

Aberaeron British
Elerch
Felinfach Board
Y Ferwig
Llanddeinol National
Llandygwydd National
Llandysul British
Llandysul National
Llanfihangel National
Llangeitho British
Llanilar
Llanon British
Llanon National
Llanrhystid
Llanwennog National
Llechryd
Newgate British
Pontgarreg British

Saint David's National
Swyddffynnon
Trefeirig Board
Tregaron National
Trewen British

Other

Aberystwyth school board minute book
Capel Bangor National punishment book
Cilcennan punishment book
Lampeter Pont Stephen school board minute book
Llanarth school board minute book
Llancynfelyn school board minute book
Llandysiliogogo Board punishment book
Llanfihangel-y-Creuddyn Lower school board minute book
Llansantffraid Board minute book
Scyborycoed school board minute book
Strata Florida school board minute book
Trefeirig school board minute book

Conwy Archives

School logbooks

Capel Curig
Cwm Penmachno National
Glanwydden
Llanddoged
Llandudno Mixed National
Llysfaen National
Rowen British
Talybont Board
Trefriw British

Glamorgan Archives

School logbooks

Aberaman Boys
Abercanaid Infants
Abermorlais

Albany Road (Cardiff)
Bodringallt
Bryncethin National
Dinas Colliery
Ferndale Board
Garth Junior Mixed
Georgetown Girls
Llwydcoed Mixed
Maesteg Garth British
Pentrebach Infants
Penyrheolgerrig Infants
St Cynon's National
St Mary's National Girls (Cardiff)
Treorchi British
Troed-y-rhiw Mixed
United Collieries (Boys) Treorchi
Ynysllwyd Board

Other

Bridgend Society for the Education of the Poor minute book
Llanfabon National school minutes
Rules of the Llantwit Major National school, est. 1831

Gwynedd Archives (Caernarfon and Dolgellau)

School logbooks

Aberdaron Deunant Board
Abergwyngregyn National
Bala British
Bangor British
Bethel Board
Brithdir
Bryncroes Board
Caernarfon British
Capel Celyn Board
Cefnfaes British
Corris British
Croesor

Dinorwic British
Dyffryn British
Y Felinheli [Port Dinorwic] British
Ffestiniog British
Garth Board
Glanypwll
Llanaelhaearn Board
Llanfrothen National
Llangian National
Llangwril Board
Llanllyfni British
Llanllechid National
Llanrug National
Llanystumdwy National
Nantlle Board
Penrhyndeudraeth British
Tanygrisiau Girls
Trefor Welsh Granite Quarry Company
Upper Bangor National

Other

Caernarfon National school minute book
Catherine Ryder exercise book
Croesor Board school punishment book
'Elementary education at Aberdovey', August 1894
Llanbedr Board school punishment book
Llandderfel Board school punishment book
Maesywaun Board school punishment book
Merioneth County Council, Education Act, 1902: County of Merioneth, Returns and Report (Conway, 1903)
W. Pryce Williams papers
William Ryder exercise book

National Archives

Davies, Williams Josh, 7 January 1869. Statement re: Aberystwith Poor Law Union: MH12/15801

National Library of Wales

Diary of Harry Thomas, Llanmaes
Let's Look at Wales: The Welsh (television script)
Niclas y Glais: Emynau a Hymnwyr (sound recording)
Oral history: atgofion cyffredinol, D. J. Morgan
Oral history: cyfweliad â William Christmas Williams gan Medwen Roberts
Oral history: Benjamin Jones
Oral history: Ellen Rogers
'Yr Hen Ysgol, 1864–7', William Williams papers

North-East Wales Archives (Hawarden and Ruthin)

School logbooks

Blaenau Llangernyw British
Bodelwyddan National
Broughton British
Dyserth National
Gresford National
Gwernaffield National
Hope Board
Llandyrnog National
Llangedwyn National
Llangernyw
Llangollen National
Llanrwst National
Nercwys National
Pentre Broughton Board
Rhydymwyn
Rhuddlan Boys
Ruabon Boys National
Tynyfelin Board

Other

Abergele National school punishment book
Autobiography of Edward Hughes
Autobiography of Samuel Nutall

Broughton school
Holywell school board minute book
Minutes of the Meetings of the Committee of Managers of Burton school
Pentre schools Girls Dept headmistress reports

Pembrokeshire Archives

School logbooks

Amblestone
Blaen-ffos
Brawdy
Bwlch-y-groes
Croes-goch
Dinas
Hermon
Mynachlog-ddu
Nevern
Picton Board
Solva

Powys Archives

School logbooks

Cemais British
Crickhowell British
Dylife National
Forden National
Glasbury Parochial
Gwenddwr National
Llidiart-y-waun
Llanllwchaearn
Llanllwchaearn National
Llyswen National
Meifod National
Montgomeryshire National
Newtown National
Pennant National, Llanbryn-mair
Penygloddfa British

Rhiwhiriaeth Board
Sarn National
Staylittle Board
Trecastell British
Trecastell National
Uwchygarreg National
Welshpool

Richard Burton Archives (Swansea University)

St David's Roman Catholic school logbook
Wilfred E. Timbrell, 'Memories of Tumble from 1894'

South Wales Miners' Library (Swansea University)

Josiah Jones interview (1972)

West Glamorgan Archives

School logbooks

Aberavon National
Baglan
Clydach
Cwm British
Cwmavon
Garnswllt
Glais Board
Gwaencaegurwen
Hafod Copperworks
Neath Abbey Boys British
Neath Abbey Girls British
Pontardawe
Pontrhydyfen
Skewen National
Tona National
Trebanos

Oral histories

Mrs Margaret Jane Williams (b.1886)

Contemporary social investigations, official reports and regulations

A Digest of Parochial Returns made to the Select Committee Appointed to Inquire into the Education of the Poor: Session 1818 (1819)

Select Committee on Education of Poorer Classes in England and Wales (London, 1837–8)

Report of the Commissioners (charity), 32 part III (London, 1838)

Minutes and annual reports of the Committee of Council on Education, 1839–1900 [CCE]

Children's Employment Commission, First Report of the Commissioners: Trades and Manufacturers (London, 1842)

Children's Employment Commission, Second Report of the Commissioners: Mines (London, 1843)

Report of the Commissioners of Inquiry for Turnpike Roads, South Wales (London, 1844)

Report of the Commissioner into the Operation of the Mines Act and State of the Population in the Mining Districts, Report on South Wales (London, 1846)

Reports of the Commissioners of Inquiry into the State of Education in Wales (London, 1847) [Blue Books]

Census of Great Britain 1851, Education: England and Wales. Report and Tables (London, 1854)

The Twenty-second Report of the Commissioners in National Education in Ireland (Dublin, 1856)

Copy of the Minutes and Regulations of the Committee of the Privy Council on Education Reduced into the Form of a Code (1860)

Reports of Assistant Commissioners appointed to inquire into State of Popular Education in England (1861) [Newcastle Commission]

Minute of the Committee of the Privy Council on Education establishing a Revised Code of Regulations (1861)

Minute Confirming the Alteration of the Revised Code of Regulations (London, 1862)

Nicolson, Alexander, Education Commission (Scotland), *Report on the State of Education in the Hebrides* (Edinburgh, 1866)

Report from the Select Committee on Education (1866) [Pakington Committee]

Schools Inquiry Commission, Vol. 1: Report of the Commissioners (London, 1868)

Schools Inquiry Commission, Vol. V: Minutes of Evidence taken before the Commissioners Part II (1868)

Schools Inquiry Commission. General Reports by Assistant Commissioners. Vol VIII: Midland Counties and Northumberland (London, 1868)

Schools Inquiry Commission, Vol. XX: Monmouthshire and Wales (London, 1870)

Commission on the Employment of Children, Young Persons, and Women in Agriculture (1867). Third Report of the Commissioners (London, 1870) [Employment of Children Commission]

Education Department, *1875. New Code of Regulations* (London, 1875)

Report of the Committee appointed to Inquire into the Condition of Intermediate and Higher Education in Wales (London, 1881)

Honourable Society of Cymmrodorion, *Preliminary Report upon the Use of the Welsh Language in Elementary Schools in Welsh-Speaking Districts* (London, 1884)

Honourable Society of Cymmrodorion, *Report of the Committee appointed into the Advisability of the Introduction of the Welsh Language into the Course of Elementary Education in Wales: The Introduction of Welsh as a Specific Subject* (Aberdare, 1885)

Royal Commission appointed to Inquire into the Working of the Elementary Education Acts, England and Wales (1886–8) [Cross Commission]

Education Department, *Code of Regulations* (London, 1889)

Ontario Education Department, *Extracts and Statements respecting Bi-lingual teaching in Great Britain, the United States and Canada* (Toronto, 1890)

Census of England and Wales 1891, vol. IV: General Report (London, 1893), section IX: Languages in Wales and Monmouthshire

Education Department, *Code of Regulations* (London, 1893)

First Report of the Royal Commission on Land on Wales and Monmouthshire (London, 1894)

Census of Ireland, 1901. Part II: General Report (Dublin, 1902)

Eleventh Decennial Census of the Population of Scotland, 1901, vol. 1 (Glasgow, 1902)

Census of England and Wales, 1901: General Report (London, 1904), section X: Languages in Wales and Monmouthshire

Royal Commission on the Church of England and Other Religious Bodies in Wales and Monmouthshire, vol. III. Minutes of Evidence. Book II (London, 1911)
Board of Education, *Patriotism: Suggestion to Local Education Authorities and Teachers in Wales Regarding the Teaching of Patriotism* (London, 1916)
The Teaching of English in England (London, 1926) [Newbolt Report]
Welsh in Education and Life: Being the Report of the Departmental Committee Appointed by the President of the Board of Education to inquire into the Position of the Welsh Language and to Advise as to its Promotion in the Educational System of Wales (London, 1927)
Ministry of Education, *The Place of Welsh and English in the Schools of Wales* (London, 1953)

Newspapers and periodicals

Aberystwith Observer
Yr Adolygydd
Amman Valley Chronicle and East Carmarthen News
Yr Arweinydd
Yr Arweinydd Annibynol
Baner ac Amserau Cymru
Brecon County Times
Y Brython
Y Brython Cymreig
Bye-gones relating to Wales and the Border Counties
Cambrian News
Cardiff Times
Carmarthen Weekly Report
Carnarvon and Denbigh Herald
Y Celt
Celt Llundain
Y Cronicl
Cronicl y Cymdeithasau Crefyddol
Cyfaill Yr Aelwyd
Y Cymro
Cymru
Cymru'r Plant
Y Darian

Y Diwygiwr
Y Drysorfa
Y Dysgedydd Crefyddol
Dysgedydd y Plant
Evening Express
The Gaelic Journal
Y Genedl Gymreig
Y Geninen
Glamorgan, Monmouth & Brecon Gazette
Glamorgan Free Press
Y Goleuad
The Grail
Yr Haul
Haverfordwest & Milford Haven Telegraph
Heddyw
Herald of Wales and Monmouthshire Recorder
Illustrated London Life
Journal of the Statistical Society of London
Y Llan
Llanelly and County Guardian and South Wales Advertiser
Llangollen Advertiser
Y Llenor
The London Kelt
Mid Wales Herald
Morning Post
Y Negesydd
North Wales Chronicle
North Wales Express
North Wales Times
Pembroke County Guardian and Cardigan Reporter
Perl y Plant
Pontypridd Chronicle and Workman's News
Pontypridd District Herald
The Principality
Rhyl Record
The Schoolmaster
Seren Cymru
Seren Gomer
South Wales Daily News

South Wales Daily Post
South Wales Echo
South Wales Star
Transactions of the Honourable Society of Cymmrodorion
Transactions of the Liverpool Welsh National Society
Transactions of the National Association for the Promotion of Social Science
Tarian y Gweithiwr
The Times
Y Traethodydd
Trysorfa y Plant
Y Tyst
Tywysydd y Plant
Usk Observer
Wales
Welsh Gazette and West Wales Advertiser
Welsh Outlook
Welsh Weekly
The Welshman
Western Mail
Wrexham Advertiser
Yr Ymofynydd
Yorkshire Post and Leeds Intelligencer
Young Wales

Contemporary books and memoirs

Ackermann's Juvenile Forget Me Not (London, 1832)
Andrews, William, Bygone Punishments (London, 1899)
Anon., A Schoolmaster's Difficulties, Abroad and at Home (London, 1853)
Arnold, Matthew, On the Study of Celtic Literature (London, 1867)
-- Reports on Elementary Schools 1852–1882 (London, 1910)
Ashton, Charles, Hanes Addysg yng Nghymru (Newtown, 1885)
Ballard, Philip Boswood, Things I Cannot Forget (London, 1937)
Bell, Andrew, The Madras School, or Elements of Tuition (London, 1808)
Benson, Arthur Christopher and Viscount Esther (eds), The Letters of Queen Victoria, vol. II (London, 1908)
Binns, Henry Bryan, A Century of Education: Being the Centenary History of the British and Foreign School Society, 1808–1908 (London, 1908)

Board of Education, *Handbook of Suggestions for Teachers* (London, 1937)
Borrow, George, *Wild Wales: Its People, Language and Scenery* (1862; London, 1977)
Bourassa, Henri, *La Langue Francaise au Canada* (Montreal, 1915)
Bowman, Anne, *Routledge's New Reading Made Easy: A First Book of Lessons in One and Two Syllables* (London, 1856)
Brinsley, John, *Ludus Literarius or the Grammar Schoole* (1612), ed. E. T. Campagnac (London, 1917)
British and Foreign School Society, *Swansea Training College 1872–1913* (Swansea, 1913)
Brown, Robert Lee (ed.), *The Letters of Edward Coppleston, Bishop of Llandaff, 1828–1849* (Cardiff, 2003)
Davies, Cassie, *Hwb i'r Galon* (Swansea, 1973)
Davies, Dan Isaac, *Yr Iaith Gymraeg 1785, 1885, 1985!: neu, Tair miliwn o Gymry dwy-ieithawg mewn Can Mlynedd* (Dinbych, 1886)
Davies, David, *Echoes from the Welsh Hills: Or Reminiscences of the Preachers and People of Wales* (London, 1883)
––– *Reminiscences of My Country and My People* (Cardiff, 1925)
Davies, E., *Cofiant Y Diweddar Barch, Morris Roberts* (Utica, 1879)
Davies, Evan, *Hanes Plwyf Llangynllo* (Llandysul, 1905)
Davies, Jonathan Ceredig, *Folk-Lore of West and Mid-Wales* (Aberystwyth, 1911)
Davies, Thomas, *Short Sketches from the Life of Thomas Davies* (Haverfordwest, 1887)
Davies, W. J., *Hanes Plwyf Llandyssul* (Llandysul, 1896)
Davies, Walter Haydn, *The Right Place, the Right Time: Memories of Boyhood Days in a Welsh Mining Community* (Swansea, 1975)
Denning, R. T. W. (ed.), *The Diary of William Thomas of Michaelston-super-Ely, near St Fagans Glamorgan, 1762–1795* (Cardiff, 1995)
Edmonds, E. L. and O. P. Edmonds (eds), *I was There: The Memoirs of H. S. Tremenheere* (Eton, 1965)
Edwards, Lewis, *Yr Athrawes o Ddifrif* (Caernarfon, 1859)
Edwards, Owen M., *A Short History of Wales* (Chicago, 1907)
––– *Clych Atgof: Penodau yn Hanes fy Addysg* (Caernarfon, 1906)
Edwards, W., *The Direct Method of Language Teaching: A Suggestion in the Education of Wales* (Newport, 1900)
Edwards, Wil John, *From the Valley I Came* (London, 1956)

Evans, Beriah Gwynfe, *Llawlyfr y Cymro ac Arweinydd yr Ymneillduwr i Ddeddf Addysg 1902* (Dinbych, 1903)
Evans, Hugh, *Cwm Eithin* (Liverpool, 1933)
Evans, Keri E. and W. Pari Huws, *Cofiant y Parch David Adams* (Liverpool, 1924)
Evans, Myra, *Atgofion Ceinewydd* (Aberystwyth, 1961)
Evans, Thomas, *A Welshman in India* (London, 1908)
Evans, William, *Cofiant y Parchedig William Evans, Tonyrefail* (Newport, 1892)
Fearon, D. R., *School Inspection* (London, 1887)
George, William, *My Brother and I* (London, 1958)
Gill, John, *Introductory Text-book to School Education, Method and School Management* (London, 1876)
Griffiths, James, *Pages from Memory* (London, 1969)
Gruffydd, W. J., *The Years of the Locust*, trans. D. Myrddin Lloyd (1936; Llandysul, 1976)
––– *Owen Morgan Edwards: Cofiant. Cyfrol 1, 1858–1883* (Aberystwyth, 1937)
Holmes, Edmond, *In Quest of an Ideal: An Autobiography* (London, 1920)
Hughes, Herbert, *Cymru Evan Jones: Detholiad o Bapurau Evan Jones (1850–1928)* (Llandysul, 2009)
Hughes, John, *Education in a Changing Wales* (Llandysul, 1932)
Hughes, William, *A Short Memoir, With Some Writings of the Rev J. A. Jackson* (Rhyl, 1877)
Humphries, E. Morgan, 'Welsh culture and education', in *National Union of Teachers Conference Souvenir: Llandudno, 1929* (Cardiff, 1929)
Isfoel, *Hen Ŷd y Wlad: Atgofion Isfoel* (Llandysul, 1966)
Jenkins, R. T., *Edrych yn Ôl* (London, 1968)
Jones, Abel J., *John Morgan MA: First Headmaster of Narberth County School* (Llandysul, 1939)
––– *I was Privileged* (Cardiff, 1943)
–– *From an Inspector's Bag* (Cardiff, 1944)
Jones, Alfred, *The Philosophy of Corporal Punishment: An Investigation into the Policy and Morality of School Coercion* (Edinburgh, 1859)
Jones, E. Pan, *Oes Gofion neu Fraslun o Hanes fy Mywyd* (Bala, 1911)
Jones, Evan, *John Jones yn yr Ysgol: Ffug-hanesyn, yn rhoddi Darluniad o Ysgolion Gwledig Cymru, oddeutru'r Flwyddyn 1840*, 2nd edn (Lampeter, 1904)

Jones, F. Wynn, *Godre'r Berwyn* (Cardiff, 1954)
Jones, Henry, *Old Memories* (London, 1922)
Jones, J. D., *Three Scores Years and Ten* (London, 1940)
Jones, Jack, *Unfinished Journey* (London, 1938)
Jones, James, *A Few Plain Hints and Suggestions on Teaching English in Welsh Country Schools, with Directions for Self-Instruction* (Bala, 1864)
Jones, John Owen, *Cofiant a Gweithiau Parch Robert Ellis, Ysgoldy Arfon* (Caernarfon, 1883)
Jones, T. Gwynn, *Gwedi Brad a Gofid* (Caernarfon, 1898)
--- 'Bilingualism in the schools', in *Aberystwyth and District: A Guide Prepared for the Conference of the National Union of Teachers* (Aberystwyth, 1911)
--- *Brithgofion* (Llandybïe, 1944)
Jones, Thomas, *Rhymney Memories* (1938; Llandysul, 1970)
Jones, William, *Parch David Davies, Bermo: Ei Gofiant a'i Bregethau* (Liverpool, 1897)
Joyce, P. W., *A Hand-Book of School Management and Methods of Teaching* (Dublin, 1863)
Kerr, John, *Memories Grave and Gay: 40 Years of School Inspection* (Edinburgh, 1902)
Lancaster, Joseph, *Improvements in Education as it Respects the Industrious Classes of the Community*, 3rd edn (London, 1805)
--- *The British System of Education: Epitome of Joseph Lancaster's Inventions and Improvements in Education Practised at the Royal Free Schools, Borough-Road, Southwark* (London, 1810)
Lewis, H. Elvet, *The Life of E. Herber Evans, DD. From his Letters, Journals etc* (London, 1900)
Lewis, H. J., *The Teaching of Welsh* (Federation of Education Committees, Wales and Monmouthshire, 1925)
Lewis, Thomas, *These Seventy Years: An Autobiography* (London, 1931)
Llewellyn, Richard, *How Green was My Valley* (1939; Harmondsworth, 1951)
Llewelyn, Michael Gareth, *Sand in the Glass* (London, 1943)
Macdonald, Tom, *The White Lanes of Summer* (London, 1975)
Mackay, William, *Urquhart and Glenmoriston: Olden Times in a Highland Parish*, 2nd edn (Inverness, 1914)
Malkin, Benjamin H., *The Scenery, Antiquities, and Biography of South Wales* (London, 1804)

Morgan, Edward (ed.), *Letters of the Rev. Griffith Jones, late Rector of Llandowror, Carmarthenshire, founder of the Welsh circulating schools to Mrs. Bevan* (London, 1832)

Morgan, J. Vyrnwy, *Welsh Political and Educational Leaders in the Victorian Era* (London, 1908)

Morgan-Richardson, C., *History of the Institution once called 'The Welsh Piety', but now known as Mrs. Bevan's Charity (Cardigan, 1890)*

Morris, W. Meredith, *The Renaissance of Welsh Literature* (Maesteg, 1908)

Owen, Daniel, *Hunangofiant Rhys Lewis, Gweinidog Bethel* (Wrexham, 1885)

--- *Rhys Lewis: The Autobiography of the Minister of Bethel*, trans. Robert Lomas (1885; 2017)

--- *Fireside Tales*, trans. Adam Pearce (1895; Talybont, 2011)

Owen, Isambard, *The Welsh Language Society: Scheme and Rules of the Society* (Bangor, 1901)

Parochial Schoolmaster, *A Plea for the Parish Schools* (Edinburgh, 1867)

Parry-Jones, D., *Welsh Country Upbringing* (London, 1948)

--- *My Own Folk* (Llandysul, 1972)

Pearse, Pádraic, *The Murder Machine and Other Essays* (Cork, 1976)

Peate, Iorwerth C., *Rhwng Dau Fyd: Darn o Hunangofiant* (Dinbych, 1976)

Phillips, Thomas, *Wales: The Language, Social Condition, Moral Character and the Religious Opinions of the People, considered in Relation to Education* (London, 1849)

--- *Life of James Davies: A Village Schoolmaster* (London, 1850)

Pillans, James, *Contributions to the Cause of Education* (London, 1856)

Powell, Lewis, *Hanes Bywyd y Parch. Lewis Powell* (Cardiff, 1860)

Price, Thomas and Janes Williams, *The Literary Remains of the Rev. Thomas Price, Carnhuanawc*, vol. 2 (Llandovery, 1854)

Pritchard, William, *Bywyd y Parch Ebenezer Davies, Llanerchymedd* (Bangor, 1879)

Ravenstein, E. G., 'On the Celtic languages in the British Isles: a statistical survey', *Journal of the Statistical Society of London*, 42, 3 (1879), 579–643

Rea, F. G., *A School in South Uist: Reminiscences of a Hebridean Schoolmaster, 1890–1913* (1927; Edinburgh, 1997)

Rhoscomyl, Owen, *Flame-Bearers of Welsh History* (Merthyr Tydfil, 1905)

Rhys, John and David Brynmor-Jones, *The Welsh People: Chapters on their Origin, History, Laws, Language, Literature, and Characteristics* (New York, 1900)
Richard, Henry, *Letters and Essays on Wales* (London, 1884)
Richard, Thomas, *Atgofion Cardi* (Aberystwyth, 1960)
Richards, Frank, *Old Soldier Sahib* (1936; Cardigan, 2016)
Roberts, O. L., *Cofiant Y Parch O. R. Owen, Glandwr a Lerpwl* (Liverpool, 1909)
Roberts, Robert, *A Wandering Scholar: The Life and Opinions of Robert Roberts* (Cardiff, 1991)
Rowlands, E. D, *Atgofion am Llanuwchllyn* (Nant Peris, 1975)
Royal Geographical Readers: First Book (For Standard II) (London, 1881)
Royal School Series, *The World at Home. Standard II* (London, 1889)
Sikes, Wirt, *Rambles and Studies in Old South Wales* (London, 1881)
Sneyd-Kynnersley, E. M., *HMI: Some Passages in the Life of One of H.M. Inspectors of Schools* (London, 1913)
Society for Utilizing the Welsh Language, *Memorial Presented by the Council to the Royal Commission on Elementary Education* (Llandilo, 1886)
--- *Welsh as a Specific Subject for Elementary Schools, Stage 1* (Cardiff, 1891)
--- *Scheme of Instruction for Use in Elementary Schools in Wales* (Caernarfon, 1893)
Southall, John E. (ed.), *Bilingual Teaching in Welsh Elementary Schools or Minutes of Evidence of Welsh Witnesses before the Royal Commission on Education in 1886–87* (Newport, 1888)
--- *Wales and Her Language* (Newport, 1892)
--- *The Welsh Language Census of 1891* (Newport, 1895)
Spencer, F. H., *An Inspector's Testament* (London, 1938)
Stanley, Henry M., *The Autobiography of Sir Henry Morton Stanley* (Boston, 1909)
Stonelake, Edmund, *The Autobiography of Edmund Stonelake* (Bridgend, 1981)
Storr, F. (ed.), *Life and Remains of the Rev. R. H. Quick* (Cambridge, 1892)
Theobald, R. M., *Memorials of John Daniel Morell, M. A., LL. D. Her Majesty's Inspector of Schools* (London, 1891)

Thirwall, Connop, *A Letter to J. Bowstead [commenting on his Letters] ... concerning Education in South Wales*, 2nd edition (1861).
Thomas, Bryn, *The Good Old Days: Notes and Jottings on Llandybie, Llandeilo, Fair Fach and the Amman Valley* (Llandybïe, 1973)
Thomas, W. C. Elvet, *Tyfu'n Gymro* (Llandysul, 1972)
Trevelyan, Marie, *Glimpses of Welsh Life and Character* (London, 1893)
Trimmer, Sarah, *Reflections upon the Education of Children in Charity Schools* (1802)
Walker, J., *The Handy Book of Object Lessons from a Teacher's Note Book*, 3rd edn (London, 1873)
Warner, Richard, *A Second Walk through Wales by the Revd. Richard Warner, of Bath, in August and September 1798*, 4th edn (London, 1813)
Watkins, Harold M., *Life has Kept me Young* (London, 1951)
Watkins, Percy E., *A Welshman Remembers* (Cardiff, 1944)
Wilde, William, *Irish Popular Superstitions* (Dublin, 1852)
Williams, D. J., *Yn Chwech ar Hugain Oed* (Aberystwyth, 1959)
Williams, J. Lloyd, *Atgofion Tri Chwarter Canrif, cyf. I* (Aberystwyth, 1941)
--- *Atgofion Tri Chwarter Canrif, cyf. II* (Dinbych, 1942)
--- *Atgofion Tri Chwarter Canrif, cyf. III* (Dinbych, 1944)
--- *Atgofion Tri Chwarter Canrif, cyf. IV* (London, 1945)
Williams, James, *Give Me Yesterday* (Llandysul, 1971)
Williams, T. Marchant, *The Land of my Fathers* (London, 1889)
Williams, W. Llewelyn, *'S Lawer Dydd* (Llanelli, 1929)
Wyn, Wactyn, *Adgofion Watcyn Wyn* (Merthyr, 1907)

Secondary sources

Aaron, Jane, 'A review of the contribution of women to Welsh life and prospects for the future', *Transactions of the Honourable Society of Cymmrodorion*, 8 (2001), 188–204
--- *Welsh Gothic* (Cardiff, 2013)
--- *Cranogwen* (Cardiff, 2023)
Adams, Matthew, *Teaching Classics in English Schools, 1500–1840* (Cambridge, 2016)
Adamson, John William, *Pioneers of Modern Education 1600–1700* (Cambridge, 1921)

Aldrich, Richard, 'The British and Foreign School Society, past and present', *History of Education Researcher*, 91 (2013), 5–11

Alexander, Michael Van Cleave, *The Growth of English Education, 1348–1648* (London, 1990)

Anderson, Robert, 'Learning: education, class and culture', in Martin Hewitt (ed.), *The Victorian World* (London, 2012), 484–99

——— (ed.), *The Edinburgh History of Education in Scotland* (Edinburgh, 2015)

Anon., *Atgofion: Canmlwyddiant Ysgol Gwynfryn, 1896–1996* (Carmarthen, 1996)

Anon., *Dunvant School Centenary, 1877–1977* (Swansea, 1977)

Anon., *Pioneers of Welsh Education: Four Lectures* (Swansea, 1964)

Ashton, Byron, 'The status of the Welsh language in the schools, 1889–1914', *History of Education*, 19, 3 (1990), 264–6

Auerbach, Sascha, '"Some punishment should be devised": parents, children and the state in Victorian London', *The Historian*, 71, 4 (2009), 757–79

——— '"The law has no feeling for poor folks like us!" everyday responses to legal compulsion in England's working-class communities, 1871–1904', *Journal of Social History*, 45, 3 (2012), 686–708

Bailey, Peter, *Popular Culture and Performance in the Victorian City* (Cambridge, 1998)

Baldauf, Richard B. and Robert B. Kaplan, *Language Planning from Practice to Theory* (Clevedon, 1997)

Barber, Henry and Henry Lewis, *The History of Friars School Bangor* (Bangor, 1901)

Bartle, G. F., 'The role of the British and Foreign School Society in Welsh elementary education, 1840–76', *Journal of Educational Administration and History*, 12, 1 (1990), 18–29

Beardmore, Carol, Cara Dobbing and Steven King (eds), *Family Life in Britain 1650–1910* (Basingstoke, 2019)

Benbough-Jackson, Mike, C*ardiganshire and the Cardi, c.1760–c.2000: Locating a Place and its People* (Cardiff, 2011)

Bennet, Gilbert (ed.), *Something Attempted, Something Done* (Llandybïe, 1973)

Breverton, Terry, *The Welsh: The Biography* (Stroud, 2012)

Birchenough, C., *History of Elementary Education in England and Wales from 1800 to the Present Day* (London, 1914)

Bischof, Christopher, *Teaching Britain: Elementary Teachers and the State of the Everyday, 1846–1906* (Oxford, 2019)
--- 'Progress and the people: histories of mass education and conceptions of Britishness, 1870–1914', *History of Education*, 49, 2 (2020), 160–83
Bragg, Melvin, *The Adventure of English: The Biography of a Language* (London, 2003)
Britain, David (ed.), *Language in the British Isles* (Cambridge, 2007)
Brockliss, Laurence and Heather Montgomery (eds), *Childhood and Violence in the Western Tradition* (Oxford, 2010)
Bronstein, Jamie L., *The Happiness of the British Working Class* (Stanford, 2023)
Brooks, Simon, *Why Wales Never Was: The Failure of Welsh Nationalism* (Cardiff, 2017)
Bunyi, Grace W., 'Language classroom practices in Kenya', in Angel Lin and Peter Martin (eds), *Decolonisation, Globalisation: Language-in-Education Policy and Practice* (Clevedon, 2005), pp. 131–52
Burchardt, Jeremy, 'Agricultural history, rural history, or countryside history?', *Historical Journal*, 50, 2 (2007), 465–81
Burke, Catherine, Peter Cunningham and Ian Grosvenor, '"Putting education in its place": space, place and materialities in the history of education', *History of Education*, 39, 6 (2010), 677–80
Burke, Peter and Roy Porter (eds), *The Social History of Language* (Cambridge, 1987)
--- *Language, Self and Society: A Social History of Language* (Cambridge, 1991)
Burnett, John (ed.), *Destiny Obscure: Autobiographies of Childhood, Education and Family from the 1820s to the 1920s* (London, 1982)
Cameron, Ewan A., 'Education in rural Scotland, 1696–1872', in Robert Anderson (ed.), *The Edinburgh History of Education in Scotland* (Edinburgh, 2015), pp. 153–70
Carruthers, Mary, *The Craft of Thought: Meditation, Rhetoric, and the Making of Images, 400–1200* (Cambridge, 1998)
Carter, Richard and Walter Jones, *Ysgol yng Nghymru tua Diwedd Oes Victoria* (Llandysul, 1994)
Claeys, Anna, 'Britannia's children grow up: English education at empire's end', *History of Education*, 47, 6 (2018), 823–39
Clement, Mary, *The SPCK and Wales, 1699–1740* (London, 1954)

——— 'Dechrau addysgu'r werin', in Jac L. Williams (ed.), *Ysgrifau ar Addysg*, vol. 4 (Cardiff, 1966), pp. 16–44
Clifford, Rebecca, *Survivors: Children's Lives After the Holocaust* (New Haven, 2020)
Colls, Robert and Philip Dodd (eds), *Englishness: Politics and Culture 1880–1920* (London, 2014)
Coupland, Nikolas (ed.), *English in Wales: Diversity, Conflict and Change* (Clevedon, 1990)
Coupland, Reginald, *Welsh and Scottish Nationalism: A Study* (London, 1954)
Cragoe, Matthew, *An Anglican Aristocracy: The Moral Economy of the Landed Estate in Carmarthenshire, 1832–1895* (Oxford, 1996)
Cregier, Don M., *Bounder from Wales: Lloyd George's Career before the First World War* (London, 1976)
Crockett, Anthony, 'Hawliau lleiafrifoedd a diwylliannol ac ieithyddol – yr âpel at gyfiawnder', *Efrydiau Athronyddol*, 57 (1994), 50–60
Crosby, Travis, *The Unknown Lloyd George: A Statesman in Conflict* (London, 2014)
Crowley, Tony, 'English in Ireland: a complex case study', in Terttu Nevalainen and Elizabeth Closs Traugott (eds), *The Oxford Handbook of the History of English* (Oxford, 2012), pp. 470–80
Crystal, David, *Language Death* (Cambridge, 2000)
Cunningham, Hugh, *Children and Childhood in Western Society since 1500* (Harlow, 2005)
——— *The Invention of Childhood* (London, 2006)
Dafydd, Myrddin ap, 'Cysgod y Welsh Not', *Llafar Gwlad*, 64 (1999), 15–17
——— 'Y Welsh Not ar waith o hyd', *Llafar Gwlad*, 79 (2003), 18–19
——— *Under the Welsh Not* (Llanrwst, 2019)
Dauenhauer, Nora Marks and Richard Dauenhauer, 'Technical, emotional, and ideological issues in reversing language shift; examples from southeast Alaska', in Lenore A. Grenoble and Lindsay J. Whaley (eds), *Endangered Languages: Language Loss and Community Response* (Cambridge, 1998), pp. 57–98
Dalby, Andrew, *Language in Danger* (London, 2002)
Daly, Mary, 'Literacy and language change in the late nineteenth and early twentieth centuries', in M. Daly and D. Dickson (eds), *The Origins of Popular Literacy in Ireland: Language Change and Educational Development 1700–1920* (Dublin, 1990), pp. 153–66

Davies, Alfred T. (ed.), *OM (Sir Owen M. Edwards): A Memoir* (Cardiff, 1946)

Davies, B. L., 'Sir Hugh Owen and education in Wales', *Transactions of the Honourable Society of Cymmrodorion*, part 2 (1971), 191–223

——— 'British schools in south Wales: the Rev. William Roberts (Nefydd), South Wales representative of the British and Foreign School Society, 1853–1863', *National Library of Wales Journal*, 18, 4 (1974), 383–96

——— 'The right to a bilingual education in nineteenth-century Wales', *Transactions of the Honourable Society of Cymmrodorion* (1988), 133–51

Davies, David Wyn, *A History of Education in Machynlleth* (Machynlleth, 1986)

Davies, E. T., *Monmouthshire Schools and Education to 1870* (Newport, 1957)

Davies, Elfed, *The Story of Hirwaun's Schools* (Hirwaun, 2013)

Davies, Eryl D., *Christian Schools: Christianity and Education in Mid-Nineteenth-Century Wales and its Relevance for Today* (Bridgend, 1978)

Davies, Griffith G., 'Addysg elfennol yn Sir Aberteifi, 1870–1902', *Ceredigion*, 4, 4 (1963), 353–73

Davies, Gwilym Prys, *Ysgol Llanegryn: Amlinelliad o'i Hanes* (Talybont, 2009)

Davies, Hazel, *O. M. Edwards* (Cardiff, 1988)

Davies, Irene Myrddin, *Welsh History: A Handbook for Teachers* (Cardiff, 1947)

Davies, J. A., *Education in a Welsh Rural County, 1870–1973* (Cardiff, 1973)

Davies, J. Ifor, *The Caernarvon County School: A History* (Gwynedd, 1989)

Davies, Jacob, *Hanes Ysgol Nantcwmrhys* (Pencader, 1957)

——— *Hanes Pedair Ysgol* (Llandysul, 1975)

Davies, Janet, *The Welsh Language* (Cardiff, 1993)

Davies, John, 'Victoria and Victorian Wales', in Geraint H. Jenkins and J. Beverley Smith (eds), *Politics and Society in Wales, 1840–1922* (Cardiff, 1988), pp. 7–28

——— *A History of Wales* (Harmondsworth, 1993)

Davies, Kate and T. Llew Jones, *Canrif o Addysg Gynradd: Ysgol Tregroes, 1878–1978* (Llandysul, 1978)

Davies, Irene Myrddin, *Welsh History: A Handbook for Teachers* (Cardiff, 1947)
Davies, Russell, *Secret Sins: Sex, Violence and Society in Carmarthenshire 1870–1920* (Cardiff, 1996)
––– *People, Places and Passions. Pain and Pleasure: A Social History of Wales and the Welsh, 1870–1945* (Cardiff, 2015)
Davies, T. Eirug. and T. Rees, *Y Prifathro Thomas Rees: Ei Fywyd a'i Waith* (Llandysul, 1939)
Davin, Anna, *Growing Up Poor: Home, School and Street in London, 1870–1914* (London, 1996)
Denvir, Gearóid, 'Decolonizing the mind: language and literature in Ireland', *New Hibernian Review*, 1 (1997), 44–68
Devine, T. M., *Scotland's Empire: The Origins of the Global Diaspora* (London, 2004)
Digby, Anne and Peter Searby, *Children, School and Society in Nineteenth-Century England* (London, 1981)
Dixon, Thomas, 'Educating the emotions from Gradgrind to Goleman', *Research Papers in Education*, 27, 4 (2012), 481–95
Doyle, Aidan, *A History of the Irish Language* (Oxford, 2015)
Dunford, J. E., 'Biographical details of her majesty's inspectors appointed before 1870', *History of Education Society Bulletin*, 28 (1981), 8–23
Durham, Mercedes and Jonathan Morris (eds), *Sociolinguistics in Wales* (London, 2016)
Durkacz, Victor Edward, *The Decline of the Celtic Languages* (Edinburgh, 1983)
Dyhouse, Carol, *Girls Growing Up in Late Victorian and Edwardian England* (London, 1981)
Eastwood, David, *Government and Community in the English Provinces, 1700– 1870* (London, 1997)
Edwards, John, *Sociolinguistics: A Very Short Introduction* (Oxford, 2013)
Edwards, Reginald, 'Theory, history, and practice of education: Fin de siècle and a new beginning', *McGill Journal of Education*, 26, 3 (1991). Retrieved from: https://mje.mcgill.ca/article/view/7991 (accessed 6 April 2024)
Edwards, Thorton B., 'The Welsh Not: a comparative analysis', *Carn*, 88 (1994–5), 10–1
Ellis, Tudor, *Back to Normal* (Caernarfon, 2014)

Enoch, D. G., 'Schools and inspection as a mode of social control in south-east Wales, 1839–1907', *Journal of Educational Administration and History*, 22, 1 (1990), 9–17

Evans, Daniel, *The Life and Work of William Williams* (Llandysul, 1939)

Evans, David, *Wales in Industrial Britain, c.1760–c.1914* (London, 1996)

Evans, Gwilym J., *The Entrance Scholarship Examination in Caernarvonshire, 1897–1961* (Caernarfon, 1966)

Evans, Howell T., *Modern Wales*, 2nd edn (Wrexham, 1937)

Evans, Hywel Gwyn, *Pum Ysgol: Ardal Cwmllynfell* (Llandysul, 2003)

Evans, John, *O. M. Edwards and the Welsh Not / O. M. Edwards a'r Welsh Not* (Cardiff, 2003)

Evans, Leslie Wynne, 'Ironworks Schools in South Wales, 1784–1860', *The Sociological Review*, a43, 1 (1951), 203–28

——— 'Sir John and Lady Charlotte Guest's educational scheme at Dowlais in the mid-nineteenth century', *National Library of Wales Journal*, 9, 3 (1956), 265–86

——— 'Colliery schools in south Wales in the nineteenth century', *National Library of Wales Journal*, 10, 2 (1957), 137–66

——— *Education in Industrial Wales, 1700–1900: A Study of the Works Schools System in Wales during the Industrial Revolution* (Cardiff, 1971)

——— *Studies in Welsh Education: Welsh Educational Structure and Administration, 1880–1925* (Cardiff, 1974)

Evans, Lyn, *Portrait of a Pioneer: A Biography of Howell Thomas Evans* (Llandybïe, 1982)

Evans, Neil and Huw Pryce (eds), *Writing a Small Nation's Past: Wales in Comparative Perspective, 1850–1950* (Farnham: Ashgate, 2013)

Evans, M. J., 'Elementary education in Montgomeryshire 1850–1900', *The Montgomeryshire Collections*, 63, 1 (1973), 1–46

Evans, Stephen, 'Macaulay's minute revisited: colonial language policy in nineteenth-century India', *Journal of Multilingual and Multicultural Development*, 23, 4 (2002), 260–81

Evans, W. Gareth, 'The Welsh Intermediate and Technical Education Act, 1889: a centenary appreciation', *History of Education*, 19, 3 (1990), 195–210

——— 'Free education and the quest for popular control, unsectarianism and efficiency: Wales and the Free Elementary Education Act, 1891',

Transactions of the Honourable Society of Cymmrodorion (1991), 203–31

——— 'The "bilingual difficulty": the inspectorate and the failure of a Welsh language teacher-training experiment in Victorian Wales', *National Library of Wales Journal*, 28, 3 (1994), 325–33

——— '"Gelyn yr Iaith Gymraeg": Y Parchedig Shadrach Pryce A.E.M., a meddylfryd yr arolygiaeth yn Oes Fictoria', *Y Traethodydd*, 149 (1994), 73–81

——— 'Education in Cardiganshire, 1700–1974', in Geraint H. Jenkins and Ieuan Gwynedd Jones (eds), *Cardiganshire County History, vol. 3* (Cardiff, 1998), pp. 540–69

Felstead, Ruth, 'How did elementary schools under the control of the Birmingham and Worcester School Boards between 1878 and 1903 contribute to the fostering of morality and patriotism in youthful future citizens?', *History of Education Researcher*, 104 (2019), 109–18

Finnemore, John, *Social Life in Wales* (London, 1922)

Firpo, Christina and Margaret Jacobs, 'Taking children, ruling colonies: child removal and colonial subjugation in Australia, Canada, French Indochina, and the United States, 1870–1950s', *Journal of World History*, 29, 4 (2018), 529–62

Fletcher, H. L. V., *Portrait of the Wye Valley* (London, 1968)

Flett, Keith, 'Sex or class revisited: the education of working-class women and men in mid-nineteenth-century England', *History of Education*, 24, 2 (1995), 159–64

Franklin, Barry M., 'The state of curriculum history', *History of Education, 28, 4 (1999), 459–76*

Franklin, Jonathan, 'Disability panic: the making of the normal school teacher', *Victorian Studies*, 62, 4 (2020), 644–67

Fréine, Seán de, 'The dominance of the English language in the 19th century', in Diarmaid Ó Muirithe (ed.), *The English Language in Ireland* (Cork, 1977), pp. 71–87

Frevert, Ute et al., *Learning How to Feel: Children's Literature and the History of Emotional Socialization, c.1870–1970* (Oxford, 2014)

Fromkin, Victoria and Robert Rodman, *An Introduction to Language*, 4th edn (Toronto, 1988)

Gallagher, John, *Learning Languages in Early Modern England* (Oxford, 2019)

Gardner, Phil, *The Lost Elementary Schools of Victorian England* (London, 1984)

--- 'The giant at the front: young teachers and corporal punishment in inter-war elementary schools', *History of Education*, 25, 2 (1996), 141–63

Gedi, Noa and Yigal Elam, 'Collective memory: what is it?', *History and Memory*, 8, 1 (1996), 30–50

George, W. R. P., *The Making of Lloyd George* (London, 1976)

Gillard, Derek, *Education in England: a history* (2018). Online at: *www.educationengland.org.uk/history* (accessed 25 March 2024)

Ginswick, Jules (ed.), *Labour and the Poor in England and Wales, 1849-51: Vol. III The Mining and Manufacturing Districts of South Wales and North Wales* (London, 1983)

Gleason, Mona, 'Avoiding the agency trap: caveats for historians of children, youth and education', *History of Education*, 45, 4 (2016), 446–59

Gramich, Katie, 'Narrating the nation: telling stories of Wales', *North American Journal of Welsh Studies*, 6, 1 (2011). Retrieved from: *https://www.academia.edu/3740391/Narrating_the_Nation_Telling_stories_of_Wales* (accessed 25 March 2024)

Green, Anna, 'Individual remembering and "collective memory": theoretical presuppositions and contemporary debates', *Oral History*, 32, 2 (2004), 35–42

Griffin, Emma, *Liberty's Dawn: A People's History of the Industrial Revolution* (New Haven, 2013)

--- 'The emotions of motherhood: love, culture, and poverty in Victorian Britain', *American Historical Review*, 123, 1 (2018), 60–85

--- *Bread Winner: An Intimate History of the Victorian Economy* (New Haven, 2020)

Griffith, D. M., *Nationality in the Sunday School Movement: A Comparative Study of the Sunday School Movement in England and Wales* (Bangor, 1925)

Griffith, William P., 'Schooling and society', in J. Gwynfor Jones (ed.), *Class, Community and Culture in Tudor Wales* (Cardiff, 1989), pp. 79–119

Griffith, Wynne G., *Yr Ysgol Sul: Penodau ar Hanes yr Ysgol Sul* (Caernarfon, 1936)

Grigg, Russell, *History of Trinity College Carmarthen, 1848–1998* (Cardiff, 1998)

--- 'The origins and growth of ragged schools in Wales, 1847– *c.*1900', *History of Education*, 31, 3 (2002), 227–43

--- '"Nurseries of ignorance"? Private adventure and dame schools for the working classes in nineteenth-century Wales', *History of Education*, 34, 3 (2005), 243–62

--- '"You should love your country and should ever strive to be worthy of your fatherland": identity, British values and St David's Day in elementary schools in Wales, c.1885–1920', *Welsh History Review*, 29, 1 (2018), 99–125

--- '"Wading through children's tears": the emotional experiences of elementary school inspections, 1839–1911', *History of Education*, 49, 5 (2020), 597–616

Gruffudd, Pyrs, 'The countryside as educator: schools, rurality and citizenship in inter-war Wales', *Journal of Historical Geography*, 22, 4 (1996), 412–23

Gwenallt et al., *Triwyr Penllyn* (Cardiff, 1956)

Halbwachs, Maurice, *On Collective Memory* (1925; London, 1992)

Hall, Catherine, 'Making colonial subjects: education in the age of empire', *History of Education*, 37, 6 (2008), 773–87

Harding, F. J. W., 'Matthew Arnold and Wales', *Transactions of the Honourable Society of Cymmrodorion* (1963), 251–72

Hardwick, G. H., *Pengam Board School* (Risca, 1980)

Harling, Philip, 'The centrality of locality: the local state, local democracy, and local consciousness in Late-Victorian and Edwardian Britain', *Journal of Victorian Culture*, 9, 2 (2004), 216–34

Harrison, Wilfred, *Greenhill School Tenby 1896–1964: An Educational and Social History* (Cardiff, 1979)

Hassard, John and Michael Rowlinson, 'Researching Foucault's research: organization and control in Joseph Lancaster's Monitorial Schools', *Organization*, 9, 4 (2002), 615–39

Hawkins, Roger, *How Second Languages Are Learned* (Cambridge, 2019)

Heathorn, Stephen, *For Home, Country, and Race: Constructing Gender, Class, and Englishness in the Elementary School, 1880–1914* (Toronto, 2000)

Hechter, Michael, *Internal Colonialism: the Celtic Fringe in British National Development, 1536–1966* (London, 1978)

Hendrick, Harry, *Children, Childhood and English Society 1880–1990* (Cambridge, 1997)

Hind, Robert J., 'Elementary schools in nineteenth-century England: their social and historiographical contexts', *Historical Reflections / Réflexions Historiques*, 11, 2 (1984), 189–205

Hobsbawm, Eric, 'Language, culture and national identity', *Social Research*, 63, 4 (1996), 1065–80

Hodson, Jane, 'Talking like a servant: What nineteenth century novels can tell us about the social history of the language', *Journal of Historical Sociolinguistics*, 2, 1 (2016), 27–46

Hoegaerts, Josephine, 'Silence as borderland: a semiotic approach to the "silent" pupil in nineteenth-century vocal education', *Paedagogica Historica*, 53, 5 (2017), 514–27

Hogan, David, 'The market revolution and disciplinary power: Joseph Lancaster and the psychology of the early classroom system', *History of Education Quarterly*, 29, 3 (1981), 381–417

Holt, Eileen, 'The Provencal Not', *Planet*, 8 (1971), 33–5

--- 'Mistral and the Welsh', *Transactions of the Honourable Society of Cymmrodorion* (1983), 157–63

Honan, Park, *Matthew Arnold: A Life* (London, 1981)

Horn, Pamela, *Education in Rural England, 1800–1914* (Dublin, 1978)

--- 'School Log Books', in K. M. Thompson (ed.), *Short Guides to Records, Second Series* (London, 1997)

Horbec, Ivana and Maja Matasović, 'Voices in a country divided: linguistic choices in early modern Croatia', in Vladislav Rjéoutski and Willem Frijhoff (eds), *Language Choice in Enlightenment Europe. Education, Sociability, and Governance* (Amsterdam, 2018), pp. 111–42

Howell, David W., *Land and People in Nineteenth-century Wales* (London, 1977)

--- *Patriarchs and Parasites: The Gentry of South-west Wales in the Eighteenth Century* (Cardiff, 1986)

--- *The Rural Poor in Eighteenth-century Wales* (Cardiff, 2000)

Howkins, Alun, *Reshaping Rural England: A Social History, 1850–1925* (London, 1991)

Howse, W. H., *School and Bell: Four Hundred Years of a Welsh Grammar School* (Halesowen, 1956)

Hughes, Colin P. F., 'A history of schools in Radnorshire: the Knighton area', *Radnorshire Society Transactions*, 65 (1995), 47–63

Hughes, J. Elwyn, *Arloeswr Dwyieithedd: Dan Isaac Davies, 1839–1887* (Cardiff, 1984)

--- *Canmlwyddiant Ysgol Dyffryn Ogwen* (Llangefni, 1995)

--- and André Lomozik, *Canmlwyddiant Ysgol y Cefnfaes Bethesda ynghyd â Hanes Canolfan Gymdeithasol y Cefnfaes* (Bethesda, 2007)

Hughes, Mary, *Gobaith a Gorthrwm: Golwg ar Addysg Elfennol a Chynradd Dalgylch Penygroes* (Penygroes, 2010)

Hughes, T. J., *The 'Old' School, Llantwit Major, A History* (1974)

Hulme, Tom, '"A nation depends on its children": school buildings and citizenship in England and Wales, 1900–1939', *Journal of British Studies*, 54, 2 (2015), 406–32

Humphreys, Emyr, *The Taliesin Tradition: The Quest for Welsh Identity* (London, 1983)

Humphries, Jane, *Childhood and Child Labour in the British Industrial Revolution* (Cambridge, 2010)

Humphreys, Melvin, *The Crisis of Community: Montgomeryshire, 1680–1815* (Cardiff, 1996)

Humphries, Stephen, *Hooligans or Rebels? An Oral History of Working-class Childhood and Youth, 1889–1939* (Oxford, 1981)

Hurt, John, *Education in Evolution: Church, State, Society and Popular Education 1800–1870* (London, 1971)

––– *Elementary Schooling and the Working Classes, 1860–1918* (London, 1979)

Jabbar, Huriya, 'The case of "payment-by-results": re-examining the effects of an incentive programme in nineteenth-century English schools', *Journal of Educational Administration and History*, 45, 3 (2013), 220–43

James, Allan, *John Morris-Jones* (Cardiff, 2011)

James, David C. and Brian Davies, 'The genesis of school inspection in south east Wales 1839–1843: issues of social control and accountability', *History of Education*, 38, 5 (2009), 667–80

––– 'Patterns of and influences on elementary school attendance in early Victorian industrial Monmouthshire 1839–1865', *History of Education*, 46, 3 (2017), 290–305

James, E. Wyn, 'Griffith Jones (1684–1761) of Llanddowror and his "striking experiment in mass religious education" in Wales in the Eighteenth Century', *Carmarthenshire Antiquary*, 56 (2020), 63–73

James, J. Douglas, *The History of Haverfordwest Grammar School* (1961)

Jenkins, Geraint H., '"An old and much honoured soldier": Griffith Jones, Llanddowror', *Welsh History Review*, 11, 4 (1983), 449–68

––– *A Concise History of Wales* (Cambridge, 2007)

––– (ed.), *The Welsh Language Before the Industrial Revolution* (Cardiff, 1997)

--- (ed.), *Language and Community in the Nineteenth Century* (Cardiff, 1998)
--- (ed.), *The Welsh Language and its Social Domains, 1801–1911* (Cardiff, 2000)
Jenkins, R. T., *A Sketch of the History of Bala Grammar School, 1713–1893* (1951)
Jernsletten, Nils, 'Sami language communities and the conflict between Sami and Norwegian', in Ernst H. Jahr (ed.), *Language Conflict and Language Planning* (New York, 1993), pp. 115–32
Johnes, Martin, *A History of Sport in Wales* (Cardiff, 2005)
--- *Wales: England's Colony?* (Cardigan, 2019)
--- 'Education, the decline of Welsh and why communities matter more than classrooms', 19 February 2020, https://nation.cymru/opinion/education-the-decline-of-welsh-and-why-communities-matter-more-than-classrooms/ (accessed 25 March 2024)
--- 'Education of the people, by the people: the elementary school in Victorian Wales', *Welsh History Review*, 32, 1 (2024)
Johnson, Richard, 'Educational policy and social control in early Victorian England', *Past & Present*, 49, 1, (1970), 96–119
Jones, Aled Gruffydd, '"One language is quite sufficient for the mass": metropolitan journalism, the British state and the "vernacular" periodical', in David Finkelstein (ed.), *The Edinburgh History of the British and Irish Press* (Edinburgh, 2020), pp. 313–36
--- 'Multilingualism in periodical studies: a social history perspective', *Journal of European Periodical Studies*, 7, 1 (2022), 61–2
Jones, Dot, *Statistical Evidence Relating to the Welsh Language, 1801–1911* (Cardiff, 1998)
Jones, E. D., 'The journal of William Roberts ("Nefydd")', *National Library of Wales Journal*, 8, 2 (1953) to 10, 3 (1958)
Jones, E. K., *The Story of Education in a Welsh Border Parish or The Schools of Cefnmawr, 1786–1933* (Wrexham, 1933)
Jones, Gareth Elwyn, *Which Nations' Schools? Direction and Devolution in Welsh Education in the Twentieth Century* (Cardiff, 1990)
--- 'Education, 1815–1974', in David W. Howell (ed.), *Pembrokeshire County History, Vol. IV: Modern Pembrokeshire, 1815–1974* (Haverfordwest, 1993), pp. 389–417
--- 'Education and nationhood in Wales: an historiographical analysis', *Journal of Educational Administration and History*, 38, 3 (2006), 263–77

— and Gordon Wynne Roderick, *A History of Education in Wales* (Cardiff, 2003)

Jones, Geraint, *'Rhen Sgŵl: Canmlwyddiant Ysgol Trefor, 1978* (Trefor, 1978)

Jones, Geraint Wyn, *Dyddiadur Ysgol: Ysgol y Manod 1867–1967* (Blaenau Ffestiniog, 1997)

Jones, Gwilym Arthur, 'David James (Defynnog) 1865–1928, in the context of Welsh education', *Transactions of the Honourable Society of Cymmrodorion*, (1978), pp. 267–84

Jones, Idwal, 'The voluntary system at work: a history of the British School Society', *Transactions of the Honourable Society of Cymmrodorion* (1931–2), 72–164

Jones, J., *Towyn, Ysgol Penwaun Cofnodion Canrif 1880–1980* (Bangor, 1981)

Jones, J. Clifford, 'A history of the schools and education in Buckley', *Flintshire Historical Society Publications*, 15 (1854–5), 83–101

Jones, J. R., *Ysgol Llangynfelyn, 1876–1976* (Talybont, 1976)

Jones, Jon Meirion, *Ôl Troed T. Llew: Deg Taith lenyddol* (Llandysul, 2011)

Jones, M. G., *The Charity School Movement: A Study of Eighteenth Century Puritanism in Action* (Cambridge, 1938)

Jones, Matthew, 'On nineteenth-century Welsh literacies, and the "Blue Book" education reports of 1847', *Branch*. Retrieved from: https://branchcollective.org/?ps_articles=matthew-jones-on-nineteenth-century-welsh-literacies-and-the-blue-book-education-reports-of-1847 (accessed 6 April 2024)

Jones, Owen E., *Deddf Addysg Ganolraddol Cymru 1889: Cloriannu Can Mlynedd* (Cardiff, 1990)

Jones, Patricia, 'The use of pupil-teachers at Newbridge-on-Wye school, 1872–1907', *Radnorshire Society Transactions*, 56 (1986), 72–80

Jones, Rachael, *Crime, Courts and Community in Mid-Victorian Wales* (Cardiff, 2018)

Jones, Rhian E., *Petticoat Heroes: Gender, Culture and Popular Protest in the Rebecca Riots* (Cardiff, 2015)

Jones, Tegwyn, 'Y "Welsh Not" yng Ngheredigion', *Llafar Gwlad*, 85 (2004), 27

Jones, W. R., *Addysg Ddwyieithog yng Nghymru* (Caernarfon, 1963)

— *Bilingualism in Welsh Education* (Cardiff, 1966)

Jones-Davies, D. Clive, 'Trinty College, Carmarthen: the early years', in Gareth Elwyn Jones (ed.), *Education, Culture and Society: Some Perspectives on the Nineteenth and Twentieth Centuries* (Cardiff, 1991)

Kaestle, Carl F. (ed.), *Joseph Lancaster and the Monitorial School Movement: A Documentary History* (New York, 1973)

Keane, Ann, 'O. M. Edwards: ei ddylanwad ar y Gymraeg mewn ysgolion', *Wales Journal of Education*, 20, 1 (2018), 26–45

--- (ed.), *Watchdogs or Visionaries? Perspectives on the History of the Education Inspectorate in Wales* (Cardiff, 2022)

Kelleher, Margaret, *The Maamtrasna Murders: Language, Life and Death in Nineteenth-century Ireland* (Dublin, 2018)

Khleif, Bud B., *Language, Ethnicity, and Education in Wales* (1980; De Gruyter, 2019)

Knight, L. Stanley, *Welsh Independent Grammar Schools to 1600* (Newtown, n.d.)

Knox, Eva, 'Welsh education sixty years ago', *Welsh Outlook*, 1, 8 (1914), 360–2

Krause, Michael, 'The condition of native North American languages: the need for realistic assessment and action', *International Journal of the Sociology of Language*, 132 (1998), 9–22

Lancy, David F., 'Unmasking Children's Agency', *AnthropoChildren*, 1, 2 (2012), 1–20

Landahl, Joakim, 'The eye of power(-lessness): on the emergence of the panoptical and synoptical classroom', *History of Education*, 42, 6 (2013), 803–21

--- 'Emotions, power and the advent of mass schooling', *Paedagogica Historica*, 51, 1–2 (2015), 104–16

Larson-Hall, Jenifer, 'Weighing the benefits of studying a foreign language at a younger starting age in a minimal input situation', *Second Language Research*, 24, 1 (2008), 35–63

Leech, Alan, *Dan Jenkins: A Biography* (Talybont, 2011)

Lewis, E. Glyn, *Bilingualism and Bilingual Education* (Oxford, 1981)

Lewis, Saunders, 'O. M. Edwards', in Gwenallt et al., *Triwyr Penllyn* (Cardiff, 1956)

Lightbown, Past M. and Nina Spada, *How Languages are Learned* (Oxford, 2013)

Lloyd, Huw Spencer, *The History of Aberystwyth County School, 1896–1973* (Aberystwyth, 1996)

Lloyd, Tecwyn, *Drych o Genedl* (Swansea, 1987)

Lloyd Jones, Gareth, 'Welsh in schools and the National Curriculum', *Transactions of the Honourable Society of Cymmrodorion* (1991), 267–83

Logan, John, 'Book learning: the experience of reading in the national school, 1831–1900', in Bernadette Cunningham and Máire Kennedy (eds), *The Experience of Reading: Irish Historical Perspectives* (Dublin, 1999), pp. 173–95

Loparco, Fabiana, 'Former teachers' and pupils' autobiographical accounts of punishment in Italian rural primary schools during Fascism', *History of Education*, 46, 5 (2017), 618–30

McCulloch, Gary, *The Struggle for the History of Education* (London, 2011)

––– 'Compulsory school attendance and the elementary education act of 1870', *British Journal of Educational Studies*, 68, 5 (2020), 523–40

MacDonagh, Oliver, 'The nineteenth-century revolution in government: a reappraisal', *Historical Journal*, 1 (1958), 52–67

MacKinnon, Kenneth, 'Education and social control: the case of Gaelic Scotland', *Scottish Educational Studies*, 4 (1972), 125–37

McLelland, Nicola, 'The history of language learning and teaching in Britain', *The Language Learning Journal*, 46, 1 (2018), 6–16

Maddox, C. W., 'Abbeycwmhir school: the chronicle of a small rural school', *Radnorshire Society Transactions*, 49 (1979), 64–74

Maguire, Moira J. and Séamus Ó Cinnéide, '"A good beating never hurt anyone": the punishment and abuse of children in twentieth century Ireland', *Journal of Social History*, 38, 3 (2005), 635–52

Mair, Laura M., '"Give my love": community and companionship among former ragged school scholars', *Family & Community History*, 21, 3 (2018), 166–79

––– 'They "come for a lark": London Ragged School Union teaching advice in practice, 1844–70', *Studies in Church History*, 55 (2019), 324–46

––– 'A "transcript of their mind"? ragged school literacy in the mid-nineteenth century', *Journal of Victorian Culture*, 24, 1 (2019), 18–32

Malmsheimer, L. M., '"Imitation white man": images of transformation at the Carlisle Indian school', *Studies in Visual Communication*, 11, 4, (1985), 54–75

Mandler, Peter, 'What is "national identity"? Definitions and applications in modern British historiography', *Modern Intellectual History*, 3, 2 (2006), 271–97

Marcham, A. J., 'The Revised Code of Education, 1862: reinterpretations and misinterpretations', *History of Education*, 10, 2 (1981), 81–99

Margolis, Eric and Sheila Fram, 'Caught napping: images of surveillance, discipline and punishment on the body of the schoolchild', *History of Education*, 36, 2 (2007), 191–211

Marsden, William E., *An Anglo-Welsh Teaching Dynasty: The Adams Family from the 1840s to the 1930s* (London, 1997)

Meacham, Standish, *A Life Apart: The English Working Class, 1890–1914* (London, 1977)

Medhurst, Andy, *A National Joke: Popular Comedy and English Cultural Identities* (London, 2007)

Meredith, R., 'Early history of the North Wales Training College', *Transaction of the Caernarvonshire History Society*, 7 (1946), 64–87

Meyerhoff, Miriam, *Introducing Sociolinguistics* (London, 2006)

Michael, Ian, *The Teaching of English from the Sixteenth Century to 1870* (Cambridge, 1987)

Middleton, Jacob, 'Thomas Hopley and mid-Victorian attitude to corporal punishment', *History of Education*, 34, 6 (2005), 599–615

––– 'The experience of corporal punishment in schools, 1890–1940', *History of Education*, 37, 2 (2008), 253–75

––– 'The cock of the school: a cultural history of playground violence in Britain, 1880–1940', *Journal of British Studies*, 52, 4 (2013), 887–907

Miller, Susan, 'Assent as agency in the early years of the Children of the American Revolution', *Journal of the History of Childhood and Youth*, 9, 1 (2016), 48–65

Millward, E. G., *Cenedl o Bobl Ddewrion: Agweddau ar Lenyddiaeth Oes Victoria* (Llandysul, 1991)

Mitch, David F., *The Rise of Popular Literacy in Victorian England: The Influence of Private Choice and Public Literacy* (Philadelphia, 1992)

Monroe, Ann, 'Shame solutions: how shame impacts school-aged children and what teachers can do to help', *The Education Forum*, 73, 1 (2009), 58–66

Morgan, J. Vyrnwy, *The Welsh Mind in Evolution* (London, 1925)

Morgan, S. E., *A Welsh Not* (published by the author, 2021)

Morgan, T. M., *Caerleon Endowed Schools, 1724–1983* (Risca, 1983)
Mostyn, J., 'Radnorshire School log books', *Radnorshire Society transactions*, vols 2–8 (1932–8)
Mugglestone, Lynda, *'Talking Proper': The Rise of Accent as Social Symbol* (Oxford, 2003)
Murray, Nicholas, *A Life of Matthew Arnold* (London, 1996)
Musgrove, P. W., *Society and Education in England since 1800* (London, 1968)
Nash, Gerallt D., *Victorian School-days in Wales* (Cardiff, 1991)
Neville, Grace, '"He spoke to me in English, I answered him in Irish": language shift in archives', in Jean Brihault (ed.), *L'Irlande ses langues: Actes du Colloque 1992 de la Sociéte Francaise d'Étude Irlandaises* (Rennes, 1993)
Ní Chiosáin, Máire, 'Language shift in early twentieth-century Ireland', *Proceedings of the Harvard Celtic Colloquium*, 26/27 (2006/7), 370–84
Nikolov, Marianne (ed.), *The Age Factor and Early Language Learning* (Berlin, 2009)
Nor, Norbahira Mohamad and Radzuwan Ab Rashidb, 'A review of theoretical perspectives on language learning and acquisition', *Kasetsart Journal of Social Sciences*, 39, 1 (2018), 161–7
Ó Ciosáin, Niall, 'Gaelic culture and language shift', in Laurence M. Geary and Margaret Kelleher (eds), *Nineteenth-century Ireland: A Guide to Recent Research* (Dublin, 2005), pp. 136–52
O'Donoghue, Tom and Teresa O' Doherty, *Irish Speakers and Schooling in the Gaeltacht, 1900 to the Present* (Basingstoke, 2019)
Offord, Derek, 'Sociolinguistics and history: An interdisciplinary view of bilingualism in imperial Russia', *Journal of Historical Sociolinguistics*, 6, 1 (2020), 1–33
Orme, Nicholas, *English Schools in the Middle Ages* (London, 1973)
——— *Medieval Schools* (New Haven, 2006)
——— 'Schools and languages in medieval England', in Mary Carruthers (ed.), *Language in Medieval Britain: Networks and Exchanges* (Donington, 2015), pp. 152–67
Olsen, Stephanie, *Juvenile Nation: Youth, Emotions and the Making of the Modern British Citizen, 1880–1914* (London, 2014)
——— 'The History of Childhood and the Emotional', *History Compass*, 15, 11 (2017)

--- 'Children and childhood', in Heather Ellis (ed.), *A Cultural History of Education in the Age of Empire (1800–1920)* (London, 2020), pp. 59–74

Ostler, Nicholas, *Empires of the Word: A Language History of the World* (London, 2005)

Osterhammel, Jürgen, *The Transformation of the World: A Global History of the Nineteenth Century* (Princeton, 2014)

Owen, William (ed.), *Bwrw Cyfrif 'Rôl Canrif* (Llanrwst, 1999)

Owen-Jones, Shelia M., 'Religious influence and educational progress in Glamorgan, 1800–33', *Welsh History Review*, 13 (1986), 72–86

Parry, Gwenfair and Mari A. Williams (eds), *The Welsh Language and the 1891 Census* (Cardiff, 1991)

Parry-Jones, D., *Welsh Children's Games & Pastimes* (Denbigh, 1964)

Parry-Williams, T. H., *John Rhŷs, 1840–1915* (Cardiff, 1954)

Parsons, Ben, *Punishment and Medieval Education* (Woodbridge, 2018)

Paulasto, Heli, Rob Penhallurick and Benjamin Jones, *Welsh English* (Berlin, 2020)

Pavlenko, Anita, *The Bilingual Mind and What it Tells us About Language and Thought* (Cambridge, 2014)

Paz, D. G., 'Working-class education as social control in England 1860–1918', *History of Education Quarterly*, 21, 4 (1981), 493–9

Peate, Iorwerth C., 'Diwylliant gwerin', *Transactions of the Honourable Society of Cymmrodorion* (1937), 241–50

Phillipson, Robert, *Linguistic Imperialism* (Oxford, 1992)

Pooley, Siân, '"All we parents want is that our children's health and lives should be regarded": child health and parental concern in England, c.1860–1910', *Social History of Medicine*, 23, 3 (2010), 528–48

--- 'Parenthood, child-rearing and fertility in England, 1850–1914', *The History of the Family*, 18, 1 (2013), 83–106

Porter, Bernard, *The Absent-Minded Imperialists: Empire, Society and Culture in Britain* (Oxford, 2004)

Powell, Glenville, 'Hanes plwyf Crai: VI addysg yng Nghrai', *Brycheiniog*, 10 (1964), 39–68

Power, Kelly, 'The influence of changing discourses of childhood on 1860s educational policy', *History of Education*, 51, 1 (2022), 1–21

Pritchard, Elfyn, 'Elin Angharad', in *Ysgol Ddoe* (Llandysul, 1978), pp. 29–37

Pretty, David A., *Two Centuries of Anglesey Schools, 1700–1902* (Llangefni, 1977)

Pritchard, John, *Rhamant Bywyd Athro* (Bala, 1927)
--- *Hanes yr Ysgol Sir ym Mrynrefail, Arfon* (Caernarfon, 1940)
Pryce, Huw, *J. E. Lloyd and the Creation of Welsh History: Renewing a Nation's Past* (Cardiff, 2011)
Pryce, W. T. R., 'Industrialism, urbanization and the maintenance of culture areas: north-east Wales in the mid-nineteenth century', *Welsh History Review*, 7 (1974–5), 307–40
--- 'The diffusion of the "Welch Circulating Charity Schools" in Eighteenth-Century Wales', *Welsh History Review*, 25 (2011), 486–519
Pugh, Martin, *State and Society: A Social and Political History of Britain*, 2nd edn (London, 1999)
Raftery, Deidre, Jane McDermid, and Gareth Elwyn Jones, 'Social change and education in Ireland, Scotland and Wales: historiography on nineteenth-century schooling', *History of Education*, 36, 4–5 (2007), 447–63
Reay, Barry, 'The context and meaning of popular literacy: some evidence from nineteenth century rural England', *Past & Present*, 131 (1991), 89–129
Reyhner, Jon, 'American Indian language policy and school success', *Journal of Educational Issues of Language Minority Students*, 12 (1993), 35–59
--- 'American Indian languages and United States language policy', in Willem Fase, Koen Jaspaert and Sjaak Kroon (eds), *The State of Minority Languages: International Perspectives on Survival and Decline* (Lisse, 1995), pp. 229–48
Ritchie, Elizabeth, '"Alive to the advantages of education". Problems in using the new statistical account of research education: a case study of the Isle of Skye', *Northern Scotland*, 7 (2016), 85–92
Rjéoutski, Vladislav and Willem Frijhoff (eds), *Language Choice in Enlightenment Europe. Education, Sociability, and Governance* (Amsterdam, 2018)
Robbins, Keith, *Nineteenth-century Britain: Integration and Diversity* (Oxford, 1995)
Roberts, Brynley F., 'Welsh Scholarship at Merthyr Tydfil', *Merthyr Historian*, 10 (1999), 51–62
Roberts, David T., 'The genesis of the Cross Commission', *Journal of Educational Administration and History*, 17, 2 (1985), 30–8

Roberts, Gwyneth Tyson, *The Language of the Blue Books: The Perfect Instrument of Empire* (Cardiff, 1998)

Roderick, Gordon, 'Education, culture and industry in Wales in the nineteenth century', *Welsh History Review*, 13 (1987), 438–52

--- 'Industry, technical manpower and education: south Wales in the nineteenth century', *History of Education*, 19, 3 (1990), 211–18

--- 'The coalowners and mining education, South Wales: 1850–1914', *Morgannwg*, 43 (1999), 36–62

--- '"A fair representation of all interests"? The Aberdare report on intermediate and higher education in Wales, 1881', *History of Education*, 30, 3 (2001), 233–50

Roehr-Brackin, K. and A. Tellier, 'The role of language-analytic ability in children's instructed second language learning', *Studies in Second Language Acquisition*, 41, 5 (2019), 1111–31

Roper, Michael, 'Re-remembering the soldier hero: the psychic and social construction of memory in personal narratives of the Great War', *History Workshop Journal*, 50 (2000), 181–204

Rose, Jonathan, 'Willingly to school: the working class response to elementary education in Britain, 1875–1918', *Journal of British Studies*, 32, 2 (1993), 114–38

--- *The Intellectual Life of the British Working Classes*, 3rd edn (New Haven, 2021)

Ross, Ellen, *Love and Toil: Motherhood in Outcast London, 1870–1918* (Oxford, 1993)

Rosser, Siwan M., *Darllen y Dychymyg: Creu Ystyron Newydd i Blant a Phlentyndod yn Llenyddiaeth y Bedwaredd Ganrif ar Bymtheg* (Cardiff, 2020)

Rousmaniere, Kate, Kari Dehli and Ning De Coninck-Smith (eds), *Discipline, Moral Regulation, and Schooling: A Social History* (London, 1997)

Seaborne, Malcolm, *Schools in Wales 1500–1900: A Social and Architectural History* (Denbigh, 1992)

Selleck, R. J., *The New Education: Background 1870–1914* (London, 1968)

Sengupta, Parna, 'An object lesson in colonial pedagogy', *Comparative Studies in Society and History*, 45, 1 (2003), 96–121

Skeel, C., 'The cattle trade between Wales and England from the fifteenth to the nineteenth centuries', *Transactions of the Royal Historical Society*, 9 (1926), 135–58

Skutnabb-Kangas, Tove and Jim Cummins (eds), *Minority Education: From Shame to Struggle* (Clevedon, 1988)

Smith, Dai, *Wales! Wales?* (London, 1984)

Smith, David (ed.), *A People and a Proletariat: Essays in the History of Wales, 1780–1980* (London, 1980)

Smith, Frank, *A History of English Elementary Education, 1760–1902* (London, 1931)

Smith, Kevin, *Curriculum, Culture and Citizenship Education in Wales* (London, 2016)

Smith, Robert, *Schools, Politics and Society: Elementary Education in Wales, 1870–1902* (Cardiff, 1999)

Snell, K. D. M., 'Deferential bitterness: the social outlook of the rural proletariat in eighteenth- and nineteenth-century England and Wales', in M. L. Bush (ed.), *Social Orders and Social Classes in Europe since 1500: Studies in Social Stratification* (London, 1992), pp. 158–84

— — — 'The Sunday-school movement in England and Wales: child labour, denominational control and working-class culture', *Past & Present*, 164 (1999), 122–68

— — — 'The culture of local xenophobia', *Social History*, 28, 1 (2003), 1–30

Soares, Claudia, 'Emotions, senses, experience and the history of education', *History of Education*, 52, 2–3 (2023), 516–38

Stead, Peter, 'Schools and society in Glamorgan before 1914', *Morgannwg*, 19 (1975), 39–56

Stearns, Peter N. and Clio Stearns, 'American schools and the uses of shame: an ambiguous history', *History of Education*, 46 (2017), 58–75

Stephens, W. B., *Education, Literacy and Society, 1830–70: The Geography of Diversity in Provincial England* (Manchester, 1987)

Stevens, Catrin, *Stori'r Gymraeg* (Llandysul, 2009)

Strange, Julie-Marie, *Fatherhood and the British Working Class, 1865–1914* (Cambridge, 2015)

Sutherland, Gillian, 'A view of education records in the nineteenth and twentieth centuries', *Archives*, 15, 66 (1981), 79–85

— — — 'Education', in F. M. L. Thompson (ed.), *The Cambridge Social History of Britain, 1750–1950* (Cambridge, 1990), pp. 119–69

Swartz, Rebecca, *Education and Empire: Children, Race and Humanitarianism in the British Settler Colonies* (Basingstoke, 2019)

––– 'Histories of empire and histories of education', *History of Education*, 52, 2–3 (2023), 442–61

Thiong'o, Ngũgĩ wa, *Decolonising the Mind: The Politics of Language in African Literature* (London, 1986)

Thody, Angela M., 'School management in the nineteenth-century elementary schools: a day of the life of a headteacher', *History of Education*, 23, 4 (1994), 355–73

Thom, Deborah, '"Beating children is wrong": domestic life, psychological thinking and the permissive turn', in Lucy Delap, Ben Griffin and Abigail Wills (eds), *The Politics of Domestic Authority in Britain since 1800* (Basingstoke, 2009), pp. 261–83

Thomas, Brinley, 'Wales and the Atlantic economy', *Scottish Journal of Political Economy*, 6, 3 (1959), 169–92

––– 'A cauldron of rebirth: population and the Welsh language in the nineteenth century', *Welsh History Review*, 13, 4 (1987), 418–37

Thomas, David, 'Brad y llyfrau gleision', *Lleufer Cylchgrawn Cymdeithas Addysg y Gweithwyr yng Nghymru*, 3, 3 (1947), 94–7

––– *Silyn: Robert Silyn Roberts, 1871–1930* (Liverpool, 1956)

Thomas, Dewi W., 'Addysg yng Nghredigion, 1800–1850, yn ôl y cofiannau', *Ceredigion*, 6, 1 (1968), 45–89

Thomas, Richard, *Bangor Normal College, 1858–1958 = Coleg Normal, Bangor, 1858–1958* (Bangor, 1996)

Thomas, M. Wynn, *In the Shadow of the Pulpit: Literature and Nonconformist Wales* (Cardiff, 2009)

Thompson, E. P., *The Making of the English Working Class* (London, 1963)

Thompson, Paul, *The Edwardians: The Remaking of British Society*, 2nd edn (London, 1992)

Thomson, Alistair, 'Anzac memories: putting popular memory theory into practice in Australia', *Oral History*, 18, 1 (1990), 25–31

Tropp, Asher, *The School Teachers: The Growth of the Teaching Profession in England and Wales from 1800 to the Present Day* (London, 1977)

Trudgill, P., *Accent, Dialect and the School* (London, 1975)

Turnbull, A., 'Learning her womanly work: the elementary school curriculum, 1870–1914', in Felicity Hunt (ed.), *Lessons for Life: The Schooling of Girls and Women 1850–1950* (Oxford, 1987), pp. 83–100

Vernon, James, *Distant Strangers: How Britain Became Modern* (Berkley, 2014)

Verstraete, Pieter and Josephine Hoegaerts, 'Educational soundscapes: tuning in to sounds and silences in the history of education', *Paedagogica Historica*, 53, 5 (2017), 491–7

Vincent, David, *Literacy and Popular Culture: England, 1750–1914* (Cambridge, 1989)

Wallace, W., 'A pupil teacher in the 1850's', *The Vocational Aspect of Secondary and Further Education*, 4, 9 (1952), 124–8

Walsh, Patrick, 'Education and the "universalist" idiom of empire: Irish national school books in Ireland and Ontario', *History of Education*, 37 (2008), 645–60

Walvin, James, *A Child's World: A Social History of English Childhood, 1800–1914* (Harmondsworth, 1982)

Ward, Stephanie, 'Miners' bodies and masculine identity in Britain, c.1900–1950', *Cultural & Social History*, 18, 3 (2021), 443–6

Wardhugh, Ronald, *Languages in Competition: Dominance, Diversity, and Decline* (Oxford, 1987)

Watts, Ruth, 'Education, empire and social change in nineteenth century England', *Paedagogica Historica*, 45, 6 (2009), 773–86

Weaver, Heather A., 'Object lessons: a cultural genealogy of the dunce cap and the apple as visual tropes of American education', *Paedagogica Historica*, 48, 2 (2012), 215–41

Weber, Eugen, *Peasants into Frenchmen: The Modernization of Rural France, 1870–1914* (Stanford, 1976)

Webster, J. R., 'Dyheadau'r bedwaredd ganrif ar bymtheg', in Jac L. Williams (ed.), *Ysgrifau ar Addysg*, 4 (Cardiff, 1966), pp. 45–75

Webster, Roger, 'Education in Wales and the rebirth of a nation', *History of Education*, 19, 3 (1990), 183–94

――― *School and Community in Rural Wales* (Aberystwyth, 1991)

Wells, Fiona G. H., 'Addysg Gymraeg: achub ydd yr iaith?', *Y Traethodydd*, 155, (2000), 94–105

Welsh Department, Ministry of Education, *Education in Wales, 1847–1947* (London, 1948)

White, John, 'Philosophy and teacher education in England: the long view', *British Journal of Educational Studies*, 67, 2 (2019), 187–200

Whitehead, Clive, 'The historiography of British imperial education policy, Part I: India', *History of Education*, 34, 3 (2005), 315–29

――― 'The historiography of British Imperial education policy, Part II: Africa and the rest of the colonial empire', *History of Education*, 34, 4 (2005), 441–54

Williams, A. Bailey, 'Education in Montgomeryshire in the late nineteenth century', *Montgomeryshire Collections Relating to Montgomeryshire and its Borders*, 52 (1952), 83–106

Williams, Chris, '"Going underground"? The future of coalfield history revisited', *Morgannwg*, 42 (1998), 41–58

Williams, Daniel G. (ed.), *Raymond Williams: Who Speaks for Wales? Nation, Culture, Identity* (Cardiff, 2021)

Williams, Elizabeth, *Brethyn Cartref* (Llandysul, 1951)

Williams, Gareth W., 'The disenchantment of the world: innovation, crisis and change in Cardiganshire, c.1880–1910', *Ceredigion*, 9, 4 (1983), 303–21

Williams, Glanmor, *Religion, Language and Nationality in Wales: Historical Essays* (Cardiff, 1979)

Williams, Gwyn A., *When was Wales? A History of the Welsh* (Harmondsworth, 1985)

Williams, H. G., 'A study of the Kynnersley educational returns for Caernarfonshire', *Welsh History Review*, 13, 3 (1987), 300–27

--- 'Longueville Jones and Welsh education: The neglected case of a Victorian H. M. I.', *Welsh History Review*, 15, 1 (1990), 416–42

--- 'Longueville Jones, Ralph Lingen and inspectors' reports: a tragedy of Welsh education', *History of Education*, 25, 1 (1996), 19–36

--- 'Learning suitable to the situation of the poorest classes: the National Society and Wales 1811–1839', *Welsh History Review*, 19, 3 (1999), 425–52

--- 'Nation state versus national identity: state and inspectorate in Mid-Victorian Wales', *History of Education Quarterly*, 40, 2 (2000), 145–68

Williams, Herbert, *Davies the Ocean: Railway King and Coal Tycoon* (Cardiff, 1991)

Williams, Jac L. and Gwilym Rees Hughes (eds), *The History of Education in Wales* (Swansea, 1978)

Williams, M. E., *Hanes Ysgol Esgerdawe* (Llandysul, 1982)

Williams, Moses, *Addysg* (Liverpool, 1944)

Williams, Tim, 'Language, religion, culture', in Trevor Herbert and Gareth E. Jones, (eds), *Wales 1880–1914* (Cardiff, 1988), pp. 73–105

Williams, Vivian Parry, 'Y Welsh Not ym Mhenmachno', *Llafar Gwlad*, 66 (1999), 14

Willinsky, John, *Learning to Divide the World: Education at Empire's End* (Minneapolis, 1998)

Wingate, Henry, 'The natural method of teaching Latin: its origins, rationale, and prospects', *The Classical World*, 106, 3 (2013), 493–504

Winter, Jay, *Remembering War: The Great War between Memory and History in the Twentieth Century* (London, 2006)

Wolf, Nicholas. '"Scéal Grinn?" Jokes, puns, and the shaping of bilingualism in nineteenth-century Ireland', *Journal of British Studies*, 48, 1 (2009), 51–75

——— 'History and linguistics: the Irish language as a case study in an interdisciplinary approach to culture', in Nils Langer, Steffan Davies and Wim Vandenbussche (eds), *Language and History, Linguistics and Historiography* (Oxford, 2012), pp. 49–64

Wolfe, Patrick, 'Settler colonialism and the elimination of the native', *Journal of Genocide Research*, 8, 4 (2006), 387–409

Wright, Arthur, *The History of Lewis' School, Pengam* (Newtown, 1929)

Wright, Susannah, 'Teachers, family and community in urban elementary school: evidence from English school log books *c*.1880–1918', *History of Education*, 41, 2 (2012), 155–73

——— 'Moral instruction, urban poverty and English elementary schools in the late nineteenth century', in Nigel Goose and Katrina Honeyman (eds), *Childhood and Child Labour in Industrial England: Diversity and Agency, 1750–1914* (Farnham, 2013), pp. 277–95

Wyn, Hefin, *Ar Drywydd Niclas Y Glais: Comiwnydd Rhonc a Christion Gloyw* (Talybont, 2017)

Yeandle, Peter, *Citizenship, Nation and Empire: The Politics of History Teaching in England, 1870–1939* (Manchester, 2015)

Yates, Paula, 'Drawing up the battle lines: elementary schooling in the diocese of Bangor in the second decade of the nineteenth century', in Nigel Yates (ed.), *Bishop Burgess and his World: Culture, Religion and Society in Britain, Europe and North America in the Eighteenth and Nineteenth Century* (Cardiff, 2007), pp. 135–44

——— 'Saving souls on a shoestring: Welsh circulating schools in a century of change', *Studies in Church History*, 55 (2019), 274–89

Zastoupil, Lynn and Martin Moir (eds), *The Great Indian Education Debate: Documents Relating to the Orientalist-Anglicist Controversy, 1781–1843* (Richmond, 1999)

Theses

Bagworth, Hazel Joy, 'The Role of Agents, Visitors and Inspectors in the Development of Elementary Education, *c*.1826–*c*.1870' (unpublished PhD thesis, Brunel University, 1998)

Dunford, J. E., 'Her Majesty's Inspectorate of schools in England and Wales 1860–1870' (unpublished MEd thesis, Durham University, 1976)

Rees, L. M., 'A Critical Examination of Teacher Training in Wales, 1846–1898' (unpublished PhD thesis, University of Wales, Bangor, 1968)

Williams, H. G., 'Elementary Education in Caernarvonshire, 1839–1902' (unpublished PhD thesis, University of Wales, Bangor, 1981)

Williams, Tim, 'Language, Identity and Education in a Liberal State: The Anglicisation of Pontypridd, 1818–1920' (unpublished PhD thesis, University of Wales, Cardiff, 1989)

INDEX

Aaron, Jane, 23
Aberaman, 268, 269, 286
Aberdare, 266, 305
Aberffraw, 77, 119, 145, 183
Abergwili, 124, 130–1, 135, 165
Aberystwyth, 44, 253, 263–4
accents, 12, 18, 115, 171, 178, 213, 240, 330, 349–50; *see also* pronunciation
Adams, William, 115
adult education, 269
Africa, 14, 15, 343–4
agency, 28, 30, 240, 252–60, 270, 280, 286, 341
agriculture, 39, 88, 127, 266, 279, 282, 284–5, 294, 295
Allen, John, 207
Amlwch, 255, 301
Anglesey, 25, 55, 95, 98, 114, 145, 183, 201, 247, 264, 266, 286, 325
Anglesey Church Schoolmasters' Association, 95, 114
Anglicanism, 42, 44, 63, 85, 97, 101, 200, 203, 206, 215, 287, 303–4
anglicisation, 97, 112, 115, 184, 306, 317–35, 352–61
aristocracy, 44, 299
arithmetic, 38, 102, 109, 122, 138, 163, 173, 181, 215, 221, 258, 284
Arnold, Matthew, 12, 23, 90, 208–9, 286, 291

attendance *see* school attendance; truancy
autobiographical accounts, 1–2, 28–9, 47, 51, 53, 93, 131, 135–6, 147, 186, 241–52, 292, 333

Bala, 48, 83, 96, 101, 160, 174, 213, 325, 330
'Baled y Welsh Not' (Iwan), 15
Bancroft, John, 216–17, 220, 221
Baner ac Amserau Cymru, 225, 305
Bangor, 47, 64, 96–7, 114–15, 116, 131, 144, 167, 330, 355
Bangor Normal College, 64, 114–15, 116, 131, 167, 330, 355
Bassett, T. M., 302
beating *see* punishment
Beddgelert, 101, 110
Bell, Alexander, 57
Bellairs, H. W., 83–4, 207
Bethel, 126, 141, 159, 169–70, 176, 178, 245, 286
Bethesda, 167, 303
Bevan schools, 39, 45, 52, 201
Bible, 43, 49, 89, 94, 97, 98, 99, 224, 229, 268, 296
bilingual textbooks, 2, 181, 183, 202, 227
bilingualism, 116, 203, 225, 264, 300, 309, 317–21, 325–8, 330, 332, 335, 338, 346, 347, 359
Binns, B. J., 215, 226–7, 268, 284
Bischof, Christopher, 27, 127, 145, 352

Blaen-ffos, 126, 161
Blue Books
　outrage in response to, 12–13,
　　24–5, 45, 200, 201, 329, 331
　on parental attitudes to education,
　　280–1, 284
　perjorative comments on Welsh
　　language, 12–13, 45, 198, 329
　on physical punishments, 55, 56,
　　291
　on pupil indiscipline, 255
　on pupil teachers and monitors,
　　87–8
　references to the Welsh Not, 5,
　　45–6, 51
　on school attendance, 280–1, 285
　on school conditions, 40
　on Sunday schools, 98
　on teacher training, 63
　on teachers' competence in English,
　　41–2, 63, 90
　on teaching of English without use
　　of Welsh, 77, 79–80, 157,
　　296–7
　on teaching of Welsh, 97, 296
　on use of Bible to teach English, 89
　on use of Welsh to teach English,
　　13, 80, 91–2, 230, 296–7, 351
　Welsh Not associated with, 13, 18
Board of Education, 2, 9, 184, 185,
　　199–200
Board schools, 17, 25, 29, 118, 280,
　　305
Bodedern, 44, 54, 120
border areas, 37, 83, 178, 300, 326
boredom, 247–8, 256, 266
Borough Road School, 62, 63
Borrow, George, 295, 333, 336
Bourassa, Henri, 241
Bowstead, Joseph, 84
Brecon, 63, 147, 302–3
Breton language, 345
Bridgend, 39, 42, 282

Bridgend Society for the Education of
　　the Poor, 39
Brithdir, 160, 219
British Empire, 328, 343–4, 352–5,
　　356–7, 360; *see also* imperialism
British identity, 230, 352–5
British schools, 42–5, 52, 64, 67, 84,
　　94, 101, 110–11, 114, 144, 200,
　　208, 215, 267, 280, 286–7,
　　290–1, 303–5
British Society, 42–4, 62, 63–4, 67,
　　84, 97, 110, 115, 133, 200, 303–4
Brittany, 208, 345
broadcasting, 17, 19
Brooks, Simon, 24–5
Bryncethin, 122–3, 268
Bryngwran, 124–5, 226
business, 7, 9, 302, 322–3, 328, 335
Bwlchysarnau, 139, 285, 289

Caernarfon Training College, 63, 116,
　　165
Caernarfonshire, 110, 126, 132, 138,
　　183, 187, 242, 266, 281, 288–9,
　　325, 341, 343, 353
Caio, 121–2, 133–4, 287
caning *see* punishment
Capel Evan, 120, 218
Cardiff, 254, 283, 306
Cardiganshire, 9, 50, 89, 124, 140,
　　167, 257, 264, 282–3, 325
Cardiganshire Teachers' Association,
　　144
caring approaches, 141–2, 159–60,
　　162
Carmarthen Training College, 24, 63,
　　115–16, 204, 206
Carmarthenshire, 80, 85, 91, 92, 144,
　　186, 211, 251, 296, 333
Carnarvon and Denbigh Herald,
　　227–8
Catholicism, 337–8, 346, 348
Celt Llundain, 241

census data, 8, 10, 18, 143–6, 165, 167, 209, 223, 261–3, 285, 302, 317–19, 321, 325–8, 332, 341, 346–8
charitable clubs, 283, 303
charitable schools, 39, 42, 119–20
Chartism, 56
child labour, 40–1, 111, 243, 266, 280, 281, 282–3, 284–5
Church of England *see* Anglicanism
circulating schools, 39, 52, 78
civilisation, 12, 84, 142, 329, 330, 355
class monitors *see* monitors
coal *see* mining
code switching, 332–4
collective memory, 3–10, 12, 20–2, 240–52
Colley, Linda, 354
colloquial language, 172, 204–5, 209, 217, 264, 265, 349–51
colonialism, 3, 199, 343–4, 356–7, 358; *see also* imperialism
Commission on the Employment of Children, 298, 329
Committee of the Privy Council on Education, 43, 197
community libraries, 269
composition, 168–9, 179, 211, 217, 221, 224, 225
compulsory education, 111, 138, 198, 280, 290
conversational skills, 177, 179
corporal punishment *see* punishment
Corris, 120, 163, 223, 287, 305
Cotton, James Henry, 304
court proceedings, 8, 294–5, 303–4
Crai, 164, 301, 302
criminal justice system, 8, 65–6, 132, 136–7, 294–5, 303–4
Croes-goch, 215–16, 253–4, 320
Cross Commission, 126, 138, 145–8, 157–8, 162, 167, 180–1, 209, 217, 220, 227, 230, 239, 295, 302, 320, 339–40
Crowther, John, 167
Crystal, David, 240
cultural capital, 7, 44, 320, 336
cultural revival, 6–7, 243–4, 331, 360
curriculum, 16–17, 109, 145–6, 168–79, 225–6, 287, 352–4, 359
Cwmcothi, 142, 161, 172
Cwmllynfell, 53, 125

Dafen Tin Plate Works, 269, 289
Dalby, Andrew, 240–1, 252, 335
Daly, Mary, 347, 358
dame schools, 39, 41–2, 56, 284
Darlington, Thomas, 184, 359
Davies, Aaron, 242–3
Davies, B. L., 112, 181
Davies, Cassie, 264, 342
Davies, D. Jones, 179–80
Davies, Dan Isaac, 38, 147–8, 225, 298, 326, 331
Davies, David, 19, 242, 284, 293–4
Davies, Hazel, 2
Davies, John, 24, 143–4
Davies, Russell, 23
Davies, Walter Haydn, 266
Davin, Anna, 349
de Fréine, Seán, 346
debating societies, 324
Denbighshire, 90–1, 147, 207, 222, 353
detention, 16, 47, 66, 121, 132, 133, 134, 138, 145, 182–3, 249
deterrence, 52, 65, 135
devolution, 17, 243
devolution referendum (1979), 17
Dewi Môn, 54
dialects, 172, 264, 332, 349–51
dictation, 168, 171, 181, 211, 215
dictionaries, 95, 206, 324
'direct method' (language instruction), 184
disruptiveness, 254–8

documentaries, 15, 16, 19
Dolgellau, 83, 101, 209
Dowlais, 40, 320, 328
Doyle, Aidan, 334
drunkenness, 44, 45, 139, 229, 253, 295
dunce's hats, 54; *see also* fool's hats
Durkacz, Edward, 24
Dyke, Sir William Hart, 182
Dyserth, 121, 285, 289

Easter Rising, 9
Eben Fardd, 49
Education Act (1870), 9, 13–14, 16, 24–6, 111–12, 114, 133, 180, 198, 226, 280, 304
Education Act (Scotland) (1872), 348
Edmunds, Mary, 144
Edwards, Owen M., 1–2, 4, 15, 17, 96, 185, 223, 258, 268, 331
Edwards, W., 331–2
Edwards, Wil John, 247
eisteddfodau, 6, 167, 285, 293
electoral reform, 111
English identity, 230, 352–5
English language
  and code switching, 332–4
  colloquial English, 264, 349–51
  compositions in, 168–9, 179, 211, 217, 221, 224, 225
  conversational skills in, 177, 179
  and court proceedings, 8, 294–5, 303–4
  examinations carried out in, 110, 112, 121–2
  forgetting of on leaving school, 320–1
  as international language, 8–9, 328
  as language of business, 7, 9, 302, 322–3, 328, 335
  learning without understanding, 78, 79–83, 116–17, 157–8, 219, 344
  levels of fluency, 263–5, 318–19
  and migration, 10, 37, 123, 306, 320–1, 323–5, 332, 347, 357, 361
  as necessary qualification for teachers, 41–2, 114
  newspapers, 317, 322, 329
  parental attitudes to teaching of, 9, 185, 280, 293–300, 308–9, 346
  regional forms of, 349–51
  relation to employment and life-chances, 8–9, 38, 201, 267–8, 280, 293–4, 347–8, 349
  school board attitudes to, 300–8
  as secular language, 7, 28, 38, 338
  songs in, 168, 353
  teachers' levels of competence in, 41–2, 63, 90, 164, 173
  teaching of internationally, 61, 343–4, 346–9
  teaching of without use of Welsh, 1, 29, 30, 77–83, 90, 137–8, 157–8, 184–5, 296–7
  teaching to infants, 173–5
  and tourism, 268, 321–2
  use of Bible in teaching of, 89, 94
  and social status, 294–6, 319, 328–9
  use of Welsh in teaching of, 3, 13, 24, 80, 82, 90–7, 100, 117, 145, 158–68, 177–85, 187–8, 201–2, 205–11, 219–21, 227, 230, 296–7, 340
  vocabulary teaching methods, 93–4, 175
  Welsh Not as tool to improve learning of, 3, 8–9, 46–7, 62, 117, 184–5, 300–1, 340
Esgairdawe, 121, 144
Evans, Beriah Gwynfe, 78, 145–6, 157, 158, 239, 294, 340
Evans, E. Herber, 96
Evans, Gwynfor, 14

Evans, John, 145
Evans, W. Gareth, 23, 112, 198–9
evening classes, 143, 324; see also night schools
examinations, 109–10, 112, 121–2, 137, 139, 158, 172–6, 181, 188, 200, 204–5, 211–17, 224–5, 266, 268
expulsion, 52, 289

farming see agriculture
'Fate of the Language' (Lewis), 12, 208
Fearon, D. R., 214–15
fees
    arrears in payment, 266, 281
    schools, 39, 41, 88, 111, 137, 266, 281–3, 291
    training colleges, 64
Felinheli, 92, 120
Felton, James, 15
feminism, 258
Few Plain Hints and Suggestions, A (Jones), 160, 163
52 Times Britain was a Bellend (Felton), 15
fines, 49, 61, 125, 134, 343
Fletcher, Joseph, 83, 205–6, 300
Flintshire, 46–7, 134, 187, 207, 283, 333, 353
fool's hats, 54, 59, 61
France, 61, 208, 345–6
free education, 198
French language, 59, 60, 345–6
French Revolution, 43, 56

Gaelic, 61, 348–9, 357
Gallagher, John, 28
gender
    and curriculum, 164, 258
    and intergenerational language transmission, 328
    and punishment, 133, 258–9
    and school attendance, 99, 258, 285
    women teachers, 133, 175, 290
genocide, 22, 23, 228, 344
gentry, 39, 44, 67, 97, 267, 328, 336
geography, 100, 144, 163, 169–71, 181, 226–7, 287, 352–5
George, William, 136, 246, 322
Gill, John, 131, 159
Glamorgan, 37, 51–2, 80, 91, 147, 217, 223, 299, 323, 326–7, 334, 338
grammar, 94, 115, 176, 183, 204, 216, 287, 324
grammar schools, 47, 59–60, 209, 263–4
grants, 43–4, 63, 67, 79, 109, 164, 169, 181, 197–8, 200, 214–16, 280, 291, 303; see also state funding
Great Reform Act, 43
Greek, 52–3, 138
Griffin, Emma, 292
Griffiths, James, 29
Grigg, Russell, 24, 100–1
Gruffydd, W. J., 21, 141, 245, 286, 337
Guest schools, 40
Gwaun valley, 118, 125–6, 260
Gwenddwr, 170, 326
Gwilym Wyn, 53, 243
Gwynedd, 295

Halbwachs, Maurice, 21
Hall, Edward Crompton Lloyd, 299
Harries, W. Carnero, 40
Heathorn, Stephen, 352
hedge schools, 346
Her Majesty's Inspectors (HMIs) see inspectors
Hermon, 143–4, 244
Highland Clearances, 348
historiography, 17–18, 19–20, 22–7, 28, 198–9
history (as school subject), 169–71, 181, 202, 266, 352–5

History Grounded (Jones), 19–20
Hobsbawm, Eric, 228
Holyhead, 254
Honourable Society of Cymmrodorion, 144, 147, 183, 296
How Green Was My Valley (Llewellyn), 10–12
How Green Was My Valley (1941 film), 10–11
How Green Was My Valley (1975–6 TV adaptation), 12
Howell, David, 268
Hughes, Edward, 254
humiliation, 15, 22, 50–1, 54, 61–2, 64–5, 68, 133–4, 250, 343, 346
humour, 248–9
Humphries, Stephen, 252–3, 340–1
Hurt, John, 214

identity *see* British identity; English identity; local identity; Welsh identity
immersive learning, 62, 102, 184
imperialism, 14, 15, 23, 202, 203–4, 352–5, 356–7, 360; *see also* British Empire; colonialism
incentivisation, 159
India, 356–7
industrial areas, 10, 37, 40–1, 88, 122–3, 183–4, 244, 264, 266, 269, 279–84, 300, 319–21, 323–4, 331–2, 336, 338, 355, 358
infants, 125, 163, 165, 173–5, 183, 214, 219, 290
inspectors
  on additional class subjects, 170–3
  attitudes towards Welsh language, 198–212, 217–21, 223–6, 229–30
  certification of untrained teachers, 114
  chief inspectors, 2, 171, 179, 185, 217, 221, 227, 265, 307
  decisions on grants, 198, 200, 214, 215, 216
  diocesan inspectors, 222
  discretion and allowances made, 214–18
  inspection day and examination procedures, 212–22, 225
  on monitors and pupil teachers, 86, 164–5
  on object lessons, 174–5, 211
  oversight of state-funded schools, 43, 79, 199–200
  on parental attitudes to education, 284, 307
  on physical punishment, 218
  on pupils' ability in English, 79, 101, 158, 171, 178, 179
  questioning of pupils by, 158, 168, 216
  relationship with teachers, 222–6
  shown what they are believed to want to see, 90, 158, 187, 199
  and social class, 200, 203, 212, 223
  and state policy, 198–9, 229–30
  on teachers' level of competence in English, 90
  on teachers with no knowledge of Welsh, 83–6, 164–5, 216, 219–20
  on teaching English without use of Welsh, 90, 297
  on teaching of infants, 174–5
  on teaching of Welsh, 225–6, 307
  on use of Welsh to teach English, 95, 145, 160, 181, 187, 201–2, 205–11, 219–21, 227, 230, 297
internalisation, 240, 252, 270, 343, 346, 358
Introductory Text-book to School Education (Gill), 131, 159
Ireland, 9, 14, 61, 187, 334, 337–8, 346–8, 357, 358
Irish language, 61, 334, 337–8, 346–8, 357, 358

Irish nationalism, 347
iron industry, 37, 279, 282, 283, 284
Isfoel, 288
Iwan, Dafydd, 15

Jacobinism, 348
Jenkins, Geraint H., 25, 329
Jenkins, John, 81–2
Jenkins, R. T., 174, 268
Jernsletten, Nils, 344
Johnson, Henry Vaughan, 77, 79–80
Johnson, Richard, 229
Jones, Abel, 136, 249, 328, 334
Jones, Benjamin, 124
Jones, R. Bowen, 296
Jones, Evan, 117
Jones, Gareth Elwyn, 25
Jones, Goronwy, 48
Jones, Griffith, 78
Jones, Henry, 53
Jones, Ieuan Gwynedd, 23, 28, 292, 299, 337
Jones, J. R., 308
Jones, J. Twyi, 7
Jones, J. W., 159
Jones, Jack, 332, 334
Jones, James, 160, 163
Jones, Josiah, 125
Jones, Longueville, 55, 92, 95, 101, 199–205, 293, 296, 299
Jones, Michael D., 357
Jones, Philip, 326–7
Jones, R. O., 330
Jones, T. Gwynn, 8, 131, 147, 244, 356
Joyce, Patrick, 350

Kay-Shuttleworth, James, 199
Kennedy, W. J., 207
Kenya, 343–4

Labour Party, 292
laissez-faire politics, 14, 198, 229
Lancaster, Joseph, 57, 62, 64–5, 85, 86, 114, 157–8
language replacement, 325–6
language transmission, 20, 265, 326–8, 330, 335, 339, 343, 349, 357–60
Lansdowne, Henry Petty Fitzmaurice, Marquess, 198
Last Note, 54
Latin, 52–3, 57–61, 138, 257
learning without understanding, 78, 79–83, 116–17, 157–8, 219, 344, 345
Legard, Albert G., 227
Letter to the Welsh People (Owen), 44
Levi, Thomas, 44, 54
Lewis, Saunders, 2, 12, 208
lines, writing of, 16, 49, 58, 66, 121, 124, 134
Lingen, Ralph Robert Wheeler, 80, 201
linguistic homogeneity, 12, 23, 208–9, 228–9, 319
literacy, 39, 41, 97, 98–9, 109, 258, 264–5, 284
Llan, Y, 305
Llanboidy, 85, 297
Llanbryn-mair, 321
Llanddewi Brefi, 48, 49
Llandovery workhouse school, 79
Llandybïe, 134, 147
Llandyrnog, 45–6
Llandysul, 48, 53, 92, 122, 216
Llanelli, 29, 40, 95
Llanfihangel (Llanfihangel-y-Creuddyn), 119, 132, 186, 219, 222, 305
Llanfrothen, 125, 132
Llanfynydd, 207, 255
Llangefni, 120–1, 159
Llangeinwen, 120, 301
Llangeitho, 124, 144, 163–4, 284
Llangernyw, 63, 186
Llangollen, 83, 256, 295
Llangunnock, 163, 253
Llanllyfni, 119, 125, 134, 140, 146, 290

Llanon, 133, 167, 175–6, 254, 287
Llanrhaeadr, 102, 294
Llantwit, 57, 58
Llanuwchllyn, 247, 268
Llanwenog, 40, 41, 171, 218
Llechryd, 96, 122, 137–8, 253
Llewellyn, Michael Gareth, 267
Llewellyn, Richard, 10–11
Llidiart-y-waun, 132, 142, 268, 342
Lloyd, Richard, 49
Lloyd George, David, 241
Llyswen, 249, 281
local government, 197–8, 359
local identity, 350–1, 354
logbooks, 23, 26, 29–30, 118–39, 142, 145–7, 158, 160–7, 171–5, 187–8, 223, 225, 256, 259, 281, 289, 290, 298, 301

Machynlleth, 305, 321
Marchant, Thomas, 295
markets, 295, 321, 322
Marryat, Joseph, 283
maths *see* arithmetic
Meirionnydd, 147, 222, 263, 325
memoirs *see* autobiographical accounts
memory, 3–10, 12, 20–2, 50, 59, 224, 240–52, 266
Menai Bridge, 126, 162, 167, 285, 320
Merthyr, 37, 40, 44, 63, 83, 115, 159, 183, 216–17, 281, 325, 327, 331–2
Methodism, 146, 287; *see also* Nonconformity
middle classes, 6, 37–8, 43, 178, 180, 200, 203, 255, 294, 299, 301, 321–2, 329, 330
Middleton, Jacob, 99, 249, 288
migration, 10, 37, 123, 306, 320–1, 323–5, 332, 345, 346, 347, 357, 361
military punishments, 65, 132

Millward, E. G., 26–7
miners' institutions, 269
mining, 37, 122–3, 266, 279, 282, 284, 358
modernity, 142, 331, 337, 358, 361
Mold, 44–5, 89, 254–5
monitors, 57–8, 62, 64, 86–8, 100, 135, 138, 164–5, 176, 256, 289
Monmouthshire, 37, 51–2, 63, 83–4, 97, 122, 158, 207
Montgomeryshire, 145, 207, 321, 323, 326, 333, 342
Moore-Colyer, R. J., 336
morality, 12, 42, 45, 162, 188, 203, 229, 337
Morell, J. D., 62
Morgan, J. Vyrnwy, 21
Morris, Hugh, 139
Mugglestone, Lynda, 178
museums, 17–18
Mynachlog-ddu, 168–9, 174

National Eisteddfod, 6, 285, 293
national identity *see* British identity; English identity; Welsh identity
National schools, 42–5, 52, 67, 94–7, 101, 110–11, 114, 200–1, 222, 243, 267, 280, 286–7, 290–1, 303–7
National Society, 42–4, 63–4, 67, 84, 97, 110, 115, 303–4
National Union of Elementary Teachers, 144, 188–9
nationalism, 14, 24–5, 182, 245–6, 303, 347
native Americans, 344–5
'Necessity of Teaching English through the Medium of Welsh' (Davies), 179–80
Nevern, 166, 290
Neville, Grace, 346
Newbolt Report, 350
Newcastle Commission, 67, 81–4, 88,

91, 96, 101–3, 109, 137, 177, 198, 213, 230, 287, 324–6, 331
Newcastle Emlyn, 245, 325
newspapers, 6, 7, 45, 226–8, 265, 296, 305, 307–8, 317, 322, 324, 329–30, 335–6, 353, 356
Nicholas, T. E., 244
Nicholas, Thomas, 299
night schools, 269; *see also* evening classes
Nonconformity, 6, 7, 12, 42, 44, 45, 63, 98, 100–1, 223, 283, 287, 303–4, 337–8
non-denominational education, 42, 287
North Wales Training College *see* Caernarfon Training College
Norway, 344
Nutall, Samuel, 254–5

obedience, 56, 139–40, 142, 159
object lessons, 163, 174–5, 211
oral history, 24, 52, 135–6, 186, 247, 248, 252–3, 332, 349
Osterhammel, Jürgen, 228, 356–7
Ostler, Nicholas, 337
Owen, Daniel, 44–5
Owen, Hugh, 44
Owen, Isambard, 339–40

Page, Robert, 338
parents
    attitudes to education in general, 280–7
    attitudes to physical punishment, 132, 249, 288–93, 297–8, 308–9
    attitudes to teaching of English, 9, 185, 280, 293–300, 308–9, 346
    attitudes to teaching of Welsh, 9, 17, 185, 280, 296, 306–7
    attitudes to use of Welsh Not, 3, 24, 293–300, 308–9
    confidence in schools, 83–4, 280, 285–7
    physical punishment by, 249, 254, 257, 292
    references to in school logbooks, 281, 289, 290, 298
Parry-Jones, Daniel, 15–16, 245, 324, 355
Parsons, Ben, 57
Patagonia, 357
paternalism, 39, 199, 301, 329–30
patriarchy, 258
patriotism, 6, 10, 144, 239, 338, 352–5
payment *see* wages
Peate, Iorwerth, 321
Pembrokeshire, 37, 58, 80, 84, 91, 115, 143–4, 216–17, 221, 260, 333
Pennant, 124, 140, 216, 219–20
periodicals, 6, 7, 45, 265, 331
Phillips, Sir Thomas, 116, 204
Phillipson, Robert, 23
physical punishment *see* punishment
Plaid Cymru, 10, 14
play, language learning through, 323–4
playground, language spoken in, 7, 22, 119, 121, 125–30, 146–7, 163, 167, 184, 245, 257, 297–8, 301
Pontgarreg, 18, 258, 288
Pontypridd, 26, 183, 325
poor law, 43
popular culture, 2, 10–12, 14–16, 21, 148, 243, 338, 354
population growth, 28, 37, 40
poverty, 37–8, 43, 140, 250, 279–80, 281–3, 292, 300, 309, 338, 348
Powell, Lewis, 47
Pretty, David, 25–6
Price, Adam, 14
Price, Owen, 302
Price, Thomas, 97
prizes, 159, 267, 296
pronunciation, 11, 82, 87, 115, 161, 176, 177–8, 247, 286, 324
professionalism, 113–17, 134, 141–3, 159–60, 188, 265

Protestantism, 337–8, 346
Provence, 345
Prussia, 111
Pryce, Shadrach, 85, 172–3, 175, 176, 209–12, 215, 217, 222, 225, 284, 297, 301, 317, 322
psychological impacts, 3, 54–5, 239–41
public services, 17, 197–8
punctuality, 126, 142, 159
punishment
   children taking pride in, 257–8
   to combat disorder and disruptiveness, 256
   in the criminal justice system, 65–6, 132
   culture of, 52–8, 146
   detention, 16, 47, 66, 121, 132, 133, 134, 138, 145, 182–3, 249
   as deterrence, 52, 65, 135
   and the difficulty of teaching jobs, 140–1, 146
   expulsion, 52, 289
   fines, 49, 61, 125, 134, 343
   fool's or dunce's hats, 54, 59, 61
   and gender, 133, 258–9
   humiliation, 15, 22, 50–1, 54, 61–2, 64–5, 68, 133–4, 250, 343, 346
   as last resort, 130, 132, 134, 135, 218, 288
   legal cases related to, 136–7
   locking into cupboards or other spaces, 53, 54
   and memory, 59, 136, 240–52
   by monitors and pupil teachers, 87, 135, 289
   parental attitudes to, 132, 249, 288–93, 297–8, 308–9
   by parents, 249, 254, 257, 292
   physical punishment, 1, 3, 9, 12–16, 22, 44–6, 49–61, 65–6, 87, 94, 100, 121, 125–6, 130–7, 140–1, 148, 159, 186, 218, 241–3, 247–60, 268–70, 288–93, 308, 342–3, 346
   post-1862 period, 109–48, 182–3, 186
   pre-1862 period, 37–68
   psychological impacts of, 3, 54–5, 239–41
   punishment books, 132–3
   recorded in school logbooks, 118–37, 146–7, 259, 290
   replaced by incentivisation, 159
   resistance of children against, 6, 27, 131, 252–60, 270
   school management attitudes to, 132–3
   social attitudes to, 65–6, 131–2, 249, 288
   standing on a chair, bench or table, 8, 54, 131, 288
   standing on one leg, 49, 54, 133, 288
   teacher training in relation to, 131
   unfairness of, 15, 54, 93, 132, 148, 242, 243, 250–1, 256, 260, 342
   writing lines, 16, 49, 58, 66, 121, 124, 134
punishment books, 132–3
pupil teachers, 86–8, 100, 135, 138, 164–5, 174, 176, 188, 206, 245, 253, 256, 289
purpose-built schools, 42, 100, 111
Pwllheli, 250, 322, 325

railways, 321, 322, 329
Ravenstein, E. G., 299, 337
reading books, 94–5, 123, 157, 169, 175, 183, 215–16, 217, 224
Rebecca Riots, 48, 293, 296, 299
recruitment
   of inspectors, 200
   newspaper job advertisements, 305, 335–6
   of teachers, 84–5, 118, 137, 305–6
   Welsh-speaking as a requirement,

305–6, 335–6
Rees, L. M., 115
religious education, 97, 98, 162, 172, 287, 304, 346, 348
resistance, 6, 27, 28, 59, 131, 240, 248–9, 252–60, 270, 280, 342, 344, 357
Revised Code, 109–14, 121–2, 137, 139, 147, 157–8, 164, 168–9, 174, 178–9, 198, 200, 205, 212–14, 222–5, 258, 303, 350
Reyhner, John, 344
Rhiwhiriaeth, 169, 219
Rhondda, 135, 136, 183–4, 289, 334
Rhydlewis, 167, 223
Rhymney, 122, 212
Rhŷs, John, 176, 177–8, 264
Rhys Lewis (Owen), 44–5, 333, 334
Richard, Frank, 136
Richard, Henry, 180
Roberts, Howell, 140, 146
Roberts, Robert, 90–1, 250, 255, 286, 289, 301
Roderick, Gordon Wynne, 25
Rose, Jonathan, 252
Rosser, Siwan M., 27
rote learning, 49, 94, 112, 117, 158, 171, 180, 206, 247, 266
Rowbotham, Judith, 131–2
Rowlands, E. D., 268
Ruabon, 164, 222, 282
rural areas, 20, 37, 39, 84–5, 88, 110–11, 118–19, 127–30, 137–40, 147, 164, 170, 261–4, 279, 282–3, 290–1, 303, 305–7, 320–5, 327, 335, 354–5, 358
Ruthin, 60, 79, 87, 143, 144, 255, 306
Ruthin workhouse school, 79

St Asaph workhouse school, 53, 55
St David's Day, 354
St Fagans museum, 17–18
salaries *see* wages

Salisbury, Enoch Gibbon, 329
Sami language, 344
Samuel, David, 135
scholarships, 64, 85, 86, 264, 269
school attendance, 13, 40–1, 67, 88–9, 111, 127, 138, 146, 159, 172, 224, 258, 266, 280–2, 285–6, 290–1, 357
school boards, 13, 111, 183, 197, 284, 300–8
school buildings, 40, 42, 45, 100, 111, 176, 187
school fees *see* fees
school inspectors *see* inspectors
school leaving age, 111, 247, 266, 280, 284, 341
school logbooks *see* logbooks
school managers, 67, 83, 109, 118, 132–3, 139, 141, 146, 183, 197, 267, 290–1, 300–8
school size, 87–8, 123–4, 138, 176
school strikes, 254
Schoolmaster, 305
Scotland, 61, 99, 348–9, 357
secondary schools, 181, 264, 269, 340; *see also* grammar schools
secularisation, 320, 338, 361
self-esteem, 240, 258, 295, 339
Seren Cymru, 329
sewing, 164, 258, 287
shaming *see* humiliation
silence, 58, 123–4, 341
Slaney, R. A., 43
Smith, Dai, 24
Smith, H., 207, 221
Smith, Kevin, 22
Smith, Robert, 26
Sneyd-Kynnersley, E. M., 213–14
snobbery, 62–3, 178, 217, 229, 330
Snowdonia 1890 (BBC), 16
social class *see* aristocracy; gentry; middle classes; upper classes; working classes

social mobility, 64, 179, 246, 269, 340, 342, 346, 347–8
social status, 294–6, 319, 328–9
Society for Utilizing the Welsh Language, 62, 180, 181, 182, 239
Solva, 117, 160–1, 169, 172, 267, 281, 287
songs, 144, 145, 168, 181, 219, 223, 224, 353, 354, 355
South Wales and Monmouthshire Training College *see* Carmarthen Training College
Southall, J. E., 147
Spectator, 329
spelling, 94, 134, 159, 161, 174, 176, 216
spelling bees, 159
sport, 6, 338
staff recruitment, 84–5, 118, 137, 305–6
staff turnover, 139–40
Stanley, Henry Morton, 53, 55
state funding, 13, 24, 29, 42–4, 63, 67, 109, 111, 164, 169, 197, 199–200, 228, 280; *see also* grants
state policy
 association of Welsh Not with, 2–3, 14, 15, 22–7, 197, 356
 on Welsh language, 2, 3, 12–13, 14, 20, 22–3, 26, 179–86, 197–9, 226–30, 355–6
Staylittle, 166, 170, 219, 223
Stonelake, Edmund, 266
Storiel museum, Bangor, 18
Strange, Julie-Marie, 241, 249
strikes, 254, 282
Sunday Closing (Wales) Act (1881), 180
Sunday schools, 38, 82, 97, 98–9, 143, 176, 188, 245, 265, 269, 302, 307
Swansea, 63, 133, 183, 254, 288, 290, 306, 336
Swansea Training College, 133

Swyddffynnon, 126, 130, 139, 175, 289, 341
Symons, Jelinger C., 80

Talk Not, 58, 124
teacher training, 41, 62–6, 68, 84–5, 96, 100, 114–16, 131, 133, 137, 173, 204–5
teaching manuals, 113, 134, 159, 160, 163, 174, 349
technical education, 269
television documentaries, 15, 16, 19
Temple, Robert, 207, 216, 219
10 Stories from Welsh History (Jones), 19
textbooks, 2, 9, 13, 16–17, 80, 82, 94–5, 169–70, 181, 183, 202, 227, 210, 227, 345, 354
Thiong'o, Ngũgĩ wa, 343
Thirwall, Connop, 207, 304
Thomas, Ben Bowen, 9
Thomas, Brinley, 323
Thomas, D., 206
Thomas, D. L., 243–4
Thompson, Paul, 252
Times, 293, 329
tourism, 268, 321–2, 329; *see also* travel
trade unions, 269, 292
training colleges, 24, 62–8, 84–5, 114–16, 131, 133, 137, 143, 160, 165, 173, 181, 204–6, 349
translation exercises, 59–60, 91, 96, 160–3, 167, 177, 181, 201, 204, 217, 225
trauma, 54–5, 239–41, 334
travel, 321, 322–3; *see also* tourism
Trecastell, 126, 143, 144, 162
Trefriw, 140, 268, 302
Tregaron, 9, 18, 165, 325
Tregroes, 160, 173
truancy, 64, 126, 133, 245, 253; *see also* school attendance
Tywyn, 127–30, 291–2
unfairness, 15, 54, 93, 132, 148, 242,

INDEX

243, 250–1, 256, 260, 342
United States, 66, 111, 328, 344–5
upper classes, 264; *see also* aristocracy; gentry
urbanisation, 43, 56

Vaughan, Gwyneth, 6, 143
Vernon, James, 330
victimhood, 27, 28, 239–40
Victoria, Queen, 197
vocabulary, 93–4, 160, 162, 175, 176–7, 324
voluntary schools, 24

wages
　for child labour, 282–3
　industrial workers, 279–80
　payment by results, 109, 121, 137, 172, 180, 188, 212
　teachers, 109, 121, 137, 139, 140, 172, 180, 188, 189, 204, 212, 291
Wales, 331
Wales in 100 Objects, 19
Warner, Richard, 46–7
Watcyn Wyn, 242, 259
Watkins, Percy, 145, 324
Watts, E. T., 187, 220–1, 223, 224
Weber, Eugen, 61, 346
welfare provision, 197–8
Welsh Assembly, 17
Welsh culture, 2, 11, 19, 25, 144–5, 180–1, 243–4, 251, 265, 270, 323, 360
Welsh Department (Board of Education), 2, 9, 185
Welsh identity, 2, 3–4, 6–7, 10, 17, 20, 143–6, 182, 243–6, 323, 331, 336, 338–9, 341, 353–4
Welsh Intermediate Education Act (1889), 180–1, 269, 340
Welsh language
　Blue Books comments on, 12–13, 45, 198, 329
　and broadcasting, 17, 19
　and code switching, 332–4
　colloquial Welsh, 172, 204–5, 209, 217, 265
　and community, 335, 336–7, 351, 358–9
　and court proceedings, 8, 294–5, 303–4
　decline of, 2, 7–10, 16, 26, 28, 306, 325–35, 339–40, 357–61
　descriptions of classroom use in school logbooks, 160–7, 171–2, 174–5
　economic benefits of speaking, 335–6
　emotional connection with, 336–7
　increasing use in schools in post-1862 period, 157–89
　inspectors' attitudes towards, 198–212, 217–21, 223–6, 229–30
　intergenerational transmission, 20, 265, 326–8, 330, 335, 339, 343, 357–60
　legal and official status of, 28, 179–86
　literature in, 7, 145, 181, 265
　migrants' learning of, 321, 323
　as necessary qualification for teachers, 305–6, 335–6
　newspapers and periodicals, 6, 7, 265, 305, 335–6, 353
　nineteenth-century revival, 6–7, 243–4, 331, 360
　parental attitudes to teaching of, 9, 17, 185, 280, 296, 306–7
　promotion of, 2, 14–15, 180–1, 185, 199–205, 225, 306
　recognised as an official school subject, 181, 183–4, 225–6, 306–7, 354, 359
　and religion, 7, 162, 320, 337–8, 360
　school board attitudes to, 300–8
　and social class, 37–8, 229, 299–300, 321–2, 330–1

and social status, 294–6, 319, 328–9
songs in, 144, 145, 181, 219, 223, 224, 353, 354
spoken by monitors and pupil teachers, 86, 100, 164–5, 188
spoken by teachers at home and in the community, 143–4, 223
spoken in the playground, 7, 22, 119, 121, 125–30, 146–7, 163, 167, 184, 245, 257, 297–8, 301
and state policy, 2, 3, 12–13, 14, 20, 22–3, 26, 179–86, 197–9, 226–30, 355–6
supposed inferiority of, 328–31
and teacher training, 114–17
teachers who do not speak, 29, 83–7, 115, 140, 144, 164–7, 188, 216, 219–20, 292, 297, 302, 306
teaching of, 9, 17, 24, 97–9, 144, 180–1, 183–5, 225–6, 265, 296, 306–7, 354, 359
training college examinations in, 204–5
use in teaching of additional class subjects, 169–73, 181, 185, 211
use in teaching of English, 3, 13, 24, 80, 82, 90–7, 100, 117, 145, 158–68, 177–88, 201–2, 205–11, 219–21, 227, 230, 296–7, 340
and Welsh identity, 17, 20, 182, 243–6, 323, 336, 338–9
Welsh-medium education, 17, 18, 19, 360
Welsh Language Society, 184
Welsh Liberal Party, 180–1
Welsh literature, 7, 145, 181, 265
Welsh-medium education, 17, 18, 19, 360

Welsh nationalism, 14, 24–5, 182, 245–6, 303
Welsh Not
associated with the Blue Books, 13, 18
associated with 1870 education act, 14, 16, 26
associated with state policy, 2–3, 14, 15, 22–7, 197, 356
associated with Welsh language decline, 2, 7–10, 16, 26, 339–40, 358–61
autobiographical accounts of, 1–2, 28–9, 47, 51, 241–52
in the Blue Books, 5, 45–6, 51
children's responses to, 6, 27, 59, 239–70
in collective memory, 3–10, 20–2, 240–52
extent of use, 3, 19, 24, 26, 30, 51–2, 67–8
in historiography, 17–18, 19–20, 22–7
methods of use, 3, 38, 46–51, 133–4, 163, 182–3, 185–6, 301
motives for use, 3, 8–9, 46–7, 57–8, 62, 184–5, 300–1, 340
mythology surrounding, 3, 19, 24, 26
names for, 4–5, 45–8
origins of, 58–62
parental attitudes to, 3, 24, 293–300, 308–9
in popular culture, 2, 10–12, 14–16, 21
post-1862 period, 117–35, 140, 147–8, 182–3, 185–6
pre-1862 period, 45–52, 67–8
psychological impacts of, 3, 54–5, 239–41
resistance of children against, 6, 27, 240, 248–9, 252–60, 270
in school logbooks, 118–37, 147
similar practices internationally, 61, 343–9

surviving physical examples of, 18
in textbooks and school materials, 2, 13, 16–18
time period of use, 5–6, 22, 26, 46–8, 51–2, 117–18, 134, 147–8, 182–3, 185–6, 340
turned into a game by children, 259–60
used alongside teaching in Welsh, 163
used as symbol in campaigns and protests, 18–19
used to improve learning of English, 3, 8–9, 46–7, 62, 117, 184–5, 300–1, 340
Welsh songs, 144, 145, 181, 219, 223, 224, 353, 354
Western Mail, 13, 51, 118, 186, 242, 307
Williams, Chris, 23–4
Williams, D. J., 10
Williams, Daniel, 25
Williams, Gwyn A., 22
Williams, H. G., 23, 202–3
Williams, J. Lloyd, 135, 267, 343
Williams, Raymond, 22

Williams, Robert, 89
Williams, T. Marchant, 110
Williams, Tim, 26
Williams, William, 187, 214, 217, 223, 249, 257
Williams, William Pryce, 160
Withers, Charles, 349
women teachers, 133, 175, 290
Woolf, Nicholas M., 347–8
Woolford, Andrew, 344
workhouse schools, 53–4, 55, 79
working classes, 37–41, 63–4, 82, 114, 132, 141–2, 229, 241, 246, 249, 253, 255, 258, 264, 269, 280, 291–2, 295, 299–301, 309, 330–1, 340–1, 346, 350, 355
Wright, Susannah, 142
writing materials, 175–6

Yiddish, 349
Ystradgynlais, 85, 283
Ystumtuen, 163, 218